Beyond the Asian Crisis

Beyond the Asian Crisis

Pathways to Sustainable Growth

Edited by

Anis Chowdhury

School of Economics & Finance, University of Western Sydney, Australia

Iyanatul Islam

School of International Business, Griffith University, Australia

Edward Elgar

Cheltenham, UK • Northampton, MA, USA

Published by
Edward Elgar Publishing Limited
Glensanda House
Montpellier Parade
Cheltenham
Glos GL50 1UA
UK

Edward Elgar Publishing, Inc.
136 West Street
Suite 202
Northampton
Massachusetts 01060
USA

A catalogue record for this book
is available from the British Library

Library of Congress Cataloguing in Publication Data

Beyond the Asian crisis : pathways to sustainable growth / edited by Anis Chowdhury, Iyanatul Islam.
p. cm.
Includes bibliographical references and index.
1. Sustainable development—Asia. 2. Asia—Economic policy.
3. Financial crises—Asia. I. Chowdhury, Anis, 1954– II. Islam, Iyanatul, 1953–
HC415.E5 B49 2001
338.95′07–dc21 2001023351

ISBN 1 84064 273 4

Printed and bound in Great Britain by MPG Books Ltd, Bodmin, Cornwall

Contents

Figures and boxes

FIGURES

BOXES

Tables

Contributors

Editors: Anis Chowdhury is an Associate Professor of Economics at the School of Economics & Finance, University of Western Sydney, Australia. Iyanatul Islam is an Associate Professor of Economics at the School of International Business, Griffith University, Australia. Both are founding co-editors of the *Journal of the Asia Pacific Economy*, and have co-authored *Newly Industrialising Economies of East Asia* (Routledge), *Asia–Pacific Economies – A Survey* (Routledge) and *The Political Economy of East Asia: Post-Crisis Debates* (Oxford University Press).

Chris Baker formerly taught Asian history and politics at Cambridge University. He has lived in Thailand for 20 years and now works as an independent writer. He has co-authored (with Pasuk) *Thailand Economy and Politics* (OUP, 1995), *Thailand's Boom and Bust* (Silkworm, 1998) and *Thailand's Crisis* (Silkworm, 2000).

Tain-Jy Chen is Professor of Economics of National University Taiwan and consultant to Chung-Hua Institution for Economic Research. His research interests are in international economics and economic development. He has co-authored *Political Economy of U.S.–Taiwan Trade* (University of Michigan Press) and edited *Taiwanese Firms in Southeast Asia: Networking Across Borders* (Edward Elgar, 1998) and *Weathering the Asian Financial Crisis: the Experience of Taiwan.*

Chia Siow Yue is director of the Institute of Southeast Asian Studies in Singapore. Her areas of specialization are international economies and development economics, focusing on ASEAN and East Asia. She has researched and coordinated projects on the Asian crisis. Her recent publications include 'The Asian Financial Crisis: Singapore's Experience and Responses', in *Southeast Asia's Economic Crisis: Origins, Lessons and the Way Forward*, edited by H.W. Arndt and H. Hill (1999) and *East Asia's Financial Systems: Evolution and Crisis*, co-edited with S. Masuyama and D. Vandenbrink (1999).

James W. Dean is Professor of Economics at Simon Fraser University in Burnaby, British Columbia, Canada and Kaiser Professor of International

Business at Western Washington University in Bellingham, Washington, USA. For the past ten years his writing and research has focused on debt, banking and financial crises and their resolution. He has lectured and consulted in most crisis regions of the world, notably Asia, Africa, Latin America and Central Europe.

Shafiq Dhanani obtained his doctorate in economics from Oxford University. An independent policy consultant based in Jakarta over the past ten years, he has undertaken extensive work for the Indonesian government as well as for several international organizations, including UNIDO, ILO, UNDP and the World Bank. His previous experience in developing countries includes a number of short- and long-term assignments in South Asia and East Africa, as well as postgraduate teaching in development economics in the Netherlands.

Syed Asif Hasnain is the UNIDO representative in Jakarta, where he has been since 1996. In his 20-year association with UNIDO, he has dealt with several industrial development issues, ranging from the development and transfer of technology to industrial development in sub-Saharan Africa and, more recently, environmental issues arising from the industrialization of developing countries.

Elaine Hutson is Lecturer in Finance at Dublin City University. Her PhD is from the University of Technology, Sydney, where she lectured in corporate finance and financial markets prior to moving to Dublin. Her published research focuses on financial regulation, mergers and acquisitions, and international finance.

Colm Kearney is Professor of Finance at Dublin City University. He holds postgraduate degrees from University College Dublin, Essex University, the University of Western Ontario and the University of Warwick. He has published widely in the areas of financial market volatility and international finance.

C.H. Kwan is a senior economist at the Nomura Research Institute and a senior fellow at the Research Institute of Economy, Trade and Industry, Japan. He has served on various policy committees of the Japanese government, including the Economic Council (advising the prime minister) and the Council on the Foreign Exchange and Other Transactions (advising the minister of finance). Dr Kwan specializes in the Asian economy and Japan–Asia economic relations, with emphasis on exchange rate issues. His publications include *Economic Interdependence in the Asia–Pacific Region*

– *Towards a Yen Bloc* (Routledge, 1994), and *Yen Block – Toward Economic Integration in Asia*, (Brookings, 2001).

O. Yul Kwon has held the Korea Foundation Chair in Korean Studies at Griffith University since 1996. He is also the Director of the Australian Centre for Korean Studies at Griffith University. Before joining Griffith University, Dr Kwon was Professor at the University of Regina, Canada, and was the Director of the university's Institute for Northeast Asian Studies. Professor Kwon has published five books, numerous articles in refereed journals and business magazines, chapters of books and special columns in newspapers. His recent research interests focus on Korean economic and business issues, and he has published extensively on Korean economic development, economic policy, the 1997 financial crisis and Korea's international business environment. He is a member of the editorial board of *Asian Studies Review* (Blackwell).

Leong H. Liew is an Associate Professor in international business at Griffith University. His major research interests and publications are in the areas of China's political economy and economics of transition. He is the author of *The Chinese Economy in Transition* (Edward Elgar, 1997) and co-editor with C.L. Chiou of *Uncertain Future: Taiwan–Hong Kong–China Relations After Hong Kong's Return to Chinese Sovereignty* (Ashgate, 2000).

Joseph Y. Lim is a Professor of Economics at the University of the Philippines, Diliman, Quezon City. He took his MS in Operations Research at the Massachusetts Institute of Technology and his PhD in Economics at the University of Pennsylvania. He has also been a visiting scholar at the University of Cambridge. He has written various articles on the Philippine economy and the East Asian crisis. His articles have appeared in the *Journal of Development Economics*, *World Development*, *Journal of Contemporary Asia* and in economics books published inside and outside the Philippines.

Pasuk Phongpaichit is a Professor in the Faculty of Economics, Chulalongkorn University, Bangkok. She has written widely in Thai and English on the Thai economy, Japanese investment, corruption and the illegal economy.

Rajah Rasiah obtained his doctorate in economics from Cambridge University (1992) and is currently Professor of Industrial Organisation at the National University of Malaysia, and Dean and Professor of Business Economics at Universiti Malaysia Sarawak. He has published several internationally refereed books and articles. He has also undertaken consultancies for several international organizations, including the World Bank, UNCTAD, UNIDO and ILO.

Amartya Kumar Sen is the 1998 Nobel Prize winner for Economics. He is the Master of Trinity College, Cambridge, and Lamont University Professor Emeritus, Harvard University. He is a Past President of the Econometric Society, the International Economic Association, the Indian Economic Association, and the American Economic Association.

Acknowledgments

We would like to acknowledge gratefully the support of our respective institutions. Our gratitude also goes to the World Institute for Development Economics Research (UNU-WIDER) and to the United Nations Support Facility for Indonesian Recovery (UNSFIR-UNDP) where the editors have been (Chowdhury at WIDER, and Islam at UNSFIR) during the final stage of editing.

This volume is dedicated to the tens of thousands of people who have been pushed to poverty and insecurity by the Asian economic crisis.

1. Introduction: responding to the challenges of the post-crisis era

Anis Chowdhury and Iyanatul Islam

The financial and economic crisis that hit the Southeast and East Asian economies in the late 1990s has generated a voluminous literature just as their successes did. Pundits, including those who were upbeat in their assessment of the continued virtuous circle of growth in these economies, have been quick in condemning the very model of development that was claimed to lie at the heart of their successes. This shows that a prevailing paradigm is in disarray, and both the successes and failures of Asian economies remain an insufficiently understood phenomenon.

The rapid transformation of a small band of Southeast and East Asian economies has been termed one of the greatest revolutions in the history of economic thought. It was seen as ushering in the dawn of a new 'Asian Century'. Sadly, with the sudden and unexpected crisis that has wreaked havoc on the lives of millions of people in the region, 'Asia approaches the new century in an introspective and apprehensive mood' (Tadashi and Chia, 1999: 7). As Asia examines the causes of a sudden fall, and searches for a way forward, there is unprecedented turmoil in current thinking on development policy.

As the dust settles after the turbulence of 1997 and as growth returns to Southeast and Northeast Asia, this collection of contributions by both Asian and international scholars adopts a reflective approach. They attempt to bring together the current thoughts on the crisis and seek to navigate pathways to sustainable development. While the individual country studies vary in terms of the importance of various factors that contributed to the crisis, most point to the necessity of paradigm changes in development policy. For those who believe that a 'strong state' is essential for economic growth, the sudden collapse of these economies means that the system of semi-democracy or 'strong state' can no longer serve the purpose of further development. For innovation-driven sustainable development, any society must be open to ideas and democratize its polity. And for those who used the success of East Asian economies as a vindication of the neoclassical orthodoxy, referred to as the 'Washington consensus', the crisis points to the follies of progressive withdrawal of the government from the economic sphere and unfettered flows of short-term capital. To appreciate the issues involved, we provide a brief review of the debate in this introduction.

IMPLICATIONS FOR THE STATIST SCHOOL

One has to accept that Southeast and East Asian political systems have, until the recent movement towards democratization, been authoritarian. They were characterized as strong states, insulated from the narrow interests of vested groups. As a result, it was argued that the leaderships in these economies were able to formulate and vigorously pursue a national goal of growth. Admittedly, rapid growth in such economies provided durable political legitimacy even in the absence of democratic institutions. In trying to attain 'technocratic insulation', attenuation of human rights and the political exclusion of the labour movement have been quite conspicuous. However, it is also the case that wealth-sharing programmes in a context of rapid growth (such as affordable public housing in Singapore and the tapping of oil wealth to alleviate rural poverty in Indonesia) have made the process of social and economic change more 'inclusive'. Thus many believe that there is a 'cruel choice' between democracy and economic growth, at least at the early stage of development.

The Asian crisis has clearly demonstrated that, even if the authoritarian regimes could deliver rapid growth, they remained fragile. According to Romer (1993: 88) 'strong, authoritarian government[s] . . . require a configuration of bureaucratic competence and ruthless dedication to national economic success that is relatively rare and may be impossible to sustain'. Olson (1982: 52) also argues in the same vein when he observes that political systems characterized by insufficient 'diversity of advocacy, opinion and policy and fewer checks on erroneous policies and ideas . . . may perform unusually badly in some periods and unusually effectively in others'. Sen (1991: 425) makes the point more forcefully: 'the view that the "harder" the state the more effective it must be, [is] dead wrong'.

Once East Asian-style governance was widely perceived as a system that could deliver spectacular results, it ended up creating a durable culture of compliance. Why question a system that has created such remarkable outcomes within one's lifetime? The political leadership in turn, inspired by its success and the legitimacy that such success confers, constructed an ideology that rewarded compliance and consensus. In investing in the unsubstantiated view that there are distinctive Asian values that promote economic growth, the political leadership may well expose their polities to the risk that ideas and human ingenuity – the wellsprings of innovation-driven growth – are insufficiently recognized and rewarded. Ideas and human ingenuity are not simply market-driven outcomes. They require a conducive institutional context characterized by a robust civil society, free-flowing information, debate and dissent. The costs and risks inherent in sustaining a culture of compliance may not become evident to the current leadership or even to society at large because input-driven growth may take a long time to experience diminishing returns.

It is in this context that one has to analyse the region's thirst for foreign capital when there was no shortage of domestic savings. To begin with, the authoritarian regimes can maintain their legitimacy only through their success in generating rapid economic growth. However, their claim to legitimacy becomes increasingly tenuous as the economy confronts diminishing returns to scale. Their inability to make the transition to an innovation-driven stage of development to counteract diminishing returns eventually causes them to crumble.

The East and Southeast Asian authoritarian regimes found, in the surge of foreign capital inflows since the early 1990s, a reprieve. The access to foreign capital helped them in at least two ways. First, it enabled them to push for grand projects that could be used to justify their continuance on nationalistic/patriotic grounds. Second, to the extent that the capital flows were private and the regime had lax control, it kept the business community happy. The general citizenry also remained placated as the economy continued to grow despite increasing inefficiency. Thus the regimes that were once hailed for their relative autonomy from interest groups and for their growth-promoting relationship with the business community soon degenerated into 'crony capitalism'.

Furthermore, a vicious circle developed in the economic front. To maintain the capital flows, governments had to follow policies that were inconsistent. First, they had to maintain a stable or semi-fixed nominal exchange rate to encourage capital inflows, but this led to an appreciation of the real effective exchange rate, to the detriment of their export growth and current account developments. Second, in order to keep the financial sector pleased, governments had either to reduce budget deficits or to maintain a surplus budget that was achieved predominantly by cutting infrastructure investment. This had adverse impacts on the productivity of, and hence returns to, private investment. In other words, the infrastructure bottlenecks added to the problem of diminishing returns as more and more investment was required with the rise in the incremental capital–output ratio (ICOR). Thus the demand for foreign capital continued to rise.

As the profitability of investment in the real sector declined, funds moved to financial and speculative investment. The investment in the financial sector was also encouraged by governments' low inflation rate policy as it removed uncertainty about real returns. However, the policies of nominal exchange rate targeting and low inflation come under increasing pressure from capital flows although, paradoxically, these policies are designed to attract capital inflows. Policy makers find it increasingly difficult to sterilize the developments in the capital account. Either they have to let the money supply increase, and hence accept higher inflation, or let the exchange rate appreciate. In both cases, they cannot avoid the adverse impact on the current account. The more they try to hold out, the more vulnerable they become to speculative attacks and capital flight.

Thus, by prolonging the durability of growth-oriented authoritarian regimes in the region, foreign capital inflows have, ironically, been responsible to a large extent for delaying the democratization of East and Southeast Asian countries and also for prolonging investment-driven growth. Furthermore, to the extent that foreign capital inflows hindered the development of a robust civil society, they contributed to the authoritarian regimes' restraining of social movements that heighten public awareness of such issues as environmental degradation, the plight of those left behind by fast-paced growth, gender discrimination and so forth. This in turn reduced the capability of the state to develop effective mechanisms for dealing with emerging social problems.

Moreover, as the contrasting experiences of Thailand, Korea and Indonesia show, the authoritarian regimes were not able to handle sudden economic shocks better as such regimes attempted to protect themselves with secrecy. They also show that the impact of short-term economic crisis falls disproportionately on poor and weaker sections of the population as they do not find a voice in an authoritarian society. This leads to a divisive social crisis and in turn deepens the economic crisis, which Sen, in Chapter 2 of the present volume refers to as 'divided we fall'.

To be fair, it has to be conceded that the financial crisis has brought the above issues into the public domain and has given impetus to democratic reform. Although the event has been dramatic, the financial crisis brought the simmering social and economic tensions to the boil, as is evident in Indonesia. It is now abundantly clear that the sustainability of the 'Asian Century' crucially depends on the ability of the Asian countries to move to a more accountable, responsive and transparent form of governance. Ultimately, such governance requires the nourishing of durable democratic traditions (see Sen, 1994; also Chapter 2).

IMPLICATIONS FOR THE 'WASHINGTON CONSENSUS'

The 'Washington consensus' reflected the intellectual imprint of Washington-based institutions: the US Treasury, the International

Monetary Fund (IMF) and the World Bank. Its emphasis was on a constellation of virtues – free markets, free flow of trade and capital across the globe, macroeconomic management characterized by sound money, fiscal prudence and limited governments – that was regarded as the source of sustained economic prosperity both for poor and rich nations. It was an important set of ideas. It was operationally powerful because of its simplicity.

However, the East Asian crisis has exposed its limitations and has demonstrated that, in important respects, it was also misguided. In a series of speeches and papers, Stiglitz has led the way in pronouncing the demise of the conventional wisdom, or the Washington consensus in the domain of development policy.[1] The success of the Washington consensus as an intellectual doctrine rests on a number of factors. 'It focuses on issues of first-order importance, it sets up an easily reproducible framework . . . and it is frank about limiting itself only to establishing the prerequisites for development' (Stiglitz, 1998a: 6). Despite its global influence, the Washington consensus could not satisfactorily explain growth in pre-crisis Asia and could not satisfactorily explain why such economies were, almost overnight, thrust into a crisis of such stark magnitude. After all, these economies were paragons of macroeconomic stability and embraced the programme of privatization and the cause of globalization as a centrepiece of their economic strategy.

One may even argue that the very Washington consensus-based policies partially contributed to the Asian crisis. First, the adoption of a consensus policy framework meant a significant departure from the 'Asian development model' (Brownbridge and Kirkpatrick, 1998) in at least two significant areas: (a) control over external borrowing and (b) state guidance of investment. Second, fiscal prudence was achieved by drastically cutting government investment in infrastructure. This removed a significant source of externality for private investment and contributed to inflationary pressure arising from shortages of critical inputs such as electricity (see Chowdhury, 1999). Third, there has been a rise in the likelihood of business cycles entailing both longer duration and higher amplitudes with the forsaking of the stabilization of economies in the presence of increased capital mobility. This has encouraged short-term speculative investment rather than longer-term investment (Porter, 1992; Eatwell, 1996).

In other words, capital account liberalization and the deregulation of the domestic financial sector (two important planks of the consensus policy) have severely constrained the macroeconomic policy mix. As pointed out by Alan Greenspan, the chairman of the US Federal Reserve:

> A consistently disciplined monetary policy is what our global financial system increasingly demands and rewards . . . While there are many policy considerations that arise as a consequence of the rapidly expanding global financial system, the most important is the necessity of maintaining stability in the prices

> of goods and services and confidence in domestic financial markets. Failure to do so is apt to exact far greater consequences as a result of cross-border capital movements than those which might have prevailed a generation ago. (*New York Times*, 21 June, 1995: A-1 and D-9)

The Asian Development Bank (1999: 19) echoes the same sentiment when it concludes:

> As the domestic capital market becomes integrated with the international capital market, domestic policy makers become subject to scrutiny by global investors. The discipline that this scrutiny brings helps to discourage the pursuit of excessive monetary and fiscal expansion (which can quickly lead to reserve outflows and currency depreciation).

Thus increased internationalization constrains governments to a conservative fiscal and monetary policy mix independent of exchange rate regimes regardless of shades of governments.

The deregulation of the financial sector has resulted in an unprecedented growth in both financial institutions and financial products. Financial institutions have a vested interest in keeping inflation low because a rise in interest rates reduces the value of fixed interest securities. Also a rate of inflation that is consistently above that in most other countries is a reliable sign that sooner or later the currency will be devalued, which adversely affects those who hold fixed foreign exchange liabilities and those who need to repatriate foreign capital income. This financial market sentiment was echoed by the former governor of the Reserve Bank of Australia, Bernie Fraser, when he commented that 'monetary policy was becoming the hostage of influential financial markets with a vested interest in making the Reserve Bank give greater weight to inflation than unemployment' (*Sydney Morning Herald*, 16 June 1996). Financial markets also worry about large budget deficits. They fear that such deficits may lead to a rise in interest rates or devaluation.

Thus what we observe is the progressive withdrawal of governments from regulating both the real and financial side of the economy since the mid-1980s in line with the Washington consensus. This meant a substantial dismantling of the Asian growth model where governments played a very vital role in terms of both high infrastructure investment and strong relationship with business. Prior to becoming hostages to financial markets (both domestic and international), governments maintained fiscal discipline through a virtuous circle of growth. Governments invested in infrastructure and human capital formation which increased the productivity of private investment and international competitiveness, as explained by the new growth theory (Barro, 1997; Lucas, 1988). This meant governments were able to maintain fiscal balance (surplus or a small deficit) through growth dividends as their revenues continued to rise, with the private sector paying more and more tax as they grew.[2]

However, the above model of fiscal balance works with substantial lags as infrastructure investment usually comes to fruition after a long gestation period. As a result, it has an inflationary bias. Given the vested interest of the financial sector in low inflation, this model becomes inoperative with the increased influence of financial markets. So governments were forced to achieve fiscal balance more quickly. Furthermore, they had to reduce tax on capital income, as higher capital tax may encourage capital to fly out. The Washington consensus also suggests that lower taxes foster entrepreneurial innovation. Hence governments had to achieve fiscal balance by cutting their expenditure. For example, as can be seen from Table 1.1, the share of tax revenues in most Asian economies remained stable between 1985 and 1995, while government expenditure as a proportion of gross domestic product (GDP) fell drastically in all except in Korea, the Philippines and Taiwan, where it increased marginally during the same period. Since cuts in current expenditure are politically difficult as they affect social services, which are meagre to begin with in Asian countries, governments chose the easier option of cutting infrastructure investment (see Figure 1.1). But the decline in public infrastructure investment was not offset by a rise in private participation in the sector as was expected within the neoclassical framework (Walton, 1997; Malhotra, 1997).

What is also disturbing is that there has been a decline in expenditure on education in some countries, such as Indonesia and Malaysia, as a percentage of their respective GDP between 1985 and 1995. This led to a vicious circle. The more reductions there were in infrastructure and education, the larger was the decline in productivity, the slower was economic growth, and hence the greater were pressures on governments to reduce expenditure (Eatwell and Taylor, 1998; Taylor, 1998).

Moreover, as Rajan and Zingales (1998) point out, when the availability of capital becomes surplus in relation to opportunities for profitable investment, the efficient allocation of capital requires a financial system which operates at arm's length and is based on a legal framework rather than on personal relations and political connections as is found in Asian economies. The domestic financial system could not change at the speed at which capital flowed in. The problem was compounded by the rapid withdrawal of the government as financial deregulation under the weight of international capital markets and IMF–World Bank pressure was taken to be synonymous with *laissez faire* or no regulation. Thus the financial system remained relations-based and lacked prudential regulation. This meant that, when the increased flow of capital was channelled through the

Table 1.1 *Government finance indicators (% of GDP)*

Economy	Tax revenue				Expenditure				Fiscal balance/deficit			
	1975	1985	1995	1996	1975	1985	1995	1996	1975	1985	1995	1996
Hong Kong	8.6	10.4	11.1	11.6	12.8 (2.7)	15.3 (2.8)	13.9 (3.1)	14.6 (3.2)	1.9	0.4	−0.3	2.2
Indonesia	16.9	18.3	14.1	14.6	21.6 (0.9)	23.5 (1.9)	15.5 (0.6)	15.1 NA	3.9	3.7	−0.4	1.2
Korea	13.8	14.8	16.9	18.6	15.7 (2.2)	16.3 (3.0	17.6 (3.6)	18.3 (3.1)	2.1	1.2	0.2	0.5
Malaysia	20.5	21.6	19.0	18.9	31.4 (6.1)	32.9 (5.6)	22.4 (4.8)	22.6 (5.0)	8.5	5.7	−0.8	0.7
Philippines	13.2	10.7	16.3	16.7	16.0 (1.9)	14.1 (2.0)	18.2 (3.2)	18.3 (3.4)	1.4	1.9	−0.5	0.3
Singapore	17.1	17.3	16.4	17.7	26.3 (3.1)	39.1 (4.6)	20.8 (NA)	NA	−0.8	4.4	NA	NA
Taiwan	16.5	8.5	10.8	9.8	21.4 (0.8)	14.0 (1.6)	15.1 (NA)	14.3 (1.5)	−1.3	0.2	1.1	−1.4
Thailand	11.5	13.7	17.0	17.0	14.9 (NA)	18.9 (NA)	15.4 (NA)	17.8 (NA)	1.7	4.3	−3.0	0.9

Note: Figures in parentheses are expenditure on education as a percentage of GDP.

Source: Asian Development Bank, *Key Indicators for Member Countries, 1998.*

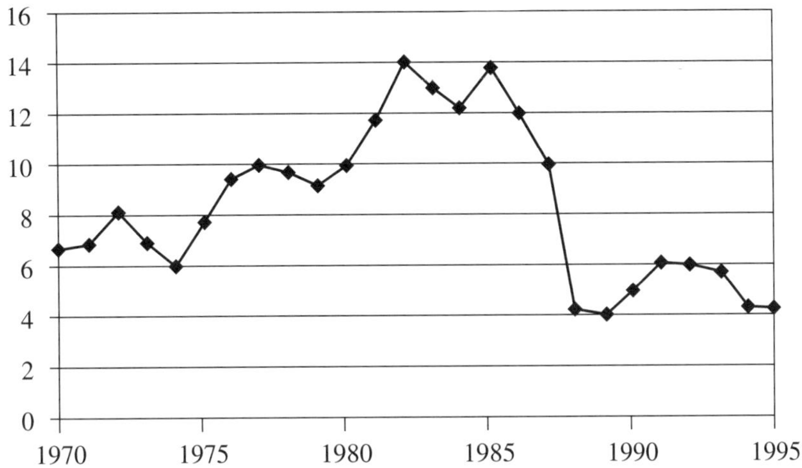

Sources: World Bank, *World Development Report* (various issues) and Asian Development Bank, *Key Indicators* (various issues)

Figure 1.1 Public investment/GDP (%)

banking sector, banks could venture into risky loans and thereby increase the fragility of the financial system.

Furthermore, inefficient uses of capital had adverse affects on productivity. As productivity of investment fell, people increasingly directed their high savings to speculative financial investment, which was facilitated by financial deregulation. The incentive for short-term speculative investment also arose from the lack of confidence in the economy as the prospect for long business cycle swings increases with governments' withdrawal from their stabilization role. The shift to short-term speculative capital had further adverse effects on productivity. As the productivity-driven economic growth tended to slow, governments needed to encourage more foreign capital to drive demand-led growth, given that a slowdown in economic growth would threaten their legitimacy. Thus they increasingly became hostages to financial markets, especially to international capital, which constrained their ability to respond to macroeconomic shocks, for which they once gained a reputation.

Furthermore, the need to win the confidence of international money markets may well lead governments towards a resolute commitment to fixed exchange rates. This may be regarded as a means of assuring the domestic corporate and financial lobby that the servicing costs of foreign currency-denominated liabilities will be protected. It is, at the same time, a signal to international money markets that governments will not allow the domestic private sector to default on its foreign debt, thus sustaining the capital flows. Unfortunately, such a 'deal' comes at potentially great costs. It builds up contingent or unfunded liabilities of the government.[3] This is a cruel paradox because it impairs the long-run fiscal position of the government, even though the need to win investor confidence pushes governments in the direction of macroeconomic conservatism in the short run.

More importantly, a strategy of attaching a premium to maintaining investor confidence exposes governments to the problem of the 'impossible trinity' in macroeconomic management (Krugman, 1998b). That is, policy makers are faced with the difficulty of managing a fixed exchange rate, an open capital account and policy independence. It can at most retain two objectives. Recent events in the wake of the East Asian crisis have shown that governments gave up – or were forced to give up – policy independence to defend the fixed exchange rate regime and open capital accounts. This means, of course, that governments forfeited the ability to fight an incipient recession through expansionary demand management policies. In the initial stages of the crisis, the policy preoccupation became, with the support and exhortation of the Washington-led international community, the need to win the 'confidence game' at all costs. Thus interest rates were raised and budgets were tightened. The Keynesian compact was broken, albeit temporarily, but its inexorable logic prevailed. A prospective recession became a stark reality.

Thus the answer to the puzzles pertaining to the sudden demise of the miracle economies of Asia now seems to lie in an undue faith in the virtues of globalization that made macroeconomic policy subservient to the interests of international money markets. In fact, prominent economists (for example, Corden, 1999; Krugman, 1998a, 1999; Sachs, 1998; Stiglitz, 1998b) have concluded that the very IMF adjustment package aggravated the crisis.[4]

LONG-TERM ISSUES AND CHALLENGES

The Asian economic crisis has understandably focused attention on rectifying errors in macroeconomic policy and achieving broad-based reform in the financial sector. The re-creation of the Asian miracle requires a vision about the future that has to go beyond the crisis and cope with a range of long-term issues and challenges. These pertain to the need to manage environmental degradation, to improve human rights and labour relations, to cope with the problem of demographic transition and growing inequality and to develop a tradition of democratic governance in order to foster and sustain productivity-driven growth.

Protection and Management of the Environment

It is generally agreed that the East Asian region has a poor record in terms of a range of environmental indicators (see Table 1.2). As the ADB (1997: 200) proclaims: 'For far too long, Asian policymakers ignored the environmental impact of rapid growth. Concern about pollution or degradation was simply not a priority.' As many as 15 of the 17 indicators pertaining to air and water pollution, access to safe water and sanitation, deforestation and land degradation, and energy consumption in East Asia show either 'very severe' or 'severe' environmental problems (ibid.: 203, Table 4.1). Most Southeast Asian countries have relied heavily on the export of their natural resources to import capital goods to support rapid growth. This has resulted in a rapid clearance of land. For example, in Malaysia, the area of land under cultivation increased from 15 per cent to 23 per cent from 1980 to 1994. Over the same period, the area of land under cultivation in Thailand rose from 36 per cent to 41 per cent. Their forestry policies have failed to recognize the scarcity of forest resources and sustainability. In Indonesia, for example, the annual sustainable harvest is estimated at 22 million m^3, but the annual production of forest products is in excess of 40

Table 1.2 Environmental indicators

	Carbon dioxide emissions per capita (metric tons)		Energy use (oil equivalent), average annual growth rate		Annual deforestation (% change)
	1980	1992	1980–90	1990–94	1980–90
Indonesia	0.6	1.0	7.4	9.3	1.1
Hong Kong	3.3	5.0	7.0	7.7	−0.5
Korea	3.3	6.6	8.5	10.2	0.1
Malaysia	2.0	3.8	9.4	11.2	2.1
Philippines	0.8	0.7	2.6	8.3	3.4
Singapore	13.2	17.7	7.2	10.5	2.3
Taiwan					
Thailand	1.9	1.7	9.5	10.0	3.5
Middle-income countries	2.9	4.8	NA	NA	0.5
South Asia	0.4	0.7	7.0	5.1	0.8
Latin America	2.4	2.3	2.5	2.7	0.7

Source: *World Development Report* (various issues).

million m^3. As a result of over-dependence on natural resources, high performing Asian economies (HPAEs) have lost more of their forest area in the last 30 years than any other region in the world (World Bank, 1998: 102).

The economic and social costs of environmental degradation are enormous. World Bank estimates suggest that the annual cost of air pollution is as high as US$3.1 billion in Bangkok, US$1.6 billion in Kuala Lumpur and US$800 million in Jakarta. These estimates would be as much as 40 per cent higher if one included additional costs due to congestion (Brandon, 1994: 22). As a proportion of GDP, economic costs stemming from environmental damage appear to be as high as 8.5 per cent in the PRC (Smil, 1984) and between 1 and 2 per cent in Indonesia, the Philippines and Thailand (World Bank, 1992, 1993).

What are the factors that have shaped this sorry evidence of environmental degradation? To some extent, this reflects the by-products of factor-driven rapid economic growth and consequent urbanization. One of the drawbacks of investment-driven or capital-intensive industrialization is that it is inevitably energy-intensive, which is notorious for its emission-related pollution. However, to a considerable extent the evidence reflects more deep-seated problems: the lack of political will and governance to tackle environmental problems; and widespread market failures compounded by inefficient policies, such as sub-optimal pricing of infrastructure services.

The countries of East Asia are slowly beginning to recognize the need for much greater vigilance with respect to managing and maintaining environmental standards. This awareness is due primarily to two factors. First, domestically, an assertive middle class is increasingly demanding reduced air, water and noise pollution. Second, internationally, industrialized countries are imposing stiffer environmental standards on trade. For example, there is a move to label all imported timber products as to whether they are from sustainable forests or not. Thus the long-run viability of export oriented HPAEs depends crucially on improving their environmental standards.

Labour Relations

There is wide agreement among the observers of HPAEs that most of them maintained relatively unfettered labour markets during their early stage of economic transformation, at the expense of workers' rights. For example, until the late 1980s labour conditions in Malaysia, Korea, the Philippines, Taiwan and Thailand were determined unilaterally by employers with or without the assistance of government (World Bank, 1998). However, observers disagree on the virtues of labour subordination. For example, neoclassical economists believe that the cost of infringement of labour rights has been more than compensated by exemplary results of rapid growth in real wages and full employment. On the other hand, critics regard the failure to uphold basic rights of workers as one of the glaring weaknesses of the pre-crisis period. In any case, progressive affluence in the region has made workers more assertive of their rights. For example, both Korea and Taiwan witnessed waves of industrial unrest in the late 1980s. In both countries, the role and power of unions have increased substantially. Malaysia agreed to allow unionization in the export-oriented, foreign direct investment (FDI)-dependent electronics sector in 1988. Both Thailand and Indonesia were forced to raise the minimum wage a number of times from the mid-1980s.

Added to the pressure is the International Labour Organization (ILO)'s determination to improve labour standards in the region. The ILO is pressing for a new 'social contract' for East Asia, which will have full respect for basic labour rights (ILO, 1998). There are also attempts to bring labour standards under the purview of the World Trade Organization (WTO). Major concerns are expressed in industrialized countries about the prevalence of child labour in countries such as the Philippines, Thailand and other countries of Southeast Asia, and the discrimination against women in terms of work conditions and pay.

Thus failure to improve labour standards and industrial relations could be very costly for HPAEs in the coming years. It may not only lead to growing industrial unrest, it is also highly likely that industrial countries will use labour standards as a protectionist device against exports from HPAEs.

Demographic Change

The high performing economies of East and Southeast Asia have gone through the demographic transition from both high fertility and mortality rates (the burden phase) to both low fertility and mortality rates (the gift phase). Between 1965 and 1990, the working-age population in East Asia grew 2.39 per cent per year, which is nearly twice the rate of annual population growth (1.58 per cent) and substantially higher than the annual rate of growth of the dependent population (0.25 per cent). Although less dramatic, the working-age population grew at a faster rate than the entire population in Southeast Asia as well. According to the estimates of Bloom and Williamson (1998), this demographic transition can explain between 1.37 and 1.87 percentage points of growth in GDP per capita in East Asia or between one-third and half of the 'miracle' in Northeast and Southeast Asia.

However, the East Asian economies are predicted to enter the final phase of demographic transition (a decline in working-age population and a rise in the older dependent population) in the immediate future. For example, according to the United Nations (1991) projections, the ratio of working-age population to non-working-age population will peak in East Asia in 2010. The Asian Development Bank (ADB, 1997) estimates show that by 2025 more than 10 per cent of the population in Singapore, Hong Kong, China and Taiwan will be aged 65 and above. The transition to this final phase of demographic transition will have at least two important implications. First, as the share of the working age population declines, the economic growth rate will fall unless either (a) the participation rate rises or (b) there is technological upgrading. According to Bloom and Williamson (1998), this is likely to shave off between 0.14 and 0.44 percentage point from the growth rate of GDP per capita. The loss is estimated to be higher for some countries such as Hong Kong (2.0–2.4 percentage points), Singapore (2.5–3.0 percentage points) and Korea (1.9–2.2 percentage points).

Second, ensuring financial security and providing age care will become a major challenge in the future. Currently, most HPAEs do not have a universal pension or social security system. Traditionally, families look after elderly persons. But as these societies are rapidly losing their traditional values with economic transformation, there will be a growing need for the state to provide age care and income support for the elderly. As a consequence, the budget deficit is likely to rise as the share of tax revenue declines and demand for public provision of age care and pensions rises (Heller, 1998). Some countries may have to depend increasingly on migrant labour, which in turn could create social tension.

The Re-emergence of Inequality

A common view – reaffirmed by Fields (1995: 103) – is that the East Asian economies are characterized by moderate degrees of inequality and trends have generally been egalitarian. Cross-country evidence compiled by Medhi (1994) suggests a less optimistic interpretation. As he observes (Medhi, 1994: 70): 'The available data indicate that the distribution of income in . . . [East Asia] . . . has shown a tendency to become more unequal in recent years. This is in contrast to their earlier periods of development where income inequality declined as the economies grew.'

Other observers have also highlighted cases of growing inequality in East Asia.[5] Focusing on the experiences of China and Thailand, Walton (1997: 5) notes that they bear the dubious distinction of registering one of the highest increases in inequality in the developing world in recent decades.

The findings of these studies have been corroborated by the World Bank (1998), which shows that inequality has risen in China, Hong Kong, Thailand and the Philippines. The World Bank (ibid.) has attributed the recent rise in inequality to two factors: (a) a rise in returns to higher education which has driven a wedge between the earnings of skilled and unskilled workers, and (b) concentration of economic activities in certain areas, which has contributed to regional income disparity.

High inequality undermines poverty alleviation. Despite substantial reductions of poverty in HPAEs, the World Bank (1998: 77) study shows that people are still very vulnerable. For example, a 25 per cent increase in the poverty line more than doubles the head-count index, from 11 to 25. It also reports a high incidence of poverty in pockets of regions. For instance, in 1990, poverty incidence in Indonesia ranged from 1.3 per cent in Jakarta to 46 per cent in West Nusa Tenggara. Likewise, northeast Thailand has the highest incidence of poverty and the highest concentration of poor people.

Table 1.3 Trends in income inequality (Gini ratio; year)

Indonesia	Hong Kong	Korea	Malaysia
0.34; 1976	0.49; 1966	0.34; 1964	0.50; 1968
0.34; 1980	0.44; 1971	0.33; 1970	0.53; 1976
0.32; 1987	0.37; 1980	0.39; 1976	0.49; 1979
0.32; 1990	0.42; 1986	0.39; 1980	0.46; 1988
0.34; 1994	0.45; 1991	0.40; 1988	0.47; 1995
Philippines	**Singapore**	**Taiwan**	**Thailand**
0.49; 1961	0.50; 1966	0.36; 1964	0.41; 1965
0.49; 1965	0.46; 1973	0.30; 1970	0.43; 1968
0.48; 1971	0.41; 1980	0.31; 1980	0.45; 1975
0.45; 1986	0.46; 1986	0.32; 1985	0.50; 1986
0.45; 1989	0.49; 1989	0.31; 1990	0.50; 1990

Sources: Medhi (1994: Table 1); Shari, I. (1998), 'Economic Growth and Income Inequality in Malaysia, 1971–1995', paper presented to the International Conference on Economic Growth, Poverty and Income Inequality in the Asia Pacific Region, UNSW, 19–20 March.

The re-emergence of inequality (see Table 1.3) is a cause of concern, particularly in ethnically diverse societies such as Indonesia and Malaysia. If the inequality is perceived to be due to the concentration of economic power in one ethnic group, this may trigger social tensions and race riots, as witnessed as recently as May 1998 in Indonesia or in 1969 in Malaysia.

It could potentially sow the seeds of demands for redistributive measures that in turn retard growth through policy distortions – a phenomenon sometimes characterized as 'distributive politics'.

TOWARDS IMPROVED GOVERNANCE

As noted, a major challenge facing East Asia in the 21st century is the need to foster and sustain democratic governance. The agenda of building democracy in the region also encapsulates issues of social protection and the nourishing of enabling institutions that could invigorate the policy-making capacities of new democracies.

Fostering and Sustaining Democracy

For a while, robust and historically unprecedented growth in East Asia led to the view among elites in the region that such outcomes were also facilitated by 'Asian values'.[6] These values, it was argued, led to a resolute commitment to the work ethic, an almost reverential attitude towards education, and respect for order and authority. Some pundits, in analysing the sources of hyper-growth in pre-crisis East Asia, also discovered quintessential Asian institutions. These were identified as close government–business relations, internal capital markets and 'technocratic insulation' by authoritarian governments that shielded policy makers from the rapacious, rent-seeking proclivities of societal groups.

Now, in the wake of the 1997 financial crises, these views have been dramatically reversed – often by the very same pundits who espoused them! Quintessential Asian virtues have become, almost overnight, conspicuous vices. As noted, 'crony capitalism' is now used as a metaphor for capturing fatal institutional weaknesses in the region. Muted concerns about past problems, particularly in the domain of human rights, have come to the forefront of discussions about designing social policy in the region that would suit the mood and the requirements of the 21st century.

A key goal is the inculcation and consolidation of democratic governance. Considerable progress certainly appears to have been made. Korea and Taiwan have continued their bold journey towards the democratization of their political systems since the mid-1980s. Thailand and the Philippines have also become important players in the pan-Asian trend towards democratization. Indonesia is the latest example of a large East Asian economy engaged in the difficult transition towards political liberalization. With the successful completion (in June 1999) of reasonably free and fair elections, after 44 years Indonesia is poised for major political and social changes.

However, the risk of the process being derailed by racial and intraregional tensions is still considerable

Also enigmatic cases and conspicuous exceptions remain. Malaysia and Singapore may be typified as 'semi-democracies', despite the trappings of parliamentary institutions, primarily because of the lack of a free press and the stringent constraints within which political dissent has to operate.[7] China is resolutely stuck in an authoritarian mould. Despite the 1989 tragedy of Tiananmen Square, China is far from showing any sign of political liberalization. It continues to profess unwavering faith in the separation of politics and economics, thus enabling it to combine communism in the political sphere with the progressive introduction of capitalism in the economic domain. Apparently, the Chinese political leadership has declared that such a system can last 'tens of generations'.[8]

Despite the fact that some countries in the region are resisting the transition to democratic governance, the spotlight on these issues will not go away. As Sen (1997: 14–15) notes, 'the case for them stands, even without having to show that democracy actually encourages growth'. Democracy and human rights are intrinsic values and may be regarded as ends in themselves as well as a means to an end.[9]

In more concrete terms, there are a number of areas in which policy makers in East Asia can work more diligently to improve on its poor record of human rights. In particular, the issue of labour rights needs a lot more attention. A start could be made by ratifying the core ILO conventions pertaining to labour standards by all the countries in the region and by incorporating 'social dialogue' with relevant stakeholders (the government itself, employers, trade unions, civil society) as a core principle of designing social policy. Korea has set an example by showing how this can be done. Indonesia agreed to ratify the core ILO conventions in the midst of considerable economic and political turmoil.

The issue of social dialogue need not simply be confined to the domain of social policy. It should become a general principle of policy formulation. Greater public discussion, openness and accountability pertaining to the policy formulation process will expedite the consolidation of democratic governance in the region.

Building a Sustainable Social Protection Policy

In the domain of social equity, the crisis has demonstrated that one cannot simply rely on rapid, employment-intensive growth to act as a *de facto* social safety net or social protection policy. Certainly, in the pre-crisis period, rapid growth brought about sustained reductions in poverty without any marked worsening of income inequality. But this proud record is now badly tarnished. Even on the eve of the crisis, countries such as China, Indonesia and Thailand exhibited evidence of rising inequality. There have been significant reversals in poverty, particularly in Indonesia.

It is now widely recognized that the sharing of the burden of the crisis has been iniquitous. Some of the most vulnerable segments of East Asian society – women, children, workers, farmers, day labourers, small businessmen – bore the brunt of the crisis even though they had no role in bringing it about. This is a reflection of a system that became hostage to the perceptions and interests of the international investor community and their domestic beneficiaries. Even worse, when the crisis struck, the vulnerable groups in society were largely left to fend for themselves. They had to seek refuge in traditional support systems (burden sharing with the help of the extended family and friends, returning to the village to participate in the family farm, finding work in the informal sector, and so on). To their credit, donor agencies ploughed substantial resources into building a social safety net system on an emergency basis, but, to be sustainable, such initiatives must eventually be financed by national governments and become a core part of their social policy.

Why have East Asian governments overlooked the need to build a sustainable social protection policy in the past (see Lee, 1998: ch. 4)? To some extent, the long boom in the pre-crisis period created a sense of complacency among policy makers that they were immune to protracted recessions and hence had no need to invest in social safety net initiatives. It is also possible that there was excessive faith in the capacity of the informal and agricultural sectors – particularly in countries such as Indonesia and Thailand, where these sectors are still significant – to act as informal social safety net schemes. Nor can one discount the possibility that elite opinion in East Asia displayed a cultural aversion to the notion of the 'welfare state' in the West. Welfare statism could have been associated with such Western stereotypes as the breakdown of the family, the destruction of the work ethic and general lack of discipline and social cohesion. Finally, it is possible that policy makers genuinely felt that the opportunity and fiscal costs of running a comprehensive social safety net system were unaffordable for the typical East Asian economy.

The crisis and its aftermath have shown that all the reasons that may be advanced to avoid the installation of a social protection policy in East Asia are largely misguided. Recessions are a real and ever-present danger in East Asia, as they are elsewhere in the world. Informal systems of social protection simply cannot cope in the wake of such a region-wide and severe recession. The cultural aversion to welfare statism is as misguided as the rationale of invoking 'Asian values' in order to justify a 'business as usual' syndrome. The issue of affordability also appears to have been exaggerated.

Some calculations show that 'an average required contribution of between 0.3 to 0.4 per cent of payroll from 1991 to 2000 would have been sufficient to provide all insured job losers over this period, including during the current crisis, with 12 months of benefits' in Korea, Thailand and Indonesia (Lee, 1998: 83).

Building Enabling Institutions: Combining Technocratic Independence with Democratic Accountability

The constellation of reform agenda that we have espoused here brings to the fore the issue of the capability of the state to manage such an agenda. In fact, when suggesting the restoration of the role of government, Stiglitz (1998c) makes it conditional on the capability of the state. This has been criticized as 'static and ahistorical . . . [and] minimalist' (Sender, 1999: 104). However, those who are advocating a 'maximalist' role of the state in response to market failure are silent about the risk of corresponding 'government failure'. There is plenty of evidence of unsustainable government budget deficits, financed by monetary expansion, which end up in high inflation, loss of competitiveness and a chronic balance of payments problem. The danger of populist macroeconomic policy is greater in a young democratic regime where politicians may easily succumb to interest group pressures.

Therefore the reform agenda in post-crisis East Asia should incorporate the building of enabling institutions. These include ensuring the independence of four core institutions from the executive arm of the government: an independent judiciary, an independent election commission, an independent central bank and an independent fiscal board.

The fundamental role of the state is the establishment of the rule of law. In many developing countries, not only is the legal system archaic, but also the judiciary is not independent of the executive branch of the government. This compounds the problems of market failure as politicians interfere with the operation of the private sector. Once the property rights are clearly defined and enforced by an independent judiciary, the area where government interventions are genuinely required becomes clearly delineated.

An independent election commission is essential for the survival of a vibrant democracy. Without such independence, money and wealth disenfranchise people and democracy becomes dysfunctional. The recent constitutional reform in Thailand gives much cause for optimism. The work of citizens' groups such as the People's Solidarity for Participatory Democracy (PSPD) in Korea and non-government organizations in exposing corrupt politicians can go a long way in political reforms.

In the macroeconomic policy making arena, the reform should begin with the central bank. The evidence shows that an independent central bank with a clear mandate for price stability enhances macroeconomic performance (Alesina and Summers, 1993; Cukierman *et al.*, 1992). Therefore the central bank's mandate should be amended to enable it to control inflation only, rather than a host of conflicting objectives. This is in line with what has been proposed above in order to enhance accountability and transparency of government departments. Note that, as emphasized by Fischer (1995), the central bank independence refers to 'instrument independence', not 'goal independence'. It is not suggested that the central bank would have the independence to pursue any goal, but that it would be constrained to fulfil a clearly specified objective.

Critics of central bank independence maintain that, as a lender of last resort, the central bank will have to cave in and monetize debt if the government remains irresponsible. This 'war of attrition' may lead to considerable political instability and larger fiscal imbalance (Alesina 1992). Therefore the credibility of government's fiscal and monetary policy lies ultimately in the accountability and transparency of the budgetary process. Here lies the importance of an independent fiscal board (IFB). The IFB must have sufficient power to review government expenditure programmes, and all new initiatives must be cleared by it. The idea of IFB is akin to an independent judiciary. Just as an independent judicial system monitors political interference with institutions for greater political efficiency, an IFB will ensure that the budgetary process is transparent and is not influenced by primarily vested interests. An IFB thus will enhance efficiency in macroeconomic management; it is a superior arrangement to a 'fiscal constitution' restricting the government to a balanced budget. Such a constitutionally binding arrangement could be unnecessarily debilitating. An IFB should work closely with an independent central bank in order to avoid any coordination problem between fiscal and monetary policies.

In pursuing the notion of enabling institutions, it is important to issue a caveat. The idea of independent institutions run by technocrats according to a clearly defined mandate always runs the risk of becoming 'too independent' and hence prejudicial to societal interests. For example, a central banker could become too inflation-averse and insensitive to the possibilities of stabilizing output relative to societal preferences. This is where the notion of combining technocratic independence with democratic accountability becomes critical. Designated technocrats in autonomous agencies (election commissioners, judges, bankers and treasury mandarins) ought to be subject to democratic accountability through public scrutiny in various forms: reporting to and questioning by elected representatives, provision of information to the public and receptivity to criticism engendered by public debate.

In sum, the agenda of building enabling institutions in East Asia through new rules and restraints cannot overlook the conventional institutions in democracies: an effective parliament, a free press, a robust civil society. The aim of independent agencies is to supplement the capability of democratic institutions, not supplant their role.

READER'S GUIDE TO THE VOLUME

Chapter 2, by Sen, touches on broader issues pertaining to development as freedom. While the crisis has exposed some of the weaknesses of past policies, Sen passionately argues that one should adhere to the proverbial injunction that the baby must not be thrown out with the bath water. The strengths of the past must be blended with the vision for the future, with a view to expanding human security and freedom. The hallmark of the Asian development model, according to Sen, was the effective use of complementary institutions – especially the state and the market. By widening economic entitlements through wider dissemination of basic education and basic heath care, and land reform, the state helped reap the benefits of markets, as the wider population shares the opportunities offered by the market. The crisis has, however, made it clear that the institutions and policies for growth may not be the same as the ones that are required for preventing transient and short-term problems which may create havoc in people's lives. 'Success in one field may not guarantee success in the other.' Among other lessons of the crisis, according to Sen, are (a) the recognition of the fact that no economy is invulnerable to short-term problems, (b) there is an asymmetry in the relation between economic growth and social security, (c) the burden of short-term problems must be shared to prevent social unrest, and (d) democratic societies, where people have a voice, can handle short-term problems much better. Thus he concludes that the old strategy of institutional complementarities must include new institutions for ensuring protective security, participatory democracy and transparent accountability.

Sen's review of the key challenges facing post-crisis Asia sets the stage for the launching of the country-specific studies. The inaugural country-specific chapter in the volume focuses on Japan. Japan was the first East Asian country to achieve spectacular economic success. The Northeast and, later, Southeast Asian countries not only followed many of Japan's development policies, but Japan also acted as a regional 'locomotive' of growth through investment and trade. Thus the slowing of the Japanese economy in the early 1990s, to some extent, contributed to the Asian crisis. Revitalizing the Japanese economy, therefore, remains a critical factor for the future of the region. Kwan's contribution argues that a key feature of the Japanese model of a cross-shareholding system of main banks, which allowed the corporate sector to pursue long-term goals instead of short-term profits, is no longer suitable after the catching-up phase is over. In its mature phase, Japan needs a new system, which promotes competition and risk taking. He highlights three new challenges that Japan faces: ageing of the population and a declining birth rate, keener competition in both manufacturing and service sectors in a globalized environment, and flexible and innovative business practices. According to Kwan, the failure of the traditional fiscal and monetary stimulus to restart the economy is a clear indication that the Japanese economy needs structural reforms. He highlights some of the reform programmes initiated by the Hashimoto government in late 1996 and concludes that the focus of policies must shift from 'equality of outcome' to 'equality of opportunity'.

Chapter 4, on the Republic of Korea (South Korea), is written by O. Yul Kwon. South Korea is sometimes referred to as the second Japan. No other Northeast or Southeast Asian economy followed the Japanese model of development as closely as South Korea did, and as a result it shares many features with the Japanese economy which are now obsolete. With the membership of the rich nations' club and the end of the cold war, Korea no longer enjoys any preferential treatment in the Western market. Yul Kwon argues that, in the new environment, protection of the Korean domestic market and industries by state intervention will become increasingly difficult. In a globalized environment, a country cannot wish to reap the benefits of international trade and capital flows and at the same time maintain national sovereignty and regulate its economy; it can have only one of the choices. Since Korea has chosen to remain engaged with the world economy, it must give up either national sovereignty or its desire to regulate the economy. According to Yul Kwon, the latter must go; instead of direct intervention in the economy, the state must play a complementary role and provide an enabling environment for the private sector. The enabling environment includes transparency, accountability and competition in both economic and political spheres. Yul Kwon also emphasizes that social development programmes and safety net must be an integral part of the new development paradigm. They not only protect those affected by short-term shocks, but also act as built-in stabilizers.

Thailand is the country from which the Asian crisis has spread to the other parts of the region. Pasuk and Baker argue in Chapter 5 that Thailand does not fit the so-called 'Asian model' of direct state intervention or labour repression. But it achieved almost similar results to others through the control of credit allocation by a few banks, Japanese FDI and exploitation of a large, resource-abundant rural sector. The relatively peaceful transition to democracy also served Thailand well in coping with the crisis and responding to it. Pasuk and Baker examine economic, social and political impacts of the crisis, and express some concern about the continued urban bias in economic strategies. They highlight some of the cross-currents in Thai rural–urban politics. According to the authors, in the vision for the future, Thailand has two models to choose from: the Singapore model, with a dominant role for multinational corporations (MNCs), and the Taiwan model, where small local entrepreneurs play a dominant role. Pasuk and Baker argue that, although the Singapore model is preferred by many technocrats, it is not suitable for Thailand, with a large rural sector. According to them, Thailand has a very lively entrepreneurial culture and it should adopt the Taiwan model, which is also favoured by Japan, Thailand's main source of FDI.

Chapter 6, by Dhanani and Hasnain, argues that the marked slowdown observed in the Indonesian manufacturing sector and manufactured exports during 1993–7 was a consequence of shallow, export-led industrialization. As a result, the country reaped only some of the advantages associated with export-oriented industrialization, while suffering most of its disadvantages. The actual pattern of industrial development in Indonesia generated a number of structural as well as institutional weaknesses which dampened manufactured growth. These included a continuously high dependence on imported raw materials and components, low value-added generated in resource-based industries, a virtually non-existent capital goods sector, limited range in export products and markets, low-productivity small and medium industries, high market concentration in many segments of industry, weak human resources, a weak technology support system and weak manufacturing capabilities of domestic firms. Owing to these weaknesses, Indonesia ran a persistent deficit in manufacturing goods ($5 billion per year) and an increasingly large deficit in the current account of the balance of payments ($2 billion to $8 billion) in the 1985–6 to 1996–7 period, which were offset by large inflows of private capital and external public borrowing. According to Dhanani and Hasnain, the structural weaknesses prevailing before the crisis will manifest again as the economy recovers, in so far as shallow export-led industrialization will once more produce a deficit in the balance of trade of manufactures. In this case, the constrained borrowing capacity of the public and private sectors that is likely to confront the country over the next four or five years will prevent the restoration of external payment balances maintained before the crisis. On the domestic front, in view of current trade liberalization, international competition as well as firm indebtedness, Indonesia is facing a real threat of deindustrialization. Thus the authors argue that a new strategy is required for the 21st century which combines the benefits of trade liberalization, export orientation and that of building the manufacturing capabilities of domestic firms, to enhance their competitiveness and resilience in the export as well as domestic markets. Since domestic firms have to undergo an arduous and risky process of learning to catch up with best international technological and business practices, a path fraught with market failures, liberalization alone will not ensure their competitiveness. The chapter calls for a changing role for government, complementary to the market, to facilitate this learning process.

Rasiah (Chapter 7) maintains that some structural weaknesses of the economy were mainly responsible for the crisis in Malaysia, although it was triggered by a sudden withdrawal of foreign portfolio capital. Among them were skill shortages, inadequate R&D support and a lack of coordination to support complementarities of industries. The lack of transparency and accountability in both political and economic spheres contributed to the build-up of these weaknesses. Although unorthodox policy experimentation with capital control and expansionary policies in defiance of the IMF dictum have succeeded in halting the decline and eventually returning the economy to a positive terrain, Rasiah expresses concerns about complacency. He fears that, with the resumption of growth, some old practices of patronage and corruption may have re-emerged. Rasiah argues that, unless the judiciary is given more authority and is made independent of the executive branch of the government, the legal instruments created for transparency and accountability could be compromised.

In Chapter 8, Lim maintains that the Philippines economy, the laggard, has been characterized by boom–bust cycles in the 1980s and 1990s. The Philippines' achievement in poverty and inequality reduction was not as impressive as in other Southeast Asian nations, and the crisis worsened the situation even further, especially for women, children and the rural sector. One of the worst casualties of the crisis, according to Lim, was the environment. The crisis came when environmental conditions had been deteriorating. The fiscal restraint affected many reforestation and conservation programmes. With the depreciation of currency, there is an added incentive for the mining and forestry industries to mine and log more intensively. The government lifted the ban on logging during the crisis in order to alleviate the problem through exports. Lim is not only critical of the IMF recovery package, he also finds the regional response inadequate. He argues that the Philippines has to improve its performance in the provision of a social safety net, protection of labour rights and management of conflicts. Although the Philippines achieved democracy, its polity is still dominated by the elite and lacks transparency. Lim also advocates an active stabilization role of the government in order to prevent boom–bust cycles.

Chia (Chapter 9) examines the strengths of the Singapore economy, which avoided the severity of the crisis. Political stability, social cohesion, a highly efficient bureaucracy and a competitive economy served it well and provide a good foundation from which it can move into the 21st century. However, according to Chia, Singapore has to change its vision and modify of the 'Singapore Inc' model, where the state played a very critical role in creating entrepreneurs. Now that it has attained a critical mass of entrepreneurs, Singapore should be less risk-averse and more innovative. Risk-taking and innovation can flourish in a society which encourages open debate and questioning of the status quo. Chia does not offer any blueprint for achieving such a society, but hopes that, with the long and successful track record, the government and people of Singapore will be able to rise to the challenge.

Taiwan is the other East Asian miracle economy which was not overwhelmed by the contagion of the Asian crisis. In Chapter 10, Chen argues that, despite the frequent lumping of all East Asian economies into one so-called 'Asian model' of development, the Taiwanese economy has some distinctive features. Among them is the dominance of smaller firms as opposed to the big chaebols in Korea. The Taiwanese firms are also less leveraged. Taiwan follows a less activist industrial policy and supports private sector R&D. Chen argues that the maturity of the Taiwanese democracy also helped avoid financial mismanagement. According to him, liberalization of the political market or democratization reinforces rather than jeopardizes free competition in the financial market. Democracy has also constrained the operation of cronyism. These distinctive features helped Taiwan avoid the region-wide financial crisis.

The People's Republic of China, too, could avoid the Asian financial crisis. Dean (Chapter 11) argues that, although China was lucky this time round, it may not be so in the future, because its economic and governance structure still remains very fragile. He characterizes the Asian model of governance as a symbiotic relationship between government, finance and industry in a triangular fashion. Problems at any one corner of the triangle can easily spread to the others and destabilize the whole economy. According to Dean, China's industrial sector is still dominated by loss-making state-owned enterprises (SOEs), and its financial sector suffers from insolvency as it has to absorb the losses of SOEs. The loss-making SOEs are also one of the main causes of fragile fiscal deficits. Despite these frailties, China could avoid the crisis due to currency inconvertibility and related capital controls, reinforced by a heavily regulated domestic financial sector. However, China's capital account is increasingly becoming uncontrollable. Flows to and from Hong Kong and Taiwan are almost impossible to monitor. Moreover, as China joins the WTO, and allows the entry of foreign banks, the capital controls will slowly disappear. Thus, if China does not reform its SOEs, it will remain vulnerable to financial crisis.

In a provocative contribution, Leong (Chapter 12) claims that, at China's current stage of transition to a market economy, the optimal political system for China in the sense of maximizing economic growth will take a form different from the Western liberal democratic model. Democracy enhances economic development, but can also impede economic growth through distributive politics and populist macroeconomic policies. According to Leong, democracy is a more crucial determinant of economic growth in circumstances of high economic development, where 'inspiration' is more important than 'perspiration', than in China's current relatively low level. Therefore, in the long run, democracy should be a goal for China, for its capacity to improve the lives of the Chinese people, beyond what it can do for economic growth. Leong claims that marketization, rather than economic growth, is driving the process of political liberalization in China. Chinese success in economic reform to date has been due more to effective government than to democracy.

The last contribution (Chapter 13), by Hutson and Kearney, gives an overview of the burgeoning debate about the future role of the IMF in the proposed new international financial architecture. It begins by reviewing the main explanations that have been advanced for the onset and contagion of the Asian financial crisis. It discusses the role played by short-term capital flows, and how the IMF attempted to mitigate the crisis. Hutson and Kearney argue that the IMF's broadening of its loan conditionalities has led to increased politicization of the institution and reduced its effectiveness in managing future crises. They conclude that a thorough review of the IMF's articles of agreement ought to be undertaken, and that the institution should be moved out of Washington and rotated around the world's main financial centres.

NOTES

1. The clearest expression of this view can be found in Stiglitz (1998a). Other highly pertinent contributions include Stiglitz (1998b, 1998c). The term 'Washington consensus' was coined by Williamson (1990). The issues discussed in this chapter also bear the influence of Sachs (1998), Radelet and Sachs (1999), Krugman (1998a, 1999) and Bhagwati (1998).
2. Matthews (1968) provides a detailed account of how industrialized countries were able to have a fiscal surplus (or a small deficit) despite high expenditure prior to financial liberalization. In short, high levels of investment by the private sector, encouraged by a public sector commitment to growth and employment, resulted in healthy fiscal balances and relatively small current account deficits.
3. The concept of unfunded government liabilities – created by the implicit and explicit guarantees of the government to finance possible defaults of private sector indebtedness – has become a major issue in the wake of the East Asian crisis. In 1997, contingent government liabilities for the crisis-affected East Asian economies fell in the top decile for a sample of 46 developing and developed economies. See Polackova (1999: 4).
4. Stiglitz now argues for the need to forge a 'Post-Washington Consensus'. See citations on Stiglitz under note 1 above.

5. See *Journal of the Asia Pacific Economy*, 5(1/2), Symposium on Poverty, Economic Growth, Poverty and Income Inequality in the Asia–Pacific Region.
6. See Islam and Chowdhury (1997: pt 1, ch. 8). The most prominent advocates of 'Asian values' are Lee Kuan Yew, ex-prime minister of Singapore and Mahathir Mohammad, current prime minister of Malaysia. For a critique, see Lee (1998: ch. 4).
7. The sad case of the imprisonment of Anwar Ibrahim in Malaysia, at one time the heir-apparent to the mantle of prime ministership, by a Mahathir-led faction in government simply highlights the problems of a 'semi-democratic' regime.
8. See interview with a leading Chinese dissident (Cao Siyuan) in *Newsweek*, 21 June 1999, p. 66.
9. Sen (1999:20) has been the most influential advocate of shifting the focus of development from a '"hard" view of development to a more "people-friendly" approach'.

REFERENCES

Alesina, A. (1992), 'Political Models of Macroeconomic Policy and Fiscal Reform', Policy Research Working Paper, no. WPS 970, World Bank.

Alesina, A. and L. Summers (1993), 'Central Bank Independence and Macroeconomic Performance', *Journal of Money, Credit and Banking*, 25, 151–62.

Asian Development Bank (ADB) (1997), *Emerging Asia – Changes and Challenges*, Manila: ADB.

Asian Development Bank (ADB) (1999), 'Economic Openness: Growth and Recovery in Asia', in *Asian Development Outlook*, New York: Oxford University Press.

Barro, R. (1997), *Determinants of Economic Growth: A Cross Country Empirical Study*, Cambridge, Mass.: MIT Press.

Bhagwati, J. (1998), 'The Capital Myth: The Difference Between Trade in Widgets and Dollars', *Foreign Affairs*, May/June (website version).

Bloom, D.E. and J.G. Williamson (1998), 'Demographic Transitions and Economic Miracles in Emerging Asia', *The World Bank Economic Review*, 12(3), 419–56.

Brandon, C. (1994), 'Reversing Pollution Trends in Asia', *Finance & Development*, June, 21–3.

Brownbridge, M. and C. Kirkpatrick (1998), 'Financial Sector Regulation: The Lessons of the Asian Crisis', mimeo, IDPM, University of Manchester.

Chowdhury, A. (1999), 'The Villain of the Asian Crisis – IMF or Thailand?', *ASEAN Economic Bulletin*, July.

Corden, M. (1999), *The Asian Crisis: Is There a Way Out?*, Singapore: Institute of Southeast Asian Studies.

Cukierman, A., S. Webb and B. Neyapti (1992), 'Measuring the Independence of Central Banks and Its Effects on Policy Outcomes', *World Bank Economic Review*, 6(1), 353–98.

Eatwell, J. (1996), 'The Performance of Liberalized Capital Markets', Center for Economic Policy Analysis, New School for Social Research, working paper no. 8.

Eatwell, J. and L. Taylor (1998), 'International Capital Markets and the Future of Economic Policy', Center for Economic Policy Analysis, New School for Social Research, working paper, no. 9.

Fields, G. (1995), 'Income Distribution in Developing Economies: Conceptual, Data and Policy-Issues in Broad-Based Growth', in M.G. Quibria (ed.), *Critical Issues in Asian Development*, Hong Kong: Oxford University Press.

Fischer, S. (1995), 'Central Bank Independence Revisited', *American Economic Review*, papers and proceedings, 201–6.
Heller, P. (1998), 'Ageing in the Asian Tiger Economies', *Finance & Development*, June, 35(2), 1–7.
ILO (1998), 'Human Rights: Human Rights in the Working World' (website version).
Islam, I. and A. Chowdhury (1997), *The Asia–Pacific Economies: A Survey*, London and New York: Routledge.
Krugman, P. (1998a), 'The Confidence Game', *The New Republic*, 5 October.
Krugman, P. (1998b), 'The Eternal Triangle', mimeo (website version)
Krugman, P. (1999), *The Return of Depression Economics*, New York and London: W.W. Norton.
Lee, E. (1998), *The Asian Financial Crisis: The Challenge for Social Policy*, Geneva: ILO.
Lucas, R. (1988), 'On the Mechanics of Economic Development', *Journal of Monetary Economics*, 22(1), 3–42.
Malhotra, A. (1997), 'Private Participation in Infrastructure: Lessons from Asia's Power Sector', *Finance & Development*, 33, 33–5.
Matthews, R. (1968), 'Why Has Britain Had Full Employment Since the War?', *Economic Journal*, 78, 555–69.
Medhi Krongkiew (1994), 'Income Distribution in East Asian Developing Countries', *Asian–Pacific Economic Literature*, 8(2), 58–74.
Olson, M. (1982), *The Rise and Decline of Nations*, New Haven: Yale University Press.
Polackova, H. (1999), 'Contingent Government Liabilities: A Hidden Fiscal Risk', Finance & Development, 35(1), 7 (website version).
Porter, M. (1992), 'Capital Choices: Changing the Way America Invests in Industry', *Journal of Applied Corporate Finance*, 5(2), 4–16.
Radelet, S. and J. Sachs (1999), 'What Have We Learned, So Far, from the Asian Financial Crisis?', Harvard Institute for International Development, January.
Rajan, R. and L. Zingales (1998), 'Which Capitalism? Lessons from the East Asian Crisis', mimeo, Graduate School of Business, University of Chicago.
Romer, P. (1993), 'Two Strategies for Economic Development: Using Ideas and Producing Ideas', *Proceedings of the World Bank Annual Conference on Development Economics, 1992*, Washington, DC: World Bank.
Sachs, J. (1998) 'Global Capitalism: Making it Work', *The Economist* (website version), 23 September.
Sen, A.K. (1991), 'Development Strategies: The Role of the State and Private Sectors', *Proceedings of the World Bank Annual Conference on Development Economics 1990*, Washington, DC: World Bank.
Sen, A.K. (1994), 'Freedoms and Needs', *The New Republic*, 31 January, 10–17.
Sen, A.K. (1997), 'Development Thinking at the Beginning of the 21st Century', London School of Economics, STICERD Development Economics Research Programme, working paper no. 2, March.
Sen, A.K. (1999), 'Interview', *Far Eastern Economic Review*.
Sender, J. (1999), 'Africa's Economic Performance: Limitations of the Current Consensus', *Journal of Economic Perspectives*, Summer, 89–114.
Smil, V. (1984), *The Bad Earth: Environmental Degradation in China*, New York: M.E. Sharpe.
Stiglitz, J. (1998a), 'More Instruments and Broader Goals: Moving Towards the

Post-Washington Consensus', The 1998 WIDER Annual Lecture, Helsinki, Finland.

Stiglitz, J. (1998b), 'Responding to Economic Crises: Policy Alternatives for Equitable Recovery and Development', North–South Institute Seminar, Ottawa, Canada, 29 September.

Stiglitz, J. (1998c), 'Redefining the Role of the State: What Should it Do? How Should it Do it?', Mimeo, World Bank, Washington, DC.

Tadashi, Y. and Siow Yue Chia (1999), *The Asian Crisis and Human Security: An Intellectual Dialogue on Building Asia's Tomorrow*, Tokyo: Japan Center for International Exchange and Institute of Southeast Asian Studies.

Taylor, L. (1998), 'Lax Public Sector, Destabilizing Private Sector: Origins of Capital Market Crises', Center for Economic Policy Analysis, New School for Social Research, working paper no. 6.

United Nations (1991), *Global Estimates and Projections of Populations by Age and Sex*, New York: UN.

Walton, M. (1997), 'The Maturation of the East Asian Miracle', *Finance & Development*, 35(3), 1–6.

Williamson, J. (1990), 'What Washington Means by Policy Reform', in John Williamson (ed.), *Latin American Adjustment: How Much Has Happened?*, Washington, DC: Institute for International Economics.

World Bank (1992), *World Development Report 1992 – Development and the Environment*, New York: Oxford University Press.

World Bank (1993), *World Bank Policy Research Bulletin*, January–February, 4(1).

World Bank (1998), *East Asia: The Road to Recovery*, Washington, DC: World Bank.

2. Beyond the crisis: development strategies in Asia

Amartya Kumar Sen[1]

ASIA AND THE GENERAL UNDERSTANDING OF DEVELOPMENT

Asia, I would argue, is a great source of understanding and knowledge about the process of development in general. A fuller analysis of Asia's achievements and problems is a good way of assessing the demands and challenges of development itself. Asia has had a variety of experiences, including extremely successful ones, in different fields. The overall result has been a reformulation not only of the answers to standard questions about development, but also of the questions themselves. Indeed, even the study of the problems and difficulties that the region has encountered can be a rich source of understanding of the demands of the process of development. Development strategies for Asia do, of course, have a specially local relevance, but ultimately they also have extensive global interest. The subject, thus, has both regional and universal significance.

ASSESSMENT OF THE PAST FOR BUILDING THE FUTURE

Let me begin with a couple of brief remarks on methodology. First, even if our primary concern is with the problems and adversities that the region currently faces, it would be appropriate to begin with an attempt to understand the special achievements – indeed the very great achievements – of the region and the general strategies that have made that success possible. We may have to look for new departures, but we also have reason to protect and build on the richness and creativity on which the region's accomplishments have been based. I shall argue that, in an important sense, the new has to emerge from the old. Second, the assessment of strategies – old and new – can be fruitfully pursued at different levels, from the very detailed to the rather general. They can serve different purposes. This chapter is at quite a general level. If that general understanding proves right, there are a great many issues of detail, including administrative particularities, that would have to be taken up in due course. But first we have to get the general picture right. At that general level, I shall argue that there is an identifiable philosophy on which the success of this region has been based – even an 'eastern strategy', first evolved in Japan and then practised very successfully elsewhere. I shall also argue that, in the philosophy underlying the older strategies, there are clues as to how the application of that general approach can be extended and improved, to deal with the problems and difficulties that have recently emerged with compelling force.

ECONOMIC DEVELOPMENT AND INSTITUTIONAL COMPLEMENTARITIES

We should start by identifying special features of the process of economic development that we have seen in this region, beginning with Japan. The world of industrialization and economic development was often assumed, earlier on, to be reserved for the West – and the West only. Japan's breakthrough in this world was so forceful and sure-footed that it cannot but be an irresistible source of learning and understanding about the nature of economic development in general. When, later on, the remarkable growth achievements of East and Southeast Asia occurred, there emerged another major source of illumination and knowledge on the nature and causation of economic development. Even though many commentators – especially in the West – took these successes to be no more than a confirmation of their prior belief in the productivity of international trade (as if there was nothing new in all this), a fuller analysis shows that the development process in Japan and in East and Southeast Asia had several strikingly new features.

The innovative features included, first of all, an emphasis on basic education as a prime mover of change. Second, it also involved a wide dissemination of basic economic entitlements (through education and training, through land reform, through availability of credit), which broadened access to the opportunities offered by the market economy. Third, the chosen design of development included a deliberate combination of state action and use of the market economy. Going further into fundamentals, these successes were based on an implicit but firm understanding that we live in a multi-institutional world, and that our ability to help ourselves and to help others depends on a variety of freedoms that we respectively may enjoy. The list of relevant freedoms includes social opportunities as well as market arrangements, and the development of individual capabilities as well as enhancement of social facilities. When, later on, I go into the recent problems and difficulties – indeed, even failures – that this successful region has experienced, I shall argue that in the fuller use of this fundamental understanding (in particular, about the multiplicity and diverse reach of different institutions) lies also the solution to present-day problems, including ways of preventing similar crises in the future. But this investigation I postpone until later.

INSTITUTIONS AND FREEDOMS

Individuals live and operate in a world of institutions. Our opportunities and prospects depend crucially on what institutions exist and how they function. Not only do institutions contribute to our freedoms, their roles can be sensibly evaluated in the light of their contributions to our freedoms. Even though different commentators have chosen to focus on particular institutions (such as the market, or the democratic system, or the media, or the public distribution system), there is a good case for viewing them *together*, for seeing what they can or cannot do, in combination with other institutions. It is in this integrated perspective that all the institutions have to be understood and examined.

The market mechanism, which arouses passion in favour as well as against, is a basic arrangement through which people can interact with each other, and undertake mutually advantageous activities. Seen in this light, it is very hard indeed to see how any reasonable critic could be against extensive use of the market mechanism. The problems that arise spring typically from other sources – not from the existence of markets per se – and include such concerns as inadequate preparedness to make use of market transactions, unconstrained concealment of information, or unregulated use of activities that allow the powerful to capitalize on their asymmetric knowledge and command over resources. These have to be dealt with, not by suppressing the markets, but by allowing them to function better and with greater fairness. Indeed, the overall achievements of the market are deeply contingent on political and social arrangements.

The market mechanism has achieved great success under those conditions in which the opportunities offered by it could be reasonably shared. In making this possible, the provision of basic education and of essential medical facilities, widely shared command over elementary resources (such as land for cultivation), and so on, demands appropriate public policies (involving such things as schooling, health care and land reform). Even when the need for 'economic reform' in favour of allowing more room for markets is paramount, the development of these vital social opportunities requires careful and determined public action going well beyond the simple fostering of markets.

JAPANESE EXPERIENCE: PUBLIC ACTION AND INDIVIDUAL OPPORTUNITIES

In the context of developing countries in general, the need for public policy initiatives in creating social opportunities is crucially important. A wide sharing of these social opportunities makes it possible for the bulk of the people to participate directly in the process of economic expansion. What the Japanese experience, followed by the success of East and Southeast Asia, did was to discredit a common – and often unargued – belief that had been dominant in some policy circles, especially in the West, that human development is a kind of luxury that a country can afford only when it grows rich. Perhaps the most important impact of the type of success that the East Asian economies have recently had (beginning with Japan, much earlier) is the total undermining of that implicit prejudice. These economies went comparatively early for massive expansion of education, and other ways of broadening the entitlements that allow the bulk of the people to participate in economic transactions and social change. This happened well before breaking the restraints of general poverty; indeed, that broad approach greatly contributed to breaking the restraints of poverty.

Consider Japan. Even at the time of Meiji restoration in the middle of the 19th century, Japan already had a higher level of literacy than Europe, even though Japan had not yet had any industrialization or modern economic development, which Europe had experienced for a century. That focus on developing human capability was intensified in the early period of Japanese development, in the Meiji era (1868–1911). For example, between 1906 and 1911, education consumed as much as 43 per cent of the budgets of the towns and villages, for Japan as a whole.[2] In this period in Japan, the progress of elementary education in particular was most rapid, and the recruiting army officers were impressed by the fact that, while in 1893 one-third of the army recruits were illiterate, already by 1906 there was hardly anyone who was not literate. By 1913, though Japan was economically still quite underdeveloped, it had become one of the largest producers of books in the world, publishing more books than Britain and indeed more than twice as many as the United States.[3] Indeed, the priority given to education and human development came very early in Japan, and even though it is massively high today, the important thing to note is that this relative priority goes back more than a century, and has not, comparatively speaking, intensified as Japan has grown richer and much more opulent.[4] The fact that human development in general and school education in particular are first and foremost an ally of the poor, rather than of the rich and the affluent, is an understanding that has informed the Japanese strategy of economic expansion throughout its entire modern history.

To a great extent, the same priority can be seen all over East and Southeast Asia, though often this came rather more hesitantly and slowly. South Korea, Taiwan, Hong Kong, Singapore, Thailand and other countries – most importantly mainland China – have made excellent use of this general approach.

HUMAN DEVELOPMENT: AN EASTERN STRATEGY

We may ask, what does human development do? It helps the lives of people in several different ways. We may see some of its contributions in terms of its role in the formation of 'human capital', but the reach of human development goes well beyond what can be adequately captured within that narrow framework.

First, the creation of social opportunities makes a direct contribution to the expansion of human capabilities and the quality of life. Expansion of education, health care and so on contribute directly to the quality of life and to its flourishing. There is every evidence that, even with relatively low income, a population that guarantees health care and education to all can actually achieve remarkable results in terms of the length and quality of life of the entire population. This is borne out particularly by the achievements of pre-reform China – prior to 1979, by which time China already had quite a high life expectancy at birth, preceding the industrial and agricultural expansion that would occur following the reforms. Indeed, the highly labour-intensive nature of health care and basic education, and human development in general, makes them comparatively cheaper in the early stages of economic development, when labour costs are low. There is a very important consideration of 'relative costs' here, which is sometimes missed in development analysis. It is often asked: how can a poor country – before much economic development – 'afford' to finance expansion of basic education and medical care? This question, which is a good one to ask, does also have a good answer. A poor country has lower wages, and labour costs are relatively moderate (often by a very long margin in comparison with the richer countries). Since basic education and medical care are also exceptionally labour-intensive activities, they are also much cheaper in the poorer countries than in the richer ones. The poorer economies, which have less money to spend on public services, also need less money to spend in achieving the same development of basic education and medical care, compared with the richer countries.[5]

So the first thing to note is the direct contribution of this strategy (what we may call the 'Eastern strategy') of going early for human development, focusing on the enhancement of basic human capabilities. It contributes to the quality of life (through more literacy, the expansion of life expectancy, reduction of morbidity rates and so on), even in the absence of its impact on economic and industrial expansion. This must be recognized first, since the object of public policy must ultimately be the enhancement of human life and freedoms. There are, however, also indirect effects.

Second, human development in the form of basic education, health care, and so on, also greatly facilitates economic and industrial expansion, and improves the efficiency and wide reach of the market economy. And these, in turn, can feed back on raising the quality of life. There are, thus, both direct gains and indirect ones.[6] Indeed, the rewards of human development go well beyond the direct enhancement of quality of life, and include also its impact on people's productive abilities and thus on economic growth on a widely shared basis.[7] Literacy and numeracy help the participation of the masses in the process of economic expansion. To use the opportunities of global trade, particularly in industrial output, 'quality control' as well as 'production to specification' can be quite crucial, and this is hard for illiterate or innumerate labourers to achieve and maintain. Furthermore, there is considerable evidence that improved health care as well as nutrition also makes the workforce more productive and better remunerated.[8]

The so-called 'East Asian miracle' was, to a great extent, based on the reach and force of the 'Eastern strategy' of focusing on human development and more broadly on acknowledging a fundamental complementarity between the state and the market. The connection between economic expansion and human development, while ignored for a long time in Western public discussion, is now more fully acknowledged. The World Bank, which had been rather sceptical in the past of these connections, has moved in recent years in the direction of greater recognition of these linkages. An important step, particularly emphasizing the role of public education, is well documented in the book, *The East Asian Miracle*, published in 1983, even though there was evidently still a residual reluctance to see more fully the larger understanding of the interlinkages of different institutions and the complementarity between the state and the market (of which public education is only one part). In more recent years, particularly under the leadership of President James Wolfensohn (and the research guidance of Joseph Stiglitz), the broader interinstitutional connections have become much more fully seized.[9] We have to see how far the far-reaching implications of this crucial recognition will be reflected in the day-to-day working of the Bank (and other institutions, such as the IMF).

Third, there is much confirmation, in the contemporary empirical literature, of the impact of education, especially female education, on reducing fertility rates (along with decreasing child mortality rates). High fertility rates can be seen, with much justice, as adverse to the quality of life especially of young women, since recurrent child bearing and rearing can be very detrimental to the well-being and freedom of the young mother. Indeed, it is precisely this connection that makes the empowerment of women (through more outside employment, more school education, and so on) so effective in reducing fertility rates, since young women have a strong reason for moderating birth rates, and their ability to influence family decisions increases with their empowerment. I have argued elsewhere that even China's achievements in reducing fertility rates does not really show the effectiveness of its draconian legal restrictions ('one-child family' and others), economic penalties and other punitive rules introduced in 1979. They are also, to a great extent, the result of the expansion of women's education and employment.

Indeed, in those parts of India where female education and empowerment are more advanced than in China (in Kerala, in particular), the fertility rate is significantly lower than in China, despite there being no compulsion whatever. Even the rate of fall of fertility rate has been much sharper in those parts of India in which female educational expansion has been faster than in China. For example, the Indian state of Kerala (the various districts of which add up to a total of 30 million people) has had a much faster expansion of female education than China. It has also, correspondingly, experienced a substantially faster decline in fertility rates. While the Chinese fertility rate fell from 2.8 to 2.0 between 1979 (when the 'one-child policy' and other coercive measures were instituted) and 1991, it fell from 3.0 to 1.8 in the same period in Kerala. Kerala has kept its lead over China both in female education and in fertility decline (currently, Kerala's fertility rate is below 1.7, China's about 1.9). Also, thanks to the process of fertility decline being freedom-based rather than coercive, the infant mortality rate has continued to fall in Kerala in a way it has not in China. By the middle of this decade, Kerala's infant mortality rate (16 per thousand for girls, 17 for boys) has become much lower than China's (33 for girls and 28 for boys), even though both regions had similar infant mortality rates around the time, in 1979, when the one-child policy was initiated in China.

Human development has extraordinary social and demographic reach, in addition to its contribution to economic development and directly to the quality of life. China should get more credit for what it has achieved through human development, rather than coercion, and less admiration for its coercive policies. The fact that, in contrast to the human development-oriented states like Kerala, the rest of India (especially the north of the country) has done so little for human development is the primary explanation of India's low performance in social as well as economic fields.

THE EASTERN STRATEGY AND THE CHINA–INDIA CONTRAST

Since I have already commented in passing on the China–India contrast, let me go on to pursue the comparison a bit further. Indeed, it is useful to see the wisdom of the 'Eastern strategy' as a point of difference from the restricted approach adopted in India. The importance of basic education and other central features of human development has been persistently neglected in India. As a result, even now nearly half the adult population of India is illiterate. It is not easy to make use of the opportunities of globalized trade if illiteracy makes it hard for the common man and woman to participate in production according to international standards and specifications, or even to have quality control.

India has also had an overpowering bureaucracy – not a good way of building the complementary relation between the state and the market. Despite the economic reforms introduced in 1991, that problem has not yet been adequately resolved. But while the need for more market-friendly policy has been much acknowledged in India, even by the government, the disastrous failure in human development has not yet received the concentrated attention it strongly needs. The advocacy of economic reforms in India in 1991 made 'liberalization' the one crucial issue and, while this was certainly an important matter, the fuller nature of what I have been calling 'the Eastern strategy' was badly missed in Indian policy making. There is, in fact, a deep complementarity between reducing, on the one hand, the over-activity of the state in running a 'licence Raj', and, on the other, removing the under-activity of the state in the continuing neglect of elementary education and other social opportunities.[10]

The contrast of India with China is relevant here. China, too, had a very bureaucratic economy prior to the economic reforms of 1979, but it had expanded – in line with its political commitment – facilities for basic education and health care much more extensively in the pre-reform period than India had. After the economic reforms of 1979, China could make excellent use of what it had already achieved in the field of educational and human development. Post-reform China greatly benefited from that part of the Eastern strategy that China had already used in the pre-reform period;

the rest of the Eastern strategy could then be added on to what had already been achieved.

In contrasting present-day India with present-day China, it is often pointed out – rightly – that China has done more to make use of the efficiency of the market than India has. This is certainly true since the Chinese economic reforms of 1979. But what is also true is that already by 1979 China had done a great deal in general human development. This was socially helpful right from the start and also provided strong support for economic development when the reforms came in 1979. Indeed, India's underdevelopment in basic education and health care – aside from reducing the quality of life of its people – is also a very big barrier to its use of the opportunities of global trade and exchange.

To be sure, India has a very extensive higher educational sector (in fact, for every university-educated person in China there are approximately six in India), and certainly India can make good use of those parts of trade and commerce that depend on highly educated skill. For example, Bangalore has become a major centre of electronic and technological activities in the world. And yet, while China is quite close to universal literacy, especially among the young, India is still very far away from it, and this is perhaps the single most important barrier to India's participation in the global economy. Even a hundred Bangalores – and all the developments of modern science and technology of which India can be genuinely proud – will not be able to penetrate the depth of rural poverty in India. I have written about this contrast elsewhere, and I shall not go more into this now.[11] What I want to particularly emphasize here is that this deficiency of Indian economic and social policy is a failure to learn more from the success of the eastern strategy in Japan and East and Southeast Asia. The remedy cannot lie only in expanding the markets and reducing the bureaucracy (important as they are). The needed strategy calls for the development of human capability taking adequate note of the complementarity between multiple institutions, so central to the Eastern strategy.

TRANSIENT CRISIS AND ENDEMIC DEPRIVATION

The time has come for me to shift gears a little and to look not only at long-run success, but also at short-run problems, which may be transient, but which can play havoc in an otherwise successful experience of long-run growth. As it happens, here too the India–China contrast is relevant, but in quite a different way – not entirely unfavourably to India.

The challenge of development includes both the elimination of persistent and endemic deprivation, and the prevention of sudden and severe destitution. The respective demands on institutions and policies of the two can be somewhat distinct and even dissimilar. Success in one field may not guarantee success in the other. For example, consider the comparative performances of China and India over the last half a century. It is clear that China has been much more successful than India in raising life expectancy and reducing mortality. Indeed, its superior performance goes back, as I have already commented, to well before the economic reforms of 1979. India is a much more diverse country than China, both because of variations of language and tradition and because of regional differences in politics (combined with a more 'federal' structure of Indian administration compared with the Chinese system). As was discussed earlier, there are parts of India (such as Kerala) in which the expansion of human development has been much faster than in China. Nevertheless, for the two countries as a whole the comparison of human development is largely in favour of China.

And yet, despite these achievements, China also experienced the largest recorded famine in history, when 30 million people perished in the famines that followed the failure of the Great Leap Forward, during 1958–61. In contrast, India has not had a famine since independence. The prevention of famines and other disastrous crises is a somewhat different discipline from that of overall increase in average life expectancy and other achievements. I shall presently argue that in ensuring security in the form of avoidance of disaster – whether originating in natural calamities or in policy blunders – democracy and participatory politics have important roles to play.

Inequality is a crucial feature of development of famines and other severe crises. Of course, the absence of democracy is in itself an inequality, in this case of political rights and powers. But we have to see particularly the relation between (a) political inequality in the form of non-democratic governance, and (b) famines and other unequal deprivations that thrive on the basis of severe and sometimes suddenly increased economic inequality. The role of economic inequality in the development of famines is illustrated by the fact that famines can occur even without a large – or even any – diminution of total food supply, because some groups may suffer an abrupt loss of market power (through, say, sudden and massive unemployment), with starvation resulting from this new inequality. Famines are very divisive phenomena.

THE RECENT CRISES IN EAST AND SOUTHEAST ASIA

Similar issues arise in understanding the nature of economic crises, such as the recent ones in East and Southeast Asia, with the accompanying feature, of selective but massive destitution and misery. Let me now turn to that. In their foreword to the volume on *The Asian Crisis and Human Security: An Intellectual Dialogue on Building Asia's Tomorrow*, Yamamoto Tadashi and Chia Siow Yue point out that 'Asia approaches the new century in an introspective and apprehensive mood'.[12] There are indeed good grounds for caution and for critical reflection. The future can be faced with greater strength and skill if we try to understand what these grounds for apprehension and introspection are. I shall argue that there are distinct elements in this overall picture that have to be clearly distinguished. We can find solutions to problems if we know exactly what the problems are. In looking for new development strategies for Asia, much of the work would have to be done through transparent identification of the problems that Asia faces, to which inadequate attention may have been given in the past.

Vulnerability and Non-monotonic Progress

Perhaps the most obvious problem relates to the recognition that the heady days of unmitigated success – with things going up and up and nothing ever falling down – are over. Even though much of Asia is already well on the way to recovery from the crisis that hit it in 1997, the sense of invulnerability has not survived. It could not have. Indeed, it is clear that severe economic crises can occur and disrupt the rushing stream of unobstructed economic progress that many Asian countries took for granted. This is an important understanding, even though it can hardly be seen as a profound recognition. Even a modest study of economic history brings out the fact, observed everywhere in the world, that economic progress is rarely monotonic. Indeed, rifts have appeared with unfailing constancy to interrupt what previously looked like the promise of an unending and unbending forward march of the economy. Asia does not have a special exemption from vulnerability. This is not a kind of 'Murphy's Law', a grand claim that, if things can go wrong, they will. Rather, it is a very modest claim that dangers of interruption are omnipresent, and no matter how robust things may look, they can – and sometimes will – go wrong. Belief in invulnerability is, in fact, a childish thought: like the way teenage car drivers often assume that accidents cannot happen to them in particular.

Even though the recognition of vulnerability is not profound, it is, in fact, extremely important to see the far-reaching implications of this simple acknowledgment. In particular, it makes it absolutely obligatory to see security as a central part of development. A view of development that judges progress by long-run growth averages and by the strength of upward trends misses out something truly central to the process of development, viz. protection against downside risk at a given moment of time. Today's miseries may coexist easily enough with speedy progress experienced yesterday and the rapid advance that may occur tomorrow.

Divided We Fall

The second point is also simple enough, even though it too is missed often enough. Even when different groups can all benefit simultaneously when rapid progress is occurring, and in this sense the interests of the different groups are substantially congruent, nevertheless, when a crisis hits, different groups can have very divergent predicaments. United we may be when we go up and up, but divided we fall when we do fall. The false sense of harmony may be torn severely asunder when things start unravelling and coming down.

The issue of divisiveness of downturns (even when upturns are harmonious) is one of the central lessons to emerge from the study of crises, often much more catastrophic than those East and Southeast Asia have recently experienced. Even when a terrible famine occurs, it may be a situation in which most groups of people in that country have no difficulty whatsoever in getting enough to eat.[13] A famine rarely affects more than 5 per cent of the population and almost never more than 10 per cent. That is one reason why famines cannot really be analysed helpfully in aggregative terms – neither in terms of total food supply, nor in terms of average gross national product (GNP) or gross domestic product (GDP) per head. The focus of causal analysis has to be the respective entitlements of different groups of people: their particular and specific abilities to buy food and other necessities and to save themselves from sudden deprivation. The entitlements of some groups can collapse severely even when other groups have only mild problems – or even remain quite unharmed and unaffected.

Exactly the same thing applies in a crisis like the one that hit East and Southeast Asia in 1997, even though the extent of deprivation was far from that of a famine or a massive disaster. Take, for example, the crises in Indonesia, or in Thailand and, earlier on, in South Korea. It may be wondered why it should be so disastrous to have, say, a 5 or 10 per cent fall in gross national product in one year when the country in question has been growing at 5 to 10 per cent per year for decades. Indeed, at the purely aggregate level this is not quintessentially a disastrous situation. And yet, if that 5 or 10 per cent decline is not shared evenly by the population, and if it is heaped instead largely on the poorest part of the population (the jobless and the marginalized, and their families), then that group may have very little income left (no matter what the overall growth performance might have been in the past). Such general economic crises, like famines, thrive on the basis of the Devil taking the hindmost.

This is why 'protective security' is such an important instrumental freedom, and why social arrangements for safety nets are an integral part of development itself. Even the otherwise highly illuminating literature on 'sustainable development' often misses out the fact that what people need for their security is not only the sustainability of overall development, but also social protection when people's predicaments diverge and some groups are thrown brutally to the wall while other groups experience nothing like that.

Security and Equity

I now turn to a third lesson, which is, in fact, closely related to the second, that is, to the issue – just discussed – of divided fortunes in a downturn. There is an important need to think of equity and economic inequality in quite a different way in the context of security from the way they are standardly treated in the development literature in the context of long-run growth. In an obvious sense, the problem of contrasting predicaments is, of course, one of inequality. There is clearly much inequality when one group falls to pieces while other groups do just fine; this reflects, in an obvious sense, a violation of equity. But it is important to recognize that this is not the same problem as the more commonly discussed challenge of 'growth with equity'.

That large literature, which is conceptually rich and practically important, is particularly suited to analysing the big – but different – problem of eliminating endemic poverty. The problem of sudden destitution can have a very different nature and may involve quite disparate causal processes from persistent deprivation and endemic poverty. For example, the fact that South Korea has had economic growth with relatively egalitarian income distribution has been extensively, and rightly, recognized.[14] This, however, was no guarantee of equitable influence in a crisis situation.[15] In particular, South Korea did not have, when the crisis hit it, a proper system of social safety nets, or any rapidly responding system of compensatory protection. The emergence of fresh inequality and unchallenged destitution can coexist with a very distinguished past record of 'growth with equity'. Different problems call for distinct analyses and understanding.

Role of Democracy

I turn now to a fourth issue – that of political democracy. It is, of course, entirely in line with the fundamental approach of the complementarity between the state and the market to see that democracy has a vital role, without that being in any way a barrier to the use of the market mechanism.

Indeed, Japan's own experience in combining democracy with the functioning of the market and other institutions illustrates this well, as do the recent experiences of more and more countries in this region. The often-repeated belief that authoritarian regimes are better at fostering economic growth (a claim largely based on selective evidence) has not received any serious general empirical support in extensive inter-country comparisons.[16] Indeed, two decades of empirical work bring out very clearly that the success of a market economy is facilitated by a supportive economic environment, rather than by the harshness of the political climate.

How does the issue of democracy relate to the problems of deprivation, security and crises that I am currently discussing? The most immediate connection lies, of course, in the fact that a denial of basic political freedom and civil rights is itself a deprivation. Prime Minister Obuchi Keizo, in his insightful 'Opening Remarks' to the earlier 'Intellectual Dialogue on Building Asia's Tomorrow,' emphasized the need to take a broad view of security:

> It is my deepest belief that human beings should be able to lead lives of creativity, without having their survival threatened or their dignity impaired. While the phrase 'human security' is a relatively new one, I understand that it is the keyword to comprehensively seizing all of the menaces that threaten the survival, daily life, and dignity of human beings and to strengthening the efforts to confront these threats.[17]

We human beings have reason to value liberty and freedom of expression and action in our lives. This can be central to our creativity as well as dignity. And it is not unreasonable for human beings – the social creatures that we are – to value participation in political and social activities without restraint. Also informed and unregimented formation of our values requires openness of communication and arguments, and political freedoms and civil rights can be central to this process. Furthermore, to express publicly what we value and to demand that attention be paid to it, we need free speech and democratic choice.

Democracy and freedoms of association and participation, thus, have a constructive role as well as intrinsic importance. In addition, there is a fundamental connection between democracy and security. The instrumental role of democracy (including elections, multi-party politics, a free media and so on) in making sure that the government does respond to people's needs and predicaments can be of great practical significance.[18] In analysing this connection, we have to consider the political incentives that operate on governments and on the persons and groups who are in office. The rulers have the incentive to listen to what people want if they have to face their criticism and seek their support in elections.

It is, thus, not at all astonishing that no substantial famine has ever occurred in any independent country with a democratic form of government and a relatively free press.[19] They have occurred in ancient kingdoms and present-day authoritarian societies, in primitive tribal communities and in modern technocratic dictatorships, in colonial economies run by imperialists from the North and in newly independent countries of the South run by despotic national leaders or by intolerant single parties. But they have never materialized in any country that is independent, that goes to elections regularly, that has opposition parties to voice criticisms, and that permits newspapers to report freely and question the wisdom of government policies without extensive censorship. Right at this moment, the two countries that are experiencing severe famines – North Korea and Sudan – are quintessentially authoritarian regimes.

SECURITY, ASIAN CRISES AND THE VOICE OF THE POOR

When things are routinely good and smooth, the protective role of democracy may not be desperately missed. But it comes into its own when things get fouled up, for one reason or another. And then the political incentives provided by democratic governance acquire great practical significance. There may be some important economic as well as political lessons here. Many economic technocrats recommend the use of economic incentives (which the market system provides) while ignoring political incentives (which democratic systems could guarantee). But economic incentives, important as they are, are no substitute for political incentives, and the lacuna of the absence of an adequate system of political incentives cannot be filled by the operation of economic inducement.

The recent problems of East and Southeast Asia bring out, among many other things, the penalty of limitations on democratic freedom. This is so in two striking respects, involving the neglect of two important instrumental freedoms, 'protective security' and 'transparency guarantee'. First, when the financial crisis in this region (from 1997 onwards) led to a general economic recession, the protective power of democracy – not unlike that which prevents famines in democratic countries – was badly missed in some countries in the region. Those who were newly dispossessed in, say, Indonesia or Korea did not get the hearing they needed. Even though a fall of 5 or 10 per cent of total national income (or of GNP) is comparatively moderate, it can decimate lives and create misery for millions, if the burden of contraction is not shared together but allowed to be heaped on those, the unemployed or those newly made economically redundant, who can least bear it. The victims in Indonesia may not have taken very great interest in democracy when things went up and up. But when things came tumbling down for some parts of the population, the lack of democratic institutions kept their voices muffled and ineffective. The protective umbrella of democracy is strongly missed exactly when it is most needed. Not surprisingly, democracy became a major issue precisely at a time of crisis, when the economically dispossessed felt strongly the need for a political voice. As the positive experience recently of South Korea shows, the workings of a democracy, even when revived only under an economic emergency, can confront, with commendable speed, severe problems of privation and insecurity.

The issue of democracy relates also to a further – a second – connection, that between the lack of democracy and the nature of the recent economic crisis. The financial crisis in some of these economies (such as Korea or Indonesia) has been closely linked with the lack of transparency in business, in particular the lack of opportunity for public scrutiny in reviewing financial and business arrangements. An effective democratic forum could have been influential in preventing malpractice, especially at the top (involving, for example, underhand arrangements between high-ranking government officials and business families). Efficient arrangements for public scrutiny of the activities and influences of selected families or groups could have made a big difference.

It is not hard to understand the motivation behind the discipline of financial reform and accountability that the International Monetary Fund tried to impose on the economies in default. Indeed, it was, to a great extent, necessitated by the lack of openness and disclosure, and the involvement of unscrupulous business linkages, that were characteristic in parts of these economies. These characteristics connect strongly with a system of non-transparent commercial arrangements. When a depositor places his or her money in a bank there may be some expectation that it will be used, along with other money, in ways that would not involve undue risk and which could be openly disclosed. Since this trust was often violated, the financial arrangements needed changing. I am not commenting here on whether the IMF's management of the crises was exactly right, or whether the insistence on immediate reforms could have been sensibly postponed until financial confidence had returned in these economies. But no matter what tactics might have worked best, the role of 'transparency freedom', or rather its absence, in the development of the Asian crises cannot be easily doubted, and the need for change was certainly strong.

Financial arrangements have many complexities, and the problems faced in different East and Southeast Asian economies are by no means the same. But there is evidence that in some of these economies, such as Indonesia or

South Korea, the pattern of extraordinary risks and improper investments could have been placed under much greater scrutiny if democratic critics had demanded that. But of course neither Indonesia nor South Korea had, over the relevant decades, a functioning democratic system that would have allowed such demands to come from outside the government. The unchallenged power of governance was easily translated into an unquestioned acceptance of the lack of accountability and openness, often reinforced by strong family links between the government and the financial bosses. In the emergence of the economic crises, the undemocratic nature of some governments played an important part.

A CONCLUDING REMARK

In this chapter I have tried to see the Asian experience in a broad framework, dealing with both successes and failures. I have seen development as a process of enhancement of human freedoms of various kinds, which are intrinsically important in themselves and which are mutually supportive. They call for a multiplicity of working institutions, of which the market is an important part, but which needs extensive and many-sided supplementation.

The arguments presented above have drawn on a somewhat fuller analysis pursued elsewhere, in particular in my book, *Development as Freedom*. That work investigates the diversity, importance and the far-reaching roles of different types of freedoms that relate with each other, and which demand a multiplicity of institutional developments. I have tried to argue here that the nature and effectiveness of the 'Eastern strategy' can perhaps be more satisfactorily understood in this general perspective. Indeed, this perspective has something to offer in explaining both the successes of the East and Southeast Asian economies and the nature of the problems and difficulties this region faces. Freedoms have to be seen both as the primary ends of development and as its principal means.

The distinct but interconnected roles of various instrumental freedoms require particular attention, covering, among other demands, economic facilities, political freedoms, social opportunities, protective security and transparency guarantee. The book, incidentally, was based on a series of lectures given at the World Bank in November 1996, just before the Asian economic crisis erupted. It was depressing to see that the worst fears expressed in these lectures were realized with alarming rapidity.

The 'old strategy' on which the major successes of East and Southeast Asia have been based is the use of the complementarity of different institutions, and in particular the creation of social opportunities through public policy that crucially supplement the functioning of the market. In this radical approach Japan led the way, followed by the successful East and Southeast Asian economies. This was not only new in the world, but those economies, even in Asia, which did not seize the wisdom of this broad approach (involving the creation of social opportunities as well as allowing the market to function efficiently) suffered substantially from that neglect. My own country, India, is a good example of that.

But development is not only a matter of long-run growth, or just a matter of long-run growth with long-run equity. Even successful economies can have sudden and severe problems and, when they occur, sections of the population may suffer from divisive fortunes. This is why security is a distinct and significant concern, which is not subsumed by the usual demands of 'growth with equity'.

In looking for new strategies for the future of this region, the need for protective security has to be firmly seized. This is important in broadening the 'Eastern strategy', for use in Asia, or anywhere else. The issue of democracy is also quite central, both because the denial of political and civil rights is itself a deprivation, and also because the political incentives provided by a participatory and open political system can be crucially important. These incentives give voice to the dispossessed, and this in turn encourages protective security. In addition, democratic and contested political systems help accountability and the prevention of the kind of financial irregularity that played a significant part in the recent Asian crises. If these lacunae point to the need for Asia to have a modified economic and social strategy, it is important to recognize that this involves, in some ways, an intensification of the basic wisdom of looking for complementarity between different institutions.

Asia has made good use of a philosophy of development based firmly on institutional complementarity. It can make better use still of that philosophy, by applying the same broad vision to the problem of security. The case for a 'new strategy' can be fitted into the basic wisdom underlying the old strategy (in particular, on the understanding of the need to take serious note of complementarity of different institutions), but applied even more broadly, covering *inter alia* protective security, participatory politics and transparent accountability.

In the 9th century, the Chinese poet and literary critic Ssu-k'ung T'u put very well the general issue of the integration of the old with the new: 'You join with the old and produce the new.'[20] This was in his classic work, *The Twenty-Four Categories of Poetry*. Of course, Ssu-k'ung T'u was talking about literary creations, not social and economic development. But the same integrative message, more than a millennium old, applies to economic and social arrangements as well. I have argued that in the present context, we need to retain the old and important understanding particularly about the complementarity of institutions and give it a new form to extend the reach and coverage of that complementarity. So let me end by echoing Ssu-k'ung T'u, and suggest that we join with the old and produce the new.

NOTES

1. This chapter is based on a shortened version of the Asia and Pacific Lecture, at the Conference on the Second Intellectual Dialogue on 'Building Asia's Tomorrow: Promoting Sustainable Development and Human Security', Singapore, 12 July 1999, and was published by the Institute of Southeast Asian Studies under its Asia & Pacific Lecture Series. It is reproduced here with the kind permission of the ISEAS with some minor editorial changes.
2. See Carol Gluck (1985) *Japan's Modern Myths: Ideology in the Late Meiji Period*, Princeton: Princeton University Press, p. 166; see also the literature cited there.
3. For these data, see Gluck (ibid.), pp. 12, 172, and the references cited by her.
4. See Hiromitsu Ishi (1995), 'Trends in the Allocation of Public Expenditure in Light of Human Resource Development – Overview in Japan' (Asian Development Bank, mimeographed, 1995).
5. On this see Jean Drèze and Amartya Sen (1987), *Hunger and Public Action*, Oxford: Clarendon Press. These issues are more fully discussed in my *Development as Freedom* (1999).
6. The nature of this connection is discussed in Drèze and Sen (1987).
7. On this, see Jere R. Behrman and Anil B. Deolalikar, 'Health and Nutrition', in Hollis Chenery and T.N. Srinivasan (eds) (1988), *Handbook of Development Economics*, Amsterdam: North-Holland.
8. See World Bank (1983), *The East Asian Miracle: Economic Growth and Public Policy*, New York: Oxford University Press.
9. See, particularly, James D. Wolfensohn (1999), 'A Proposal for Comprehensive Development Framework', World Bank, mimeographed. See also Joseph E. Stiglitz (1998), 'An Agenda for Development in the Twenty-first Century', in J. Pleskovi and J.E. Stiglitz (eds), *Annual World Bank Conference on Development Economics 1997*, Washington, DC: World Bank.
10. On this, see Jean Drèze and Amartya Sen (1995), *India: Economic Development and Social Opportunity*, Delhi: Oxford University Press. See also my 'How Is India Doing?', *New York Review of Books*, 21 (Christmas Number, 1982), reprinted in D.K. Basu and R. Sissons (eds) (1986), *Social and Economic Development in India: A Reassessment*, London: Sage.
11. See particularly Jean Drèze and Amartya Sen (1995).
12. *The Asian Crisis and Human Security: An Intellectual Dialogue on Building Asia's Tomorrow*, Tokyo: Japan Center for International Exchange and Institute of Southeast Asian Studies, 1999, p. 7.
13. On this, see my *Poverty and Famines: An Essay on Entitlement and Deprivation*, Oxford: Clarendon Press, 1981, and jointly with Jean Drèze, *Hunger and Public Action*, Oxford: Clarendon Press, 1989.
14. See Torsten Persson and Guido Tabellini (1994), 'Is Inequality Harmful to Growth? Theory and Evidence', *American Economic Review*, 84; Alberto Alesina and Dani Rodrik (1994), 'Distributive Politics and Economic Growth', *Quarterly Journal of Economics*, 108; Albert Fishlow, C. Gwin, S. Haggard, D. Rodrik, and S. Wade (1994), *Miracle or Design? Lessons from the East Asian Experience*, Washington, DC: Overseas Development Council. See also the contrast with India (and South Asia in general), in Jean Drèze and Amartya Sen (1995).

15. Indeed, as Jong-il You (1998) has pointed out, in these countries (including in South Korea) 'low inequality and high profit shares coexisted primarily due to the unusually even distribution of wealth' ('Income Distribution and Growth in East Asia', *Journal of Development Studies*, 34). In this achievement, prior land reforms, widespread development of human capital through educational expansion, and other influences reducing inequality in basic wealth, were important. But all this does not, in any way, ensure a commitment to protective security when a crisis develops. Participatory politics can be an important influence in that direction.
16. See, for example, Adam Przeworski *et al.* (1995), *Sustainable Democracy*, Cambridge: Cambridge University Press; Robert J. Barro (1996), *Getting It Right: Markets and Choices in a Free Society*, Cambridge, MA: MIT Press. See also the rather vast literature cited there.
17. Obuchi Keizo, 'Opening Remarks', in *The Asian Crisis and Human Security*, Tokyo: Japan Center for International Exchange and Institute of Southeast Asian Studies, 1999, pp. 18–19.
18. These issues are more fully discussed in my *Development as Freedom* (1999).
19. On this, see my 'Democracy: Which Way Now?', *Economic Journal*, 93 (December 1983) and *Resources, Values and Development*, Cambridge, MA: Harvard University Press, 1984.
20. English translation from Stephen Owen (1992), *Readings in Chinese Literary Thought*, Cambridge. MA: Harvard University Press, p. 309.

3. Revitalizing the Japanese economy

C.H. Kwan

INTRODUCTION

The 1990s will be remembered as Japan's lost decade, with economic growth lagging far behind not only the high level it used to achieve in the past but also that of other major industrial countries. Two sets of factors combined contributed to the stagnation of the Japanese economy during this period. On the one hand, falling asset prices had an immense negative impact on domestic spending, and macroeconomic policies failed to restore production to its potential level. On the other hand, the traditional 'Japanese model', which seemed to work so well in the past when Japan was catching up with the West, had become impotent once this phase was over. It has also come to be widely recognized that structural reform is essential for Japan to cope with a new environment characterized by globalization, an ageing population and the transition to a post-industrial society.

In an attempt to revitalize the Japanese economy, the Hashimoto Administration initiated a comprehensive reform programme covering six major areas in late 1996. Led by the financial Big Bang, major efforts have been made to enhance competition through deregulation. Japanese companies have responded by changing business practices, with more emphasis on the market mechanism as the guiding principle. Mergers and acquisitions (M&As) across corporate groups and national borders, for example, have become a common tool of restructuring. The success of Japan's reform programme hinges on how it handles the trade-off between short-term and long-term growth and that between equity and efficiency.

COPING WITH THE AFTERMATH OF THE BUBBLE ECONOMY

The bursting of the asset-price bubble was by far the most important event determining the course of the Japanese economy in the 1990s. At its trough in October 1998, the benchmark Nikkei average index was down to one-third its peak level recorded in late 1989. Prices of land for commercial use

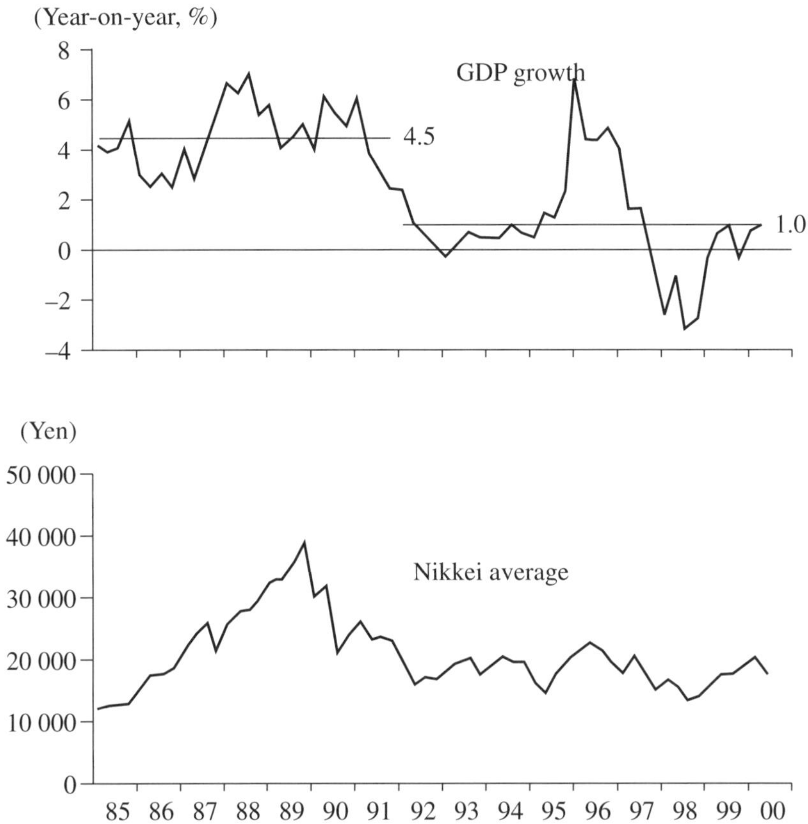

Sources: Economic Planning Agency, *National Income Statistics*, and Tokyo Stock Exchange.

Figure 3.1 Falling growth rate and stock prices in Japan, 1985–2000

and residential use have dropped 70 per cent and 45 per cent, respectively, since 1991. The government has tried to boost the economy with several rounds of fiscal stimulus packages, and the Bank of Japan has allowed interest rates to fall to a historically low level. The overall impact on economic growth, however, has been disappointing, with GDP expanding by only 1.0 per cent a year between 1992 and 1999 (Figure 3.1).

Disappointing Macroeconomic Performance

Ten years after the asset-price bubble burst, the Japanese economy is still struggling with its aftermath. During the boom years in the late 1980s, banks and other financial institutions provided vast amounts of credit collateralized against land and stocks whose values surged to levels totally out of line with economic fundamentals. The reckoning began in 1990, when stock prices plummeted, soon followed by real estate prices. Most financial institutions were left holding very large volumes of non-performing loans, forcing them to take a much more cautious stance in extending new loans. Households and companies also suffered immense capital losses, prompting them to cut spending in an attempt to repair their balance sheets.

On closer examination, the Japanese economy experienced two recessions during the 1990s, interrupted by two years of relatively strong growth in FY1995 and FY1996.[1] The second recession was deeper than the first, with the banking sector pushed to the brink of a major crisis.

The first recession started in 1992 and lasted for three years, with the economic growth rate averaging a disappointing 0.5 per cent between FY1992 and FY1994. When the economy began to show clear signs of slowing down in 1992, both the private sector and the government perceived the downturn primarily as part of a normal business cycle and expected it to be short-lived. Falling asset prices notwithstanding, capital gains (particularly on assets acquired before the bubble period) and retained earnings accumulated during boom years were still large enough at this stage for Japanese companies to take a wait-and-see stance instead of implementing drastic restructuring. Japanese banks also wrongly believed that their deteriorating bad debt problem would be easily solved as the economy recovered and asset prices picked up again. The authorities were slow in responding to the looming banking crisis partly because they failed to grasp the full extent of the problem owing to inadequate disclosure by financial institutions. With hindsight, the macroeconomic economic policy implemented during this period, which seemed aggressive at that time, was too little and too late.

The economy picked up in 1995, thanks to the temporary impact of two fiscal stimulation packages implemented in that year and the reconstruction demand following the Kobe earthquake in January. GDP grew 3.0 per cent in FY1995 and 4.4 per cent in FY1996, while stock prices rose over 50 per cent between July 1995 and June 1996. However, the bad debt problem of non-bank financial institutions started to surface, with a number of small financial institutions going bankrupt.[2]

Economic performance deteriorated again in FY1997 shortly after the government shifted to a fiscal consolidation policy by raising taxes and reducing public expenditures. When Prime Minister Ryutaro Hashimoto took office in January 1996, he put top priority on reducing the fast-growing budget deficit. Owing to a misjudgment that the economy was on its way to a robust recovery, the consumption tax rate was raised from 3 per cent to

5 per cent as scheduled, while the temporary tax cut amounting to ¥2 trillion implemented since FY1995 was terminated in FY1997. The Fiscal Structural Reform Act was passed in November 1997, stipulating that the government deficit be reduced to below 3 per cent of GDP by FY2003 when new issues of deficit-financing government bonds should also be terminated. These fiscal-tightening measures had adverse effects on consumption, dragging Japan's economic growth rate down to −0.4 per cent in FY1997 and to −1.9 per cent in FY1998, its worst performance in the postwar era.

The downturn that started in 1997 was aggravated by the financial malaise at home and the currency crisis in neighbouring Asian countries. Two major financial institutions, Yamaichi Securities and then Hokkaido Takushoku Bank, failed in the autumn of 1997. Concerns that more Japanese banks might follow suit drove the so-called 'Japan premium' – the interest rate premium they paid when borrowing in dollars in international inter-bank markets – up to as much as 1 per cent in late 1997. At the same time, attempts by banks to restructure their balance sheets in anticipation of the 'Prompt Corrective Action Plan', coming into effect the following April, aggravated the credit crunch problem.[3] Meanwhile, in Asia, the currency crisis that started in Thailand in July 1997 quickly infected the whole region, and Japan was not spared from its repercussions.

As the crisis deepened, the government was forced to reverse its tight fiscal policy stance, announcing a stimulating package (the 'Comprehensive Economic Measures') totalling ¥16 trillion on 24 April 1998.[4] The return to an expansionary fiscal policy stance accelerated after Keizo Obuchi took office as prime minister in July 1998. Another fiscal package (the 'Emergency Economic Package') totalling ¥17 trillion was announced in November, while the Fiscal Structural Reform Act was suspended in December the same year to accommodate this major shift in fiscal policy. The expansionary initial budget for FY1999, which contained permanent tax reductions (national and local) for individuals and corporations exceeding ¥6 trillion and generous tax incentives for home purchases, was followed by yet another fiscal package ('Policy Measures for Economic Rebirth') totalling ¥17 trillion in November 1999.

The Obuchi administration also lost no time in restoring confidence in the soundness of the financial system. Major laws were enacted in October 1998 to allow the government to put failing banks under public control temporarily, and to use public funds to recapitalize banks that are considered viable. A total of ¥60 trillion, equivalent to 12 per cent of Japan's GDP, was earmarked for these schemes. Of this amount ¥17 trillion was for guaranteeing bank deposits. With the backing of these funds, all the deposits and debentures of Japanese financial institutions would be fully guaranteed until March of 2001 (later extended to March 2002).[5] Another ¥18 trillion was set aside for the reorganization of failed financial institutions. The remaining ¥25 trillion was to be used for the recapitalization of viable financial institutions. The troubled Long-term Credit Bank and Nippon Credit Bank were soon nationalized under the new framework. In addition, 15 banks received capital injections from the government amounting to ¥7.5 trillion in March 1999, allowing them to write off bad debts at a faster pace. This financial stabilizing programme succeeded in restoring public confidence in the soundness of the financial system, as reflected in the subsequent elimination of the Japan premium as well as the recovery in the stock prices of Japanese banks.

At the same time, measures were taken to cope with the credit crunch problem plaguing small- and medium-sized companies. In addition to providing them with ample funds through government financial institutions and credit guarantees, a special credit programme was set up in October 1998 with total guarantee authorization amounting to ¥20 trillion, which was subsequently increased to ¥30 trillion. These measures have helped alleviate the credit crunch problem, and reduced the rate of bankruptcies of small- and medium-sized companies.

Monetary Policy

Since the bursting of the asset-price bubble in the early 1990s, monetary policy has been relaxed in steps to stimulate the economy. The official discount rate has been reduced eleven times since July 1991, from its peak level of 6 per cent to 0.25 per cent since March 2001. The uncollateralized overnight call rate has been kept at virtually zero per cent since February 1999 (except for a short period between August 2000 and March 2001.)

While monetary relaxation has been accompanied by a sharp increase in the monetary base, it has failed to boost the broad money supply, let alone aggregate demand (Figure 3.2). There are two major schools of thought explaining why monetary policy has failed to stimulate the economy: the 'liquidity trap school' led by MIT economist Paul Krugman and the 'credit crunch school' led by Nomura economist Richard Koo. While a heated debate is going on between these camps, the two approaches are better interpreted as complementing, rather than competing with, one another.

The first school focuses on the 'interest rate channel' of transmission and argues that the Japanese economy has fallen into a liquidity trap, 'that awkward condition in which monetary policy loses its grip because the nominal interest rate is essentially zero, in which the quantity of money becomes irrelevant because money and bonds are essentially perfect substitutes' (Krugman, 1998). Given immense excess capacity in traditional industries and the slow emergence of new industries, a sharp reduction of

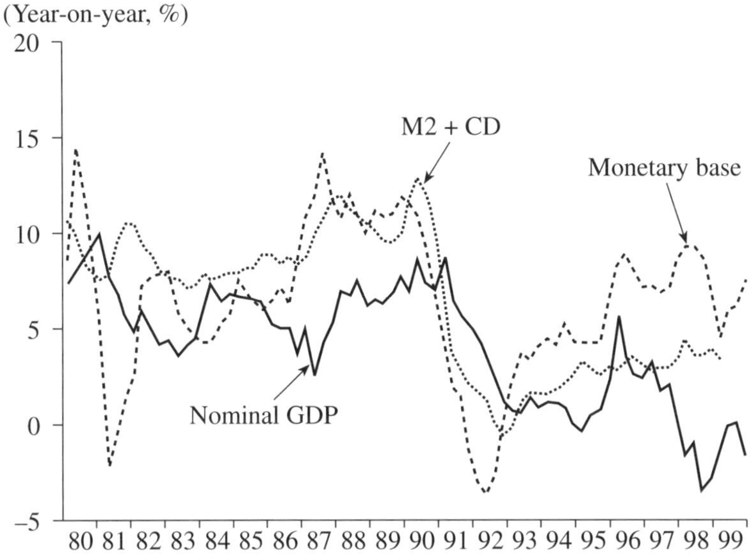

Note: CD denotes certificate of deposit.

Sources: Bank of Japan, *Financial and Economic Statistics Monthly*, and Economic Planning Agency, *National Income Statistics*.

Figure 3.2 Weakening links between monetary base, money supply and nominal GDP

real interest rates, probably to a negative level, would be needed to restore full employment.[6] Since there is little room for nominal interest rates to fall further, Krugman advocates that the central bank should commit itself to a policy of managed inflation – announcing a target rate of inflation over the long term and committing itself to do whatever is necessary to achieve that rate. The aim is to raise inflation expectations (for example, up to 4 per cent) so that, given nominal interest rates, real interest rates should decline to stimulate investment (see Box 3.1). In addition, further monetary loosening is expected to be accompanied by a sharp depreciation of the yen, with positive effects on net exports.

While Krugman's proposal has gained wide attention, if not support, from economists in both Japan and the United States, it has been rejected by the Bank of Japan on the ground that it is difficult not only to set a specific target (in terms of which price index to go for and at what level) but also to achieve it (Okina, 1999).[7] With interest rates already down to a historically low level, there is little room left for further monetary loosening to

BOX 3.1 INFLATION TARGETING IN A SIMPLE *IS–LM* MODEL

Inflation targeting is a framework for conducting monetary policy in which the central bank makes an explicit commitment to meet a publicly announced numerical inflation target within a particular time frame.

The effectiveness of inflation targeting can be analysed using the standard *IS–LM* model, where a liquidity trap is represented by a flat *LM* curve lying close to the zero interest rate level. Here we need to distinguish between nominal and real interest rates, the difference being the rate of expected inflation. It should also be noted that, while money demand (and thus the *LM* curve) is a function of the nominal interest rate, aggregate spending (and thus the *IS* curve) depends on the real interest rate. With the vertical axis denoting real interest rate, the *LM* curve shifts downward in proportion to the increase in inflation expectations. Should the central bank be successful in raising inflation expectations, output expands as aggregate spending responds to the fall in the real interest rate to a negative level (although the nominal interest rate stays at zero per cent).

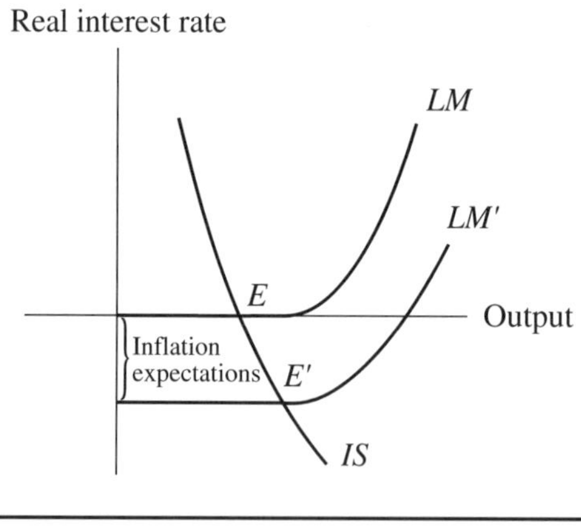

raise inflation expectations.[8] The Bank of Japan also worries that inflation may get out of control once it gains momentum. In that case, using monetary policy to pursue a higher rate of inflation may result in higher nominal interest rates and a weaker yen. Rising nominal interest rates would offset the expected reduction in real interest rates resulting from higher inflation (expectations). Trying to export its way out of the recession by allowing the yen to fall is also likely to put downward pressure on the crisis-hit Asian countries and delay their export-led recovery, while at the same time heightening trade frictions with the United States. By reducing the capital–adequacy ratio of Japanese banks that have large exposure in dollar-denominated lending, this strategy also runs the risk of worsening the credit crunch problem facing Japanese companies.[9]

In contrast, the credit crunch school emphasizes the breakdown of the 'lending channel' as undercapitalized banks are unable to provide firms with adequate credit (Koo, 1999).[10] Deterioration in the quality of banks' balance sheets following the bursting of the asset-price bubble has reduced their ability to lend. In particular, the need to meet the BIS capital–adequacy ratio may act as a binding constraint on lending. Small- and medium-sized companies are particularly hurt, as they have no access to alternative sources of financing, such as issuing bonds in capital markets. The credit crunch problem cannot be solved by the central bank increasing the supply of base money, as this would result only in an accumulation of excess reserves by banks. Rather, the capital base of banks needs to be revamped by injecting public funds.

The transmission of monetary policy through the lending channel has also been hampered by the weakening propensity and ability of companies to borrow as their net worth declines in value. Most Japanese companies have been forced to pursue a backward-looking strategy of reducing borrowings in an attempt to restructure their balance sheets. Even those with a forward-looking strategy may not be able to offer land or securities as collateral when borrowing to invest in new projects. This should be distinguished from the credit crunch problem, which reflects the supply-side problem of unwillingness or inability of banks to lend. Indeed, the injection of public funds in March 1999 has not been followed by a recovery in lending, suggesting that the current stagnation in lending can better be explained by a lack of demand for funds than by a lack of supply.[11] This conclusion is consistent with the liquidity trap hypothesis if the 'balance sheet scare syndrome' that causes the stagnation in bank lending also explains the weakness in private investment despite very low interest rates.

Fiscal Policy

According to standard macroeconomic models, when the economy is under a liquidity trap, fiscal policy is supposed to be most effective in stimulating demand because, even if the government spends more by borrowing, it will put little upward pressure on interest rates.[12] Thus both the crowding-out effect on private investment and the negative impact on net exports as the yen rate appreciates on the back of higher interest rates (the

Mundell–Fleming effect) should be minimal. The burden of repaying public debt issued now to finance the fiscal deficit should have a relatively light repayment burden due to the historically low level of interest rates. This situation represents a golden opportunity for the government to improve the country's meagre infrastructure.

This optimistic scenario, however, has been betrayed by Japan's recent experience. The Japanese government has implemented a wide range of economic stimulus measures of over ¥100 trillion since 1992, but these so far have failed to stimulate the economy. The disappointing performance of fiscal policy can be explained largely by the decline in the multiplier reflecting the following factors. First, the corporate sector's marginal propensity to invest has declined following the bursting of the asset-price bubble because of excess capacity and the debt overhang problem facing Japanese companies. This is particularly true for construction companies, which are by far the largest beneficiary of fiscal stimulation. Second, the marginal propensity to consume of the household sector has also fallen (and the marginal propensity to save has increased) because of rising concern about unemployment as well as expectations of tax increases in the future to compensate for the widening fiscal deficit now (the Ricardian equivalence hypothesis). Third, the marginal propensity to import has increased in recent years because of stronger competition with developing countries in Asia. Since savings and imports by the corporate and household sectors represent leakages in the multiplier process, these changes mean that income increases have a smaller second-round effect on aggregate demand than they previously had.

Some economists have argued that fiscal stimulus in the 1990s was insufficient, rather than ineffective, in restoring self-sustaining economic growth. Posen (1998), for example, dismisses the claim that the attempts at fiscal stimulus failed. Rather, he argues that a serious fiscal stimulus was attempted on only one occasion, September 1995, and that this was followed by strong growth in the next year. By contrast, misguided contractionary fiscal policies, notably the consumption tax increase in April 1997, slowed the economy. On the basis of this diagnosis of the prolonged recession, Posen prescribes a sizeable fiscal stimulus, with income tax cuts as a major component, to bring about economic recovery.

Judging from the sharp deterioration in the government's fiscal deficit, however, it is fair to say that fiscal policy on the whole has been expansionary since 1992. According to the Organisation for Economic Co-operation and Development (OECD, 2000), Japan's general government financial balance as a percentage of GDP worsened from −0.6 per cent in 1990 to −8.8 per cent in 1999. This share was by far the highest among OECD countries and significantly higher than the peak share of −6.7 per cent reached in the United States in 1992 (Figure 3.3). The implementation of aggressive economic stimulus packages, coupled with the sharp decline in tax revenues resulting from the economic slowdown, has contributed to the widening of the deficit.

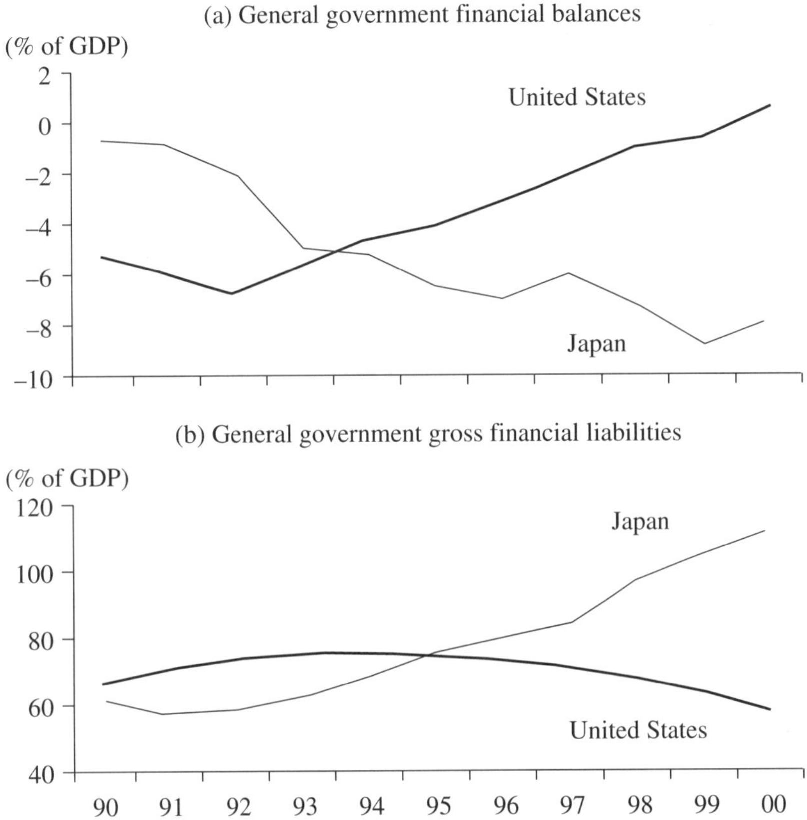

Note: General government financial balances exclude social security.

Source: OECD, *OECD Economic Outlook*, 68, December 2000.

Figure 3 .3 Japan's deteriorating fiscal position: a comparison with the United States

The need to finance a chronic fiscal deficit has resulted in a sharp increase in public borrowing. Gross financial liabilities of the public sector surged from 57.9 per cent as a percentage of GDP in 1991 to 112.3 per cent in 2000, the highest among all OECD countries. Nominal interest rates (ten-year government bond yield) averaged 3.1 per cent between 1992 and 2000, well above the 0.9 per cent growth rate of nominal GDP during the same period. Thus the debt-to-GDP ratio will continue to increase even if new borrowing is limited to financing interest payments. In addition to a recovery of the Japanese economy, drastic cuts in public spending and/or increases in taxes will be needed to redress Japan's fiscal position.

STRUCTURAL REFORM

As efforts to restore economic growth through fiscal and monetary expansion have failed repeatedly, the need to pursue structural reform has become more and more apparent.[13] Furthermore, the prospect of a shrinking work force means that, Japan will have to focus even more sharply on higher productivity through supply-side structural reform to sustain economic growth over the long term.

What Went Wrong?

Japan's economic growth rate has declined in steps since the early 1970s, from 10.4 per cent in the 1960s to 5.2 per cent in the 1970s, to 3.8 per cent in the 1980s, and to 1.7 per cent in the 1990s. Since investment (as measured by gross capital formation) as a percentage of GDP was about the same (at about 30 per cent) in both the 1980s and the 1990s, the decline in the growth rate in recent years can be attributed to a decline in investment efficiency, as reflected in a sharp increase in the incremental capital–output ratio (ICOR).[14] Indeed, the ICOR is now substantially higher, and thus efficiency of investment much lower, in Japan than in the United States (Figure 3.4). Above all, the potential economic growth rate slowed as a natural result of Japan closing its technology gap with the industrial powers. The rate was further dragged down because both the government and the corporate sector failed to adapt the institutions that had contributed to the economy's past success to the new environment.

In retrospect, the postwar 'Japanese model' played an important role in supporting Japanese industry during its catch-up phase when technology was readily available from abroad and corporate goals were clear and investment risk was small. A spirit of national consensus promoted close cooperation between business and government, helping to concentrate resources in promising areas that needed substantial initial investment. A high savings rate reduced the cost of capital and promoted investment in an era when capital controls prevented domestic interest rates from converging to the overseas levels, while the emergence of new industries

Note: Based on 5-year moving averages of 'gross capital formation as a percentage of GDP' and the 'GDP growth rate'.

Source: Compiled by the author, based on IMF, *International Financial Statistics*.

Figure 3.4 Incremental capital–output ratio: Japan versus the United States

ensured that the marginal efficiency of investment stayed high. A cross-shareholding system centred on main banks allowed the pursuance of long-term corporate goals (including a lifetime employment system and market share maximization) instead of short-term profits. Combined with a dedication to the production of high-quality products, Japanese manufacturers quickly established themselves as a major force in international markets.

Now that the catch-up process is over and Japan needs to develop its own economic frontiers, a new system that promotes competition and risk taking has become all the more important. Furthermore, Japan is facing three new challenges. First, its working population is expected to shrink as a result of an ageing society and a declining birth rate. Second, the trend towards globalization implies keener international competition not only in the manufacturing sector but also in the service sector (finance, distribution, telecommunications and so on). Third, rapid developments in information technologies call for more flexible and innovative business practices. Many of the structures and institutions that proved so valuable in helping to develop Japan's industrial power in the past are thus no longer sufficient to meet the needs of a more mature, service-oriented economy. To revitalize the Japanese economy in this new environment, the following structural problems need be redressed.

Industrial policy and government regulations

As argued by Katz (1998), the overall thrust of Japan's industrial policy has switched from market-conforming 'accelerationism' to market-defying 'preservatism'. The purpose is to preserve already existing industries in order to protect sunk costs, to prevent unemployment and to maintain wage equality. The recession cartels formed under the initiative of the Ministry of International Trade and Industry (MITI) to protect declining industries have reinforced inefficiency. In the name of egalitarianism, members of a recession cartel are obliged to cut production in proportion to their share of the market or their share of capacity. To help out the weakest, the bigger or stronger firms are sometimes pressured to take an extra-large cut. Under Japan's 'convoy' system, the whole convoy can move no faster than the slowest ship.

At the same time, excessive government regulations and a high corporate tax rate have sustained domestic prices at an artificially high level. The gap with overseas prices is particularly marked for public utilities charges and transport and distribution costs. Protection of the agricultural sector has also led to higher food prices and land prices. Since services and land are important inputs for the manufacturing sector, their high prices adversely affect the competitiveness of Japanese products in international markets, forcing companies to relocate production offshore. Furthermore, constrained by the notorious 'Large-scale Retail Store Law', the Japanese retail sector has traditionally been composed of small stores and complex distribution networks. The resulting inefficiency and wide mark-ups have made consumer product prices much higher in Japan than overseas.

Banking and finance

Until recently, the convoy system also applied to the financial sector, whereby the government ensured that all financial institutions (banks in particular) would not go bankrupt. In the case where a bank had become insolvent, the Ministry of Finance would arrange for it to merge with another bank in order to protect the interests of depositors and borrowers. The presence of this 'safety net' created moral hazard problems, prompting banks to take excessive risks, as they did during the late 1980s. This sowed the seeds of the bad debt problem that emerged with the bursting of the asset-price bubble in the 1990s.

Japan needs to establish a financial system capable of allocating funds based on the market mechanism instead of direction by the government. The traditional financial system was originally established to assist the formation of a mass production society, soaking up funds from the public at large to lend them out to standardized mass production type industries. Uniform interest rates and government protection adopted for this system meant that major corporations could rely on low-cost borrowing from commercial banks. This system, however, encouraged inefficient uses of capital, rewarding marginally profitable firms by penalizing more efficient competitors. It also limited the access of Japanese consumers to a full range of competitive financial products. In addition, under the traditional system, venture businesses have difficulty borrowing from banks because they do not have land to offer as collateral. To develop new industries, Japan should take steps to facilitate venture businesses to raise funds through capital markets, including listing on stock markets, to ensure that savings are channelled to industries that may involve high risks.

At the same time, there is an urgent need to reform the postal savings system, which is the largest deposit-taking institution in the world. This state-run system enjoys a competitive advantage over private banks because it does not have to pay any corporate taxes or deposit insurance premiums and it is not subject to reserve requirements. Postal savings are used to finance policy loans (channelled automatically through the Ministry of Finance and then government-related financial institutions) based more on political than on economic considerations. Some of these borrowers are public corporations that are running very large deficits, raising doubts over their ability to repay without additional financial support from the government.

Public finance

The immense amount of public expenditures, including those incurred in the name of pump-priming fiscal expansion, may not have been efficiently used. At 6.0 per cent of GDP in FY1998, public fixed capital formation is significantly higher than in other industrial countries (1.9 per cent for the United States for example). The lack of transparency in awarding contracts has provided fertile soil for corruption and collusion among construction companies to raise prices. Public works have also been used as tools to create jobs and transfer income (to the construction sector and to the countryside) rather than as investment to yield a return. Making matters worse, under a very rigid budget system, public expenditures continue to be channelled into declining sectors while such new areas as information infrastructure receive insufficient public funds. This backward-looking public spending strategy has led to a misallocation of social resources and retarded economic growth.

Corporate governance

The Japanese corporate system characterized by long-term relations has led to inefficiency as companies come to be plagued by excess capacity, overemployment and debt overhang. The lifetime employment system and corporate groupings (*keiretsu*) centred on main banks played important roles in the development of Japan's manufacturing industry, which requires on-the-job training, technology transfer to subcontractors, and a stable supply of low-cost funds. However, flexibility in combining various factors of production is more important in new areas such as information and finance. To facilitate industrial restructuring, the government should eliminate obstacles to the mobility of labour, mergers and acquisitions and development of venture capital.

In recent years, the supervisory function of the main banks has greatly weakened. There is an urgent need to rebuild corporate governance based on market principles. As part of that process, it is necessary to form a mobile market of senior executives to replace the present practice of promoting managers from within the corporate hierarchy. In addition, managers ought to be monitored using objective market indicators, and one way to achieve that is to link their compensation to company share prices by granting them stock options.

Recent Attempts at Reform

While the structural problems facing the Japanese economy are well known, attempts at reform have always met with resistance from vested interests. In a sharp break from its traditional gradual and piecemeal approach, in December 1996 the Japanese government under Prime Minister Ryutaro Hashimoto adopted a comprehensive reform programme that covered six key areas: economic structure, finance and banking, public finance, health and welfare, public administration and education. The aim of this reform programme was to revitalize the economy and to create a free and fair socioeconomic system that was fully opened to the international community and based on the rules of accountability and market principles. This was to be achieved by eliminating or relaxing regulations and transferring the responsibilities of the government to the private sector. The regulatory role of the government would be shifted from *ex ante* approval to *ex post* monitoring of compliance with general rules in this process.

Among the six key areas, reform of economic structure, which aims at shifting resources to growth areas that will underpin domestic employment over the long term, will have the largest direct impact on productivity growth. The government aims to facilitate corporate restructuring by reducing restrictions that hinder mergers and acquisitions, cross-border investments, alliances and financial transactions both within and across national borders. Specifically, current reform and deregulation initiatives include the following measures (JETRO, 1999).

Changes in corporate taxation

The government implemented a permanent tax cut in FY1999, reducing the corporate tax rate from 46 per cent to 40 per cent, making it competitive with tax rates in the United States and Germany.

Promotion of new industries

The government is supporting the creation of new industries and business start-ups by private entrepreneurs. To this end, it is implementing deregulation, technological development and human resource development to create a business environment conducive to the growth of 15 industries selected for their high growth potential in the next generation. [15]

Changes in anti-monopoly regulations

Japan's anti-monopoly law has been revised to facilitate mergers and acquisitions. The ban on pure holding companies (companies with more than half of their assets being shares of other companies) was lifted (effective from December 1997 for non-financial firms and March 1998 for financial institutions). In addition, where once all mergers and acquisitions were required to be reported to the Fair Trade Commission, now only those transactions above a certain amount need to be registered.

Changes in commercial law

Corporate acquisitions by stock transfer rather than cash purchases have been approved. Regulations concerning the legal structure of Japanese companies, including rules governing corporate spin-offs and divestitures, are now being reviewed and altered.

Changes in corporate pension systems

A new pension contribution system modelled on the 401(k) plan in the United States will be introduced in 2001. This allows employees to contribute a portion of their compensation, before income taxes, to a company-sponsored retirement plan. Under the new scheme, the employees decide how the contributions are to be invested, and continuity is guaranteed when they change jobs.

Changes in accounting regulations

To improve transparency and disclosure, beginning in FY2000, Japanese companies have been required to report consolidated financial statements that cover subsidiaries at current market prices. Under the new rules, the Japanese accounting system has become consistent with international standards.

A Closer Look at the Financial Big Bang

Another pillar of Japan's comprehensive reform programme is the financial Big Bang, whose aim is to transform Tokyo into an international financial centre on a par with New York and London by the year 2001. The three underlying principles are to be (a) free, a free market where the market mechanism prevails, (b) fair, a transparent and reliable market, and (c) global, an international market ahead of its time. The Big Bang covers all major areas of the financial sector, including banking, securities and insurance. It drastically reduces restrictions on products, services, and organizational structures on the one hand, and tries to improve fair trading rules for customer protection and the framework for dealing with failures on the other. The measures to stabilize the financial system discussed earlier aim at remedying problems inherited from the past, while the Big Bang represents a forward-looking strategy of preparing for the future.

The financial Big Bang was initiated in November 1996 and formulated into a formal agenda in June 1997. As the first step, the Foreign Exchange Law was revised to liberalize cross-border transactions completely in April 1998. Then the Financial System Reform Law, a package of revisions of laws including the Banking Law the Securities and Exchange Law, and the Insurance Business Law, came into effect in December 1998. Almost all measures have been subsequently implemented as planned, bringing drastic changes to the financial sector (MOF, 2000).

First, efforts were made to provide attractive services by enhancing competition. Major measures include promoting entry of banks, securities companies and insurance companies into each other's business, switching from the licensing system to a registration system for securities companies, liberalizing cross-border capital transactions and foreign exchange business, and liberalizing brokerage commissions and insurance premium rates. Many new securities companies, including foreign ones, have been established since switching to a registration system. (A total of 32 companies were newly registered during the 13 months since December 1998.) Furthermore, the liberalization of brokerage commissions has led to expansion of securities trading through the Internet (on-line trading). Financial institutions have also taken advantage of deregulation to increase the range of financial instruments and services available to investors, including financial derivatives and new investment trusts and over-the-counter sales of investment trusts by banks and other financial institutions.

Second, new markets and channels for fund raising were created by abolishing the requirements to trade equities only through stock exchanges, and by introducing electronic trading systems. The Tokyo Stock Exchange established a new market for promising start-ups, the so-called 'MOTHERS' (Market of High Growth and Emerging Stocks), in November 1999. This was followed by the establishment of the NASDAQ-Japan market at the Osaka Stock Exchange in May 2000.

Finally, a framework for prudential surveillance was established by improving the disclosure system, setting up fair trading rules, such as stricter insider trading control, and protecting customers when financial institutions fail. Since the accounting period ending March 1999, financial institutions have been required by law to disclose information on their non-performing assets on a consolidated basis according to standards equivalent to the ones set by the Securities and Exchange Commission of the United States, with possible penalties for non-compliance.

EARLY SIGNS OF CHANGE

Thanks to the continuing efforts to reform, the Japanese economy has shown positive signs of change. Japanese corporations are responding to keener competition resulting from globalization and deregulation, and consumers have benefited from this process in terms of lower prices and better services.

Progress in Corporate Restructuring

Japanese corporations are undergoing a restructuring process that involves not only 'downsizing' but also drastically changing their traditional business practices. Greater emphasis is given to profitability than to market share. Labour mobility is increasing, and merit is gradually replacing seniority as the basis of remuneration. The main bank and *keiretsu* systems are also losing their influence, and mergers and acquisitions among companies belonging to different corporate groups have become a common means of restructuring.

First, Japanese companies are paying more attention to the rate of return on their investment, with return on equity (ROE) and return on assets (ROA) followed closely by both managers and investors. During the bubble period, fuelled by very low cost of capital, Japanese corporations actively increased their asset portfolios with little regard to profitability. The resulting negative economic growth, rising debt and bankruptcies, and inefficient use of management resources, further reduced corporate profits and prompted a change in corporate strategy. A survey by the Economic Planning Agency (EPA, 1999) confirms that an increasing share of Japanese corporations is focusing on the rate of return rather than the absolute levels of sales and profits in their corporate strategies (Figure 3.5). The same survey shows that many corporate managers see both the cross-shareholding system and the main bank system weakening. From now on, their investment decisions will be closely monitored by shareholders and creditors, who are demanding a rate of return commensurate with the risk on their investment. At the same time, more and more corporate managers have been granted stock options in recent years, so that they now have a stronger incentive to maximize profit.

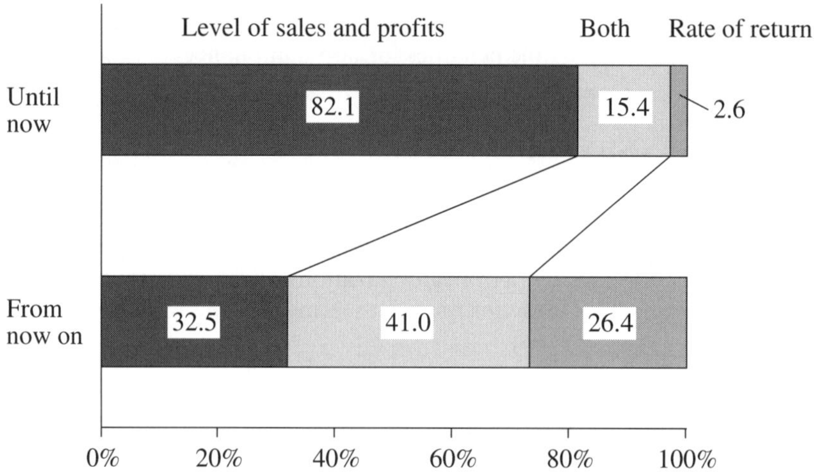

Source: Economic Planning Agency, '1998 Survey of Corporate Behaviours', April 1999.

Figure 3.5 Focus of corporate strategy: market share versus capital efficiency

Second, the lifetime employment system is giving way to a more flexible one. During the recent recession many companies restructured through layoffs, introduction of early retirement schemes, and limiting their hiring of new employees. As a result, the unemployment rate has reached a historically high level, and the government has responded by launching diverse initiatives to create employment. In the past, the government's employment policy was designed to maintain workers in their present jobs, but the emphasis has shifted to promoting the transfer of human resources to new growth areas. Higher labour mobility in turn has made it difficult for

Japanese companies to sustain a remuneration system based on seniority, prompting them to shift to a new system based more on merit. This is particularly true for financial institutions, which are losing some of their brightest professionals to foreign competitors expanding their operations in Tokyo.

Finally, mergers and acquisitions have become widely used in corporate reorganization and restructuring to achieve economies of scale and economies of scope. M&A activity is increasing not only in the service sector, which is responding to deregulation, but also in the manufacturing sector, which is facing keen competition in the global market.

The increase in M&As has been led by the banking sector. Following the merger between Mitsubishi Bank and Tokyo Bank in 1996, Dai-ichi Kangyo Bank (DKB), Fuji Bank and Industrial Bank of Japan (IBJ) joined hands to form the Mizuho Financial Group in the autumn of 2000. Subsequently, alliances were formed between Sanwa Bank, Tokai Bank and Toyo Trust Bank, and between Sumitomo Bank and Sakura Bank in the spring of 2001. At the same time, Bank of Tokyo-Mitsubishi was joined by Mitsubishi Trust Bank and Nippon Trust Bank. As a result, Japan's biggest banks have effectively been consolidated into four major groups.

In many cases, recent M&As in the financial sector have involved foreign partners that are eager to cash in on the Big Bang. When Yamaichi Securities was liquidated in 1998, Merrill Lynch took over its branch network. GE Capital acquired Toho Life Insurance Company and then Japan Lease Corporation, Japan's fifth-largest consumer finance company. In 1998, Traveler's Group invested in Nikko Securities, one of the Big Three in Japan's securities industry, by purchasing 25 per cent of its stock. More recently, Ripplewood, a US-led investment group that includes General Electric and the Mellon Bank as major partners, acquired the temporarily nationalized Long-term Credit Bank from the government.[16]

Japan is also part of the global wave of M&As in the motor industry. Renault of France invested $5.3 billion in Nissan in 1998, giving it a 36.8 per cent ownership share of Japan's second-largest carmaker. This was followed by GM's investment in Fuji Heavy Industry in 1999 and DaimlerChrysler's acquisition of a 33.4 per cent stake in Mitsubishi in 2000. As a result, seven out of Japan's 11 major carmakers have come under the control of foreign companies. Of the remaining four, Toyota now has a majority holding of Daihatsu and Hino, and only Honda has decided to go it alone.[17]

The rise in cross-border M&A activity has been reflected in a sharp increase in foreign direct investment into Japan. According to the Ministry of Finance, inward foreign direct investment reached $28.3 billion in FY2000. The current pace of investment in Japan by foreign companies is about seven times as high as that five years ago.

Consumers Benefiting from Deregulation

Meanwhile, Japan's deregulation programme is moving steadily ahead according to the original schedule. In addition to the changes in the financial sector noted earlier, the positive effects of deregulation have been most apparent in the retail and telecommunications sectors.

Following two major amendments implemented in 1992 and 1994, the Large-scale Retail Store Law was finally abolished in June 2000 to reduce entry barriers. As a result of moves to deregulate, the number of large-scale retail stores increased by 41.1 per cent between 1991 and 1997, compared with only 16.7 per cent in the previous six years, despite a sharp slowdown in economic growth. Keener competition is raising the efficiency of the retail sector, presenting Japanese consumers with lower prices and a greater array of choices than before. The Large-scale Retail Store Law has been replaced by a new Large-scale Retail Store Location Law which stipulates that regulation of large stores will no longer be based on supply/demand considerations but on the degree to which a large store opening or expansion affects the local environment.

In the telecommunications sector, deregulation has allowed businesses and consumers to gain access to a far wider range of services at reduced prices. For example, long-distance telephone rates have now fallen by more than 75 per cent since 1985. Cellular telephone subscriptions have also increased rapidly, from 2.13 million in 1993 to 69.2 million in June 2001 since reform efforts allowed the introduction of a new sales system in 1994.[18] The expanding scope and size of the market have not only lowered telecommunication costs drastically, but also provided opportunities to a number of foreign firms such as Nokia and Motorola to enter the Japanese market. Investors also recognize the emerging opportunities, as reflected in the highly successful public offering of NTT Mobile Communications Network (DoCoMo) in October 1998.

The Unfinished Agenda

Although there are early signs of change, Japan's 'transition to a market economy' is far from complete, and many barriers to reform remain to be overcome.[19]

Trade-off between short-term and long-term growth

Structural reforms in some areas have been delayed because of the need to maintain employment and financial stability. In addition to building roads leading to nowhere using taxpayers' money, there are more implicit forms of serious resource misallocation. Subsidizing money-losing banks and companies has the adverse effect of locking resources in stagnant sectors instead of shifting them to more dynamic ones. Guaranteeing bank loans to small- and medium-sized companies and bailing out troubled financial institutions, in particular, have led to immense moral hazard problems.

Moreover, the current level of fiscal deficit is certainly too high to be sustainable and the frozen Fiscal Structural Reform Act should be revived once private demand is back in the driver's seat. It is necessary not only to increase tax revenues and to reduce expenditures, but also to improve the fiscal structure itself. This requires redefining the division of labour between the public and the private sectors as well as between the national and local governments, based on cost–benefit calculations.

Resistance from vested interest groups

Resistance from vested interest groups has remained a major barrier to reform. Administrative reform, for example, has so far achieved no more than a nominal reshuffling of the ministries. In addition to allowing the private sector and local governments to play a more important role in providing public services, a lot more needs to be done in improving administrative transparency, accountability and adaptability. As pointed out by the Organisation for Economic Co-operation and Development (OECD, 1999), Japan suffers from a deeply conservative policy process that slows decision making, discourages open debate, encourages 'clientelism' and allows special interests to block needed changes. New incentives, participants and controls in the regulatory processes are needed to reorient old relationships with producer groups, to break up information monopolies in the bureaucracy and to narrow administrative discretion to regulate in the name of public interest.

The failure to privatize the postal savings system provides a typical example where vested interests continue to obstruct the reform process. As proposed in the interim report of the Administrative Reform Council, an ad hoc panel headed by Ryutaro Hashimoto when he was prime minister, there is a broad consensus that the postal savings system should be privatized to improve the allocation of financial resources. With strong opposition from the Post and Communications Ministry, however, the plan has not been realized.

The egalitarian way of thinking

The egalitarian way of thinking remains deep-rooted in the current debate on economic reform, even though the importance of competition has been greatly emphasized. For example, many people are concerned that competition may increase income inequality, with adverse effects on social stability. Since probably nowhere in the world is the income distribution as equitable as it is in Japan, however, the efficiency gain that competition creates is likely to be much greater than any harm it causes by increasing income inequality. Japan needs a change of mind-set: a shift from pursuing equality of outcome to equality of opportunity, so as to provide more rainbows to chase for those who wish to put their talents to work.

NOTES

1. The Japanese fiscal year runs from 1 April to 31 March in the following year.
2. In 1996, public funds amounting to ¥685 billion (about $6 billion) were used to rescue troubled housing loan companies (*jusen*), which are non-banks that do not take deposits directly from the public. It was widely believed that the government aimed to bail out the politically influential agricultural deposit-taking institutions, which had lent substantial sums to these companies. This distrust of the government's intention made subsequent use of public funds to bail out financial institutions very difficult, even when the soundness of the whole financial system was at risk.
3. Prompt Corrective Action is a new administrative means by which the supervisory authority, using capital–adequacy ratios as an objective indicator, issues necessary correction orders to banks in a timely and proper manner. Prompt Corrective Action is classified into three levels: (1) an order to make and implement a plan prepared by banks themselves to improve their management (for financial institutions with a capital–adequacy ratio between 4 and 8 per cent if they have international operations, and 2 and 4 per cent if otherwise); (2) an order to implement specific measures, including raising new capital and 'downsizing' business operations (for financial institutions with a capital–adequacy ratio between 0 and 4 per cent if they have international operations and 0 and 2 per cent if otherwise); (3) suspension of business for financial institutions with a capital–adequacy ratio of under 0 per cent).
4. ¥1 trillion is approximately $10 billion dollars. Japan's GDP currently stands at about ¥500 trillion.
5. From April 2002, the amount guaranteed will be limited to ¥10 million for each person.
6. While Krugman attributes Japan's liquidity trap to such domestic factors as the lack of technology innovation and an ageing population, McKinnon and Ohno (1997) suggest that it has been externally imposed and trace its roots to the 'ever-higher-yen syndrome'. The yen has been following an upward trend against the US dollar at an annual rate of about 4 per cent on average, reflecting efforts by the USA to pressure Japan to allow the yen to appreciate in an unsuccessful attempt to reduce the bilateral trade imbalance. Interest rate arbitrage based on this expectation has forced Japanese interest rates about 4 per cent below US rates. This was not a problem when nominal interest rates in the USA were high, due to high inflation there. However, in the mid-1990s, when US interest rates came down, Japanese interest rates were driven down to zero. McKinnon and Ohno propose a solution to Japan's liquidity trap problem consisting of two complementary sets of policies: a commercial agreement limiting bilateral sanctions in trade disputes and ending (future) pressure from the USA to push the yen up, and a monetary accord to stabilize the yen–dollar rate over the long term. Should these bilateral commitments become credible, interest rates in Japan would rise to the levels in the USA.
7. The current IT (information technology) revolution and deregulation have led to price declines through the improvement in productivity and development of new products. It is difficult to distinguish these effects from deflation using traditional price indexes, which may even fail to capture fully the impact of this 'new price revolution'.
8. Some economists have argued that there is still room for long-term interest rates to fall from the current level of over 1 per cent if the central bank buys long-term government bonds either through open market operations or by underwriting them directly in the

primary market. The Bank of Japan, however, warns that this would actually raise long-term interest rates as investors ask for a risk premium to compensate for the resulting deterioration in the creditworthiness of the Japanese government.

9. The capital–adequacy ratio (also known as the BIS ratio) is defined as the ratio between capital and risk assets. International banks are required to maintain this ratio at a minimum level of 8 per cent. For Japanese banks, capital is denominated in yen, while 80 per cent of their overseas lending (which comprises about 30 per cent of their risk assets, the rest being domestic lending) is denominated in dollars. A weaker yen increases the value of risk assets (the denominator) in yen terms, and thus lowers the ratio. Other things being equal, in order to meet the minimum capital–adequacy ratio, Japanese banks need to reduce lending either at home or abroad. The ability of Japanese banks to lend is estimated to fall by ¥1 trillion for each one-yen of depreciation against the dollar (Koo, 1998).
10. The bank lending channel is based on the view that banks play a special role in the financial system because they are well suited to deal with certain types of borrowers, especially small firms where the problems of asymmetric information (and thus adverse selection and moral hazard) are especially pronounced. An increase in money supply, by increasing bank lending, leads to an increase in output. Bernanke and Blinder (1988) show how the lending channel can be integrated into the conventional IS–LM model by abandoning the assumption of perfect substitution between bonds and bank loans.
11. In addition to capital injection, the subsequent appreciation of the yen and increase in stock prices also imply an improvement in the BIS ratios of banks, and thus their ability and willingness to lend. Indeed, the *Short-term Economic Survey of Enterprises in Japan* (*Tankan*) published by the Bank of Japan confirms that the lending attitude of financial institutions as seen by borrowers has turned more accommodative since early 1999.
12. In terms of the IS–LM framework in Box 3.1, an expansionary fiscal policy shifts the IS curve to the right. With a flat LM curve, this results in higher output without raising the interest rate.
13. The growing concern over the 'hollowing out of industry' amidst large-scale outflows of foreign direct investment has added a sense of urgency. Until the onset of the latest economic crisis in Asia, some people wrongly viewed growing competition with Asia's developing countries as the cause of Japan's economic slowdown and the hollowing out problem. Subsequent developments have clearly shown that it is in Japan's national interest to be surrounded by prosperous and peaceful countries rather than by poor and unstable ones.
14. The incremental capital–output ratio is calculated by dividing 'gross capital formation as a per centage of GDP' by the 'GDP growth rate.' The higher its value the less efficient is investment in raising output.
15. The 15 selected fields are (1) medical care and welfare, (2) lifestyle and culture, (3) information and telecommunications, (4) new manufacturing technology, (5) distribution and logistics, (6) environment, (7) business supporting services, (8) ocean and maritime, (9) biotechnology, (10) urban environment, (11) aviation and space, (12) new energies and energy conservation, (13) human resource development, (14) economic globalization, and (15) housing and construction.
16. Nippon Credit Bank, another major bank temporarily nationalized, has been sold to an investment group led by Softbank, whose chairman, Masayoshi Son, is Japan's most successful venture capitalist.
17. Other examples of recent M&As in the manufacturing sector include the merging of Nippon Oil and Mitsubishi Oil in April 1999, and Japan Tobacco acquiring Asahi Chemical's food business in January 1999 and Asahi Beer's pharmaceutical subsidiary in November 1998. In addition, General Electric, Hitachi and Toshiba agreed in April 1999 to create an international atomic fuel company, and Toshiba and Mitsubishi Electric established an industrial motor company in October 1999. Nippon Paper and Daishowa, the nation's second- and fourth-largest paper firms have also merged under a holding company in the spring of 2001. In the telecommunications sector, DDI, KDD and IDO merged on 1 October 2000 to compete against NTT, Japan's largest telecom

group. Meanwhile, NKK and Kawasaki, Japan's second- and third-largest steelmakers have agreed to integrate their operations in October 2002.

18. Before that, users could only subscribe on a rental basis and were required to pay a lump-sum deposit. Subsequent innovations that allow direct access to the Internet have also boosted subscriptions
19. For a critical view of Japan's reform process, see Lincoln (1998).

REFERENCES

Bernanke, B.S. and A.S. Blinder (1988), 'Credit, Money, and Aggregate Demand', *American Economic Review*, 78(2), May.

EPA (1999), '1998 Survey of Corporate Behaviors' (in Japanese), Economic Planning Agency, http://www.epa.go.jp/99f/19990420ank/menu.html.

JETRO (1999), 'Japan Moves to Adopt New Business Practices', *Focus Newsletter* (30 April), Japan External Trade Organization (USA), http://www.jetro.org/newyork/focusnewsletter/focus 5.html.

Katz, R. (1998), *Japan: The System that Soured*, New York: M.E. Sharpe.

Koo, R. (1998), 'The Weak Yen and Japan's Credit Crunch Problem', mimeo, Nomura Research Institute, Tokyo.

Koo, R. (1999), 'Foreign Menace', *The International Economy* (November/December).

Krugman, P. (1998), 'It's Baaack: Japan's Slump and the Return of the Liquidity Trap', *Brookings Papers on Economic Activity*, no. 2, Washington, DC: Brookings Institution.

Lincoln, E.J. (1998), 'Japan's Financial Mess', *Foreign Affairs* (May/June).

McKinnon, R.I. and K. Ohno (1997), *Dollar and Yen – Resolving Economic Conflict between the United States and Japan*, Cambridge, Massachusetts: MIT Press.

MOF (2000), 'Japanese Big Bang', Ministry of Finance (January), http://www.mof.go.jp/english/big-bang/ebb37.htm.

OECD (1999), *Regulatory Reform in Japan*, Paris: Organization for Economic Co-operation and Development.

OECD (2000), *OECD Economic Outlook* 68 (December), Paris: Organization for Economic Co-operation and Development.

Okina, K. (1999), 'Monetary Policy under Zero Inflation – A Response to Criticism and Questions regarding Monetary Policy', IMES Discussion Paper, no. 99-E-20, Institute for Monetary and Economic Studies, Bank of Japan, Tokyo.

Posen, A.S. (1998), *Restoring Japan's Economic Growth*, Washington, DC: Institute for International Economics.

4. Paradigm shift in Korean economic policy in the wake of the 1997 financial crisis

O. Yul Kwon

INTRODUCTION

The objective of this chapter is to examine critically a shift in the paradigm of South Korean economic policy in the wake of the 1997 financial crisis. After a successful performance over the last three decades, the South Korean economy (hereafter South Korea will be referred to as Korea) fell into financial crisis in 1997, and was rescued by the IMF. No one would repudiate the fact that the government has played the pivotal role not only as regards the prodigious growth of the Korean economy over the last three decades, but also in the recent developments of the financial crisis and the ensuing restructuring process. Its economic policy has extensively permeated and affected all the factors related to recent economic developments, rendering it of overriding importance.

A few burning questions have therefore arisen, including the following. Why did Korean economic policy work well over the three decades of the economic success period? Why should the economic policy that had worked well in the past have suddenly failed, thereby resulting in the financial crisis? How would the Korean policy paradigm change in the wake of the financial crisis? It appears that these questions have not been dealt with systematically and comprehensively. Therefore the specific purposes of this chapter are (a) to examine the policy paradigm during the economic success period, (b) to relate the failure of economic policy to the causes of the financial crisis, (c) to examine the shift in economic policy paradigm, and (d) to appraise the prospects for Korean economic policy into the new millennium.

THE KOREAN ECONOMIC POLICY PARADIGM PRIOR TO THE 1997 FINANCIAL CRISIS

Extensive State Intervention in the Economy

There is a general consensus that Korea maintained a state-led economy during the economic success period (1962–97). Evidence of state intervention in the Korean economy can be found in every field of economic activity over the last three decades (Kwon, 1997). Since 1962, economic activities have been geared to the achievement of targets set by the consecutive five-year economic plans. The economy has thus been tightly controlled and extensively subject to intervention by the central government. It was therefore the government, not market forces, which controlled the direction and pace of industrialization under the successive authoritarian regimes until the late 1980s.

The underlying thrust of Korea's economic policies has been rapid economic growth, although their directives have gone through different stages as the economy developed. During the 1960s, under the Park regime, Korea sought to achieve maximum growth through export-led industrialization by developing light, labour-intensive industries. This was the genesis of industrial policy that Korea implemented as an integral part of its maximum growth policy. The outward-looking development strategy was aimed at overcoming a lack of natural resources and a small domestic market.

During the 1970s, under the Park regime, Korea carried out an industrial policy to promote key heavy and chemical industries (steel, petrochemicals, metals, shipbuilding, electronics and machinery). In the early 1980s, the Chun regime introduced structural adjustments and comprehensive stabilization measures as the main policy direction. The new policies were less industry-specific and followed an economic liberalization policy based on 'a private sector-guided, market-rational economic system'. Concurrently, under the mounting pressure from developed trade partners, trade liberalization was seriously embarked on during the mid-1980s.

In the late 1980s, the Roh regime pursued political democratization, ending the authoritarianism of over four decades. The political transition imposed tremendous economic adjustment costs on the country. Labour disputes, which had remained suppressed under the authoritarian regimes for the sake of maximum economic growth and political stability, became rampant and violent, and wages rose far in excess of productivity. Real estate speculation flared up again, and economic injustice was exacerbated. Throughout this adjustment process, the Korean economy lost part of its economic growth vitality and international competitiveness.

Against this political and economic background, the Y.S. Kim regime, the first civilian regime in three decades, was launched in 1993 with the banner of a 'New Korea through change and reform'. It embarked on 'A Five-Year Plan for the New Economy' for the period 1993–7 with a focus on 'globalization'. This implied further liberalization and internationalization of the economy. One result of these efforts was that Korea was admitted to the OECD as its 29th member in 1996.

One of the most salient features of Korea's rapid development over the last three decades is that extensive state intervention has been an integral part of the government development strategy. All possible policy tools were mobilized in the process of intervention, and they may be classified into incentive schemes and domestic market protection. The former included tax, credit, foreign exchange allowances and interest rate policies, and the latter included trade policy, foreign direct investment policy and other forms of intervention with a plethora of regulations. State intervention based on these two types of tools was an indirect measure in that it was not reflected in the government budget. As a result, the size of the government sector, as measured by its expenditure to GNP ratio, was relatively small. Among the incentive schemes, the most powerful tool was the allocation of credit at preferential interest rates for specific purposes such as exports and investments in specific target industries or projects during the 1960s and 1970s.[1] The extent of subsidies for exports in the form of preferential loans was reflected in differences in interest rates charged. An average interest rate for export loans was 8.4 per cent over the 1961–81 period, while the interest rate for general loans was 19.6 per cent and the average inflation rate was 16.0 per cent over the same period (Ahn and Kim, 1997: 361). In addition, the government implemented a foreign exchange rate policy as an important tool for promoting exports. It maintained stable effective exchange rates over time in the presence of a relatively high inflation rate in Korea and variations of official exchange rates with trading partners.

As part of its drive for heavy and chemical industrialization, the government allocated 56.4 per cent of all investment funds available to policy loans during the period 1973–81, of which the majority was allocated to heavy and chemical industries. The interest rate on these policy loans was an average annual rate of 13.9 per cent, compared with 17.7 per cent charged on general loans and a 17.7 per cent inflation rate (Stern *et al.*, 1995: 66). On the basis of these incentives, the effective subsidy rate (the sum of financial incentives plus the amount of domestic value-added divided by the value-added in the world market) for the manufacturing sector was estimated at 12 per cent in 1968, increasing to 23 per cent in 1988 (Ahn and Kim, 1997: 366).

The Korean government has protected the domestic producers of strategic manufacturing sectors – including heavy and chemical industries – by erecting high barriers to imports through regulations, tariffs and non-tariff barriers. At the same time, the government used a licensing procedure to block the entry of domestic and foreign competitors into the target industries. For instance, Korea implemented a singular FDI policy that discouraged and restricted inward FDI in order to protect domestic firms from foreign competition. This resulted in an amount of FDI in Korea that fell far below that in its competitor countries. The ratio of FDI to Korea's fixed capital formation averaged only 0.9 per cent over the six-year period 1992–7, displaying the lowest level in the world, with the exception of Japan's 0.1 per cent (Kwon, 1999). High protection of the domestic market was also reflected in high effective protection rates (the ratio of the domestic value-added to the value-added in the world market) particularly for consumer durables, machinery and transport equipment, with the rates ranging from 17 per cent to 163 per cent over the 1968–88 period (Ahn and Kim, 1997: 366).[2]

One of the most remarkable features of Korean economic development over the last decades was the ability to develop and utilize the nation's abundant human resources. Demand for labour increased rapidly with the rapid industrialization. The supply of human resources increased through population growth, mobilization of underemployed farm labour towards industrial sectors and high education levels. Government promotion of education together with the strong educational zeal of Koreans accelerated the education level and quality.

The Korean government intervened extensively in the labour market until the late 1980s. The focus of government labour market policy was directed at the maximum generation of employment in line with maximum growth policy (Kwon, 1997). To this end, anti-competitive institutional arrangements such as minimum wage laws and labour protection laws and union monopolies, which could raise real wages and labour costs, either did not exist or were not implemented until the late 1980s. Instead, the government frequently imposed wage guidelines. At the same time, labour laws prohibited the laying off of workers, which was never a serious labour issue because of the continuous expansion of companies and practices of lifetime employment. As part of the manpower policy, the government promoted the rights of management at the expense of labour, suppressing union activities and intervening in labour disputes. Management, taking advantage of government policy and intervention, applied an authoritarian method of labour management. Whenever labour disputes occurred, management often relied on the government to resolve the disputes, instead of learning and practising appropriate methods of dispute resolution. Therefore the labour market did not progress towards the sort of labour market seen in advanced countries, and remained inflexible with regard to the laying off of the workforce for business reasons.

Why Was the Policy Successful?

The extensive state intervention in the Korean economy raises a critical question: did the intervention contribute to economic development? This question has been discussed extensively in the literature and comprehensive surveys of Korea's state intervention have been undertaken by Pack and Westphal (1986), Westphal (1990), Chang (1993), Smith (1994), the World Bank (1993), Stern *et al.* (1995), Cha *et al.* (1997) and Kwon (1997). However, these surveys were all undertaken before the 1997 financial crisis, and failed to fully comprehend the problems that had been generated over time and that lurked behind the veil of the opaque operation of government, business and banks and the euphoric and inertial attitudes of policy makers. It therefore appears necessary to reassess Korea's state intervention.

State intervention going beyond rectification of neoclassical market failure could be easily justified at the initial stage of Korean economic development. The market size was too small and too primitive to function efficiently, and the institutions required for information and efficient market operation did not develop. Korea's economic growth required overseas knowledge and technology, for which international markets were imperfect, with pervasive inequality of bargaining power. These features of underdevelopment, as well as technological externalities and economies of scale, could be justifiably held to require state intervention and promotion of the Korean economy.[3]

Although the efficacy of state intervention could have been abated over time, international and domestic environments and institutional infrastructure were all conducive to the success of state intervention until the mid-1980s. Consecutive authoritarian military regimes, which took a grip on political power until the mid-1980s, maintained vision and objectives consistent with the national interest of rapid economic development as their way of legitimizing the political power. Nationalism, which has always been strong in Korea, generated a powerful incentive for all citizens to assign high priority to economic growth of the nation. In this context, predatory behaviour of state officials for their own self-interest (Islam, 1994) would not be of serious concern in Korea.

The international environment was also conducive to the Korean economic strategy of state intervention. Korea played an important role for the advanced Western allies in the Cold War because of its strategic location. Besides, the Korean economy was relatively small in size and underdeveloped until the mid-1980s. Hence Korea's export-led economic development strategy coupled with state intervention and the protection of domestic industries did not raise serious ire from advanced countries. This helped

Korean products penetrate into advanced countries, thereby rendering Korea's industrialization strategy successful.

From the early stages of its economic development, Korea established the appropriate institutions required for economic development and operated them effectively. A powerful Economic Planning Board, established in 1962, was assigned the central economic policy-making role and a broad budgetary authority. Integration of planning and budgeting eliminated possible conflicts of interest among different ministries. The government secured competent economic technocrats through highly competitive civil service examinations. Almost every ministry of the government established its own research institution staffed by academics, mostly with doctorates from abroad.

A bureaucracy staffed by talented technocrats ensured a high degree of autonomy from political interference under the authoritarian regimes. Shielded by their powerful, prestigious and highly reputable organizations of economic policy-related ministries and affiliated research institutions, and guarded by the respect of society, the core technocrats have been able to formulate and implement policies in pursuance of national goals. They were to answer directly to the top authoritarian leader, maintaining significant independence from the legislature and other sources of political pressure. In order to maintain close interactions between the public and private sector, the government has established a number of deliberation councils under various ministries and for special policy tasks. They were forums for government officials and relevant representatives and experts from the private sector and academic community to discuss policy issues and to exchange views and information. These councils facilitated the transmission of information in both directions between the government and the private sector, providing both sides with the opportunity to synthesize the information into their action plans. Furthermore, both government and business were monitored and checked by experts from the private sector and academic community in the councils, restraining self-interested behaviour.[4]

In summary, not only was state intervention easily justified at the initial stage of Korean economic development during the 1960s and 1970s, but also the organizations related to state intervention were well established to maximize organizational capabilities. Strong nationalism and nationalistic zeal for economic prosperity prevailing in society were conducive to the pursuance of the national goal of economic development. The bureaucracy was staffed by reputable and competent experts, and well protected behind high authoritarian shields, whereby technocrats were persistently able to formulate and implement national policy, maintaining autonomy and insulation from political pressure and business lobbying. The government established close government–business interactions through deliberation councils, through which communication and cooperation were facilitated between the two sectors. It is therefore reasonable to draw a conclusion that Korean society, policy and its implementation mechanism were conducive to the efficacy of state intervention.[5]

STATE INTERVENTION AS THE MAJOR CAUSE OF THE FINANCIAL CRISIS

The effectiveness of state intervention changes with environments and institutions. State intervention in Korea, which could be efficacious during the 1960s and 1970s, might not be so in different international and domestic environments. After the Cold War was over, at the beginning of the 1990s, the world economy in general became less receptive to the industrial policies of individual countries. In particular, Korea was no longer treated in a preferential way by advanced Western countries. Under the rising globalization with increasing economic integration and competition, protection of the Korean domestic market and industries by state intervention would have become increasingly difficult.

Domestically, the high organizational capabilities under old authoritarian regimes could not be maintained under the new internal environment. Since the late 1980s, Korea has been undergoing rapid political change, whereby authoritarianism has been on the wane, and ensuing democratic regimes have been relatively unstable. The government has also lost its strong policy direction, as attested by the seventh five-year economic plan (1993–7) being left unattended. Political changes have altered the government–business interface. The relative size and importance of the business sector had been enlarged over time, so that the balance in the government–business relationship has swung remarkably towards business. As the world economy has become increasingly interdependent and complex, with free flows of goods, services, information and capital, the government has lost its advantage over the business sector in collecting and understanding information required to pursue appropriate economic strategy. These changes in government–business relations have rendered government control over the private sector less effective. Concomitantly, the labour market which had been extensively hindered and repressed by the government was democratized with political democratization from the late 1980s, as a result of which labour disputes have flared up, and state intervention in the labour market has become politically impossible.

Over time, not only has state intervention lost its efficacy, but also it has sown the seeds of the 1997 financial crisis in Korea. The causes of the

Korean financial crisis, which have been extensively investigated in the literature (Cha, 1999; Jaw and Yi, 1999; Kwon, 1998; Pyo, 1999), include the following: (a) excessive expansion and diversification of chaebols with debt capital, (b) the inefficient financial sector inflicted by moral hazard, (c) lack of transparency in business operations, (d) low productivity and loss of international competitiveness, and (e) rigid labour market practices. Each of these causes of the Korean financial crisis was directly related to state intervention; or, in order words, the fundamental factor underpinning all these causes was state intervention.

Korea has developed its own singular government–business relations from the beginning of its export promotion and industrial policy. The government nourished a limited number of chaebols with which to pursue its economic development strategy by providing a variety of incentives, protection and institutionalized privileges. These privileges included cross-subsidiary loan guarantees, cross-subsidiary ownership, prevention of the takeover of chaebols by means of hostile M&A by domestic and foreign firms, and a lopsided corporate governance system in favour of the majority shareholders.[6] This process brought about the collusion between the government and chaebols, and generated a perception that chaebols were 'too important and too big to fail' or guaranteed to be 'bailed out by the government if needed'.[7] Taking advantage of these privileges and government protection not only against potential domestic and international competitors but also from minority shareholders, chaebols expanded and diversified excessively. In doing so, it was debt capital that they relied on for investment purposes, because of perceived low risk, together with readily available loans to them at preferential interest rates. This was reflected in a high debt–equity ratio of 519 per cent held by the top 30 chaebols in 1997 (Joh, 1999). It follows that the collusion with the government and the lopsided corporate governance system would lead to a lack of transparency in the operation of chaebols.

The unhealthy structure and financial weaknesses rendered chaebols vulnerable to a financial crisis. In 1997, a number of the major chaebols became insolvent because of their excessive expansion and diversification with debt capital together with their operational inefficiency.[8] By allowing a number of chaebols to become bankrupt, the government signalled that it would no longer bail out large companies, causing their creditworthiness to crumble. These bankrupt companies eventually dumped their non-performing debt on domestic financial institutions, thereby weakening the already weak financial system. This was part of the genesis of the financial crisis.

The inefficiency and lack of transparency and accountability of financial institutions, together with the inefficient supervision thereof, which were among the major causes of the 1997 financial crisis, were attributable to government intervention. In order to control credit allocation for its own purposes of industrial policy, the Korean government controlled and protected financial institutions as the owner as well as the legitimate regulator. From the 1960s until the mid-1980s, the government was the major shareholder in a number of banks, and intervened extensively in bank management, including the appointment of bank managers. It was therefore the government – not the banks – that decided credit allocation. As a means of protecting the financial sector, the government imposed protective measures, thereby safeguarding the financial sector from domestic and international competition. The overall financial sector (banks, securities, foreign exchange markets) remained shielded from international competition by limiting the entry of foreign banks. Chaebols were prohibited from being controlling shareholders of commercial banks. Thus the ownership of banks was widely diversified, and minority shareholders had little power in terms of corporate management. Accordingly, Korean banks were regarded as 'entities without owners'. Banks were therefore accountable to no one except their political masters, and thus their operation lacked transparency and accountability.[9] At the same time, there was a strong prevailing perception that 'banks will never fail' because of government protection, thereby generating moral hazard. As a result, the banking sector was inefficient, inexperienced in risk assessment, and undercapitalized.

Banking regulation and supervision was fragmented and inefficient over a long period of time. Part of the financial policy maintained the strict separation of financial industries (commercial banks, securities firms and insurance companies) until the early 1990s. Regulation and supervision of each of these sectors was separated. The task of regulation and supervision of banking institutions was divided between the Bank of Korea (the central bank) and the Ministry of Finance and Economy. Commercial banks were under the central bank's supervision, while specialized banks and all non-bank financial institutions (including merchant banks) were under the direct supervision of the Ministry of Finance and Economy. Furthermore, the insurance and securities sectors were regulated by their own supervisory bodies that were in turn under the control of the Ministry of Finance and Economy. It was well known that the supervisory infrastructure was not well established in the ministry. As a result, proper supervision and coordinated prudential regulations for the financial sector did not develop.

Korea started to liberalize and internationalize the financial market in 1993, and the liberalization process was speeded up to fulfil the membership requirements for admission to the OECD. As a consequence, banks were allowed to gain access to the international financial market. However, the supervisory structure of banks did not adapt to the liberalization of the financial sector, and the appropriate restraints on the risk-taking behaviour of banks were not in place. The lack of prudential regulation of banks encouraged them to borrow excessively from offshore financial markets, as soon as they were allowed access to international financial markets in 1993. Faced by domestic interest rates substantially higher than those in the international market and by the insatiable demands for funds from chaebols, Korean financial institutions took advantage of international financial markets.

Korean financial institutions relied heavily on short-term borrowings from abroad rather than long-term funds, because of lower interest rates for short-term foreign loans and the prevailing perception of low risk under the government protection. This was reflected in the surge in short-term capital inflows, from an annual average of approximately $600 million over the period 1990–3 to $5.2 billion in 1996, and in short-term debt amounting to $107.3 billion, or 66.6 per cent of the total foreign debt of $161.8 billion in November 1997. In the presence of mounting short-term foreign debt, foreign reserves held by the Bank of Korea dwindled quickly to $7.3 billion in November 1997 (Kwon, 1998). Moreover, the Korea currency was kept appreciated from 1988 by state intervention in the foreign exchange market (ibid.). The Korean financial situation was therefore certainly ripe for speculative financial attack, propagating financial panic.

The inflexibility of the Korean labour market contributed to the 1997 financial crisis. Under government interference and repression until the late 1980s, the skill of conciliatory labour management did not develop. Nor did a proper workforce retrenchment mechanism develop because of the continuously rising demand for labour over time with sustained rapid economic growth and lifetime employment practices, leading to the lack of flexibility in the labour market. The labour market democratization at the end of the 1980s brought about rampaging militant union activities. This raised labour costs rapidly, and by 1995 Korea had the highest labour cost among Asian countries, with the exception of Japan (ibid.). This led to the loss of international competitiveness, contributing to economic recession from the beginning of 1996 and to the current account deficit, an important source of the financial crisis.

A paradox of domestic market protection has materialized in Korea. As mentioned earlier, the Korean government imposed a variety of restrictive measures on imports of consumer goods, inward FDI and business takeover by means of M&A in order to protect the domestic market and industries as part of its industrial policy.[10] This policy would have contributed to the rapid growth of industries and banks until the end of the 1980s. However, this protection generated excessive economic power concentration in a limited number of chaebols, which practised monopolistic business operations within the country, depriving chaebols and banks of the opportunity to equip themselves with international competitiveness.[11] As McKinsey (1998) points out, the protection policy led to a slow growth in productivity and eventually the loss of national competitiveness. This was, according to Pyo (1999), the key cause of the financial crisis.

Another important cause of the Korean financial crisis was the failure of the government to take appropriate action in advance. The critical factor underlying the causes of the financial crisis, as examined above, appeared to be the failure of economic institutions and structure to adapt to emerging changes in the domestic and international environments. Institutional and structural impediments developed over a long period of time out of the collusion between the government, chaebols and banks, which was in turn attributable to extensive government intervention, repression and protection of the business and banking sectors. Although these institutional and structural problems had been extensively analysed and remedies prescribed, the government failed to take appropriate action to remedy them for several years (Kwon, 1998). Instead, the government maintained its excessive intervention policy and multitudinous regulations over business and banks – indicating the structural and institutional dysfunction of the policy process.[12]

In conjunction with the November 1997 financial crisis, a couple of conclusions can be drawn with regard to Korea's policy apparatus. First, the Korean government did not realize that state intervention was the fundamental factor underpinning all the causes of the financial crisis. Second, it did not introduce appropriate measures in time to stem the financial crisis in the presence of numerous emerging symptoms and evidence. This clearly signified the demise of the old paradigm of economic policy. The deterioration of macroeconomic fundamentals was obviously revealed from the beginning of 1997, with a number of insolvency cases of chaebols. The sustained appreciation of the currency value, the rising current account deficit and short-term foreign debts, falling foreign reserves and the emerging contagion effect of the financial crisis from East Asia were all indicative enough of the imminence of a financial crisis. The actual financial crisis in November 1997 and the ensuing enormous economic damage have made the country understand the multiplying problem of moral hazard, political cronyism and the resulting institutional and structural dysfunction behind the facade of rapid growth under the old policy process. This has led the country to realize the necessity of shifting the policy paradigm. Moreover, the country was coerced by the IMF with its rescue package to discard the old paradigm and undertake a new paradigm of economic policy.

THE SHIFT IN THE ECONOMIC POLICY PARADIGM

Upon request by the Korean government, the IMF agreed to provide financial assistance of $58 billion to save Korea from foreign debt default, but under a strict policy package imposed on Korea. The IMF policy package consisted of three components: macroeconomic policy, financial sector restructuring and other structural reform measures.[13] Macroeconomic policy was to restrain aggregate demand, to maintain a flexible exchange rate without state intervention and to build up foreign reserves. The objectives of the macroeconomic policy have been achieved, in that interest rates came down below the crisis levels, the exchange rate has been stabilized under the flexible exchange rate system without state intervention, and foreign reserves accumulated beyond the agreed level.

In accordance with the IMF policy package, the restructuring of the financial sector was intended to increase the independence of the banking sector from the government, to consolidate and strengthen the supervision of all financial institutions, to liquidate and restructure insolvent financial institutions and to recapitalize viable ones. Added to this was the liberalization of the financial sector, which allowed competition from abroad and M&A of banks. At the same time, the financial sector was required to adopt international standards regarding capital adequacy, risk management, disclosure and auditing in order to improve the efficiency and transparency of the sector.

The Korean government has been quite successful in this respect, so that the policy framework of the financial sector has changed remarkably. The new financial bills, which were passed in December 1997, enhanced the independence of the Bank of Korea (the central bank) from the government.[14] The new bills consolidated and strengthened all the supervisory functions of the financial sector (including banks, securities, insurance and trust companies) under the new Financial Supervisory Commission, and improved the commission's independence from the government (Kwon, 1998). This will certainly improve the prudential supervision of the financial sector. The government closed or suspended 96 banks and non-bank financial institutions, including five commercial banks, 16 merchant banks and two securities firms (MOFE, 1998a: 29). The remaining domestic banks were recapitalized to obtain the 'sound bank' status, with BIS ratios ranging from 10 to 13 per cent by September 1998 (ibid.: 33). In achieving this, the government provided funds to purchase non-performing loans through the Korea Asset Management Corporation (KAMCO) or to fund bank restructuring.[15]

Under the new financial framework the operational efficiency as well as transparency and accountability of financial institutions will improve.

Financial institutions are required not only to conduct external audits by internationally recognized accounting firms but also to establish a board of directors with director members selected by shareholders. The new financial framework introduces greater competition into the financial sector by opening the sector to foreign capital and allowing M&A of banks by foreign investors. Currently, barriers against advancement of foreign investors into the domestic financial industry have been almost entirely lifted and capital markets have been fully opened (*Korea Herald*, 20 September 1999). In particular, since the ownership of banks by foreigners was permitted with a few nominal restrictions in March 1998, foreigners' participation in domestic banks' equity capital has increased remarkably. As a result, for two banks, the number one majority shareholders are foreigners, and for three banks foreigners participate in the management (SERI, 1999b).[16] Finally, the decision was made in September 1999 to sell a troubled bank (Korea First Bank) to a group of American investors (Newbridge Capital), marking a watershed change in the Korean financial sector.

The advancement of foreign capital into the domestic financial industry not only improves competitiveness of the domestic financial system but also weakens the influence of the government on the financial market. The advancement of foreign capital will contribute directly to the resolution of financial institutions' bad debt problems. At the same time, with the introduction of advanced management skills in regard to credit evaluation and risk controls by foreign institutions, the efficiency of the domestic financial system will be enhanced. As the control of major financial institutions is transferred to foreigners with increasing foreign capital advancement, the government's direct intervention in the management of financial institutions will be difficult, signifying an end to the old practice of government-controlled finance. As a result, the market economy principle will be able to take root in the industry. In particular, putting one bank (Korea First Bank) in the hands of experienced foreign managers will help discard the traditional practice of lending on the basis of size or political connections rather than sound credit analysis. As Korea First Bank is transformed, so that it lends on objective criteria and shows strong profitability, the rest of the financial industry will have little choice but to follow its lead.

With the introduction of the new financial laws, the government has changed its policy direction, from the separation of banks from insurance, securities and trust firms to universal banking. This is to improve the efficiency and competitiveness of the financial sector by bringing the system in line with the systems of advanced countries.[17] Banks are now permitted to engage in various businesses, such as the securities business, either directly or through their subsidiaries. There will be a merging of securities firms, investment trust companies and merchant banks into a single type of institution.

A consolidation of the supervisory functions of the financial sector is already in place under the new Financial Supervisory Commission.

In the past, the Bank of Korea maintained money supply as the target of its monetary policy. Since the financial crisis, however, the overnight call rate has become the key target of the central bank's monetary policy. The government started interest rate liberalization in 1991 and completed it in July 1997 for all the lending and borrowing rates (SERI, 1999c: 15). This will allow interest rates to recover their market function of allocating funds and balancing supply and demand in the financial market. With the role of interest rates recovered in the financial market, the direction of monetary policy shifted from outright control of money supply to a more flexible and subtle approach to using the money and capital market by means of interest rates, as in advanced countries.

Although substantial progress has been made in financial sector restructuring, the basic approach to the restructuring has not been appropriate. Under the urgency of recovering the international financiers' confidence in the Korean financial sector, the government has stressed the speed and intensity of the financial sector restructuring. Yet the government has attempted to impose structural reforms on financial institutions by coercion and intervention, instead of relying on market principles. The forced amalgamation of non-viable banks with seemingly viable ones is a case in point. This approach amounts to an encroachment on the autonomy of the financial sector, and begets another type of collusion between the government and banks, as well as the problem of moral hazard. For the long-term health of the financial sector, the government should let the financial sector operate on market principles after the transitional period.

THE PARADIGM SHIFT IN POLICY TOWARDS CHAEBOLS

Korea has made a marked shift in its policy toward chaebols in the process of complying with the IMF rescue package. Chaebols excessively expanded and diversified by means of debt capital with government support and protection, together with their collusive relations with the government. This led to the lack of transparency and accountability in their operation. As a result, chaebols were one of the main causes of the 1997 financial crisis, and therefore the reform of chaebols in terms of their financial structure, corporate governance standards, business structure and operation is a critical part of the IMF policy package.

One of the most significant achievements in the area of chaebol reforms is the so-called 'five-point agreement' between the government and chaebols on corporate restructuring in January 1998. The agreement requires mandatory reporting of consolidated financial statements by chaebols; eliminating the practice of cross-subsidiary loan guarantees; improving corporate financial structure; focusing on a limited number of core operations; and making majority shareholders and executives more accountable (*Newsreview*, 17 January 1998: 6). This agreement, once fulfilled, will enhance the transparency of operation, financial soundness, corporate governance and concentration on core competence areas, and as a result address the endemic problem of the collusive relationship between the government and chaebols.

In order to improve the business structure, the government has undertaken a three-pronged approach. It has ordered credit banks to assess the viability of client firms and to distinguish between the viable and the non-viable. The non-viable firms were encouraged to exit through the refusal of new credit and the prohibition of financial assistance (or fund shifting) across affiliate companies. Viable firms were required to formulate their self-rescue ('debt work-out') plans together with their credit banks, and the government would then provide some assistance in implementing the programmes. The five largest chaebols, because of the preponderance of their market share and economic influence, have been coerced into taking part in the so-called 'big deals', which aim to make the five chaebols focus on their core competencies, and to reduce over-capacity in key industrial sectors through mergers and business exchanges among them.

Substantial progress has been made in the reform of chaebols in accordance with the 1998 agreement between them and the government. Chaebols adopted the use of consolidated financial statements, beginning in fiscal year 1999. They were expected to eliminate cross-subsidiary debt guarantees from March 2000 and to reduce their debt–equity ratio to 200 per cent by the end of 1999 (MOFE, 1999: 45). As a way of upgrading corporate governance, listed companies (chaebols) are appointing outside directors and have removed restrictions on the voting rights of institutional investors, and strengthened minority shareholders' rights by lowering the representation requirement for class action suits from 1.0 per cent to 0.01 per cent of the total share in May 1998 (MOFE, 1998a: 34). Also a number of chaebols have entered into debt work-out programmes with their credit banks.

Although the tasks of attaining transparency, securing financial soundness and upgrading corporate governance have made substantial progress, the most difficult part of the reform task is the restructuring of chaebols specified by the 'big deals' programme. Only a little progress has been made in consolidating chaebols' businesses into core competence areas and in exchanging businesses between them. By the end of March 1999, the top five chaebols had reduced the number of their subsidiaries by 57, from 272 to 215, still well below the target number of 135 which was the number agreed with the government (MOFE, 1999: 50). Negotiations in regard to business swapping have run into a number of snags, and conclusion of the deals appears to be far way.

It appears that the basic way in which the new government has been tackling the structural reform of chaebols has not been appropriate. The government has attempted to enforce structural reforms on chaebols by means of guidelines, threats, coercion and intervention, as is reflected in the so-called 'big deals'. Instead, it should be the companies involved in an industry – not the government – that decide whether or not to stay in the industry on the basis of their core competence and market disciplines. The government approach has caused chaebols to drag their feet in implementing the process of reform, and has led chaebols to ask the government for financial and regulatory support. The 'big deals' approach will generate another set of monopolies in key industries and beget other regulations. Furthermore, the companies involved are under constant pressure from the government and labour unions to minimize lay-offs in conjunction with business exchanges. Under these circumstances, the big deals may do little to reduce excess capacity in the key industrial sector, running counter to their original objectives.

In view of the fact that most areas of the Korean economy have been opened to international standards, there is very little chance of success for state intervention to choose appropriate industries and business structures. The solution to the structural problems of chaebols should be sought by further liberalizing the market and by eliminating the institutionalized privileges bestowed upon chaebols, such as cross-guaranteeing and cross-ownership, unfair internal transactions, fund shifting among affiliates, and the expectation of a 'bail-out' by the government. In the absence of those privileges for chaebols, financial institutions will lend to them only if they have evidence of sound business operation. A liberalized market will also allow competition from overseas competitors and freer mergers and acquisitions. These will force chaebols to concentrate on their core competent areas and to divest themselves of the marginal ones.

Even if the government attempts to interfere in the nation's industrial structure, the chances of success dwindle in the emerging international and domestic circumstances. Foreign capital has substantially penetrated the Korean business sector. As a way of improving their financial soundness, the five chaebols attracted US$3.9 trillion foreign capital by the end of March 1999 (MOFE, 1999: 50). Following the abolition of foreign investment ceilings in domestic companies and permission for hostile M&A, the number of listed firms, whose combined foreign interests exceed those of the largest domestic shareholder, increased to 42 by the end of January

1999 (*Newsreview*, 1999: 26). This will promote competition among firms. As foreign companies gain more access to inside information as shareholders, domestic firms will become more vulnerable to hostile M&A by foreign investors. Once some companies that are influenced by foreign investors become resistant to state intervention, the government will have little choice but to give up its intervention in the business sector.

The government is also losing its power of credit allocation that has been the critical tool of business control and interference. As discussed earlier, the financial sector has been liberalized, and foreign investors participate in management of some of the financial institutions. As a result, the government will not be able to allocate credits at preferential interest rates to special sectors of the economy. Besides, the government no longer provides protection of business from overseas competition and takeover by M&A. Hence there is no compelling reason why the business sector, and particularly chaebols, have to be cooperative with government intervention, once the current transitional period is over. This will result in breaking the government–business nexus that gave rise to moral hazard and economic inefficiency. It is thus safe to draw a conclusion that the old paradigm of state intervention in the business sector will shift towards an economic policy based on market principles.

As discussed earlier, another important facet of the Korean policy paradigm in the past was protection of the domestic market and industries (including financial and securities industries) by means of restriction and intervention on imports, capital flows and FDI. This has contributed to the lack of efficiency, transparency and accountability – a cause of the financial crisis. The IMF policy package therefore required trade liberalization and capital account liberalization. Trade liberalization aims at advancing the timetables of compliance with Korea's WTO commitments, including the elimination of trade-related subsidies and trade restrictions, and streamlining import procedures. Capital account liberalization is to open up the securities market to foreign investors, eliminate restrictions on incoming foreign direct investments and allow Korean corporations to borrow from abroad.

Substantial progress has been made in these areas. The government fulfilled the trade liberalization requirements by the end of 1998 (MOFE, 1998b: 27). In order to increase Korea's access to foreign capital, the government has complied fully with the IMF requirements of capital account liberalization. All controls on capital movements, including Koreans' overseas investment and borrowing and incoming FDI, and the establishment of financial institutions, have already been abolished. Foreign exchange transactions were fully liberalized on 1 April 1999. Foreign equity ownership ceilings have been eliminated, and foreigners are now able to invest in local bonds and short-term money market instruments without restrictions. All this amounts to a marked shift in the policy paradigm.

Finally, another important shift in the policy paradigm has occurred in the labour market. Under government repression and interference, the Korean labour market developed in a singular way and lacked flexibility in the adjustment of the workforce, thereby contributing to the financial crisis. In order to comply with the IMF policy package which required labour reform, a tripartite commission including labour, government and business representatives was established, and made it possible to revise the labour laws in February 1998. The revised law instituted labour market flexibility by allowing for the first time in history lay-offs in the event of urgent management need such as business transfers and M&A caused by extreme financial difficulty. This amendment has facilitated the necessary corporate sector restructuring and allowed firms to function more competitively.

PROSPECTS FOR KOREAN ECONOMIC POLICY INTO THE NEW MILLENNIUM

The paradigm of Korean economic policy has shifted from a government-led economy by means of extensive state intervention towards a market economy. This shift has been reflected in the continuing institutional and structural reforms of financial institutions and chaebols. The Korean economy is thus in transition. Even though economic recovery symptoms are readily observable since the early 1999, the transition period will probably take a few more years until the reforms are completed and the economy has fully recovered.[18] At this juncture, an important question arises as to the prospects of economic policy under the new paradigm during the transitional period and thereafter. More specifically, what types of policy should or would the government apply from now on, taking for granted that markets are at the centre of the economy?

A policy paradigm would be predicated on the vision that the society attempts to pursue and on internal and external environments. Although it is a daunting task to identify a social consensus on nation's vision in Korea, sustainable, equitable economic development under market principles and political democracy seems likely to describe the underlying social feeling of the vision. This is quite consistent with President Kim Dae-jung's proclaimed dual objective of democracy and a market economy (Kim, 1999). During the 1960s and 1970s, all citizens, including policy makers, were mobilized under a strong vision of maximum growth out of the war-stricken poverty. The 1997 financial crisis has also been a force that united

Koreans to rally their cooperation for the task of resolving the crisis and helped in generating a social consensus on nation's vision. Because of the bitter experience of the 1997 financial crisis and the ensuing economic setback, together with a strong feeling of economic injustice, the importance of sustainability and equity in the process of economic development has been emphasized. It appears that Korean society has taken the market economy and political democracy for granted from the onset of the financial crisis and the presidential election in 1997.[19]

As discussed earlier, economic liberalization based on free market principles has taken place with regard to trade, the capital market and the foreign exchange rates as well as the banking and business sector. Macroeconomic stabilization has been restored, remarkably, with the enhanced autonomy of the Bank of Korea with its clear mandate of stabilization. Externally, globalization or global economic integration is continuously and forcefully rising, and Korea appears to have taken globalization for granted. Under these circumstances, what should the government do in order to meet the challenge of sustainable, equitable economic growth? As Stiglitz (1997, 1998, 1999) cogently argues, the government should play a complementary role for the private sector.[20] That is, under the new policy paradigm, the role of the government should be to guarantee the economic freedom of the private sector and create environments conducive to the development of a strong, competitive and efficient private sector. As Korea has learned painfully, from the onset of the financial crisis, the private sector prospers under the emerging global environment by enhancing transparency, accountability and competition. To this end, the government is required to establish a comprehensive and robust regulatory infrastructure (legal and institutional frameworks) to safeguard the key success factors for the private sector.

The complementary role of the government economic activity would be subject to constraint under the emerging global economic integration. Korea, like any other country, wishes to take advantage of the benefits of globalization in the form of greater realization of the efficiencies available from specialization and competition, and from foreign technology and capital. At the same time, Korea wishes to manage or regulate the domestic economy and to maintain national sovereignty. As Summers (1999) points out, the three goals are incompatible. If Korea wishes to maintain sovereignty and yet allow international economic integration, it must accept, in a world of capital mobility, an entirely free market at the global level, thereby abandoning its regulatory powers over the domestic economy and international flows of goods, services and capital. If Korea embraces economic integration and its own economic regulation, it ends up forfeiting sovereignty, as do member countries of the European Community.

Finally, Korea will not be able to derive full benefits from international economic integration while maintaining its sovereignty and regulatory powers.

It appears that economic liberalization has gone beyond the returning point, and Korea obviously aims to take advantage of the benefits arising from international economic integration. In view of a high level of nationalism and no particular prospect of regional integration in the near future, Korea will maintain its sovereignty. Under these circumstances, Korea has little choice but to align domestic policy in consistence with international standards – including the WTO and OECD standards. In this respect, first, openness, transparency and accountability are demanded for the policy-making process as well as policy contents up to the international standards. The lack of openness and transparency in the policy contents and policy-making process increases the influence and financial benefits that the government officials and special interest groups can share, as evidenced in the recent past in Korea. Secrecy makes it more difficult to correct errors and to evaluate officials, and creates profits for those who have information, which is a source of collusion with interest groups.[21] Accountability will improve when errors made by involved officials are easily corrected and officials are easily evaluated. Hence openness is required to improve accountability.

Maintaining its own openness, transparency and accountability, the government should establish transparent standard regulatory rules based on market disciplines, which are consistent with the international standards, and impose them on everyone fairly and impartially. For instance, the transparency of banks and chaebols should be aligned with international standards. So too should the Korean accounting systems, corporate governance standards, competition and bankruptcy laws. This would amount to a redrawing of the government relationship with the private sector, coupled with transparent and democratic oversight of chaebols and banks, thereby minimizing political cronyism.

Social development programmes should be an integral part of the new policy paradigm, to which Korea has paid minimal attention over the past three decades of economic success. Korea has carried on its economic development strategy based on a 'growth first, then equity' ideology since the early 1960s. Thus social development programmes have not developed in parallel with economic growth. In particular, systems of social safety nets such as unemployment insurance have not been developed, not only because of government's low priority attached to them but also because of the cultural heritage of family members supporting each other during difficult times. Besides, continuously high demand for workers, with minimum levels of unemployment over the long period of economic success, coupled with the lifetime employment practices, minimized the necessity for safety net systems. This is reflected in the small portion of government budget allocated for social development programmes, which was well below that of advanced countries (National Statistical Office, 1998). The portion was consistently below 10 per cent throughout the three decades up to 1997, except for 1991, with a share of 10.2 per cent.

The circumstances surrounding the equity issues have now changed remarkably, particularly from the onset of the 1997 financial crisis. Unemployment has risen to an unprecedented level, and become a serious social issue. The social fabric has been changing to a discernible extent, in such a way that nuclear family units increase and the culture of family safety nets erodes. Furthermore, the long-cherished lifetime employment practices are disappearing as the lay-off system takes root. Therefore it is increasingly incumbent on government to provide support for the rising number of people who cannot support themselves. Equitable development with advanced social development programmes will be justified not only for purposes of equity, but also on grounds of efficiency. Not only do social safety nets protect those adversely affected by macroeconomic shocks like the financial crisis, but also they play the so-called 'built-in stabilizer role' against economic fluctuations.

CONCLUSION

In light of the overriding importance of economic policy for Korean economic development over the last three decades, this chapter has examined why and how the Korean economic policy paradigm has shifted in conjunction with the 1997 financial crisis. The Korean economic policy paradigm before the crisis can be best described as an extensive state intervention in the process of implementing its industrial policy and consecutive five-year economic plans. State intervention worked well until the late 1980s because of a clear social consensus on the nation's vision of maximum growth, high organizational capabilities and cooperative external environments. From the late 1980s, however, not only was the effectiveness of state intervention eroded because of adverse changes in the internal and external policy environments, but also it turned out to be the major underlying cause of the 1997 financial crisis.

State intervention rendered the private sector vulnerable to financial crisis. Government control and protection of chaebols led them to become lacking in transparency and accountability in their operation, and to expand and diversify excessively with debt capital. State intervention in financial markets led financial institutions to be inefficient, undercapitalized and heavily reliant on short-term foreign borrowings. Government protection of domestic industries from international competition by means of restrictions of imports, incoming FDI and M&A resulted, paradoxically, in the loss of efficiency and competitiveness of domestic industries. Government repression and intervention in labour markets resulted in inefficiency in labour management and the lack of flexibility in the markets. Finally, the government failed to introduce appropriate measures in time to stem the final crisis in the presence of emerging symptoms and evidence of the crisis. This signified a demise of the old paradigm of economic policy.

After a painful realization of the limitations of the old policy paradigm through the financial crisis, the policy paradigm has shifted from state intervention towards a market economy. Under the new policy paradigm, with a vision of sustainable, equitable economic development based on market principles and political democracy, the government should play a complementary role to the private sector. The government must guarantee the freedom of the private sector and provide the environment conducive to the development of the private sector. In an era of globalization, the private sector prospers through transparency, accountability and competition in its operation. Hence the critical role of government is to provide a comprehensive and robust infrastructure to safeguard the key success factors of the private sector. Added to this is a higher emphasis than before on equity as an important facet of the new paradigm.

From the present case study of Korea's economic policy paradigm over the last three decades, it is evident that the policy paradigm of a nation should change over time with internal and external circumstances and the vision of the nation. To maintain economic development over time, the country should be diligent in identifying changes in the policy environments and adapt its policy paradigm to the emerging changes in time. Otherwise, the country would experience economic setbacks at times, as Korea has recently witnessed.

NOTES

1. Policy can be classified according to its targets, such as promotion of manufactured exports, development of heavy and chemical industries, improvement of productivity, human capital development and labour market, and high investment and saving rates. For this type of policy classification, see Kwon (1997).
2. As a result of protection of the domestic market and industries, Korea has long been regarded as the most difficult market in Asia (Kwon, 1999).
3. Stiglitz (1997) argues that state intervention contributed strongly to the United States' growth at the end of the 19th century.
4. The World Bank (1993: 187) argues that any predatory self-interested behaviour has been constrained by the repeated nature of this collaboration through deliberation councils. C.H. Lee (1992) argues that deliberation councils have worked as quasi-internal

organizations of the capital market, through which government intervention has been internalized as part of the overall economic operation, thereby improving efficiency of the capital market more than without government intervention.

5. Stiglitz (1997, 1999) argues strongly that the government intervention has actually had an enormous effect in promoting the rapid growth in East Asia as well as in Korea.
6. The low standard of corporate governance was reflected in the board of directors system that consisted only of employees hired by the companies – not outside directors representing minority shareholders. Furthermore, institutional investors could not exercise the voting rights, and the representation requirement of minority shareholders for class action was set too high (1 per cent of the total shares) to be practical. As a result, the chairmen of the top 30 chaebols exercised the managerial control over their groups by owning, on average, only 2 per cent of their overall assets (Chung, 1998).
7. There were a number of incidences from 1972 in which the government actually bailed several large companies out of financial difficulties, and large-scale bankruptcy was almost non-existent until the 1997 financial crisis (Joh, 1999).
8. The excessive investment and diversification by chaebols resulted in a 2.2 per cent rate of return on equity capital in 1996 (Lee and Lee, 1998).
9. The Korean banking sector generated the typical principal–agent problem. Since the agents (bankers) existed without owners, the agents were bound to collaborate with regulators and politicians (the government).
10. According to the International Institute for Management Development (IMD), cited in Booz, Allen & Hamilton (1997: 28), Korea was regarded as the most difficult market in Asia in 1996. The *Far Eastern Economic Review* (1998a), Booz.Allen & Hamilton (1997) and McKinsey Global Institute (1998) were all saying that Korea had been the worst place to invest among Asian countries.
11. Hwang (1998) has estimated the loss from monopolistic business practices in Korea as ranging from 0.12 per cent to 2.89 per cent of GDP.
12. According to an executive poll conducted by the *Far Eastern Economic Review*, Korea had the highest degree of government influence over business among Asian countries (*Far Eastern Economic Review*, 1998b: 36). Also, according to an index complied by the Canada-based Economic Freedom Network, Korea ranked far behind its Asian rivals, let alone advanced countries, in terms of economic freedom. Korea ranked 44th in 1998 out of 110 countries surveyed. It ranked 39th in 1990 (*Korea Herald*, 12 Nov 1998).
13. From investigations of the Latin American economic woes during the 1980s, a general consensus was formed by the end of that decade that state intervention was not likely to deliver economic progress. This is the so-called 'Washington consensus'. Policy prescriptions arising out of the Washington consensus, forged between the World Bank, IMF and US Treasury officials, include liberalization, macroeconomic stabilization and privatization. The IMF policy package imposed on Korea appears quite consistent with policy prescriptions of the Washington consensus. For the Washington consensus, see Williamson (1990) and Stiglitz (1997, 1998, 1999).
14. According to a survey by the Bank of England, the Bank of Korea still has a long way to go in terms of independence from the government; it ranked 37th in the category of political independence among 77 central banks around the globe (*Korea Herald*, 22 June 1999).
15. By the end of March 1999, 43.5 trillion won had been injected into banks by the government, and, by the end of 1999, the amount escalated to 64 trillion won. This is compared with an estimate of the total scale of non-performing loans of 130 trillion won held by financial institutions – or about 30 per cent of GDP (SERI, 1999a: 16–17).
16. With the rapid advancement of foreign capital, the market share of foreign bank branches in terms of deposits and loans grew from 1.8 per cent at the end of 1997 to 2.5 per cent at the end of 1998. If those banks whose number one majority shareholders are foreigners are included as foreign banks, the market share of foreign banks amounts to 20.6 per cent (SERI, 1999b).
17. This is consistent with the recent development of the financial sectors of advanced countries in which the compartmentalization of the financial sector (banks, securities,

insurance and trust sectors) has disappeared and competition-inhibiting structures have been dismantled.

18. From their empirical studies based on a large number of samples of financial crisis-inflicted countries, Khan and Knight (1985) and Conway (1994) argue that it takes a few years to complete structural reforms. Stiglitz (1999) argues that the Mexican economy had not fully recovered from its 1994 financial crisis by 1999 even though the Mexico crisis was declared over some time in mid-1995.
19. Cha (1999) has proposed a similar vision for Korean economic policy.
20. There are debates in the literature on what governments should do under an economic situation similar to that of the Korean economy. According to the Washington consensus, there is little left for the Korean government to do for its economy, as it has more or less fulfilled the policy prescriptions of liberalization, privatization and macroeconomic stabilization. The World Bank (1993) and Stiglitz (1997, 1998, 1999) argue for the important and complementary role of the government beyond the policy prescriptions of the Washington consensus.
21. Secrecy and lack of transparency surrounding foreign reserves were among the main sources of financial speculation related to the financial crisis in Korea.

REFERENCES

Ahn, Chung Yong and Joo-Hoon Kim (1997), 'The outward-looking trade policy and the industrial development of South Korea', in Dong-Se Cha, Kwang Suk Kim and D.H. Perkins (eds), *The Korean Economy 1945–1995: Performance and Vision for the 21st Century*, Seoul: Korea Development Institute.

Booz.Allen & Hamilton (1997), *Revitalizing the Korean Economy toward the 21st Century*, Seoul: Booz.Allen & Hamilton.

Cha, Dong-Se (1999), 'The Korean economy into the new millennium: reform and revival', paper presented at the Conference of Australia and Korea into the New Millennium, Griffith University, 5–6 August 1999.

Cha, Dong-Se, Kwang Suk Kim and D.H. Perkins (eds) (1997), *The Korean Economy 1945–1995: Performance and Vision for the 21st Century*, Seoul: Korea Development Institute.

Chang, Ha-Joon (1993), 'The political economy of industrial policy in Korea', *Cambridge Journal of Economics*, 17(2), 121–57.

Chung, Un-Chan (1998), 'IMF rescue financing and macroeconomic policy', mimeo.

Conway, Patrick (1994), 'IMF lending programs: participation and impact', *Journal of Development Economics*, 45, 365–91.

Far Eastern Economic Review (1998a), 'Asian executives poll', *Far Eastern Economic Review*, 15 January, 30.

Far Eastern Economic Review (1998b), 'Asian executives poll', *Far Eastern Economic Review*, 18 June, 36.

Hwang, Inhak (1998), *Market Structure and Social Efficiency* (in Korean), Seoul: Korea Economic Research Institute.

Islam, Iyanatul (1994), 'Between the state and the market: the case of eclectic neoclassical political economy', in Andrew MacIntyre (ed.), *Business and Government in Industrialising Asia*, pp. 91–112, Sydney: Allen & Unwin.

Jaw, Sung Hee and Insill Yi (1999), 'Korean financial crisis: evaluation and lessons', paper presented at the Conference of Australia and Korea into the New Millennium, Griffith University, 5–6 August 1999.

Joh, Sung Wook (1999), 'The Korean corporate sector: crisis and reform', paper presented at the Conference of Australia and Korea into the New Millennium, Griffith University, 5–6 August 1999.

Khan, M., and M.D. Knight (1985), 'Fund-supported adjustment programs and economic growth', IMF Occasional Paper no. 41, IMF, Washington, November.

Kim, Dae-jung (1999), 'Toward a parallel pursuit of democracy and a market economy', *Economic Bulletin*, 21(3), 49–54

Korea Herald (1998), 12 November.

Korea Herald (1999a), 22 June 1999.

Korea Herald (1999b), 20 September 1999.

Kwon, O. Yul (1997), 'Korean economic developments and prospects', *Asian–Pacific Economic Literature*, 11(2), 15–39.

Kwon, O. Yul (1998), 'The Korean financial crisis: diagnosis, remedies and prospects', *Journal of the Asia Pacific Economy*, 3(3), 331–57.

Kwon, O. Yul (1999), 'The Korean financial crisis and Implications for Australia', paper presented at the Conference of Australia and Korea into the New Millennium, Griffith University, 5–6 August 1999.

Lee, Chung H. (1992), 'The government, financial system, and large private enterprises in the economic development of South Korea', *World Development*, 20(2), 187–97.

Lee, Young-Sup and Jong-Uk Lee (1998), 'Was it possible to foretell Korea's currency crisis' (in Korean), paper presented at a symposium sponsored by Korea Finance and Economic Research Institute, Seoul, 14 February 1998.

McKinsey Global Institute (1998), *Productivity-led Growth for Korea*, Seoul: McKinsey Seoul Office.

Ministry of Finance and Economy (MOFE) (1998a), *The Year in Review: Korea's Reform Progress*, Seoul: MOFE.

Ministry of Finance and Economy (MOFE) (1998b), *Economic Bulletin*, 20(12), December.

Ministry of Finance and Economy (MOFE) (1999), *Economic Bulletin*, 21(8), August.

National Statistical Office (1998), *Major Statistics of Korean Economy*, Seoul: National Statistics Office.

Newsreview (1998), 17 January.

Newsreview (1999), 'Corporate raiders looming', 13 February, 26–7.

Pack, Howard and Larry E. Westphal (1986), 'Industrial strategy and technological change', *Journal of Development Economics*, 22 (June), 87–128.

Pyo, Hak K. (1999), 'The financial crisis in Korea and its aftermath: a political–economic perspective', paper presented at the Conference of Australia and Korea into the New Millennium, Griffith University, 5–6 August 1999.

Samsung Economic Research Institute (SERI) (1999a), 'Accomplishments of one year's restructuring of the banking sector', *Korean Economic Trends*, SERI, 26 June, 13–21.

Samsung Economic Research Institute (SERI) (1999b), 'The advancement of foreign capital into the domestic financial industry and its effects', *Korean Economic Trends*, SERI, 18 September, 13–21.

Samsung Economic Research Institute (SERI) (1999c), 'The Direction of future financial policy', *Korean Economic Trends*, SERI, 22 May, 13–21.

Smith, Heather (1994), 'Korea's industry policy during the 1980s', *Pacific Economic Papers*, no. 229, March

Stern, Joseph D., J.H. Kim, D.H. Perkins and J.H. You (1995), *Industrialisation and the State: the Korean Heavy and Chemical Industry Drive*, Cambridge, MA: Harvard University Press.

Stiglitz, Joseph (1997), 'The state and development: some new thinking', mimeo (website: www.worldbank.org).

Stiglitz, Joseph (1998), 'More instruments and broader goals: moving toward the post-Washington consensus', mimeo (website: www.worldbank.org).

Stiglitz, Joseph (1999), 'Back to basics: policies and strategies for enhanced growth and equity in post-crisis East Asia', mimeo (website: www.worldbank.org).

Summers, Lawrence H. (1999), 'Distinguished lecture on economics in government: reflections on managing global integration', *Journal of Economic Perspectives*, 13(2), 3–17.

Westphal, Larry E. (1990), 'Industrial policy in the export-propelled economy: lessons from South Korea's experience', *Journal of Economic Perspective*, 4 (summer), 44–54.

Williamson, John (1990), 'What Washington means by policy reform', in John Williamson (ed.), *Latin American Adjustment: How Much Has Happened?*, Washington, DC: Institute for International Economics.

World Bank (1993), *The East Asian Miracle*, Washington, DC: World Bank.

5. Beyond Thailand's crisis: impact and implications

Pasuk Phongpaichit and Chris Baker[1]

INTRODUCTION

Thailand was the fastest-growing economy through the Asian boom of the early 1990s, and the starting point for the subsequent crisis. Yet, ironically, while Thailand was at the centre of Asia's economic rise and fall, it was not at all typical of it. None of the variants of an Asian model fit Thailand at all well. It does not have a strong state. It never had anything which could be dignified as industrial policy. It did not participate at all in the debate on Asian values. Relationships between rulers and businessmen have little in common with either the Korean or Indonesian versions stigmatized as crony capitalism. Regional studies of Asian success and international analyses of the crisis have often skipped deftly past Thailand because it will not fit easily into the general theory.

The objective of this chapter is to suggest some key trends in the Thai political economy in the exit from the crisis. However, this is preceded by two introductory sections. The first sketches key features of the Thai political economy during its era of rapid growth in order to clarify the differences from an Asian model and to provide a baseline for the subsequent account. The second summarizes the major changes wrought by the crisis, to the extent that they can be perceived in early 2000.

We argue that the crisis has had a dramatic impact on the Thai political economy. It has shifted the country significantly in the direction of the neoliberal agenda of economic restructuring through financial reform, greater foreign penetration and reduction of government's interventionist role. However, in the aftermath of the crisis, government is likely to face a fiscal crisis, worsening income distribution and increased demands from civil society. An emerging but as yet unfocused debate presents two visions of the economy's future. The first sees Thailand serving as a host for international capital. The second hopes for a resurgence of entrepreneurship among small and medium enterprises.

THE THAI ECONOMY BEFORE THE CRISIS

Versions of a Japan-derived Asian model of economies in the period spanning the 1960s to 1980s share some key features: a powerful, authoritarian state which sought economic growth through market-defying industrial policy and an assertive role in the allocation of credit; close cooperative or dependent relationships between an economic technocracy and the leaders of business; high levels of domestic savings and their conversion into industrial investment; the creation of a docile urban working class through repression and paternalism; high investments in education, skill and technology development; and relatively high insulation of the economy from external forces through exchange controls, trade barriers and other filters.[2]

Very few of these features hold good for Thailand for the single reason that the government played a much more limited role in industrialization. There was no industrial policy, virtually no guided credit, low levels of investment in skill and technology, relatively distant relationships between business and technocracy, and a trend away from dictatorship to parliamentary rule. Yet many of the achievements of the Asian model do hold good for Thailand: high rates of savings, a growth-oriented allocation of credit, and plentiful supplies of cheap labour. However, in the Thai case, the mechanisms were different, and the resulting industrial structure rather different from East Asian examples.

Capital Market

Until the early 1990s, there were two main sources of capital formation: the Thai commercial banks and foreign direct investment. Government set out incentives to attract foreign investment into sectors prioritized by government, but this incentive regime was only minimally restrictive, and more investment took place outside the incentive framework than within it. Foreign investment was conditioned more by international business's perception of Thailand than by specific Thai government policies. After 1975, the United States, previously the largest foreign investor, saw Thailand as unsafe and unpromising. Apart from oil companies and a few consumer goods vendors, very little Western investment flowed into Thailand until the late 1990s. By contrast, Japan identified Thailand as a site for offshore manufacture, and cultivated its knowledge of and relations with Thailand over the long term. From the mid-1980s, there was a large inflow of manufacturing direct investment into Thailand from Japan and, to a smaller extent, from other East Asian countries.

The Thai government took only a minimal role in the allocation of domestic credit, but provided protection for a cartel of Thai commercial banks. Four or five major banks became such a large factor in the whole economy that their decisions on allocating credit were fundamental not only to their own profits but to the overall direction and health of the economy. These banks became the centres of sprawling business networks. Government had no overt policy to favour these corporate groups, but government machinery was highly susceptible to their great influence. Government agencies sometimes policed business competition by creating monopolies, but this was relatively rare. Government preferred instead to be ringmaster to competing oligopolies which were more efficient and more competitive in sharing their profits with the regulators (Khan, 1998). The result was a high degree of concentration under 30 or so major business conglomerates, mostly focused on the four or five major banks. Because government encouraged foreign investors to enter into joint ventures with domestic partners, foreign direct investment (FDI) also became part of this process (Suehiro, 1989; Pasuk and Baker, 1995).

A key factor in this crudely developed capital market was knowledge. The Thai banks and the Japanese investors built their own data banks and information networks about the Thai economy, its prospects and its participants. The major banks developed economic research departments which gathered statistical data often more extensive than official coverage. The heads of the banks cultivated extensive networks of trust with allied entrepreneurs. The Japanese government funded information gathering and personal networking through institutions such as JICA (Japanese International Cooperation Agency) and JETRO (Japan External Trade Organization), while major Japanese firms developed relationships with counterpart Thai business groups in order to acquire market knowledge and other advantages.

Until 1990–92, the capital account was closed, and the rate of capital accumulation was dictated by domestic savings and FDI inflows – with the former being much the larger component (Jansen, 1990, 1997). The rate of savings was consistently high, partly because of government savings, but more because of the success of the commercial banks in gathering up the savings of the large rural population and the small business sector. With a little encouragement from the technocrats and with a lot of attention to their own profit lines, the major banks channelled this capital towards promising areas of growth. In the 1960s and 1970s, investment was concentrated in trading and processing the produce of expanding agriculture. When this frontier growth delivered rising domestic demand, some investment was diverted to import substitution, but very much as a subsidiary activity. When the rural frontier was exhausted, the emphasis turned first towards the export of services (tourism, labour export) and then more emphatically towards export-oriented manufacture in the conditions for capital relocation around Asia created by the Plaza Accords of 1985. By

1990, as the export industries came more and more under multinational control, domestic capital turned more towards investment in local services (finance, real estate, retail) and in infrastructure (Pasuk and Baker, 1998).

Labour Market

Thailand has a large rural sector whose population increased from 20 million in 1960 to over 40 million in the late 1990s.[3] From around 1980, investment in agriculture declined, and this sector's rate of growth fell behind that of the economy as a whole. From this point on, the countryside was managed as a source of labour and other inputs for urban growth (land, water, electricity generation). Until the final years of the financial bubble, the countryside released plentiful supplies of labour into the urban economy, at a price which was subsidized by the village's role as a social welfare system providing unemployment relief, retirement support and many other social functions. This labour force remained cheap and largely docile, requiring only selective and periodic exercises of repression, and careful control over labour laws. When the labour market tightened sharply in the early 1990s, the government tacitly opened the borders to allow large inflows of illegal or semi-legalized labour.

Technology and Skills

The openness to FDI provided access to technology, relieving the government of any imperative to divert funds towards technology development, or to force firms to do likewise (Westphal, 1989). Similarly, government's role in education and skill development was limited. School education concentrated on creating mass basic literacy, while higher education was oriented to staffing the bureaucracy. Secondary schooling and technical education were neglected. Until the late 1980s, the demand for high-level educated manpower in industry and commerce was met by local supplies supplemented by self-financed overseas education. Labour skills were largely acquired on the job. When the pace of industrial growth changed dramatically in the late 1980s, bottlenecks quickly developed, particularly in the supply of skilled middle-level manpower and specialists such as engineers. Government reacted by increasing its own investments in secondary and tertiary education, expanding overseas scholarships, licensing private expansion of education and allowing a large inflow of foreign expertise to overcome the shortage.

Politics

This economic framework coexisted with an expansion of democratic politics and civil society. This contrasts with most other Asian countries, where rapid economic expansion took place under authoritarian regimes. In Thailand, the end of the Cold War and the decline of US tutelage in the 1970s paved the way for a gradual transition from military dictatorship to parliamentary systems. The transition was not totally smooth. Generals and their coalitions of supporters were reluctant to cede power, and there was a continuous series of clashes and stand-offs from 1976 to 1992. But the trend was clear.

The new parliamentary politics became an arena of competition between business interests, and between competing claims on the government budget. The resulting public life – characterized by fluid parliamentary coalitions, immature parties, fierce electoral competition and raucous public debate – provoked concern about 'stability' and 'corruption'. But in the absence of severe rural disorder or strident labour demands, attempts to revive dictatorship or one-party statism to defend urban growth from internal threats found only limited support. From the mid-1980s, party politics, press and civil society organizations developed very rapidly (Hewison, 1997).

In sum, Thailand did not approximate to any Asian model of state-driven growth, but delivered some of the same results, namely high savings, reasonably well-directed allocation of scarce capital, export-oriented manufacturing relying on plentiful supplies of docile and cheap labour, access to technology and the absence of major political threats to urban-based economic growth. These were achieved not through directed credit, industrial policy, labour repression and dictatorship, but rather through the control of capital allocation by a handful of major banks and one major FDI source (Japan), the exploitation of a large and dependent rural sector and a relatively smooth transition away from military dictatorship to parliamentary democracy.

IMPACT OF THE CRISIS

The dismantling of the above model started during the boom which began in the mid-1980s. The liberalization of the capital account in 1990–92 not only opened up an unprepared financial market to eccentric movements of short-term money, but also destroyed the existing mechanism for allocating capital within the economy. The dominant role of the major Thai banks was diminished by the multiplication of domestic credit institutions, and by domestic borrowers' direct access to overseas financial markets. At the same time, the ranks of foreign direct investors expanded, with increasing inflows from non-Japan sites in East Asia and from the West. In addition, the dominant form of capital inflows changed from FDI to bank loans and portfolio investments (Table 5.1). Capital was no longer scarce: between

Table 5.1 Thailand: capital account, 1985–96 (baht 000 mn)

	85	86	87	88	89	90	91	92	93	94	95	96
Capital account balance	51	11	21	73	145	248	288	241	266	306	545	494
govt and monetary auths	32	−1	5	−1	−9	−42	8	−8	−4	−1	7	10
private	20	13	17	75	153	290	281	249	270	307	538	483
direct investment	4	7	5	28	46	62	47	50	40	22	29	36
portfolio	4	3	13	11	36	11	1	16	131	45	99	78
loans	3	−4	−16	8	69	151	172	124	111	223	391	232
currency & deposits					28	34	52	45	68	51	84	74
other	8	7	15	28	−27	32	9	14	−79	−35	−66	64
GDP (current prices)	1056	1133	1300	1560	1857	2184	2507	2831	3170	3631	4189	4598

Note: Pre-1989 data do not allow separation of currency and deposits.

Source: Bank of Thailand.

1988 and 1990, net private inflows quadrupled, and then maintained that new level until a final bubbly surge in 1995–6.

Foreign debt accumulated rapidly. Between 1988 and 1996, the private sector's foreign debt increased almost tenfold (Table 5.2). Much of the inflow came from new sources, through institutions which were new to the market and which made little investment in local knowledge. The opportunities for profitable investment did not expand at this rate. As a result, much investment was poorly planned and redundant, resulting in falling rates of return, rising over-capacity in certain sectors and then a self-feeding bubble in finance and real estate (Phatra Research Institute, 1997). Much of the evidence cited to condemn Thai firms for malpractice comes from this terminal, money-mad period.

By 1996, Thailand's total foreign debt stood at 90.5 billion US dollars (equivalent to half of GDP), of which 81 per cent was held by the private sector. As several commentators have shown, Asia's debt-based credit systems, once exposed by financial liberalization, proved highly vulnerable to collapse in the event of capital flight (Wade and Veneroso, 1998; UNCTAD, 1998; Bhanupong, 1999). The sudden withdrawal of capital undermined the asset base of financial institutions. It also caused the currency to depreciate and hence increased the foreign exchange-based liabilities of these financial institutions. The result was a double blow which affected all corporations which had borrowed overseas, and especially those which had acted as financial intermediaries.

The crisis had an especially sharp impact on Thailand because of the scale of capital flight. Given the excessive inflows, growing over-capacity and falling rate of return in Thailand by the mid-1990s, some level of capital outflow was inevitable. But the IMF package and IMF politicking in late 1997 ensured the outflow would be panicky and excessive. The package, designed for a Latin American country where the government faced bankruptcy, was totally inappropriate for an Asian country swamped by private foreign debt. The sharply deflationary implications of the macroeconomic package (budget surplus, tax increases, tight money) promised that things would get worse rather than better for private investors. This, together with the rather meagre size of the IMF loan, provided an incentive for foreign investors to get out quickly. The IMF's forcing of the government to guarantee foreign liabilities made exit easy. The IMF's statements about political instability added to a sense of panic.

In the two years following the float (July 1997–June 1999), total private outflows net of FDI ran at a rate of almost a fifth of GDP. In total these outflows were roughly equivalent to the total inflows under the same categories back to 1990. They were balanced somewhat by inflows of public sector borrowing and of FDI and portfolio money acquiring cheap assets.

Table 5.2 Foreign debt (US dollars bn)

	88	89	90	91	92	93	94	95	96	97	98	99*
Private sector	7.8	10.7	17.8	25.1	30.6	37.9	49.2	66.2	73.7	69.1	54.7	40.7
Public sector	12.6	11.8	11.5	12.8	13.1	14.2	15.7	16.4	16.8	17.2	20.3	23.7
Monetary authorities	0.7	0.3	0.0	0.0	0.0	0.0	0.0	0.0	0.0	7.2	11.2	12.8
Total	21.1	22.9	29.3	37.9	43.6	52.1	64.9	82.6	90.5	93.4	86.2	77.2
Per cent of GDP	*34.0*	*31.5*	*34.2*	*38.4*	*39.0*	*41.5*	*44.8*	*48.9*	*49.7*	*60.0*	*75.5*	*67.2*

Note: *November.

Source: Bank of Thailand.

But the capital account was in deficit by 776 billion baht (18.4 billion US dollars) over two years.[4]

The currency collapsed from 25/US$ before the float to a low point of 54 in January 1998 before recovering to a range of 37–40. The combined effect of such sharp capital flight and currency depreciation rendered the entire financial sector first illiquid and then effectively bankrupt. In addition, starting with the IMF-ordained closure of 56 finance companies in late 1997, the credit system effectively collapsed. The closures left many small firms without a source of working credit. Many big firms (for example, Siam Cement) withdrew from credit relationships and converted as many as possible of their domestic transactions to cash. From mid-1998, increasing numbers of creditor companies stopped repaying the bankers ('strategic non-performing loans') – at first as a strategy to survive, and later as a means to remain competitive against other firms which had already stopped repaying. Over the second half of 1998, total non-performing loans (NPLs) rose from 8 to 45 per cent of all commercial credit (TDRI, 1999, p. 7).

In March 1998, the government under IMF direction set out a two-year programme for financial institutions to raise their bad debt provisioning to Basle standards. This programme, combined with the double blow and the rise of strategic non-payment, left the banks with little chance of survival. On 14 August 1998, the government announced a financial rescue package which made government funds available for recapitalization, but only on conditions which threatened to deprive the existing shareholders of both ownership and control. A handful of the large banks attempted to survive by floating international share issues, and by scaling down their businesses. The smaller banks gave up.

Financial Devastation

Perhaps the major impact of the crisis on the Thai political economy has been the devastation in the financial sector.

On the eve of the crisis, Thailand had 15 commercial banks and 92 finance companies. In the early years of the boom, the finance companies played an important role in financing the rapid expansion of domestic manufacturing firms which helped to create the export boom. After 1987, when government began to promote the stock market, they became more involved in developing brokerages and lending money for stock speculation. After capital account liberalization in 1990–92, they could make the highest profits in the short term simply by borrowing funds in the offshore market and relending locally. After government imposed some restrictions on banks (but not finance companies) lending to the overheating real estate sector in 1994, the finance companies' lending was oriented more to real estate. By the time of the crash, most finance companies were hopelessly exposed to foreign short-term borrowing on the one hand, and to real estate loans, consumer credit and advances to stock speculators on the other. A total of 56 finance companies were closed down by government in December 1997. Others subsequently closed, merged or were absorbed into a parent. Currently, 23 are still in operation. Ultimately, only one or two merged groups are expected to survive in the form of limited banks.

The banks fall into four groups (see Table 5.3, read bottom upwards). First, six small and medium banks were taken over by the Bank of Thailand in early 1998. Two were closed down, and the remaining four slated for sale to foreign interests. Second, three small banks negotiated private sale of a majority interest to foreign banks during 1998–9.[5] Third, Krung Thai (owned by the government) and Thai Military Bank (owned by the army) enjoyed special status. In mid-1998, the government had hopes of using Krung Thai (and other smaller state-owned financial institutions) as a mechanism for absorbing some of the damage to the financial sector, and for stimulating recovery in the real economy. A new management was installed, including several high-profile technocrats and financial managers. However, it quickly emerged that Krung Thai was suffering a sharp version of the balance-sheet damage and strategic non-payment which characterized the whole sector. In addition, the high-profile technocrats and financial managers had little experience in the world of personal connections of Thai corporate banking. By mid-1999, Krung Thai was in the worst shape of all the remaining local banks. However the government, committed to maintaining its existence, pumped in 185 billion baht of new capital, and installed another batch of management. The Thai Military Bank was similarly damaged and its future is unclear.[6]

Fourth, the four remaining larger commercial banks struggled to survive and maintain the existing management control. All except the more 'establishment'[7] Siam Commercial Bank viewed the government's financial rescue package (14 August 1998) as a poison pill, and refused to accept inputs of government capital. The smallest of the four, Bank of Ayudhya, survived by selling off other assets of the group (principally its cement plant). The other three floated international share issues which raised the foreign-owned share of their capital to 49 per cent. All four converted some of their domestic deposits into share capital (at high cost). However, their situation is still highly uncertain. The government has stated that it does not wish to see the whole financial system converted to foreign ownership (as happened in some Latin American countries), but at the same time is highly nervous of being seen to give any direct support to the major banks.

Table 5.3 Thai commercial banks, 1997–9

Bank	Controlling interest pre-crisis	Employees 1997	Deposits 1997 (bt bn)	Status, end 1999	Foreign share (%)
Bangkok Bank	Sophonpanich family	25958	947		49
Thai Farmers Bank	Lamsam family	19158	588		49
Siam Commercial Bank	Crown Property Bureau	12908	559		49
Bank of Ayudhya	Rattanarak family	11530	389		34
Krung Thai Bank	Government	16286	580		
Thai Military Bank	Thai army	8165	258		13
Thai Danu Bank	Tuchinda family	2993	90	Acquired by DBS (Singapore).	62
Bank of Asia	Phatrapraisit family	2519	80	Acquired by ABN Amro.	75
Nakhon Thon Bank	Wang Lee family	2162	47	Acquired by Standard Chartered.	75
Bangkok Bank of Commerce	Jalichandra family	5391	110*	Closed down. Good assets to Krung Thai.	
Siam City Bank	Mahadamrongkul family	6260	158	Taken over by BoT. Being sold.	
Bangkok Metropolitan Bank	Tejaphaibul family	5916	80	Taken over by BoT. Being sold.	
First Bangkok City Bangkok	Charoen Siriwattanaphakdi	3765	132	Taken over by BoT. Merged with Krung Thai.	
Laemthong Bank	Chansrichawla family	1162	27	Taken over by BoT. Sold to UOB (Singapore).	75
Union Bank of Bangkok	Cholvijarn family	2805	48	Taken over by BoT. Merged with 13 finance companies as BankThai. To be sold.	

Notes: *1996 figure.

Sources: Bank of Thailand; press reports.

Attrition of the Conglomerates

Large foreign debts and the collapse of the banks at the core of the pre-crisis economy caused wider damage among the major business groups which clustered around these banks.[8] A few of these business groups may be totally wiped out. An example is the Sukree textile group, which was already in decline because of failure to invest in new technology in line with the changing structure and competitive advantage of the economy (*Nation*, 22 July 1998).

Many others are being severely scaled down. At present, the extent and details of this collapse are difficult to document. The fate of the Siam Cement Group (SCG) may give some indication, even though this group cannot be called typical. Despite a reputation as one of the best-managed of any Thai corporation, SCG was caught with massive unhedged foreign loans at the time of the depreciation. In 1997, it recorded a loss of 53 billion baht, largely on foreign exchange (*Bangkok Post*, 26 February 1998). The group reacted by putting a third of its total assets up for sale (*Bangkok Post*, 28 February 1998). These assets include many joint ventures in electronics and automotive parts which the group acquired when incoming foreign investors sought a politically powerful ally as local partner. This scaling down will shed most of the fruits of the group's expansion since the early 1980s.[9] A similar trend can be seen in the major retail empire (Central), the steel industry (Sahaviriya, NTS group) and others.

A few of the conglomerates suffered rather less. The CP group, for instance, managed its foreign exchange losses largely by selling off assets in China (brewery, motorcycle manufacture), while its core agri-business continued to deliver a reasonable cash flow.

Foreign Penetration

The collapse and sell-offs by the Thai groups has enabled a much higher foreign penetration of the modern economy. These asset transfers have a certain geo-economic pattern. Many manufacturing enterprises have been transferred to Asian owners – mainly Japanese. Many service businesses (financial and retail) have been taken over by Western firms – principally American and continental European.

In October 1997, the government effectively relaxed remaining restrictions on foreign ownership of corporations, with the exception of a small reserved list.[10] Over the next year, many of the manufacturing enterprises originally set up as joint ventures were converted into full or majority foreign ownership. In the automotive sector, Mitsubishi bought out its local partner. Honda injected new capital, resulting in a halving of the already small local shareholding. Toyota injected 4 billion baht of new capital, further diluting the local partner's minority stake. Toyota also bought three auto-parts companies sold off by Siam Cement (*Nation*, 8 July 1999). Yamaha bought a majority stake from its joint venture partner. One of the largest auto-parts producers, the Somboon group, reduced its stake in nine of its companies from 51 to 5 per cent. By early 1999, half of the 1200 local auto-parts makers had reportedly closed down (Brimble and Sherman 1999, p. 21).

The same was true in electronics and electrical goods. Matsushita bought out the local National joint venture. Samsung and NEC bought out their local partners completely. The SVOA computing business sold 51 per cent to Acer and 10 per cent to Epson.

In heavy industry and infrastructure, the results were mixed. The largest steel producer, Sahaviriya, was forced to sell majority control in two of its three core companies to Japanese partners (*Nation*, 27 April 1998; *Bangkok Post*, 22 June 1999). The Nakhonthai steel group is preparing to sell an 80 per cent stake to foreign creditors (*Nation*, 20 January 2000). Jalaprathan cement sold 80 per cent to Ciment Français, and Siam City Cement sold 25 per cent to Holderbank. Other large steel (SSP), petrochemical (TPI) and infrastructure (BTS) groups survived temporarily by simply not paying their creditors but are the targets of foreign buyers and are unlikely to survive.

Many service businesses passed into the ownership of Western firms. ABN Amro and Standard Chartered bought two of the bank. Virtually the whole brokerage industry was taken over, largely by European firms.[11] The ownership mix in the insurance industry also tilted as some local firms were bought out by their foreign partner (for example, Prudential), others were reduced in size, and Western firms established before the crisis (AIA, John Hancock) took the opportunity to expand.

The pattern was similar in the retail sector. The largest Thai business group in this sector, the Central group, sold off the supermarkets, discount warehouses and megastores which had represented most of its corporate expansion of the past decade or more, in order to hang on to its original core business of department stores. The two main purchasers were the Dutch Ahold group and French Groupe Casino. The CP group, similarly, sold its main retail holdings to Tesco of the UK and Delhaize of Belgium. In addition, the established Carrefour and Makro took the opportunity to expand into the space created by the collapse of other retail businesses. On a smaller scale, 7-Eleven stores continued a rapid expansion into space vacated by the collapse of corner-store businesses.[12]

In some areas of the economy, local firms did reasonably well through the crisis because their foreign debts were limited and the currency

Table 5.4 Thailand: foreign acquisitions, October 1997–May 1998

	Number	Value (US$mn)	Per cent of number	Per cent of value
Total	130	4526.5	*100*	*100*
Finance	36	1772.7	*28*	*39*
Electronic	19	586.5	*15*	*13*
Automotive	19	199.4	*15*	*4*
Japan	39	586.9	*30*	*13*
Europe	31	1772.4	*24*	*39*
USA	25	789.3	*19*	*17*
East Asia	17	628.6	*13*	*14*
Majority (51–90%)	38	2685.0	*29*	*59*
Outright (91–100%)	32	451.6	*25*	*10*

Source: Brimble and Sherman (1999).

depreciation boosted demand. Examples are food processing, hotels and other businesses related to tourism. But overall, there was a clear upward step in foreign ownership and foreign penetration.

There are no complete data on the numbers or scale of these ownerships transfers. Brimble and Sherman (1999) tracked 130 acquisition deals by foreign capital between October 1997 and May 1999 representing a total value of US$4.5 billion (Table 5.4).[13] Roughly a third of this amount represented deals in the financial sector, and the largest source of capital was Europe. In addition, Brimble and Sherman tracked 135 deals worth US$1.5 billion made under a special provision for foreign investors to acquire a majority stake in firms promoted by the Board of Investment (BoI) on condition of the local partners' consent. Almost half of these deals were in the automotive sector, with others spread across chemicals, electronics and light industry.

The figures on investment inflows (Table 5.5) give some indication of the overall scale. The total net inflow of foreign direct investment in the two years following the float of the baht in July 1997 was 493 billion baht, or 12.5 billion US dollars. For comparison, this two-year total is higher in baht terms (and 82 per cent in dollar terms) than the total FDI inflows over the 1986–95 boom – a boom often attributed to high FDI. In other words, after the float, FDI flowed in four to five times faster than ever before.

Of this post-crash inflow, around 140 billion baht went into the buy-outs and recapitalization of the banks. Another 149 billion baht went into

Table 5.5 Thailand: foreign investment

		Billion baht		Billion US$	
		1986–95	7/97–6/99	1986–95	7/97–6/99
Total FDI	*including banks*	388.7	492.5	15.4	12.5
	excluding banks	386.3	352.4	15.3	10.1
Industry		147.4	149.5	5.8	4.3
Financial institutions		26.7	31.0	1.1	0.8
Trade		66.3	79.9	2.6	2.4
Construction		36.0	9.3	1.4	0.3
Mining & quarrying		13.7	2.4	0.5	0.1
Agriculture		3.0	0.1	0.1	0.0
Services		14.0	30.8	0.6	0.9
Real estate		81.5	24.4	3.2	0.7
Others		−2.4	26.2	−0.1	0.7
Japan		116.6	100.6	4.6	2.6
Hong Kong		63.3	33.5	2.5	0.9
Taiwan		26.9	8.0	1.1	0.2
USA		53.0	67.4	2.1	1.7
EU		35.1	62.0	1.4	1.6
Singapore		34.1	55.2	1.3	1.4
Other		57.4	25.7	2.3	1.7
Total portfolio investment		197.5	124.8	7.8	3.3
Hong Kong		79.3	88.6	3.1	2.4
Singapore		99.9	82.4	4.0	2.1
USA		21.3	−57.1	0.8	−1.5
Taiwan		2.6	0.1	0.1	0.0
Japan		2.3	1.2	0.1	0.0
UK		34.7	25.0	1.4	0.7
Other		−42.4	−15.5	−1.7	−0.4

Source: Bank of Thailand.

industry (the same figure as over the ten boom years), especially into automotive, electrical and metal industries. Other major destinations were the financial sector (31 billion), services (31) and trade (80). The major source was Japan (101 billion baht, or 2.6 billion US dollars). In addition, 67 billion came from the United States and 62 billion from the European Union (EU). Other large amounts came from Hong Kong and Singapore, some of which possibly represent investments through subsidiaries of

Table 5.6 Thailand: government debt

	92	93	94	95	96	97	98	99*
Domestic debt (baht bn)	278.9	293.0	293.6	311.0	322.6	325.5	727.5	952.4
Foreign debt (US$ bn)								
Public sector	13.1	14.2	15.7	16.4	16.8	17.2	20.3	23.7
Monetary authorities	0.0	0.0	0.0	0.0	0.0	7.2	11.2	12.8
Total (baht bn)	611.5	652.5	689.6	720.5	749.4	1091.3	2037.2	2340.9
As % of GDP	*21.6*	*20.6*	*19.0*	*17.2*	*16.3*	*23.1*	*43.7*	*50.1*

Note: *November.

Source: Bank of Thailand.

Western firms. In addition, over the two post-float years, there was a net inflow of portfolio investment of 125 billion baht or 3.3 billion US dollars, with the major sources being Hong Kong, Singapore and the UK.[14]

Government Debt

Prior to the crisis, the public sector's foreign debt (including monetary authorities) had stood at 17 billion US dollars, equivalent to around 10 per cent of GDP (Table 5.2). By late 1999, the foreign debt had doubled to 36 billion US dollars, and was predicted to increase further. (See Table 5.6.) The increase in public sector foreign debt resulted only partially from obligations to the IMF. The two other major sources were loans contracted through the World Bank, ADB (Asian Development Bank) and the Miyazawa Plan to fund the fiscal stimulus launched from mid-1998, and the bonds launched to finance the debts of the financial firms taken under government control in late 1997 and early 1998.

In addition, the public sector's domestic debt also accumulated as a result of the budget deficit and financial bail-outs. The central government's domestic debt (including debts of state enterprises) tripled, from 323 billion baht before the crisis to 952 billion in November 1999, equivalent to half of annual GDP. With the continuing deficit and full fiscalization of the money pumped into the financial industry, the total government debt was predicted to rise further.[15]

Constitutional Reform

Besides the major changes in the economy, the crisis has also prompted several changes within politics and civil society. Here we will just note three changes of major importance (Baker, 2000).

In September 1997, in the eye of the crisis, the parliament approved a new constitution. The process to draft the new charter extended back many years, and it was by chance that the final decision, whose timing had been determined 18 months earlier, would coincide with the crisis (the IMF package was agreed on the same day the constitution draft was finalized). However, this coincidence was critical in securing the constitution's passage. The original draft of the new charter had been opposed by almost everyone occupying positions of formal power, and certainly by a majority of those in the two houses of parliament. Yet the shock of the economic crisis prompted a movement of revulsion against the current political leadership, and this movement seized on the constitution as a symbol of hope for change. The prospect that rejection of the charter would lead to public disorder at a time when the economic crisis thrust

Thailand into the international spotlight prompted several power centres (starting with the army) to back the charter's passage.

The charter is complex and, for the purpose of this chapter, we will only draw attention to two of its many aspects. First, the charter's reformatting of the parliament attempts to increase the importance of Bangkok against the provinces. This is a reaction against the politics of the mid-1990s when provincial politicians dominated the parliament, and when the combined forces of the technocracy and Bangkok business lost control of economic policy making. The main mechanism of this Bangkok bias is the 'party list' – an additional 100 MPs (on top of the existing 400) elected by a national vote.

The second main change of the new charter is a range of innovations demanded by NGOs and civil society groups to counter the over-centralization of the Thai state, and shift the balance of power between the state on the one hand and the individual or local community on the other. These innovations include an extensive listing of civic and human rights, foundation of many new quasi-judicial institutions (human rights commission, freedom of information, administrative court) and a range of state commitments (on decentralization, liberalization of the media, community control of local resources). In essence, these provisions amount to an attempt to secure through the constitution a range of changes which civil society groups despair of achieving through the parliamentary process. Whether this strategy will succeed is still uncertain. Already, many of these measures have run into heavy opposition. But the effort – and the opposition – indicate some of the conflicts which are likely to dominate public life in the near future.

Neoliberal Politics

A second major political change which has come with the crisis is the increased exposure of politics and economic policy making to outside influence, particularly influence from Washington. The neoliberal agenda for change in the world economy demands many reforms at the national level, and this has led those institutions involved in the neoliberal project to pay more attention to national-level politics. The World Bank has shifted its focus to include more attention to political matters. USAID has returned to Thailand after a long absence with a programme to influence political reforms rather than to distribute economic aid. Several Western foundations and lobby organizations have also been active. The desired programme of change runs under the heading of 'good governance' or sometimes the more vague 'reform'. In practice the main items on the agenda are control of corruption, changes in the legal system to approximate more to a Western model, privatization of public-sector enterprises and insulation of economic policy from political pressures by increasing the role of the central bank and other supposedly rule-based technocratic institutions.

In the context of this outside pressure, Thailand's dominant party, the Democrats, has made a significant if incomplete shift towards the neoliberal camp. In the early 1990s, the Democrat party resembled other major Thai parties – a coalition between provincial businessmen whose main agenda was to pull more resources into their localities, and Bangkok business groups whose main agenda was to maintain the partially protective regime for the development of national capital. In the mid-1990s, when ruling coalitions were dominated by other parties with a strong provincial bias, the Democrat party was converted into a counterweight party representing Bangkok and the protection of the modern urban economy. Under this flag, the Democrats were pitched into power in November 1997 to manage the crisis. While the Democrat government rebelled against the IMF macroeconomic programme, it accepted the IMF–Washington blueprint for transformation of the financial system, and conditionally accepted much else on the neoliberal agenda (Pasuk and Baker, 2000). It supported privatization but was slowed down by public opposition. It is engaged in recasting the role of the central bank under the tutelage of the World Bank. It has made initial steps on legal reform, particularly with a bankruptcy law and related legislation. More broadly, the Democrats have become more distanced from dominant business interests than any other government in recent memory, and appear to have abandoned almost all responsibility for the state to nurture domestic capitalism.

Rural Politics

Finally, the crisis has seen an adjustment in the politics of rural society. Over the boom period, agriculture stagnated, the income gap between urban and rural grew wider, and rural households became more dependent on income transfers from the urban economy, principally through migrant labour. From around 1990, there was a sharply rising trend of rural protest. These protests fell into two types. First, there were reactions against attempts by state and urban business to claim resources of land, water and forests on which rural communities depended. Second, there were campaigns against high debts and low crop prices – the symptoms of declining profitability of agriculture. This trend of protest climaxed with a 99-day demonstration by rural groups under the umbrella of the Assembly of the Poor in Bangkok in early 1997 (Praphat, 1998).

The crisis increased the economic pressure on rural society. Income transfers from the urban economy were severely reduced. Many disemployed migrants were forced to fall back on the village family as their social welfare system. In 1998 and again in 1999, farmer groups demanded debt relief. In early 1999, some landless groups, swollen by unemployed migrants, launched 'land invasions' into state-claimed forest areas. These movements were contained by a mixture of repression and compromise.

Rural groups largely withheld protest campaigns during the latter stages of the crisis on the grounds that such campaigns would alienate urban sympathy, invite government repression and bring no tangible benefit. However, the crisis changed the context of rural politics in several ways. It demystified the supposed superiority of the urban economy, and emboldened groups which promote rural self-reliance and groups which demand greater government attention to agricultural development. It halted – at least temporarily – the gradual transfer of population from village to city, undermined faith in the reliability of urban employment and increased the importance of the village as a social cushion.

BEYOND THE CRISIS

Restoration of Selective Export-led Growth

While exports fell in dollar terms between 1995 and 1998, the sectoral pattern has been very uneven. Agricultural exports have dropped sharply because of international price trends (see Table 5.7). Exports of textiles and other classic cheap-labour manufactures have also fallen in the face of competition from China and elsewhere. But exports of technology-based manufactures have continued to grow through the crisis, albeit at a reduced rate. This extends the trend which first appeared in the early 1990s.

On this evidence, Thailand still appears to have a competitive standing in electronics, electrical goods, automotive and similar areas. Thailand is now one of the world centres for final production of disk drives. Both Japanese and US carmakers are developing Thailand as an Asian export centre. Many of the processes carried out in Thailand are simple fabrication and assembly, and the rates of value-added can be very low (10–30 per cent). However, technology-based exports now contribute almost half of total Thai exports. Some of the plants (particularly in electronics) are very footloose, but others, such as the automotive assemblies, represent large investments in plant and in manpower development. They are not likely to disappear soon. Much of the inflow of Japanese investment over 1997–99 has gone into buying full Japanese ownership of such firms, and hence

Table 5.7 Thai exports by segment, 1996–9

	Value, US$ billion				Annual growth (%)				Shares	
	1996	1997	1998	1999	1996	1997	1998	1999	1996	1999
Agriculture	6.58	5.84	5.08	4.87	2.5	−11.2	−13.1	−4.0	11.8	8.4
Resource-based	7.05	6.92	6.37	6.66	−2.5	−1.8	−7.9	4.5	12.7	11.4
Labour-intensive	11.00	10.25	9.06	9.45	−14.9	−6.8	−11.6	4.4	19.8	16.2
Process	4.56	5.24	4.65	5.43	15.4	14.8	−11.2	16.7	8.2	9.3
Technology-based	22.10	23.92	24.00	26.89	3.0	8.3	0.3	12.1	39.7	46.1
Other	4.32	5.22	4.88	5.01	−0.6	20.7	−6.4	2.7	7.8	8.6
Total	55.61	57.39	54.05	58.33	−1.3	3.2	−5.8	7.9	100.0	100.0

Source: Bank of Thailand.

increasing the parent companies' commitment to make them profitable. The markets for these industries are largely within Asia, and should regain their dynamism as the region as a whole emerges from the crisis.

In sum, Thailand is likely to continue in the pattern of export-led growth, with the lead coming from the technology-based areas of electronics, electrical and automotive goods. The extent to which this growth benefits the economy as a whole will depend on measures to increase the level of local value-added by developing more supplier industries.

The Prospects for Domestic Firms

The prospects for domestic firms are much more mixed. Established Thai firms will continue to prosper in growth areas such as tourist-related services and food processing. But the prospects for a broader trend of growth are poor. The two key supports of the pre-crisis phase – the central role of the banks and the loosely protective role of government – have been knocked away. The domestic banks will take a long time to recover and overcome the antagonisms that developed between creditor and debtor during the crisis. The international banks are likely to favour international firms because the systems and relationships are already in place. They will concentrate on consumer banking and risk management, where they have clear advantages through technology and experience. They are much less likely to take over the Thai banks' old role of funding ambitious entrepreneurship on the basis of personal relationships and personal market knowledge.

Indeed, it is becoming clear that financial liberalization destroys the form of entrepreneurial banking pursued by many Asian banking sectors. In the old world of Bretton Woods, fixed exchange rates and closed capital accounts, all the regulation of the international financial system took place at the international level. This created a relatively stable environment in which banks inside national economies could be very entrepreneurial. Now all the international regulation has been removed. The international financial system is a barely restrained anarchy. All the regulation now has to take place at the national level or, more exactly, at the level of each bank. Hence governments clamp very stringent rules onto the way banks operate – rules which extend to the procedures banks have to follow before making each and every loan. In this new world, old Asian-style entrepreneurial banking becomes impossible.[16]

While the corporate devastation may look dramatic, it is worth pointing out that this is not the first such occasion. Akira Suehiro's study of the development of Thai capital since the 1880s documents three earlier occasions when many of the leading firms were wiped out in a crisis of international instability – first in the worldwide recession of the 1890s, second in the post-First World War crisis, third in the 1930s depression (Suehiro, 1989). In each case, the cycle of revival took many years. Besides, on these earlier occasions, the assets were largely transferred among Thais or among Sino-Thais.

However, this overall picture could be modified by two factors: local politics and Japan. While the Democrats are firm on a hands-off policy towards industrial assistance, other parties take a very different line. Taksin Shinawatra has pitched his new Thai Rak Thai party as supportive of entrepreneurship and small and medium enterprise. The Chat Phatthana party remains closely involved with some of the stronger of the surviving Thai conglomerates, and has argued (unsuccessfully so far) for a more proactive industrial policy. In early 1999, it proposed government should directly support the resurrection of a wafer fabrication project which collapsed at the onset of the crisis.

From before the crisis, Japan warned Thailand over the neglect of direct industrial policy. Through the crisis, it occasionally signalled dissent from the neoliberal, finance-accented trend of the IMF's anti-crisis strategy. MITI has been working to persuade the Thai Ministry of Industry to adopt a sector-based industrial promotion strategy based on Japanese experience. However, the Japanese voice has been undermined by the weakness of Japan's own economy, and by the sheer noise level of the neoliberal advocacy. The Japanese effort is also vulnerable to the criticism that it focuses aid in areas which are directly supportive of Japanese export firms in Thailand. However, since the Miyazawa Initiative in late 1998, the Japanese voice in policy making has become significantly stronger. In November 1998, the Thai finance minister met the head of MITI and agreed a programme of support for small and medium enterprises based on Japanese funding and expertise (Suehiro, 2000).

In sum, there is some chance that a changed political regime, stronger Japanese advocacy and Japanese technical support could lead to a faster recovery of domestic business, but, on present evidence, the possibility seems remote. Far more likely is that the scaled-down Thai firms will find it difficult to expand and compete, and will cede most of the opportunities arising from renewed growth to further international penetration.

Government in the Economy

The role of the government in the economy will shrink, partly as a result of neoliberal pressure, and partly as a result of severe budget constraints. At present around 64 per cent of the budget is devoted to current expenditure (salaries and overheads), while 36 per cent or around 300 billion baht per year goes on capital expenditure. Already in the budget for fiscal year 2000, interest payments on public debt will eat away a fifth of the budget allocation for capital items. If the public debt does rise over 2.5 trillion baht, as expected, a ten-year repayment programme would require *all* of the current capital expenditure budget for that decade.

The World Bank claims the Thai government will be able to reduce this debt rapidly, in the same way that it did in the 1980s, when the upturn in the economy resulted in a high budget surplus. But this time it may not be so easy. First, the surplus accumulated quickly in the 1980s because the economy (and tax receipts) accelerated very fast. Second, revenue depends heavily on trade taxes which are due to be reduced under regional ASEAN Free Trade Area (AFTA) agreements.[17] Third, expenditure was low in the 1980s because government failed to invest in infrastructure, but this may no longer be an option. Government will undoubtedly attempt to increase tax demands and reduce budget leakage, but will face considerable resistance in both endeavours. Privatization will only partially reduce the budget load.

Besides, government will also be under great pressure to devote whatever funds are available to programmes which assist the foreign-owned export-oriented segment of the economy which will be driving growth. Such programmes are likely to include certain forms of education and infrastructure development. As a result, government is unlikely to have funding for other major initiatives in the economy.

Income Distribution

On a long trend, while average per capita income has increased, distribution has become steadily worse. In the boom years, the worsening was dramatic. The gap between the top and bottom deciles of the income range widened from a multiple of 17 in 1981 to a multiple of 37 in 1994 (Pasuk and Baker, 1998, p. 285). Also in the boom years, rural land passed from small farmer-operators into the hands of urban speculators and investors. Accurate statistics are not available, but it is most likely that the ownership of land has become more skewed, and the numbers of landless and insecure farmers have increased.

The main factors driving the maldistribution trend were the concentration of growth in certain sectors of the urban economy, the continued weakness of agriculture and the poor distribution of economic assets (land ownership), social assets (education) and political assets (organizational strength and access). The crisis temporarily halted the trend of worsening distribution by severely cutting incomes at the top end of the range. But, in the exit from the crisis, the trend towards maldistribution may resume and intensify. Even more than before, growth will be concentrated in specific areas of the urban economy, and especially in those attractive to foreign capital. With no measures to revive the rural economy, the countryside will continue to release manpower into the urban economy. However, the more moderate pace of growth and the bias towards technology-based and moderately capital-intensive industries will ensure that the labour market remains weak, and that prospects remain especially poor for the majority of the labour force who still have no more than elementary education. The urban bias built into the reformed parliament will obstruct pressure to reverse the trends through any refocus on agriculture or any serious restructuring of the allocation of economic, social and political assets. The tight fiscal constraints, and the overriding neoliberal ideology, will stand in the way of any significant advance in social security.

Political Trends

The combined impact of the crisis and the new constitution is likely to lead to an extended period of political reorientation. The urban bias of the constitution, the strength of outside pressure and the dominant position acquired by the Democrat party suggest that the ruling coalition will remain generally committed to a strategy of external orientation and further liberalization. While opposing agendas may be present in the parliamentary arena, they are likely to exert even more pressure in public politics outside the formal political arena.

One key unknown is how the remnants of domestic big business will behave. In the eye of the crisis, domestic business proved unable to defend the forms of state protection and assistance it had earlier enjoyed. The instincts of big business are to work behind the scenes of parliamentary politics, but this proved ineffective in the circumstances of crisis. Some sections of business attempted to raise a standard of economic nationalism, but were unable to generate any widespread movement either within the business community or within a wider population because Thailand has no tradition of mass nationalism stemming from anti-colonial struggles, and no strong record of economic–nationalist policy making.

Rural political expression is likely to return to the rising trend of the 1990s. At the height of the crisis, the government implemented its Keynesian stimulus of the economy by pushing funds (from the Miyazawa scheme and budget deficit) into the rural localities on the grounds that this would both cushion distress and deliver the fastest multiplier. On the exit from the crisis, rural demands which have been temporarily repressed are likely to re-emerge strongly. As past governments have tried to minimize rural pressure by denying space for rural politics, there are no good mechanisms for handling such demands. Government will find it hard to scale down palliative schemes such as the Miyazawa funding. It will face more serious demands to devise a convincing agricultural policy, and to handle the many conflicts between community and state on the control and use of natural resources.

Two trends in rural politics established before the crisis are likely to re-emerge. First, conflicts over resources of land, water and forest will lead to increasingly more radical demands for the relaxation of central control, and for the devolution of power from centre to locality. Second, the rear-guard action against the declining profitability of agriculture will throw up demands for more government attention to debt relief and crop pricing and for more diversion of national resources to the rural sector.

Urban civil society activism will press harder to dismantle the remnants of the old centralized bureaucratic state by implementing the agenda of the 1997 constitution on such matters as decentralization, liberalization of the media, reform of the civil service and activation of the new institutions (human rights commission, ombudsman, freedom of information act) which empower individual and community against state.

Finally, there is likely to be a surge of 'establishment radicalism'. In the past, in periods of heightened political conflict or worsening distribution, conservative forces often rooted in the established bureaucracy have come out to promote ideologies of national unity and programmes of economic redistribution. In the early stages of the crisis, such forces were enthusiastic about the notion of 'good governance'. However, as the crisis deepened, they became more concerned over growing social division and the increased foreign penetration of the Thai economy. This is not because they are anti-foreign in any cultural or political sense. Most of the individuals involved are very westernized. But they are concerned that the speed and extent of foreign penetration may be too difficult for the society to absorb. They fear some chemical reaction between increasing social division and economic nationalism.

How these different forces of business nationalism, rural radicalism, urban civil society activism and establishment radicalism will react together is impossible to predict. What is clear, however, is that Thailand's relatively open public politics will provide space for these forces. The government's ability to respond to these demands will be limited by the fiscal crisis, and by neoliberal pressure to constrict the scope of government intervention. Initially, this is likely to lead to a fractious period of competing demands, confused alliances and petulant reactions by government and bureaucracy under attack. In the longer term, this public space will provide an arena for compromise.

CONCLUSION

While pre-crisis Thailand lacked the strong state, directed credit and industrial policy at the heart of the East Asian model, it achieved some of the same benefits through other means: a relatively efficient mobilization of capital by a protected banking system and Japanese-dominated FDI; the existence of a large rural society which could be squeezed to supply cheap labour; and access to technology and scarce skills through selective opening of both capital and labour markets.

The crisis has resulted in a sharply increased foreign penetration of the Thai economy. It has also removed two key features of the pre-crisis economy: the central role of the domestic banks in planning capital allocation, and the ability of the government to provide a limited amount of protection and market policing for domestic firms.

Thailand has progressed some considerable way towards the neoliberal goals of greater market liberalization, greater foreign penetration and reduced government intervention in the economy. However, as the economy returns to a more even keel, this new regime will have to cope with three long-run trends in the Thai political economy which do not feature in the neoliberal model. The first is the long-run trend towards a skewed income distribution in general, and more particularly to a gaping divide between the rural and urban economies. The restructuring during the crisis is likely to accentuate this trend in the future, rather than diminish it. The second is the long-run trend to a more open public politics which gives space to business interests and social segments which feel displaced or disadvantaged by the neoliberal trend. The third is the role of Japan, which has consistently backed a rather different model of Thailand's economic development, and whose investment commitment to the Thai economy has significantly increased over the crisis.

While the crisis has thus seen Thailand move along the neoliberal path, the future trend is not at all clear and uncontested. In the past year, international institutions, led by the World Bank, have placed greater emphasis on an agenda of democratization, governance, social safety nets and support for civil society. This new agenda – dubbed the 'New' or 'Post Washington' Consensus – recognizes that the earlier neoliberal agenda lacked social and political aspects, and that social and political reactions can threaten the economic programme (Jayasuriya and Rosser, 1999). This new agenda enshrines a belief that more open politics will strengthen the prospects for the success of the neoliberal economic agenda of open markets. In Thailand, where politics are already more open than in most Asian countries and where the crisis has stimulated participation and competition, this belief is likely to be put to the test. The groups which we expect to assert themselves after the crisis – small and medium businessmen who do not understand why their businesses were wrecked; farmers who have borne much of the social strain; civil society activists who are emboldened to build on recent success; and establishment radicals who are concerned about whether the society can absorb such a sudden change in foreign economic penetration – these groups have many good reasons not to support open markets without reservation.

At present two competing visions of the future are available, though neither is yet sharply defined in public debate. The first accepts and welcomes the fact that Thailand is moving from an era in which the main aim of economic policy was to develop a local capitalism, to an era in which Thailand will prosper as a host for multinational capital. This is the vision implied by the neoliberal agenda, and also favoured by many Thai technocrats who have become increasingly antagonistic to the old business conglomerates. The model is Singapore. The major problem lies in managing the social consequences. Singapore confronted this problem by building one of the world's most extensive systems of social welfare, concentrating public investment on education and infrastructure, and disposing of its rural sector (to Malaysia). Not all of these options are available to Bangkok. However, educational reform has risen to the top of the national agenda, while the World Bank and ADB are supporting schemes to extend social welfare at low cost by mobilizing and strengthening existing non-state provisions by family, community and self-help associations. Yet the fiscal constraint imposed by high levels of public debt, and the possibility of competing political demands for public expenditure, mean that this solution will require a significant retreat from democracy.

A second vision sees a resurgence of local capitalism among small and medium firms. This vision starts from the proposition that Thailand's entrepreneurial culture is still alive, and that the collapse of the conglomerates creates a more open space for the growth of small and medium firms. The model is Taiwan. Advocates suggest that this model is more appropriate to Thailand than the earlier concentration of growth in big domestic conglomerates, and that the benefits will be more widely distributed. This view finds support among formal business lobbies and some political parties (Thai Rak Thai, Chat Phatthana). It is roughly congruent with the Japanese vision to develop Thailand's foundation of service and subcontract businesses to support another wave of region-wide growth based on an outflow of Japanese manufacturing. However, the prospects for this vision depend on the construction of a political coalition able to defeat the neoliberal-inclined Democrat-led regime and its background support from Western business lobbies and international organizations. This model also faces the problem of budget constraints and competing political demands.

The prospects for this model depend on the performance of the Japanese economy. If the Japanese economy revives and delivers a new phase of regional growth, Thailand's economy and its economic policy will be pulled into line with Japanese strategy. But if the Western economies remain significantly stronger, the Singapore model will come more to the fore. More than ever, Thailand's political economy is hostage to the fortunes of the major forces in the global economy.

NOTES

1. The writers wish to thank the Thailand Research Fund and the Centre for Southeast Asian Studies at Kyoto University.
2. The two major pre-crisis versions of an Asian model are World Bank (1993) and UNCTAD (1996).
3. Definitions of the urban and rural population are not straightforward. Officially, only around 13 million live in the municipal area and 48 million outside. But this classification understates the extent of urbanization. Meanwhile around half of the total of 61 million belong to households whose main employment is in agriculture.
4. These figures include Errors and Omissions in private flows. The two-year total including the countervailing inward flow of FDI was equivalent to 29 per cent of annual GDP. See Pasuk and Baker (2000: Table 2).
5. In the case of Nakhon Thon Bank, the private negotiation stalled and government stepped in, took over the bank and completed the sale to Standard Chartered.
6. Thai Military Bank failed to raise new capital through an international roadshow in late 1999. The bank's advisers knew the project was doomed when some of the directors turned up to the meetings with foreign buyers dressed in full uniform.
7. The principal shareholder is the Crown Property Bureau.
8. 'We [bankers] are upset that the regulators are giving the country's economy to foreigners. First of all, the banking industry – which is the main blood of the economy – will be taken over by foreigners, then other industries will follow suit since they lack the liquidity to recapitalise . . . We are now in the third world war. It is the economic war and we are losing' (an anonymous banker in *Nation*, 13 November 1997).
9. With the exception of petrochemicals, which the group retained as a core business despite doubts about the over-capacity and comparative advantage of the Thai petrochemical industry.
10. In October 1997, 100 per cent foreign ownership was allowed in financial institutions (previously restricted to 25 per cent), but with a ten-year limitation which is seen as only a cosmetic touch. The 49 per cent limitation on businesses other than those US-owned or covered by specific export-promotion concessions was effectively lifted by a Board of Investment (BoI) provision. The Alien Business Law, which reserves certain sectors for Thai-only investment, has been revised and is currently at the final stages in parliament. Full foreign ownership of land is still restricted, but leasehold has been significantly liberalized.
11. Firms buying majority stakes included Merrill Lynch, Vickers Ballas, Société Générale. Crosby, AIG group, ING Barings, Indosuez W.I. Carr, Lehman Brothers, BNP, Bankers Trust and two Singaporean (DBS, Kim-Eng) and one Taiwanese (KG) firm (*Bangkok Post*, 25 August 1998).
12. In 1999, the number of chain convenience stores increased by 15 per cent, and the market leader, 7-Eleven, increased its turnover from 11 to 13 billion baht (*Bangkok Post*, 10 November 1999).
13. Brimble and Sherman's sample included deals in which the foreign participant put in at

least US$1 million *either* to buy an initial stake of at least 10 per cent *or* to convert a minority stake into a majority or outright ownership.

14. Between July 1997 and mid-1999, 45 large companies listed on the Stock Exchange of Thailand had offered their shares to foreign buyers. These included seven commercial banks, eight securities companies, three insurance companies and 27 others (Report of the Stock Exchange Commission, cited in Kamon, 1999).
15. The governor of the Bank of Thailand, Chatumongkol Sonakul, said government debt would rise to 2.5 trillion baht once it absorbed the debts incurred by the Financial Institutions Development Fund from the rescue of collapsed banks and finance companies. Chatumongkol commented: 'Outside your country it's a dog-eat-dog world and little dogs that don't behave get their heads bitten off' (*Nation*, 21 October 1999).
16. Several leading Thai bankers (for example, Chartsiri Sophonpanich of Bangkok Bank, in *Nation*, 4 May 1999) have stated that they too will focus on consumer banking and compete with the international banks. Less convincingly, they claim they will develop more lending to small and medium enterprises – a claim which is rather more politically correct than realistic. Chartsiri stated: 'Relationship banking used to generate 70 per cent of business, now it's probably 30 per cent' (*Nation*, 30 June 1999).
17. Import tariffs on 85 per cent of goods traded within ASEAN were cut to a range of 0–5 per cent from 1 January 1999.

REFERENCES

Baker, Chris (2000), 'Politics of crisis: failure, reform and division', in Peter Warr (ed.), *Thailand Beyond the Crisis*, London and New York: Routledge.

Bhanupong Nidhiprabha (1998), 'Economic crises and the debt–deflation episode in Thailand', *ASEAN Economic Bulletin*, 15 (3), December.

Brimble, Peter and James Sherman (1999), 'Mergers and Acquisitions in Thailand: The Changing Face of Foreign Direct Investment', prepared for the United Nations Conference on Trade and Development, 20 May.

Hewison, Kevin (ed.) (1997), *Political Change in Thailand: Democracy and Participation*, London and New York: Routledge.

Jansen, Karel (1990), *Finance, Growth and Stability: Financing Economic Development in Thailand, 1960–1980*, Aldershot: Avebury.

Jansen, Karel (1997), *External Finance in Thailand's Development*, London: Macmillan.

Jayasuriya, Kanishka and Andrew Rosser (1999), 'Economic orthodoxy and the East Asian crisis', working paper no. 94, Asia Research Centre, Murdoch University, November.

Kamon Kamontrakun (1999), 'Ongkon lok lae aphi maha thun tang kam chat amnat setthakit thi ying yai nai kan khrop khrong lok' (Global organizations, large global enterprises and their power of global control), in Phittaya Wongkun (ed.), *Withithat: Lokaphiwat 12: wikrit lok phan world bank yut chat thai* (*Vision: globalization series no. 12: world crisis and the World Bank's plan to seize Thailand*), Bangkok: Amarin Printing.

Khan, Mushtaq H. (1998), 'Patron–client networks and the economic effects of corruption in Asia', *European Journal of Development Research*, 10 (1), June.

Pasuk Phongpaichit and Chris Baker (1995), *Thailand: Economy and Politics*, Kuala Lumpur: Oxford University Press.

Pasuk Phongpaichit and Chris Baker (1998), *Thailand's Boom and Bust*, Chiang Mai: Silkworm Books.

Pasuk Phongpaichit and Chris Baker (2000), 'Thailand's crisis: neoliberal agenda and local reaction', in Ha-Joon Chang, Gabriel Palma and Hugh Whittaker (eds), *Financial Liberalization and the Asian Crisis*, London: Macmillan.

Phatra Research Institute (1997), 'The way out of the economic crisis', unpublished paper, Bangkok, 30 September.

Praphat Pintoptaeng (1998), *Kan muang bon thong thanon: 99 wan samatcha khon chon* (*Politics on the street: 99 days of the Assembly of the Poor*), Bangkok: Krirk University.

Suehiro, Akira (1989), *Capital Accumulation in Thailand 1855–1985*, Tokyo: Centre for East Asian Cultural Studies.

Suehiro, Akira (2000), 'The Asian crisis and economic and social restructuring: Americanization and social governance', unpublished paper.

Thailand Development Research Institute (TDRI), Macroeconomic Policy Program (1999), 'Financial reforms in Thailand', *TDRI Quarterly Review*, 14 (4), December.

UNCTAD (1996), *Trade and Development Report, 1996*, New York and Geneva: UNCTAD.

UNCTAD (1998), *Trade and Development Report, 1998*, New York and Geneva: UNCTAD.

Wade, Robert and Frank Veneroso (1998), 'The Asian crisis: the high-debt model vs. the Wall Street–Treasury–IMF complex', *New Left Review*, 228, March–April.

Westphal, Larry (1989), *Assessing Thailand's Technological Capabilities in Industry*, Bangkok: Thailand Development Research Institute.

World Bank (1993), *The East Asian Miracle: Growth and Public Policy*, New York: Oxford University Press.

6. Indonesia: beyond shallow, export-led industrialization

Shafiq Dhanani and Syed Asif Hasnain[1]

INTRODUCTION

Export orientation can lead to rapid industrialization and higher living standards, as forcefully demonstrated by the experience of the newly industrialized countries (NICs) of Southeast Asia in the past three decades. Among the usual advantages of export-orientation are foreign exchange earnings (provided manufacturing is not overly dependent on imported inputs and foreign capital), exposure of domestic firms to international competition and consequent increase in their efficiency, transfer of technology, the fuller utilization of resources in which the country has comparative advantage, particularly natural resources and labour, and employment generation.

There are nevertheless several disadvantages, as well as inherent limitations, which have to be addressed in the course of export-led industrialization. First, an open economy highly dependent on a few markets for its exports is likely to be quite vulnerable to external shocks such as price changes in imported inputs and exports, and movement in exchange rates, largely outside its control. Second, other lower-cost producers can rapidly erode the comparative advantage of low-wage production. Third, the more successful a country is in the export of manufactured goods, the more likely it is going to face import barriers or to reach its quota limits. Fourth, changes in technology such as robotization and computer-controlled manufacturing can significantly reduce the competitive advantage of labour-intensive methods of production, while computer-aided inventory systems and lean production processes often require component manufacturers to be located nearby. Finally, a growing balance of trade surplus is likely to put upward pressure on exchange rates.

Following a sharp decline in oil revenues and increasing balance of payment difficulties in 1982, the Indonesian government adopted an export-led industrialization strategy, with the emphasis on private sector-led growth and the promotion of resource-based and labour-intensive export products. This contrasted with the previous import-substitution strategy pursued since the mid-1970s, which focused on public investment in state-owned industries in steel, chemical, cement, fertilizer and other basic industries. Growth in the manufacturing sector accelerated in the 1985–8 period, and was particularly rapid in the period 1989–92. However, the growth of the manufacturing sector and of manufacturing exports slowed down noticeably in the subsequent period, 1993–7, four years before the crisis.

This chapter argues that the observed slowdown was primarily a consequence of shallow, export-led industrialization. As a result, the country reaped only some of the advantages associated with export-oriented industrialization while suffering most of the disadvantages of such a strategy noted above. Following a review of industrial policy since the mid-1960s in the next section, the third section reviews some of the major structural as well as institutional weaknesses which marked the actual pattern of industrial development in Indonesia, and which eventually dampened manufactured growth. These include a continuously high dependence on imported raw materials and components; low value-added generated in resource-based and labour-intensive industries; a virtually non-existent capital goods sector; limited range in export products and markets; singular specialization in labour-intensive but demand inelastic manufactured products combined with fierce international competition in the export markets from lower cost producers; low-productivity in small and medium industries; high market concentration in many segments of industry; weak human resources; weak technology support systems; and weak manufacturing capabilities of domestic firms.

The fourth section discusses how the economic crisis, begun in mid-1997, as well as the emerging challenges of liberalization and globalization, will further exacerbate these inherent weaknesses in the patterns of manufacturing development. To regain the momentum of the early 1990s and to take industrialization to its next stage of broader and technologically more resilient development, this section suggests the adoption of a comprehensive industrial strategy to be implemented at three levels.

The fifth section of the chapter concludes that, just as the import-substitution strategy of the 1960s and 1970s gave way to an export-oriented strategy in the 1980s and 1990s, the full benefits of the export-led strategy as well as the changing international environment call for more creative and innovative strategies which rely on closer public–private partnerships. While a liberal trading and investment environment is necessary, the full benefits of an export-oriented strategy will not accrue automatically. The government must play a more active and complementary role to the market, but different from that in the past. It should not only get prices right and continue to improve the business environment and physical and human resources, but also implement concrete and practical public–private measures to directly improve the competitiveness of manufacturing firms in Indonesia.

INDUSTRIAL DEVELOPMENT POLICY, 1965–2000

Indonesian industrial development policy since President Soeharto came to power in 1965, can be divided into three broad phases. The first period, between 1965 and 1975, was characterized by an open-door economic strategy, aimed at producing maximum economic growth and relying heavily on investment by international corporate capital. Having inherited a debt-ridden and chaotic economy, the government was desperate to renegotiate debts and attract foreign investment. Following government guarantees to foreign investors, this period witnessed the re-entry of foreign capital, short-term foreign loans in the form of import credits to finance extensive commodity imports in the late 1960s, so crucial to bringing rampant inflation under control, and long-term foreign loans to rehabilitate infrastructure (Robison, 1986: 138).

The second period, 1975–81, buoyed by high oil prices and substantial state revenues, saw the resurgence of economic nationalism in which the state played a more active role in financing, protecting and subsidizing domestic capital, and in direct investment. In addition, the stated policy was the creation of a national heavy industrial capacity, based on major resource projects in steel, natural gas, oil refining and aluminium, and on import substitution. Japan, eager to penetrate the previously US-dominated energy and resource sectors, provided finance outside the normal channels of IGGI (Inter-Governmental Group for Indonesia) finance to build basic industries. Manufacturing growth averaged 8 per cent per annum between 1975 and 1981 (Table 6.1).

Efforts were initiated in this period to increase non-oil exports by offering tax and other incentives to investments to increase foreign exchange earnings. In 1978, a 34 per cent devaluation was carried out to increase the competitiveness of non-oil exports. However, its effectiveness was short-lived and, by 1981, the rupiah was almost back to its pre-devaluation level.

The third period, starting in 1982, began with the collapse of oil prices, and of domestic and foreign exchange revenues. The ensuing economic crisis prompted the government to seek larger IBRD (International Bank for Reconstruction and Development) and IGGI loans, making the government increasingly susceptible to pressures to facilitate foreign capital entry, the adoption of free-market, open-door policies, and the restructuring of the Indonesian economy in a less protectionist environment. The state-led drive to achieve an integrated, national, industrial capitalist economy

Table 6.1 Indonesia: manufacturing sector performance (non-oil and gas), 1975–99

	75–81[1]	82–84	85–88	89–93	94–97	98–99
Average growth rates (% p.a.)						
Manufacturing value-added	8	5	13	20	12	−7[2]
Manufactured exports (SIT categories 5–8)	34	29	27	27	8	2
Export of plywood, textiles, garments, footwear	94	64	32	28	2	−7
Structural change (end of period)						
% manufacturing value-added in GDP[3]	8	11	14	19	23	23
% manufactures in total exports	4	11	31	54	50	57
Balance in manufactured trade (US$ bn)[4]						
Exports	0.8	1.8	3.9	13.4	24.4	27.2
Imports	6.3	10.3	8.8	18.6	29.5	16.9
Balance	−5.5	−8.5	−4.9	−5.2	−5.1	10.3

Notes:
1. 1978–81 instead of 1975–81 for exports, imports and trade balance.
2. Growth rate for 1998 only.
3. Manufacturing value-added from national accounts (includes household and small industries).
4. Annual average.

Sources: Manufacturing value-added: *Large & Medium Industrial Statistics*, annual publication, CBS (back-cast series; nominal value-added deflated by 3-digit industry-specific wholesale price index); exports and imports: *Foreign Trade Statistics* (in US$), Central Bureau of Statistics; GDP: national accounts, Central Bureau of Statistics.

slowed down considerably, largely as a result of the decline in oil income, which had financed the huge investments in infrastructure and industrial and resource projects (Robison, 1986: 375). An export-oriented industrialization strategy was adopted, without however renouncing the protection of several industries serving the domestic market. The requirement for foreign investors to form joint-venture partnerships with local firms remained.

In addition to a 28 per cent devaluation in April 1983, an export promotion package was introduced, providing low interest rates for export credits. However, these efforts produced disappointing results. Manufacturing exports reached just 11 per cent of total exports in 1984 (Table 6.1). Other elements of the strategy consisted of reforms such as the deregulation of investment licensing, the deregulation of the banking and financial sector, the removal of credit ceilings and preferences in credit provision, the reform of the custom and excise administration system and the import duty drawback system for exporters of manufactured goods. Export competitiveness was given a major boost by a third devaluation of 30 per cent of the rupiah in 1986, followed by a managed 5 per cent annual devaluation against the dollar in the following years.

The 1985 Plaza currency realignment accord led to the rapid reevaluation of the currencies of many advanced countries, resulting in a restructuring of regional manufacturing capacity. Many Japanese companies, particularly in the consumer electronics and automotive industries, shifted production abroad. In the Southeast Asian region, the major beneficiaries were Thailand, Malaysia and Indonesia. This move was facilitated by the liberalization of the Japanese financial markets and government assistance in relocation for enhanced markets and cheaper production costs (Pempel, 1999: 67). These investments continued to flow into Indonesia during the 1990s, and they were followed towards the late 1980s by labour-intensive garment and footwear firms from South Korea, Taiwan, Hong Kong and Singapore, whose rapidly expanding export-oriented economies led to higher current account surpluses, higher currency values, labour shortages and rising production costs. As a result of these large inward investments, as well as substantial domestic investments, Indonesia's manufacturing growth rate accelerated from 13 per cent per annum during 1985–8 to 20 per cent per annum during 1989–93.

However not all free-market arguments were accepted in this period. To promote higher value production in the forest sector, for example, the government imposed a ban on the export of logs to encourage the export of plywood. There also remained an extensive negative list of investment closed to foreign investment, which was only gradually reduced. A number of import-substitution sectors, where the interest of state-owned firms and domestic business groups of military bureaucrats and private capital predominated, remained protected, including auto assembly, cement, steel, heavy engineering, metal fabrication and pharmaceuticals. The requirement to form partnerships with local firms remained.

In mid-1994, a new foreign investment regulation finally lifted the local partner requirement, allowing foreign firms to hold 100 per cent equity in Indonesia for the first time. The negative list was also reduced considerably, effectively barring foreign direct investment (FDI) only from strategic and environmentally undesirable industries. Foreign investment inflows surged in the 1994–7 period as a result of this package, as well as being partly driven by the worldwide boom in FDI (Soesastro *et al.*, 2000). Nevertheless, manufacturing growth began to slow down in the period 1994–7, four years before the economic crisis. While still rapid by international standards, the growth of manufacturing value-added nearly halved, from an annual average of 20 per cent in 1989–93 to 12 per cent in 1994–7. This was partly the result of the slowdown in the growth of manufacturing exports, from 27 per cent to 8 per cent per annum in these two periods. In fact the growth rate of earnings of Indonesia's four major export products (plywood, textiles, garments and footwear) reached a plateau by 1993, and stagnated during 1994–7. A number of factors contributed to the slowdown of manufacturing growth, some of them long-standing, while others resulting from rapid, export-led industrialization. These are discussed in the next section.

Since the onset of the economic crisis in mid-1997, both domestic and foreign investment resources have plummeted. By 1999, gross domestic capital formation declined from 32 per cent to 19 per cent of GDP, while FDI inflows had dried up, from US$6.5 billion in 1996/97 to $1.6 billion in 1997/98, and nil in 1998/99 (Dhanani, 2000: 67). Since 1998, the Indonesian government has been particularly sensitive to the need to increase investment resources, and has embarked on an intensive promotional campaign to woo foreign investors back into the country. In fact, as far as official pronouncements are concerned, industrial policy has been equated with re-establishing investor confidence to attract FDI in the manufacturing sector. A 1998 regulation focused on simplifying approval and licensing procedures, and reducing the negative list of industries closed to FDI (Soesastro *et al.*, 2000). Otherwise, the authorities were preoccupied with resolving the substantial debt problems of domestic corporations and the financial restructuring of large manufacturing firms, under the tutelage of the Indonesian Bank Restructuring Agency.

As part of the its recovery programme with the International Monetary Fund, Indonesia has reaffirmed its commitment to trade liberalization, and to agreements made under the Asian Free Trade Association and World Trade Organization rules. Notwithstanding a sharp drop in manufacturing production (−7 per cent growth rate in 1998) and the weak predicament of most manufacturing firms, the government pressed ahead with tariff reductions and the removal of non-tariff barriers. As a consequence, Indonesia may have possessed one of the most liberalized economies in Southeast Asia by 2000.

Finally, a new investment regulation of June 2000 imposed certain restrictions on foreign investment, such as the need to establish a joint venture with a local partner and limited equity ownership. However, such conditions applied mainly to sectors outside manufacturing, such as media, energy, ports, transport, trade and restaurants (*Jakarta Post*, 7 August 2000). As in the past, restrictions affected environmentally damaging or strategic industries such as sawmills and those sectors utilizing certain types of chemicals.

STRUCTURAL AND ORGANIZATIONAL WEAKNESSES

While the government has assiduously promoted export-oriented industrialization since 1985, neither the government nor the private sector accompanied this drive with the necessary measures to diversify export products and markets, to deepen and diversify the manufacturing base, and to enhance the competitiveness of Indonesian firms. The absence of these measures to compensate for known market failures in building up manufacturing capability, such as inadequate information, high risks and a long and expensive learning process (Lall, 1993, 1995), and the sheer rapidity of industrialization, led to a relatively shallow industrial structure, while the promised foreign exchange earnings failed to materialize.

A number of other structural problems emerged. The oil and gas sector generated only limited net revenues. Low productivity plagued the small and medium-scale industries, while significant market concentration by a few large firms prevailed in large segments of manufacturing. Manufacturing production remained concentrated in Java, and in Greater Jakarta in particular. The capacity to absorb, adapt and develop process and product technology as well as human resources remained weak. Finally, little effective institutional support from government departments or from industry associations was available to manufacturing firms.

Deficit in Merchandise Trade

The overall fragility of industrial development in Indonesia is most apparent in the persistent deficit in the balance of trade of manufactured products. Despite 15 years of rapid industrialization, the balance of trade in manufactures was in deficit from 1985 until the onset of the crisis in 1997. The gap between manufactured imports and manufacturing exports remained at US$5 billion per year throughout this period (Table 6.1). As a result, Indonesia ran increasingly large deficits in the current account of the balance of payments, from $2 billion in 1985–6 to $8 billion in 1996–7, which were offset by large inflows of private capital and external public borrowing.

More recently, the balance of trade in manufactures has shown a surplus in 1998 and 1999. While part of this is due to the recovery of exports, most of the surplus generated over the past two years was due to a collapse of imports, primarily of capital goods, reflecting the drastic slowdown in investment over the last two years. It is highly likely that, as the economy and investments recover, the trade deficit in manufactures will reappear. It remains to be seen whether this will be offset by a capital account surplus as in the past.

Reliance on a Limited Number of Export Products and Markets

Manufacturing development relied to a great extent on the rapid expansion of exports in which Indonesia had a comparative advantage in terms of plentiful, fairly good quality labour, good infrastructure and natural resources. However, exports were highly concentrated in terms of both products and markets. Thus four products accounted for half of exports (plywood, garments, textiles and footwear; see Figure 6.1). Market access for two of these, textiles and garments, was seriously constrained by non-tariff barriers to countries abiding by the Multi-fibre Agreement (MFA), while the domestic supply of timber had reached its limit of sustainability. Furthermore, three countries accounted for over half of exports (the United States, Japan and Singapore), while one country, the United States, absorbed nearly half of the total exports of garments and footwear. Ten products provided 80 per cent of all the country's manufactured export revenues. Exports were thus highly vulnerable to the changing fortunes of these few products in limited markets.

More importantly, many of the labour-intensive exports selected by Indonesia have suffered from a secular decline in world prices due to intense international competition, particularly from China, Latin America and other low-cost producers in the North American market, and from Eastern Europe in the West European market. Indonesian labour-intensive exports also faced a relatively inelastic demand in industrialized country markets. External factors rather than internal factors such as rising wage rates were thus responsible for the declining competitiveness of traditional Indonesian exports. Indonesian firms managed to contain unit labour costs by increasing labour productivity, and also maintained profitability before the economic crisis.

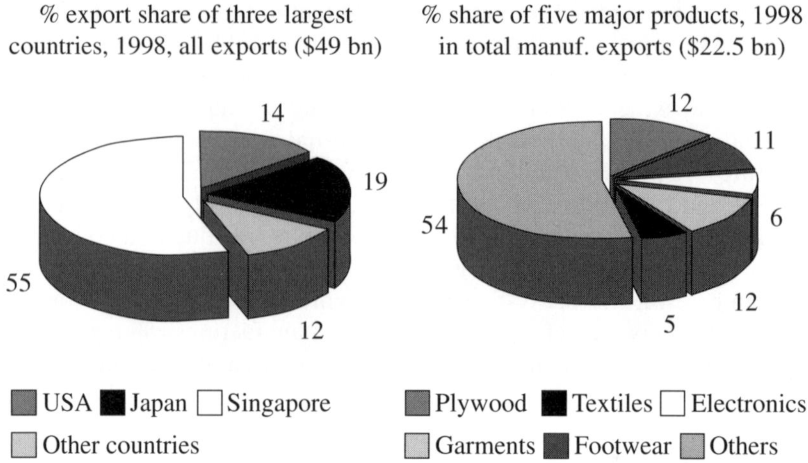

Source: CBS, *Foreign Trade Statistics, 1998*.

Figure 6.1 Indonesia: Export product and market concentration, 1998

In many ways, Indonesian export products behaved similarly to agricultural export commodities, especially since many of them were exported with minimal processing and therefore limited value-added (plywood, pulp, paper, palm oil). The massive devaluation of the rupiah following the onset of the crisis has restored the overall competitiveness of these Indonesian export products. Export volumes have risen in some cases (garments, textiles); however, export revenues have risen only slightly in dollar terms owing to the devaluation and the continuing decline in the world price of textiles, garments, wood, footwear and furniture.

Import Dependence

The manufacturing sector was heavily dependent on imported components and machinery. Many industries have consisted primarily of simple blending, packaging and assembly operations, with the result that, in 1997, the value of imported raw materials, intermediate inputs and components ranged from 45 per cent in chemical industries to 53 per cent in machinery, 56 per cent in transport equipment industries and 70 per cent in electrical goods industries (Figure 6.2). Even labour-intensive industries relied heavily on imported raw materials, intermediate inputs and components, ranging from 40–43 per cent in the textile, garment and leather industries to 56 per cent in the footwear industry. Moreover, this extent of import dependence changed little during the course of the 1990s. The development of the capacity of domestic supplier and support industries is a demanding task because firms face high risks and a lengthy and costly learning process. Market failures in this respect suggest the need for the government to assist domestic firms in building up their manufacturing capacity.

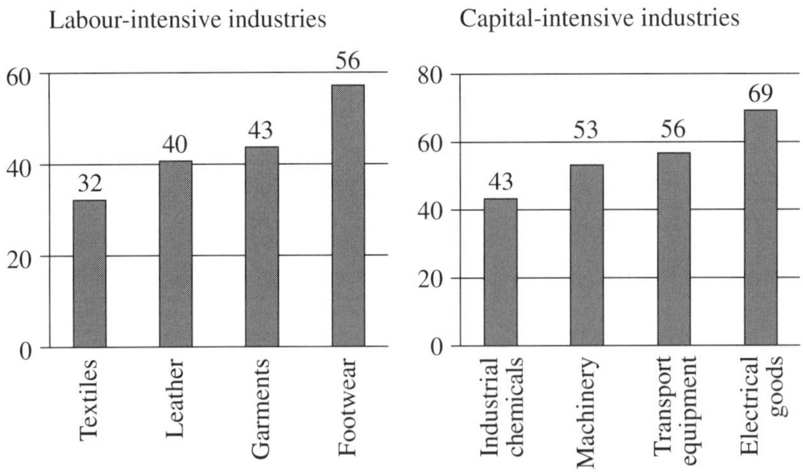

Source: CBS, *Large and Medium Industrial Statistics, 1997 (special tabulations)*.

Figure 6.2 Import content of manufacturing inputs, 1997 (%)

As for capital goods, most plant and equipment originated abroad. Capital goods accounted for nearly half of the total manufactured imports. Unlike the case of China and India, the capital goods industry is very small in Indonesia (2 per cent versus 9 per cent of manufacturing value-added in China and India). Efforts to establish a machine tool industry, as well as a motor vehicle component industry, have met with very limited success. Yet the production of capital goods and intermediate components plays a very special role in industrialization because they engage firms in developing their manufacturing capabilities through activities such as reverse engineering and adapting foreign technology to domestic markets, products and scales of production. They also provide the technological base for further industrial diversification and the deepening of production.

Lack of Industrial Depth

The pattern of Indonesian industrialization differed from that of other countries with similar degrees of industrialization. Between 1985 and 1997, the contribution of higher technology industries to manufacturing value-added did not increase, while the production of low-technology industries expanded, mainly at the expense of medium-technology industries (Figure 6.3). The increase in the share of low-technology industries was due to the rapid growth of labour-intensive industries such as textiles, garments and footwear, and to a lesser extent to the expansion of the resource-based food, paper and wood industries. In contrast to the decline of medium-technology industries in Indonesia (including the rubber and plastic industries, fertilizer, cement, basic metals and the simple fabricated metal industry) virtually all countries in the region and elsewhere have maintained the share of medium-technology industries in their manufacturing output. Similarly, the contribution of physical capital-intensive products to total exports also declined during this period.

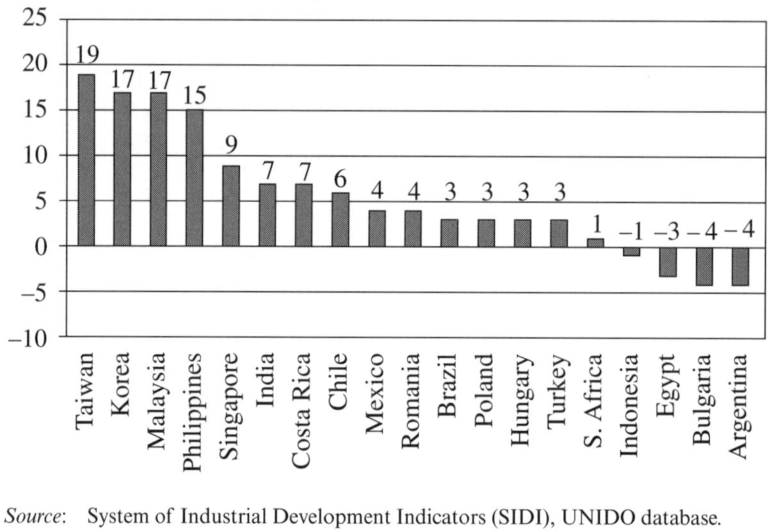

Source: System of Industrial Development Indicators (SIDI), UNIDO database.

Figure 6.3 Percentage change in share of higher technology industries in manufacturing value-added, 1985–97

Starting in 1990, Indonesia made substantial progress in investing in higher-technology industries such as pharmaceuticals, chemicals, consumer electronics, electrical appliances, motorcycles and motor vehicles. The exports of consumer electronics and electrical goods in particular are a good example of manufacturing and export diversification. However, since they were mainly final assembly manufacturers of imported raw materials and intermediate inputs, as noted above, they generated limited domestic value-added, associated mainly with inexpensive labour. In other words, industries in this category were similar to labour-intensive industries, relying on good-quality assembly labour, efficient infrastructure and good trading links in the region.

Foreign Direct Investment

Despite the much heralded success in attracting foreign investment to Indonesia, the manufacturing sector enjoyed rather limited benefits in terms of exports, employment, tax revenues, linkages with the rest of the manufacturing sector and technology transfer in the 1990s. FDI amounted to just 3–6 per cent of total capital formation (Lall, 1998; Dhanani, 2000: 56), though most of this was directed at the manufacturing sector. The persistent gap in production efficiency, labour productivity and higher wages between foreign and domestic firms further suggests minimal adoption of best manufacturing practices by the latter. Foreign firms may even have prolonged the manufacturing sector's dependence on foreign suppliers of raw materials and components.

According to a recent study by the United Nations Industrial Organization (UNIDO), foreign establishments accounted for about 25 per cent of medium and large-scale manufacturing production, and 35 per cent of total manufactured exports in 1996 (Table 6.2). However, because foreign establishments also imported more than half of their inputs, their net export earnings were lower than for domestic firms as a proportion of total production (8 per cent versus 12 per cent). Even these limited foreign exchange earnings may have been offset by the outflows of repatriated profits, royalties and fees. Moreover, owing to their higher capital intensity, foreign establishments employed just 15 per cent of the manufacturing workforce, and equivalent to less than 1 per cent of the total Indonesian workforce. Thus domestic firms continued to account for the bulk of manufacturing production, employment and export earnings.

Foreign establishments did not develop linkages with domestic firms, or promote industrial diversification and technological deepening. They operated rather like enclave industries, establishing fewer linkages with the rest of the manufacturing sector than their domestic counterparts. While the latter bought only a quarter of their inputs from abroad, foreign establishments imported 55 per cent of their inputs in most sub-sectors, even in relatively simple industries such as garments and footwear. This proportion in fact rose to 60 per cent following the onset of the crisis. In higher-technology industries such as medicines, machinery, electronics and vehicle components, foreign establishments bought around 90 per cent of their inputs from abroad and transformed them into components and finished products, using inexpensive Indonesian labour and good infrastructure, for the domestic and export markets. That higher linkages were possible in many of these

Table 6.2 Indonesia: contribution of FDI to manufacturing, 1990–98 (percentage of total)

	1990	1993	1996	1998
Value-added	100	100	100	100
Foreign	19	21	27	25
Domestic private	74	73	60	52
Public	7	6	13	24
Gross exports	100	100	100	100
Foreign	20	26	35	33
Domestic private	75	72	62	65
Public	5	2	3	3
% production exported, gross	12	20	27	14
Foreign	12	28	35	15
Domestic private	12	20	25	15
Public	9	6	9	5
% production exported, net*	0	6	10	−3
Foreign	−9	1	8	−15
Domestic private	3	9	12	3
Public	3	−4	1	−4
Employment (000s)	237	480	694	619
Percentage	100	100	100	100
Foreign	9	13	16	19
Domestic private	82	80	78	74
Public	9	7	6	27
Import content of inputs (%)	31	28	32	33
Foreign	54	55	55	57
Domestic private	25	22	24	23

Note: *Net exports = gross exports minus imports of raw materials, inputs and components.

Source: S. Dhanani (2000: 59), *Indonesia: Strategy for Manufacturing Competitiveness*, Jakarta: United Nations Industrial Development Organization (based on special tabulations of the *Large and Medium Industrial Statistics*, annual publication, Central Bureau of Statistics).

industries is indicated by the significantly higher local content of inputs procured by domestic establishments in similar industries.

The extent and quality of technology transfer from FDI to domestic firms and to the domestic economy is more difficult to assess. The lack of progress in four indicators used in the above UNIDO study – difference over time in production efficiency, trends in the development of domestic supplier and support industries, training and growth of external linkages – suggest that, though foreign establishments are likely to have shared their technology with their joint-venture partners, particularly with respect to production organization and quality management, they had only a limited impact in the upgrading of technology of domestic firms at large.

As noted, the post-1985 restructuring of manufacturing within the East Asian and Southeast Asian region drove industrialization and export growth in Indonesia. The influx of foreign direct investment, particularly from Japan and the newly industrialized countries of Taiwan, South Korea and Singapore, brought the technical, managerial and marketing skills needed to produce goods for the world markets. These were able to plug Indonesia into the world trade system almost overnight by incorporating local producers in the manufacturing and trading chain of foreign buying agents and intermediaries. Given the rapidity of investment growth and the transfer of entire components of regional manufacturing systems, technology transfer to Indonesian partners in the broad sense (including technical, management, organizational and marketing skills, quality management, technical information, product development and external linkages) was necessarily limited. Perhaps the rapid exposure to FDI may also have slowed down the development of indigenous manufacturing capability of domestic firms, and their ability to move up the value chain through indigenous product development, own brand names and own marketing channels.

Limited Net Revenue Generated by the Oil and Gas Sector

The large oil and gas sector generated relatively limited surplus. Balance of payment data show that the total exports of $13 billion were to a large extent offset by imports of oil products amounting to $5 billion and oil-related services of another $4 billion, leaving a surplus of just $4 billion or 35 per cent of gross revenues in 1996–7. In fact, Indonesia ran an overall deficit in services both in the oil and gas sector and in other services.

Low Employment Generation

The medium and large-scale manufacturing establishments employed some 4 million workers about 4 per cent of the total workforce of around 90 million. Starting in 1992, manufacturing wages began to rise by about 10 per cent per annum. Employers managed to contain unit labour costs by raising labour productivity, but at the cost of slowing down the recruitment of new workers. The annual surveys of medium and large-scale manufacturing industries show that the value-added–employment elasticity declined from 0.5 in 1989–93 to 0.3 in 1994–7 in the manufacturing sector as a whole, and from 0.4–0.3 to 0.1 in textiles and garments. The low elasticities in these two relatively labour-intensive industries were the result of very small additions to the workforce, of the order of 1 per cent as against 10–15 per cent per annum in the previous period, while continuing to post healthy 10–15 per cent annual growth rates in output.

Regional Concentration

Medium and large-scale manufacturing industries were heavily concentrated in Java and in Greater Jakarta in particular (Figure 6.4). Despite special incentives offered by the government, overall manufacturing production continued to be concentrated in Java. Jakarta and West Java in fact increased their share of manufacturing employment and value-added to around half of the country's total by 1997, due to factors such as large market size, good infrastructure and proximity to government officials (role of market, infrastructure, proximity to government officials). The total manufacturing sector in Outer Java was about the same size at that of East Java (20 per cent) and about half the size of Jakarta–West Java.

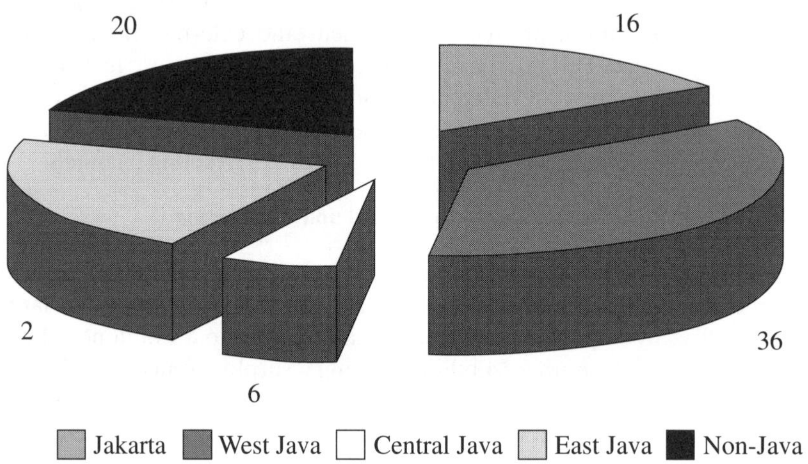

Source: CBS, *Large and Medium Industrial Statistics, 1997.*

Figure 6.4 Regional distribution of manufacturing value-added, 1997

Underdeveloped Small and Medium-scale Industries

Small and medium-scale industries (SMIs) contributed relatively little to manufacturing value-added. Large establishments (100+ workers/establishment) employed a third of the manufacturing labour but produced 80 per cent of manufacturing value-added in almost all sub-sectors, and thus dominated the Indonesian manufacturing sector (Figure 6.5). Medium-scale, small-scale and household industries employed an average of 37, eight and two workers per establishment, respectively, and accounted for just 5–6 per cent each of total manufacturing value-added while employing two-thirds of the manufacturing workforce, denoting low productivity. SMIs were concentrated in the food and wood sub-sectors. They produced final consumer goods and not many raw materials, intermediate inputs and components for the rest of the manufacturing sector. In other words, subcontractor–supplier linkages between SMIs and larger establishments were virtually non-existent.

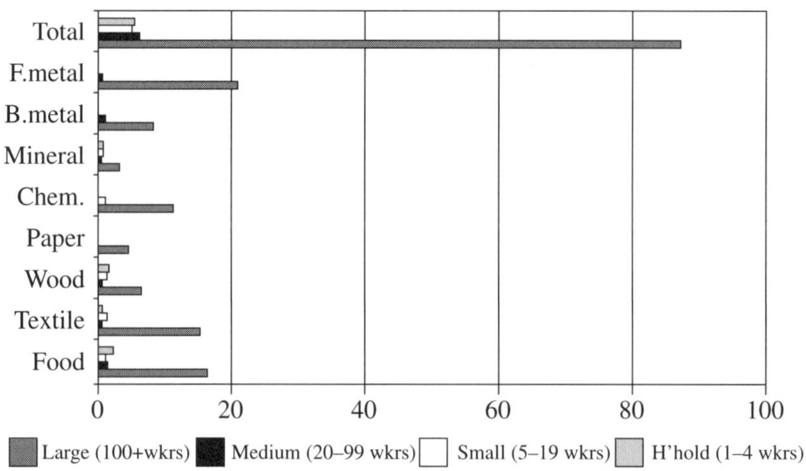

Source: CBS, *Large and Medium-scale Industrial Statistics, 1996*, *Small-scale Manufacturing Industry Statistics 1996* and *Household and Cottage Industry Statistics 1996*.

Figure 6.5 Size distribution of manufacturing value-added, 1996

Market Concentration

High levels of concentration were found across large segments of manufacturing, potentially stifling domestic competition. The output share of the four largest firms (CR4) amounted to more than three-quarters of the total output of nearly half of the industrial branches. The average unweighted four-firm concentration ratio remained high, at nearly 70 per cent in 1997 (Dhanani 2000: 22).

As expected, some of the largest CR4 ratios occurred in capital-intensive industries such as pulp (90 per cent), industrial papers (92 per cent), single fertilizers (82 per cent), compound fertilizers (100 per cent), tyres (87 per cent), glass sheets (90 per cent), cement (66 per cent), basic iron and steel

(87 per cent), electronics (65 per cent), motor vehicles (93 per cent) and motorcycles (99 per cent). However, they were also high in other industries, such as wheat flour mills (100 per cent), cigarettes (96 per cent), pharmaceutical products (97 per cent) and soaps and toothpaste (73 per cent) (CBS, 2000). Foreign firms were important players in many of these industries.

Weak Technology Development

Three entities could have played an important role in harnessing foreign technology and know-how to improve the competitiveness of the manufacturing sectors, namely: foreign direct investment, Indonesian conglomerates and the state-assigned R&D institutions. Recent assessments of technology transfer have concluded that none was successful in this regard, and institutions involved in technology transfer remain particularly weak and ineffective (Thee and Pangestu, 1994; Thee, 1998; Lall, 1998).

Many foreign investors in the domestic consumer-durable industries came to Indonesia for high profits under protection (World Bank, 1993). Those in the export-oriented sector came for low-cost labour. As noted earlier, they did not transfer technology (technical information, organizational, managerial skills and marketing skills, R&D) or develop significant domestic supplier or support industries.

The Indonesian conglomerates worked on the basis of establishing multi-sector, diversified business interests, manufacturing usually being one component of a diverse business portfolio. The advantage of this strategy was the rapid accumulation of capital and consequent growth through a broad front of corporate activity and a diversification of business risk. The disadvantage was the lack of concentration on building core competencies in manufacturing by most conglomerates.

As for the government, Indonesia has relied on an outdated model of state intervention for developing or adapting technology, characterized by direct state control of R&D and production activity, high levels of protection and state subsidies to high-technology industries. Though the strategic industries may have absorbed and adopted technology within their own environment in their quest for technological leapfrogging, they did not interact or provide technical leadership to the private sector, while even competing with the private sector in areas such as shipbuilding. Thus they have not produced or disseminated technology of use to commercial enterprises.

Weak Human Resource Development

Several assessments of the Indonesian education and training system at the primary, secondary, vocational and professional levels indicate that it does not meet the needs of industry. School leavers and graduates are thus not equipped with the knowledge and skills required for a more complex and diversified manufacturing sector, and are thus unlikely to benefit fully from in-plant training.

At the primary and secondary school levels, surveys to test student competencies and other diagnostic surveys consistently reveal that schools rely on rote learning and do not develop adequate mastery of basic literacy, basic numeracy, and thinking and creative skills (for primary schools see, for instance, Sweeting, 1997; Blazely, 1999, for secondary schools, see Blazely *et al.*, 1996; Sadtono *et al.*, 1996; Somerset, 1996).

At the vocational level, the senior secondary technical vocational schools, mostly in the private sector, are poorly equipped and staffed, and do not impart sufficient practical knowledge. As a result, the labour market does not differentiate between general and vocational senior secondary school leavers, paying them the same wage and allocating to them the same jobs in industry (Dhanani, 1995). Post-secondary vocational technical education is provided primarily by the government, under the Ministry of Manpower and the Ministry of Industry, and not the private sector. The changes in technology and product mix taking place in the economy have not been substantial enough to bring about corresponding market changes in the demand and therefore the supply of the required training from the private sector (ibid.).

At the higher education level, employer surveys show that science and engineering institutions are producing poor quality graduates, unable to work independently, and with inadequate general skills in problem solving, technical problem analysis, teamwork, technical report writing and oral presentation skills. As a result, many employers have to provide training in these basic skills to graduates upon recruitment (Dhanani and Sweeting, 1995).

As for in-plant training, the majority of firms do not undertake on-the-job training because they find it unnecessary given the dominance of simple processes in their plants. Those that do, mostly in the higher-technology category, do not do it extensively or systematically (Dhanani, 1992).

Fragmented Responsibility for Industrial Promotion and Policy

Owing to the complexity of the industrial sector, various aspects of industrial policy and promotion are shared among ten government departments. Taking sectoral agencies first, besides the Ministry of Industry and Trade, the Departments of Agriculture and Health are respectively in charge of selected agro-processing and pharmaceutical industries, while the Ministry of Cooperatives and Small-scale Enterprises is responsible for small-scale industries, and the Ministry of Mines and Energy for oil and gas production and refineries. Next, all tariff changes and VAT matters are handled by the Ministry of Finance, while the State Ministry for Investment and State-owned Enterprises is responsible for the formulation of investment policies, the approval of foreign direct investment, and for managing all the state-owned enterprises.

The National Development Planning Board is responsible for planning and resource allocation, as well as approving and monitoring all industrial projects funded by bilateral, multilateral and national agencies. The Board for Science and Technology is charged with developing technology. Since the onset of the crisis, the Indonesian Bank Restructuring Agency (IBRA) has owned a large number of manufacturing establishments and has appointed its officials on the board of directors of companies pledged as collateral by banks.

As a result of the shared responsibility at the central level, and the increasingly important role played by provisional and district governments in the wake of regional autonomy, there is a need for more strategic and tightly coordinated industrial policy and promotion.

Relatively Narrow Focus of Industry Associations

Interactions between government officials and the existing industry associations have been mostly limited to taxation and regulations. They have not often taken the form of meaningful public–private dialogue and collaboration in important areas such as investment and trade promotion strategy, industrial and export diversification, productivity enhancement and mastery of product and process technology, international competitiveness and skills development. The analytical capacity of most industry associations needs to be upgraded to enable them to contribute effective arguments and ideas related to industrial development and increasing competitiveness, especially needed in the face of regional and global liberalization.

EMERGING CHALLENGES AND IMPLICATIONS

Emerging Challenges

In addition to the numerous existing weaknesses outlined above, the manufacturing sector will face a number of new challenges and constraints in the coming years due to the globalization of world manufacturing and serious competition from emerging exporters both in the export and domestic markets. These include the increasingly stiff competition, in the export markets, from lower-cost producer countries, and the real threat of de-industrialization due to rapid import liberalization and corporate indebtedness. Additional pressure will be felt on the balance of payments owing to inflows of imported manufactures, while, at the same time, aggressive competition from equally reform-oriented countries will reduce foreign direct investment funds.

There will be little scope for continuing the expansion of manufacturing based on domestic natural resources such as timber and petroleum, since their limits may have already been reached due to finite supplies and/or environmental constraints. Guaranteed export quota markets will disappear with trade liberalization, while the country's large external debt burden will constrain its ability to borrow offshore. Growing demands for regional autonomy and decentralization will bring the problems associated with achieving balanced regional development to the fore.

The above challenges suggest that a strategic realignment in industrial policy is required to regain the momentum of industrialization of the early 1990s, both to maintain market share in the world and to compete successfully against increasingly cheaper imported manufactures. Indonesia cannot indefinitely continue to rely on a narrow range of labour-intensive and resource-based products such as plywood, textiles, garments and footwear to spearhead manufacturing development, as in the past. Indonesia faces the challenges of channelling domestic investment resources, attracting more foreign direct investment and directing more technology and other support infrastructure to transform its industrial sector successfully. On the other hand, now that production, sourcing and distribution have all become globalized, it has the opportunity to attract the kind of FDI that increases the technological and industrial competitiveness of the Indonesian manufacturing sector.

As markets liberalize, and investment becomes ever more mobile, the determinants of industrial development will increasingly shift from trade, tariff and price-dependent strategies of nations to the business strategies of firms. In other words, the focus of competition will move from nations to firms. Indonesia's price-dependent trade and industry strategy must give way to an industrial strategy which strengthens the competitiveness of firms and which spans the patterns of investment, innovation, industrial organization and structure. There may thus be little alternative but to design an overall industrial strategy to transform the manufacturing sector in the context of open, deregulated and increasingly liberalized markets (Rodrik, 1997) and in the context of transparent and competitive pricing in all transactions between government agencies and private sector firms. Ideally, however, the process of economic liberalization should be a gradual and controlled process of opening up, which should be accompanied by a strategy of industrial restructuring and upgrading in collaboration with the private sector.

Furthermore, while trade reforms and transparency are necessary to address the immediate, short-term constraints of the manufacturing sector, they are not sufficient by themselves for the next stage of industrial development. In other words, progress will not evolve naturally in the context of Indonesia's present endowments and policy framework, or in the international context of fierce competition in the globalized market place. A reassessment of the effectiveness of industrial policy in Indonesia has concluded that industrial policy played a crucial role in the development success of Indonesian manufacturing since the mid-1960s. The neoliberal interpretation, that industrial policy was incoherent, subject to rent seeking and irrelevant to Indonesia, may oversimplify the policy objective of creating a strong, integrated, diversified and outward-oriented industrial economy, which the state achieved in part as a result of the development of an effective government–business partnership (Rock, 1999).

In sum, just as the import-substitution strategy of the 1960s and 1970s gave way to an export-oriented strategy in the 1980s and 1990s, the changing international environment calls for more creative and innovative strategies which rely on closer public–private partnerships, as the regulatory or dirigiste approach becomes increasingly incompatible with the current free-trade era. However, the role of government in industrial development, while necessary, needs to change from that in the past. The government should redefine industrial strategy as the attainment of a common public–private vision of industrialization, and the basic implementation mechanisms as shared public–private efforts (Sercovich, 1999). It should also be more selective, and intervene in areas where it can be most effective (Rodrik, 1995).

Policy Implications

In close collaboration and formal partnership with the private sector, the government should formulate and implement policies at three levels (Sercovich, 1999). Industry-wide policies should aim at reducing country costs and enhancing transaction efficiency for business, including the necessary macroeconomic, regulatory and business environment, the physical infrastructure and the educated and skilled labour force under which manufacturing firms can invest and grow (Figure 6.6). At the sub-sectoral level, the government can support the development of strategic initiatives and promotional activities in priority industries. And at the firm level, the government can aim to increase the manufacturing capabilities of local enterprises. This new approach to industrial strategy is elaborated further below.

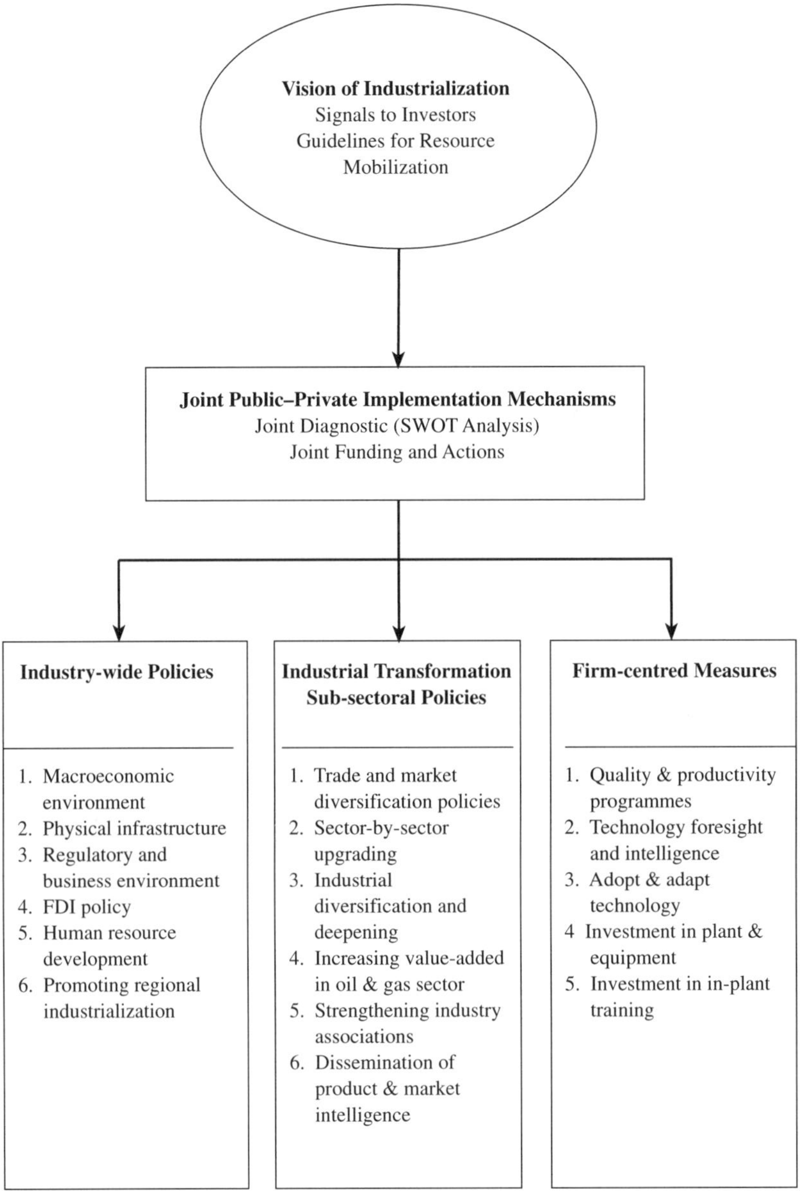

Figure 6.6 Strategy for enhancing manufacturing competitiveness

Vision of industrialization
At the outset, the government and the private sector should jointly produce a joint public–private sector long-term vision of where Indonesia wants to be in terms of industrialization (what types of products it would like to produce and export, and what other types of goods it should continue to import), to provide broad signals to investors, and to develop guidelines for public–private resource mobilization. This collaborative process is by itself very important to reach a common vision, which can be articulated in a joint public–private strategy on industrial competitiveness. The strategy should identify a number of priority industries and export products which the government and the private sector can jointly promote, without however prejudicing other industries. It should contain a realistic assessment of the competitive potential of various sectors and, since government resources for industrial promotion are limited, a promotional strategy focused on priority areas. Intervening in a large number of unrelated activities will risk diffusion and failure. A common strategic vision of industrialization will also assist in coordinating the efforts of the central government departments concerned with implementing various aspects of industrial policies, as well as all provincial and district authorities, which will become increasingly involved in regional industrial development.

An industrial strategy, which can elicit desirable responses from the largely private manufacturing sector in a free-trade environment, will necessarily be more complex to formulate and implement. Nevertheless, the private sector may welcome the opportunity to contribute to a common overall strategic vision as to the desirable directions of manufacturing development in the medium and long term. Critical to this is the need to initiate and maintain close public–private dialogue. The government can accelerate the process of industrial transformation and the establishment of a more competitive industrial sector by sending signals and switching government resources to build critical endowments in support of priority private sector needs.

Industry-wide policies to reduce country costs

Macroeconomic environment A stable macroeconomic environment, such as was provided by Indonesia in the second half of the 1980s and the 1990s, adds to a country's competitive standing. It is a requirement for attracting foreign and domestic investment, and for firms to engage in modernizing and technological upgrading. Stable and competitive exchange rate, interest rate and tax rates are three key elements of macroeconomic stability. An overvalued exchange rate makes exports less competitive, while high interest rates dampen investment, and end up attracting short-term capital, thus pushing up the exchange rate and resulting in a high-cost economy. Moreover, savings rate should be increased through the development of financial and capital markets. In addition to the above, manufacturing enterprises intending to invest and trade should have access to funds from the banking sector.

Physical infrastructure Good-quality transport, telecommunications and power are the three most important components of physical infrastructure sought by investors (Rodrik, 1995) and these were important factors in Indonesia's success in attracting both domestic and foreign investments in the manufacturing sector. It is important for government to consult the private sector as to the requirements and location of necessary additional infrastructural investments. The private sector involvement in the provision of telecommunications and power should be encouraged through the establishment of a supportive regulatory framework for private investment, and the commercialization and privatization of existing transport, telecommunications and energy generation assets.

Adequate transport facilities and economical freight costs and port charges are important; however, time and reliability are increasingly dominant factors in the production of higher-value goods. The availability of efficient traditional (telephone, facsimile) and new (Internet) telecommunication services will enable manufacturers to take advantage of globalization and regionalization trends in location, as well as allowing clients to request rapid response to inquiries and orders through electronic commerce.

Regulatory and business environment The regulatory and business environment is an important element of country costs, and is often cited as the major impediment in facing foreign investors in Indonesia. The government should hold regular consultations with the private sector to listen to their concerns, to identify the most serious bottlenecks in these areas, and to provide an undertaking to rectify them in a given period of time.

The judicial system and the rules and institutions that affect FDI, including contract enforcement, bankruptcy law and competition policy regulations and enforcement, are recognized factors in attracting and retaining investors, and of country competitiveness. Effective anti-dumping legislation, institutions and enforcement should also receive priority to protect manufacturing enterprises from unfair competition. To lower transaction costs, the government should be unrelenting in its efforts to reduce unnecessary administrative and bureaucratic procedures to speed up the investment approval process, as well as to simplify tax and customs systems for existing enterprises. Unnecessary labour regulations, such as rigid salary schedules for expatriate workers according to occupation and nationality, should be abolished.

FDI policy In addition to investment in physical infrastructure, education and training, and in the improvement of the regulatory and business environment, the following measures are specifically required to attract foreign direct investment. First of all, experience in other countries indicates that incentives play a relatively minor role in a good promotion programme, since long-term investors are not susceptible to short-term inducements (UNCTAD, 1999). In view of the limited benefits of FDI accruing to Indonesia in the past, the government should dispense with preferential measures such as tax breaks and holidays, accelerated depreciation and various duty exemptions, which tilt the level playing field in favour of FDI and discriminate against domestic investors, who after all produce most of the output, employment, exports and foreign exchange.

Second, it is more important for investment promotion agencies to strive to discover the special needs of transnational corporations (TNCs) and other foreign firms, and then to take steps to cater to them. Effective promotion should be mounted to establish a distinct image or to alter the perception of potential investors by providing more and better information. However, such promotional efforts are highly skill-intensive and can be expensive, and they need to be undertaken carefully to maximize their impact.

Third, despite the institution of a one-stop approval process, investors still have to obtain additional licences from other government agencies (Soesastro *et al.*, 2000). Decentralization and the future relationship between the central and local administrations have further heightened their concerns, thus necessitating clear and simplified regulations. The government can strengthen the opportunities for domestic firms to do business with foreign firms by building up local capabilities and a strong group of domestic firms which can develop linkages with foreign establishments (see the sub-section on firm-centred policies below).

Fourth, FDI should be used as a vehicle for the development of new industries and for maximizing technology development. Owing to lack of information, high transaction costs and high risks involved, the government can undertake the crucial role of selective investment promotion to match technology-based medium-scale foreign companies with suitable domestic partners to promote technology-based supplier industries in such areas as capital goods, component manufactured and high technology.

Human resource development The current secondary education system is more suited to producing school leavers for the repetitive nature of shop floor manufacturing processes currently in use in many export-oriented labour-intensive industries. As the country moves up the technology ladder and begins to produce more complex products such as capital goods and advanced chemicals in greater volumes, manufacturers will require workers able to use judgment and other thinking skills in the operation of advanced manufacturing processes and in the maintenance and repair of complex automated production equipment.

The industry associations and the Ministry of Industry and Trade (representing the users of educated and trained manpower) and the Ministries of Education and Manpower (representing the producers of skills and knowledge) should establish a forum to continually identify the problems and agree on improvements to develop the skills, knowledge and attitudes required by the increasingly knowledge-based industry at the secondary general school, secondary vocational school, post-secondary vocational technical and tertiary education (university and diploma) levels. The private sector should be encouraged to establish and operate demand-driven technical training centres through financial and other incentives, under a very carefully designed quality control and accreditation system.

Promoting regional potentials and regional industrialization The strong impetus given by the present government to decentralization and regional autonomy will provide the provinces with a new and powerful channel to build their manufacturing base by formulating policies to attract both domestic and foreign manufacturing investment. While this process will create many new opportunities, the competition for scarce investment funds between provinces will at the same time raise new challenges to make optimum use of available investment funds. The provincial governments will need to intensify cooperation among them to avoid being played one against the other by potential domestic and foreign investors. In addition, central government's role will be crucial to coordinate their individual industrial policies to achieve maximum benefits from their relative comparative advantages and local resources.

Proactive central government policies and guidelines will be necessary to achieve effective cooperation and coordination between the provincial government in the areas of identification of regional potential, specializations and priorities, taking into account economies of scale; the creation of industrial clusters and provision of relevant information regarding business opportunities; the adherence to common minimum national standards regarding labour conditions and environment; and the harmonization of investment incentives, particularly concerning tax holidays and other fiscal incentives.

Sub-sectoral policies

Non-discriminatory policies such as those outlined above have gained favour over those with a sub-sector or industry focus. They require less detailed information and less implementation capacity on the part of government agencies, while averting the risk that policy makers would pursue capacity creation in non-competitive industries. However, the practice of policy implementation has shown that many policies need to address sub-sector issues. Trade and commercial policies, beyond an initial thrust towards trade liberalization and reform with universal rules, need to be formulated according to the specific needs of different industries, for instance to deter anti-dumping and unauthorized subsidies, as well as offering temporary relief when necessary. Export promotion programmes often involving industry associations are usually sub-sector-specific. Industrial restructuring programmes and cluster support policies are industry-specific. Some sub-sectors are characterized by significant market failures, externalities or technological economies of scale, calling for selective support for capacity creation. Government–private sector networks are generally organized around sub-sector issues. Sub-sector policies are a natural response in addressing issues of competitiveness.

However, when specific sectors are selected for promotion, an appropriate industrial strategy is one that acts selectively. It should identify a narrow group of industries and set out transparent policies to promote them, as well as clear-cut guidelines against which their success can be evaluated (Rodrik, 1995).

Trade and market diversification policies Exports must continue to grow, not only to provide valuable foreign exchange, but to speed up industrial transformation, reap externalities and master international best practice, which all come from competing and trading in international markets. Exports are also necessary to maintain balance of payment viability, in view of the country's large external debt. Indonesia's share in world markets is still small, and the scope for expansion still substantial.

Exports should be rapidly diversified, in terms of both products and markets. The selection of export products and markets to promote should be made jointly with the private sector, and could focus on other labour-intensive products (for example, food products), more processed export products (for example, secondary wood and paper processing, processed foods) and higher value-added products. Export promotion policies should be made in terms of net benefits; that is, taking into account export earnings and the need to import inputs. Promotion policies should carefully study price trends, and avoid promoting products likely to face a decline in world prices due to competition and low demand. Biased government policies and regulations against exports should be identified through frequent government–private sector consultations, and eliminated. Existing mechanisms for providing trade financing and inputs at world prices are still cumbersome and should be greatly improved. Trade promotion efforts must be accelerated with existing trading partners (for example, the United States, Europe, Japan) as well as with new countries (the Middle East, Latin America, South Asia and Africa).

Industrial transformation programme The industrial transformation programme should begin with stocktaking, industry-by-industry, analysing strengths and weaknesses (SWOT analysis) in various industries, to reach public–private consensus on medium-term objectives for sub-sector development. This should be followed by designing an implementation programme consisting of project ideas of common interest to all firms in priority sectors. These ideas should be compiled by industry associations and other public and private sector representatives, and initial costs should be prepared (bottom-up approach). Resource mobilization should follow, by identifying sources of funding for the industry-specific operational programmes, and agreeing on cost-sharing arrangements between the private (domestic and foreign) sector, the public sector and overseas development funds. Finally, an implementation plan should be drawn up, to develop procedures and mechanisms for implementing the industry-specific operational programmes for industrial transformation, and for monitoring and evaluating the programmes.

Industrial diversification and deepening The broadening of the manufactured base should be achieved through the establishment of supplier and support industries to produce intermediate inputs and components including those in the chemical, consumer electronics, electrical appliance and motorcycle and motor vehicle industries (backward linkages), the promotion of downstream industries to increase value-added in exports (forward linkages), the production of basic machine tools and other industrial equipment. The production of capital goods and components should be promoted both domestically and for FDI because of their special role in the manufacturing learning process and technological mastery, and in the expansion of medium-technology industries (plastics, paper products, rubber, iron and steel, non-mineral metallic products, and iron and steel).

Past government efforts at deepening and diversifying the industrial base, for instance in establishing a component industry for motor vehicle manufacturing and a machine tool industry, have not succeeded (Aswichahyono *et al.*, 2000; Braadbaart, 1996). The factors responsible for this lack of success should be evaluated, and on the basis of this new policies and strategies should be designed. Furthermore, government policies should also take into account the inherited structure and organization of the manufacturing sector such as size and location, which have evolved for historical as well as technological indivisibility reasons, and build upon this to promote core competencies and improve competitiveness.

Increasing value-added in the oil and gas sector The oil and gas sector is characterized by large trade imbalances as well as substantial discontinuities in the value chain of petrochemical products. Domestic value-added should be increased and import dependence reduced by increasing the domestic production capacity of refineries and petrochemical feedstock, and encouraging domestic firms to supply services to the oil and gas sector including freight, insurance, exploration and other related services.

Strengthening industry associations The government and the private sector should work together to strengthen private sector industry associations, particularly in the areas of competitiveness analysis, the dissemination of international best practice (industrial organization, management, quality management, manufacturing techniques), the establishment and operation of industry-level and customer-oriented productivity centres, and the joint management and operation of existing government-owned technical centres, with eventual transfer of ownership in the future.

Dissemination of product and market intelligence The industry associations, with assistance from government, can provide a very useful service to domestic and foreign entrepreneurs who wish to invest in the production of inputs or final products for both the domestic and the export markets. Product-based information would include the market prospects both at home and abroad, price trends and quality requirements, information referral services of prospective clients, and machinery and equipment suppliers, estimates of investment costs and sources of investment funding, and guidance in negotiating contracts with foreign investors and equipment suppliers.

Firm-centred policies to develop manufacturing capability

The government should encourage indigenous firms to develop their manufacturing capability by acquiring and applying technology in its broad sense, including skills (technical, managerial, industrial organization and marketing), technical information, manufacturing techniques, quality management, product development and external linkages to enhance their competitiveness. Firm-level policies can encourage producers towards best-practice standards in the following areas in particular: adoption of total quality and productivity programmes, technological upgrading and investment in plant and industrial skills.

Total quality and productivity programmes The application of continuous improvement, minimum waste of energy, materials and time, zero defects and other aspects of quality can greatly reduce production inefficiencies and enhance the competitiveness of firms. To reach companies, productivity centres and technical institutes and centres should be in a position to provide effective and competent extension services. In addition to expanding the existing programmes of on-the-job transfer of production know-how by technical experts from Japan and elsewhere, additional incentives can also be provided to companies to finance specialized consultant services.

Technological upgrading While quality and productivity programmes are a prerequisite for most Indonesian firms at their current level of development, their productivity gains will eventually be exhausted. Firms will then need to compete on the basis of product differentiation and innovation, as well as cost and quality. Firms will need to build the capacity to undertake product adaptation and development by upgrading their technology. Domestic firms and affiliates of foreign firms need not aim to innovate at world frontiers, but should be encouraged to adapt and assimilate new technologies and create new products on the basis of existing technologies. For example, the government and the private sector can jointly present awards of excellence to particularly innovative firms to give them public and international recognition. Firms should also be encouraged, through the dissemination of relevant information, to acquire arm's-length technology through technology licensing, technology transfer agreement, reverse engineering and adaptation to build their own capabilities.

Investment in equipment and training The government should consider tax and other incentives for upgrading plant and equipment, and the skills of workers and managers through in-plant technical and management training.

CONCLUDING REMARKS

The dramatic increase in industrial investment, manufacturing output and exports since the mid-1980s would suggest that Indonesia possessed a fairly articulated and developed industrial structure. The evidence presented here suggests that this was not the case. Despite the relatively large size of Indonesia's industrial economy, the industrial structure is characterized by significant weaknesses, and international competitive threats pose the risks of de-industrialization and wiping out the gains experienced in the past decade and a half of rapid growth.

Three years before the crisis, there were already tendencies towards dampened growth in manufacturing exports, due mainly to increased competitive pressures from other emerging economies across the limited range of products and in the few markets which Indonesian industry managed to penetrate. The inability of Indonesian firms to deepen their technological base or to move beyond the assembly stage of manufacturing contributed to persistent deficits in balance of trade, caused largely by imported inputs and capital goods. Following the spectacular growth of export-led manufacturing in the early 1990s, some slowdown was expected, since the manufacturing sector could not continue to grow at over 20 per cent per annum indefinitely. Nevertheless, the rapid deterioration in export revenues in the four years before the economic crisis of mid-1997, and the consequent halving of the growth rate of the manufacturing sector, took many by surprise.

Also the preconditions for investment-driven growth were beginning to change. The regional restructuring of manufacturing capacities in the mid-1980s resulted in a massive flow of investments by Japanese, South Korean, Taiwanese, Hong Kong and Singaporean firms to what were then the three or four most open and labour-abundant ASEAN economies (Indonesia, Thailand and the Philippines). By the early 1990s, however, the investment liberalization process had become fairly widespread across Asia, with some of the newly liberalized economies offering equivalent, if not higher, productivity–wage rate ratios, and comparable investment incentives.

The economic crisis hit Indonesia amidst growing competitive threats both in the investment and the product markets. More recently, exports have recovered, and a current account surplus was posted in 1998 and 1999. However, the export boom in manufactures has been caused by a (delayed) response to favourable prices resulting from the massively depreciated rupiah, and the trade surpluses are due to a collapse of imports rather than a change in the pattern of shallow export-led industrialization. When growth resumes, there is little to suggest that the balance of trade will not display its recurrent deficit. Only, this time, there will be constrained opportunities for offsetting current account deficits through a positive capital account, given the large private and public debt overhang resulting from the financial collapse of 1997.

The threats of stagnation or de-industrialization also pose significant political challenges. It was observed that most of Indonesia's industrial capacities are located in people-abundant but resource-poor Java, which, consequently, would have the most to lose from a process of de-industrialization. By contrast, the devaluation of the rupiah has caused an increase of economic advantage in relatively sparsely populated but resource-abundant islands. A probable shift in economic weight among the constituent provinces has implications for regional balances within the country, as well as the pattern of revenue sharing implied by the recent moves towards decentralization adopted by the government in the post-Soeharto era.

This chapter has argued that there is little choice but to maintain the pace of industrial development and to redress past weaknesses. Even in the context of liberalized investment and trade flows, public policy can go a long way towards influencing the nature and direction of industrialization, without resorting to distortive pricing policies or firm-specific incentives. Public–private partnerships in the formulation and implementation of industrial strategy could provide the necessary framework for the coordinated action of various government agencies involved in industrial development. In addition, policy-makers and institutions will need to be insulated from lobbying for special favours from interest groups. However, to guard against bureaucratic authoritarianism, technocratic independence would need to be accompanied by public accountability.

Whether these initiatives can be realized and implemented with the imagination required remains to be seen, as the government struggles to cope with the numerous economic and political reforms that occupy its policy agenda.

NOTE

1. The material presented here is based on the findings of a recently completed UNIDO/UNDP project entitled "Policy Support for Industrial Recovery," no. NC/IWS/99/004. The views expressed here are those of the authors: and should not be attributed to the above organizations.

REFERENCES

Aswichahyono, H., M.C. Basri and H. Hill (2000), 'How Not to Industrialize: Indonesia's Automotive Industry', *Bulletin of Indonesian Economic Studies*, 36(1).

Blazely, L. (1999), *Review of Primary School Science Curriculum*, Jakarta: Curriculum Development Centre–British Council Curriculum Capacity Project.

Blazely, L., M. Samami, Y.S. Rahayu and R. Purwati (1996), *Junior Secondary Education Science: Diagnostic Survey*, technical report no. 10, Jakarta: Directorate of Secondary Education–World Bank Junior Secondary Education Project.

Braadbaart, O. (1996), 'Machine Tools and the Indonesian Engineering Subsector: Consumption Trends and Localization Efforts', *Bulletin of Indonesian Economic Studies*, 32(2).

CBS (2000), *Large and Medium Manufacturing Indicator 1998*, Jakarta: Central Bureau of Statistics.
Dhanani, S. (1992), *Indonesian Manufacturing Employment and Training: Major Findings of the 1992 Enterprise Surveys*, technical reports 1, 2and 3 (West Java, East Java and North Sumatra), Jakarta: Regional Manpower Planning and Training Project, Bappenas Bureau of Manpower–World Bank Professional Human Resources Development loan 3134-IND.
Dhanani, S. (1995), *Indonesia: Public Vocational Training Centres in the Ministry of Manpower*, Jakarta, World Bank Consultant Report, EA3PH.
Dhanani, S. (2000), *Indonesia: Strategy for Manufacturing Competitiveness*, volume II (main report), UNDP/UNIDO Policy Support for Industrial Recovery Project No. NC/INS/99/004, Jakarta: United Nations Industrial Development Organization.
Dhanani, S. and E. Sweeting (1995), *Employment, Remuneration and Training of Technical Graduates in Indonesia: Findings of a 1994 Tracer Study*, Technical report, Jakarta: Regional Manpower Planning and Training Project, Bappenas Bureau of Manpower–World Bank Professional Human Resources Development loan 3134-IND.
Lall, S. (1993), 'Policies for Building Technological Capabilities', *Asian Development Review*, 11(2).
Lall, S. (1995), 'Government and Industrialization: The Role of Policy Interventions', *Global Forum on Industry: Perspectives for 2000 and Beyond*, New Delhi: United Nations Industrial Organization.
Lall, S. (1998), 'Technology Policies in Indonesia', in H. Hall and K.W. Thee (eds), *Indonesia's Technological Challenge*, Singapore: Institute of Southeast Asian Studies.
Pempel, T.J. (1999), 'Regional Ups, Regional Downs', in T.J. Pempel (ed.), *The Politics of the Asian Economic Crisis*, Ithaca and London: Cornell University Press.
Robison, R. (1986), *Indonesia: The Rise of Capital*, Sydney: Allen and Unwin, in association with Asian Studies Association.
Rock, M.T. (1999), 'Reassessing the Effectiveness of Industrial Policy in Indonesia: Can the Neoliberals be Wrong?', *World Development*, 27(4).
Rodrik, D. (1995), 'Trade Liberalization, Competitiveness and Industrial Policy: Major Conceptual Issues', in UNIDO (ed.), *Policies for Competition and Competitiveness: The Case for Industry in Turkey*. General Studies Series, Vienna: United Nations Industrial Development Organization.
Rodrik, D. (1997), *Has Globalization Gone Too Far?*, Washington: Institute for International Economics.
Sadtono E., Handayani and M. O'Reilly (1996), *Junior Secondary Education: English Diagnostic Survey with Recommendations for In-Service Training Programme for SLTP Teachers*, technical report no. 8a, Jakarta: Directorate of Secondary Education–World Bank Junior Secondary Education Project.
Sercovich, F. (1999), *Competition and the World Economy*, Cheltenham: Edward Elgar, in association with the United Nations Industrial Development Organization.
Soesastro, M.H, K.W. Thee and W. Chandra (2000), 'Foreign and Domestic Direct Investment in Indonesia since the Early 1990s', mimeo, Jakarta.
Somerset, A. (1996), *Junior Secondary Education Mathematics: Diagnostic Survey of Basic Number Skills*, technical report no. 12, Jakarta: Directorate of Secondary Education–World Bank Junior Secondary Education Project.

Sweeting, E. (1997), *The Three R's: Their Assessment and Development in PEQIP Schools*, technical report no. 17, Jakarta: Directorate-General of Primary and Secondary Education–World Bank Junior Secondary Education Project.
Thee, K.W. (1998), 'Determinants of Indonesia's Industrial Technology Development', in H. Hall and K.W. Thee (eds), *Indonesia's Technological Challenge*, Singapore: Institute of Southeast Asian Studies.
Thee, K.W. and M. Pangestu (1994), 'Technological Capabilities and Indonesia's Manufactured Exports', in D. Ernst, T. Ganiatsos and L. Mutelka (eds), *Technological Capabilities and Export Success in Asia*, London and New York: Routledge for the United Nations Conference on Trade and Development (UNCTAD).
UNCTAD (1999), *World Investment Report: Overview*, New York and Geneva: United Nations Conference for Trade and Development, United Nations.
World Bank (1993), *Indonesia: Industrial Policy: Shifting into High Gear*, report no. 12153-IND, Washington, DC: World Bank.

7. Malaysia's recovery from the burst bubble

Rajah Rasiah

INTRODUCTION

Unlike the other crisis economies of Thailand, South Korea, Indonesia and the Philippines, Malaysia did not face default and therefore did not need to visit the International Monetary Fund (IMF), cap in hand. Malaysia managed to keep its short-term debt commitments below its serviceable limit. Thus Malaysia enjoyed the economic space to experiment with policies unconventional to IMF operations. While some of the strategies used by Malaysia are similar to those of the IMF packages, fundamental differences differentiate the former from the latter. Another point to note is that Malaysia allowed the crisis to wreak considerable damage before instituting capital controls, while Hong Kong, Taiwan and Singapore introduced different scales of controls to shield their economies from the contagion.

This chapter examines the causes of the financial crisis and rescue efforts made by Malaysia. It is divided into four main sections. The first looks at pre-crisis macroeconomic conditions comparatively. The second presents the causes of the slowdown and crash. The third evaluates the capital control measures undertaken by the Malaysian government. The fourth draws implications for sustainable long-term growth.

PRE-CRISIS MACROECONOMIC CONDITIONS

A number of the macroeconomic fundamentals of Malaysia were sound at the time of the financial rupture. As with other East Asian economies, rapid growth helped sustain low inflation and falling unemployment rates over the last decade (see Table 7.1). Only the Philippines faced low growth and high unemployment rates over that time. Like the remaining three crisis-affected Southeast Asian economies, Malaysia was fuelled by a massive wave of foreign direct investment (FDI) from Japan and the Asian newly-industrialized economies (NIEs), which was triggered by their appreciating currencies following the Plaza Accord of 1985, and the withdrawal of the Generalized System of Preferences (GSP) from the latter in 1988. GDP growth of Malaysia averaged 8.9 per cent in the period 1990–95. Malaysia's growth rate continued to hold strong, recording 8.6 and 7.7 per cent respectively in the years 1996 and 1997. Only China's and Thailand's GDP growth rates exceeded Malaysia's in East Asia. The dependent variables of inflation and unemployment rates remained low (see Table 7.1). Inflation rates remained remarkably low despite a rise in domestic purchasing power following rapid growth and a gentle appreciation of the ringgit vis-à-vis foreign currencies. Rapid growth also helped lower unemployment rates in Malaysia. Its unemployment rate not only fell to a record low of 2.5 per cent in 1997, the share of foreign labour in the labour force rose from around 15 per cent to 30 per cent in the period 1992–7.

Savings as a share of GNP of Malaysia in the period 1996–7 was only exceeded by Singapore among the East Asian economies (see Table 7.1). Its investment levels were also among the highest in East Asia. Moreover, unlike the deficits experienced by most of the East Asian economies, Malaysia's savings–investment gap improved prior to the financial crisis. Rising savings levels ensured that high investment did not create a burgeoning savings–investment deficit in Malaysia. Indonesia, the Philippines, South Korea and Thailand faced such deficits throughout the 1990s. Malaysia's imbalances over 1990–95 were reversed in 1996–7. However, as with the other crisis affected economies, Malaysia faced worsening current account deficits throughout the 1990s.

Overall, macroeconomic expansion in Malaysia appeared to be grinding to a halt owing to a burgeoning growth in current account imbalances. Malaysia's savings–investment gap was still favourable at the time of the crisis, but its current account deficit was rising sharply. Also, with its investments growing faster than outputs, the incremental capital–output ratios began to rise prior to the crisis. Nevertheless, there was a significant advantage Malaysia enjoyed over the other crisis-affected economies: Malaysia did not face a savings–investment deficit and overall imbalances with international payments commitments. The former was possible because of strong surpluses recorded in the capital account.

The bulk of short-term foreign capital came through the banking system rather than borrowing. As a result, Malaysia's debt-serving burden was lower than that of other crisis economies (see Table 7.2). Hence, despite growing current account deficits, Malaysia was not under immediate pressure to seek IMF resettlement.

Table 7.1 Macroeconomic statistics of East Asia, 1990–98

	GDP growth rate			Inflation rate			Unemployment rate		
	90–95	96	97	90–95	96	97	90	96	98
Indonesia	8.0	7.8	4.9	8.7	7.9	6.6	—	4.1	9–12
Malaysia	8.9	8.6	7.7	3.7	3.5	4.0	6.0	2.5	6.7
China	10.7	9.6	8.8	11.3	8.3	2.8	—	3.0	5–6
Philippines	2.3	5.8	5.2	10.6	9.1	6.0	—	7.4	13.1
Singapore	8.6	6.9	7.8	2.7	1.4	2.0	—	1.8	4.5
South Korea	7.8	7.1	5.5	6.6	5.0	4.5	—	2.6	7.6
Taiwan	6.4	5.7	6.8	3.8	3.1	0.9	—	—	—
Thailand	9.0	5.5	−0.4	5.0	5.9	5.6	—	1.1	4.4

	Savings/GDP			Investment/GDP			(Savings–investment)/GDP		
	90–95	96	97	90–95	96	97	90–95	96	97
Indonesia	31.0	27.3	29.9	31.3	30.7	31.3	−0.3	−3.4	−1.4
Malaysia	36.6	42.6	43.8	37.5	41.5	42.0	−0.9	1.1	1.8
China	40.8	40.5	41.5	38.8	39.6	38.2	2.0	0.9	3.3
Philippines	16.6	18.5	20.3	22.4	23.1	23.8	−5.8	−5.3	−3.5
Singapore	47.0	51.2	51.8	34.9	35.3	37.4	12.1	15.9	14.4
South Korea	35.6	33.7	33.1	36.8	38.4	35.0	−1.2	−4.7	−1.9
Taiwan	26.9	25.1	24.8	24.0	21.2	22.0	2.9	3.9	2.8
Thailand	34.4	33.7	32.9	41.0	41.7	35.0	−5.6	−8.0	−2.1

	Incremental Capital–Output ratios*			Fiscal balance/GDP			Current account/GDP		
	87–89	90–92	93–95	90–95	96	97	90–95	96	97
Indonesia	4.0	3.9	4.4	0.2	0.2	0.0	−2.5	−3.4	−1.4
Malaysia	3.6	4.4	5.0	−0.4	0.7	1.8	−5.8	−5.0	−5.3
China	—	—	—	−1.0	−0.8	−0.7	1.2	0.9	3.2
Philippines	3.3	22.8	6.0	−1.1	0.3	0.1	−3.7	−4.7	−5.3
Singapore	—	—	—	9.4	6.8	3.3	0.6	15.4	15.4
South Korea	3.5	5.1	5.1	0.2	0.5	−1.4	−1.2	−4.7	−1.8
Taiwan	—	—	—	−5.0	−6.6	−6.3	4.2	4.0	2.7
Thailand	2.9	4.6	5.2	3.2	2.4	−0.9	−3.9	−7.9	−2.0

Sources: *Radelet and Sachs (1998: Table 11); others from ADB (1999).

Table 7.2 Debt service and short-term debt, 1980–96

	Debt service as a proportion of exports (%)			Short-term debt (US$bn)*				Current account deficit plus short-term debt as proportion of international reserves (%)**			
	1980	1992	1995	1992	1994	1995	1996	1992	1994	1995	1996
Indonesia	13.9	32.1	30.9	18.2	14.0	16.2	17.9	191	139	169	138
Malaysia	6.3	6.6	7.8	3.6	7.6	7.5	8.5	29	46	60	55
Philippines	26.6	27.7	16.0	4.4	9.7	11.0	12.0	100	212	203	149
South Korea	—	—	—	—	—	—	—	—	—	—	251
Thailand	18.9	14.1	10.2	14.7	29.2	41.1	44.0	101	127	152	153

Note: *Year end figures; **as percentage of reserves, measured by dividing the current account deficit plus short-term debt by international reserves (1992 figures computed from World Bank data).

Sources: UNCTAD (1997: Table 14); World Bank (1994: Tables 20, 23, 1997: Table 17).

SLOWDOWN AND CRASH

While Malaysia achieved rapid growth, and low inflation and unemployment rates, serious problems that were masked earlier began to slow down growth by the mid-1990s. Four key domestic problems that contributed to the weakness of the economy prior to the crisis are discussed here.

Structural Change and Liberalization

Malaysia abandoned instead of modernizing agriculture, so that a significant share of its consumption has increasingly been imported. Obsessed with myopic arguments that manufacturing value added will always be significantly higher than agriculture, the government even promoted relocation of food supplementation to neighbouring Indonesia, Thailand and the Philippines. The typical structural argument posited a circular price relationship between agriculture and manufacturing, so that structural change would start with agriculture supporting manufacturing, but once agricultural productivity rose its subsequent support for manufacturing's modernization would lead to some equalization of the terms of exchange between the two. The gradual reduction in emphasis on agriculture since the 1980s left a serious complementarity gap. The share of agriculture in GDP dropped sharply from 1990 (Table 7.3). In Malaysia, the disregard for agriculture in preference for industrial widening has opened basic consumption to massive imports. Food imports in 1996 alone exceeded 10 billion ringgit.

Table 7.3 Malaysia's GDP structure, 1970–97 (%)

	1970	1980	1990	1997
Agriculture	31	22	19	13
Industry	26	38	41	46
Manufacturing	13	21	27	34
Services	40	40	41	41

Sources: World Bank (1998: Table 12); Malaysia (1981, 1993).

The 1990s have also been characterized by increased liberalization which, given the domestic political structure, magnified crony privatization. Privatization efforts demonstrated the classic workings of the market and state in a capitalist economy (see Polanyi, 1957; Kornai, 1962). Powerful private interests dominated the markets – enjoying strong political backing – gaining substantial profit, generated by the privatization initiatives. The excesses did not seem too draining in the late 1980s and early 1990s, owing to rapid growth and the consequent widespread profit-generating opportunities. When the real sectors began slowing down from 1996, shrinking rents and unsustainable expenditures involving mega projects began to undermine both the current account and government finance (see Jomo, 1998). The number of public institutions privatized in Malaysia rose from two in 1983 to 72 in 1993 (Rugayah, 1995). The government also began divesting shares of public companies considerably in the 1990s (Malaysia, 1996; Rasiah and Ishak, 2001). Contrary to neoliberal references to privatization in the country as being state-driven, private interests working hand-in-hand with the politically powerful began to dominate the financially profitable but rentier activities (see Gomez and Jomo, 1997). In the absence of risk bearing – as several of such ventures enjoyed state guarantees of domestic market control – a significant section of the newly created managerial class hardly showed critical elements of entrepreneurship.

External pressures influenced the removal of a number of incentives and tariffs, pushing private interests into other rentier activities in Malaysia. The World Trade Organization's (WTO) formation in 1995 and other regional trade deregulation efforts, such as the ASEAN Free Trade Area (AFTA) and the Asia–Pacific Economic Cooperation (APEC), accelerated the liberalization process. Incentives that were used to subsidize exports, such as the double deduction incentives for export and the export abatement allowance, were selected for removal. Rising production costs, including wages, in the face of falling tariffs and imminent removal of export subsidies, scared away several local firms. Tariffs were already falling even before the onset of AFTA (see Rasiah, 1998a). Rent-dependent ventures – both those thriving on pure deadweight loss in consumer welfare and those gaining efficiency gradually in innovative activities – shifted operations to other sectors such as the real property sectors. Despite operating behind tariffs exceeding 55 per cent for a range of steel products and with subsidized loans from the government, Perwaja (a government-owned steel company) continued to run up losses throughout the 1980s and 1990s. Meanwhile, local garment and textile firms such as Malayan Weaving, South Island Garment and Kamunting Textiles enjoyed tariff protection until the 1990s and export subsidies even into the 1990s. Hence the once lucrative local manufacturing activities that relied on tariffs and subsidies, but without state sponsorship in Malaysia, and not having achieved international competitiveness moved away to less risky sub-sectors.

Unproductive ventures, including property and share purchases, attracted financing from banks and other financial institutions which, given their huge assets in the 1990s, launched aggressive lending strategies.[1] While a number of the mega projects of the government can be argued to contain potential ammunition for substantial multiplier effects, the failure of several, such as the Bakun dam, also drained the country of scarce resources. For example, the Bakun project sapped RM2.5 billion, and Perwaja reported a loss of over RM2.5 billion in the 1990s. Private banks and finance companies facing liberal regulations began to extend loans based on quick returns, collateral and links with powerful politicians.[2] While loans to the construction sector in Malaysia rose from 7.0 per cent in 1990 to 8.9 per cent in 1996, the amount going to the productive sectors of agriculture, manufacturing and trade and transport had fallen from 44.2 per cent in 1990 to 36.5 per cent in 1996. The rest went to services and construction. The bulk of the loans with preferential interest rates to manufacturing were directed at government-sponsored projects such as Proton, Perwaja Steel and other heavy industry projects, including infrastructure.[3]

Overexpansion in construction and services before industrial maturity had been achieved created a big dent in Malaysia's capacity to finance industrial and technology development. Unlike other successful industrializers where the transition to services was achieved after extensive industrial deepening and productivity increments (see Rowthorn and Wells, 1987), the accelerated expansion in construction and services in Malaysia has come while its manufacturing sector is still dominated by low value-added simple and original equipment manufacturing (OEM) activities. To make matters worse, the limited learning experience has restricted its capacity to export service and construction items, thereby aggravating the trade imbalance. Construction and services have contributed to massive increases in imports in the 1990s. Unlike the late 1980s, when the mid-1980s recession was turned around by a massive relocation of East Asian investment, the scale of FDI inflows likely to emerge over the late 1990s appears much less.

Debt-driven Investment

The rapid deceleration of growth by the mid-1990s left a gaping investment vacuum. The financial institutions in the country, accustomed to rapid credit growth, did not scale down their lending activities (Table 7.4). The availability of deposits from abroad raised the liquidity in the financial institutions far beyond domestic capabilities. The amount of Malaysia's loans drawn from foreign banks rose from US$16.8 billion at the end of 1995 to US$28.8 billion by mid-1997.

Although Malaysia's foreign debt situation was more favourable than South Korea's, Thailand's, the Philippines' and Indonesia's (see Tables 7.1

Table 7.4 Loans and advances by commercial banks, 1990–96 (%)

	Indonesia		Malaysia		Philippines		Thailand	
	1990	1996	1990	1996	1990	1996	1990	1996
Agriculture	9.0	6.0	6.4	2.4	13.8	6.5	6.2	3.5
Manufacturing	35.0	27.0	21.3	22.0	38.5	32.3	23.7	23.1
Construction	—	—	7.0	8.9	2.7	3.9	3.8	4.1
Trade and transport	34.0	24.0	16.5	12.1	18.2	22.2	25.5	21.7
Finance and real estate	—	—	39.5	39.2	16.9	21.8	19.2	21.5
Service industries	18.0	31.0	—	—	—	—	—	—
Households	—	—	2.4	3.7	—	—	13.8	16.3
Others	3.0	11.0	6.9	11.8	10.0	13.3	7.9	9.7

Source: ADB (1999).

and 7.2), unproductive investment also characterized the country in the 1990s. As a proportion of GDP, gross fixed capital formation (GFCF) has shown a trend rise (see Rasiah, 1998b; Tham, 1998). Given the faster rise in investment over GDP, Malaysia's ICOR has continued to rise (see Table 7.1),[4] supporting the assertion that the country's growth was achieved more by expanding inputs and factors of production than by disembodied technical change.[5] Total factor productivity studies by Tham (1998) and Young (1995) confirm these observations. In addition, FDI, which contributed considerably to growth in investment in Malaysia, began to fall after 1996 (see Figure 7.1).

Falling foreign investment was replaced by loans drawn primarily from domestic sources. Many of the loans in Malaysia were drawn from local financial institutions or through foreign funds deposited domestically. The private sector's share of such foreign banks' claims of Malaysia rose from 67.5 per cent at the end of 1995 to 93.4 per cent in mid-1997.[6] Malaysia did face considerable loosening of banking policies in the 1990s, which, given the slowdown in the real sectors of manufacturing and agriculture, accelerated the bubble. The easy expansion of credit, especially in the 1990s, raised the loans–equity ratios to extremely high levels. The collapse in share prices aggravated such imbalances further. Loans and advances as a share of GNP at purchasers' value in Malaysia rose from 133 per cent in 1992 to 170 per cent in 1997 (computed from Bank Negara, 1997) as investment in the real sectors slowed down and loans built up from 1996.

Slowdown of Capital Inflows

From virtually negligible participation in Malaysian stock markets, foreign portfolio equity investment rose sharply from the mid-1980s following aggressive promotion by the finance ministry. However, portfolio investment fell sharply during the period 1993–5 (Figure 7.1). Although it recovered slightly in 1996, the level remained far below its peak in 1993.

FDI has traditionally been a major contributor to economic growth in Malaysia. Its significance became most important from 1987. Gross FDI as a proportion of GDP reached 22 per cent for Malaysia in 1995 (UNCTAD, 1997: Figure 11.19). Without repayment pressures, FDI complemented local capital to enhance growth. While the high savings rates made FDI less necessary, the latter enjoyed greater employment and export capabilities than local capital because of its superior technological capabilities. However, as indicated above, FDI to Malaysia began to fall from 1996 (see Figure 7.1). The Southeast Asian share of overall FDI going to South, East and Southeast Asia fell from 61 per cent in 1990–1 to 30 per cent in 1994–6. Declining FDI alongside an electronics glut depressed manufacturing growth in Malaysia. The fall in FDI and its exports reduced domestic demand for services and construction, since these are functions of GDP growth.

The fall in FDI to Southeast Asia from late 1996 can be said to be a

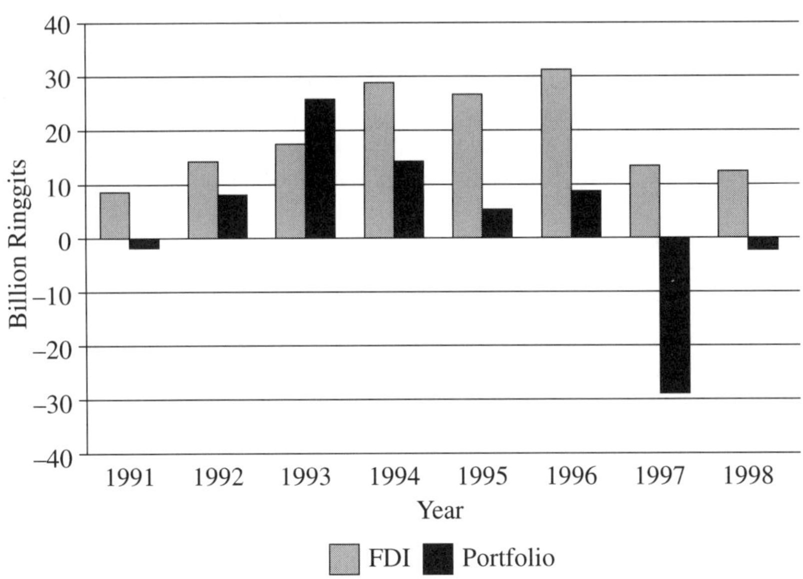

Figure 7.1 Net foreign investment, Malaysia, 1991–8

consequence of a number of factors. The most important among them is the exhaustion of labour reserves since the mid-1990s. Malaysia had a foreign labour force exceeding 1.5–2.5 million in 1996, which accounted for 15–30 per cent of the country's labour force. While Malaysia's migrant workers' policy has enabled the sustenance of a relatively low wage regime, it has also restricted production in the country to a low value added level. Hence the government changed the incentive structure in the early 1990s so that labour-intensive firms faced pressure to relocate to less developed locations within the country, or abroad (see Rasiah, 1999b).

Slow Technological Progress

While industrial policy equipped the first-tier Asian NIEs with strong institutional support for driving technical change, it has yet to do so in Malaysia. Singapore successfully developed and maintained the institutions necessary to sustain its leading role as the Southeast Asian regional hub for medium to high technology-intensive production and services. South Korea and Taiwan have successfully developed the necessary institutions not only to speed up the absorption and development of technologies, but also to strengthen their capacity to support new product development. With the exception of resource based industries, such as palm oil processing, many of the manufacturing firms in Malaysia have yet to go beyond OEM capabilities, and do not have the institutions adequately to generate the requisite human and other technological capabilities to support rapid technical change. Institutional deficiencies in Malaysia can be seen in three major areas: (a) human resource gaps, (b) instruments supporting technological deepening and technology diffusion mechanisms (that is, R&D support), and (c) complementary disciplinary mechanisms.

Human capital

Human capital development in Malaysia has evolved in a lopsided manner. While the supply of general schooling facilities has been encouraging, Malaysia ranked well below other rapid industrializers in tertiary and technical fields. This weakness has stifled firms' efforts to shift to higher value-added and skill-intensive stages of production. For example, drawing on a survey of 2200 firms, Rasiah and Osman (1997: Table 1) reported labour supply and workers' quality as the prime deficiencies confronting manufacturing firms in Malaysia. All 231 firms interviewed in 1995 revealed lack of skilled workers as their biggest problem.[7] The critical nature of this problem becomes clear when comparisons are made across economies. Malaysia's participation rates in education fall short of those of South Korea and the developed economies, especially at the tertiary level (see

Table 7.5). Shortages in the supply of technical graduates has become more serious. It had only 2 per cent of secondary students enrolled in technical fields compared with 19 per cent in South Korea (Table 7.6). Interestingly, Indonesia – which is less developed than Malaysia – enjoyed a 12 per cent share of secondary students in technical education. Systematic governmental promotion of technical education in Taiwan led to the transformation of the ratio of vocational high school (VHS) graduates to academic high school (AHS) graduates from 1:1.7 in 1950 to 1:1 in 1975 and 2:1 in 1988 (Lee, 1994: 5–6). On the other hand, serious skill shortages in Malaysia have been reflected in the high wage premium enjoyed by skilled occupational categories (World Bank, 1995a).

Table 7.5 Educational enrolment, 1970–92

	% of age group enrolled in educational institutions					
	Primary		Secondary		Tertiary	
	1970	1992	1970	1992	1970	1992
Japan	99	102	86	—	31	32
United States	—	104	—	—	56	76
Sweden	94	101	86	91	31	34
Germany	—	107	—	—	27	36
France	117	106	74	101	26	46
Canada	101	107	65	104	42	99
United Kingdom	104	104	73	86	20	28
Korea	103	105	42	90	16	42
Turkey	110	112	27	60	6	15
Brazil	82	106	26	39	12	12
Malaysia	87	93	34	58	4	7
Thailand	83	97	17	33	13	19
Indonesia	80	115	16	38	4	10
Jamaica	119	106	46	62	7	9
Kenya	58	95	9	29	1	2
Bangladesh	54	77	—	19	3	4

Source: World Bank (1995b: 216–17).

Malaysia launched serious efforts to develop the institutions necessary to support firms' competitiveness, and to correct supply shortages emerging in the labour market only from the late 1980s. The Double Deductions on Training Incentive (DDTI) was introduced in 1988 to encourage in-house

Table 7.6 Public education and technical orientation

	Public education (as % of GNP)		Secondary technical enrolment (as % of all levels)	Tertiary natural and applied sciences enrolment (as % of total tertiary)	Science graduates (as % of total graduates)
	1960	1990	1988–91	1990–91	1988–90
Japan	(4.9)	5.7 (5.0)	28	26	26
United States	(5.3)	5.5 (7.0)	—	14	15
Sweden	5.9	6.5 (6.5)	73	43	26
Germany	(2.4)	4.0 (5.4)	80	42	32
France	(3.6)	5.4 (6.0)	54	31	27
Canada	(4.6)	(7.4)	—	14	16
United Kingdom	3.4	5.3	20	39	26
Korea	2.0	3.6	19	42	29
Turkey	2.6	—	25	33	36
Brazil	1.9	4.6	—	31	19
Malaysia	2.9	6.9	2	30	28
Thailand	2.3	3.8	19	22	18
Indonesia	2.5	—	12	—	11
Jamaica	2.3	6.1	4	35	19
Kenya	4.6	6.8	2	32	24
Bangladesh	0.6	2.0	1	27	16

Note: Figures in parentheses refer to private funding.

Sources: UNDP (1995: 158–9, 192–3).

training in firms. The Human Resource Development Fund (HRDF) replaced the DDTI in 1993. The DDTI, which existed from 1988 until its termination in 1992, was found to have been utilized generally by foreign transnationals who would generally have trained their workers even in its absence (see Rasiah and Osman, 1997). The HRDF requires firms to submit a levy of 1 per cent of their payroll to the Human Resource Development Council, which they can then reclaim using approved training expenses. The Fund penalizes firms that do not train according to the criteria defined in the eligible conditions. The prime problem associated with this penalty system is the absence of proximate training institutions in several locations. Firms in Sabah and Sarawak have been seriously disadvantaged owing to a lack of training institutions.

Special mechanisms and incentives were introduced by the government in the mid-1990s to expand the supply of science and technology graduates. Training suppliers, from low-level technical and vocational trades to engineering degrees, were expanded and modernized to overcome the growing supply–demand gaps besetting the labour market. The Private Universities Bill of 1996 helped open the way for the growth of more universities, especially in engineering disciplines.

Private initiatives to boost training followed indirect incentives and motivation offered by the government. The Penang Skills Development Centre (PSDC), founded in 1989, coordinated by transnationals, local firms and the local state's development corporation (the Penang Development Corporation) has managed to generate generic and firm-specific skills tailored to meet cutting-edge production operations. The PSDC has subsequently become the model for similar training institutions in the western corridor states. The political structure of Penang, with strong relations between businesses and the ruling Gerakan government, where the business community and the state political leadership have historically enjoyed good relations, has ensured effective state–business coordination to minimize both government and market failures (Rasiah, 1999b). The same cannot be said of the remaining western corridor states.

R&D support

Industries in Malaysia carry out little in the way of R&D activities. As shown in Table 7.7, Malaysia only had four R&D scientists and technologists per 10 000 people, compared with 22 in Korea, in 1988–9. Investment in R&D in 1987–92 was only 0.4 per cent of GNP, compared with 2.1 per cent in South Korea. These figures were even higher in the more industrialized economies. Malaysia's relatively low R&D endowment places it at the bottom of the technology trajectory. The depth and width of R&D participation is generally a function of the structure and levels of development of an economy (see Rasiah, 1999b). Malaysia's industrial structure is dominated by electronics assembly activities in manufacturing. Most of these firms are still engaged in simple and OEM activities and do not have serious plans to move up the technology trajectory. Thus they do not seek R&D support or employ R&D scientists and technologists (see also Lall *et al.*, 1996). Foreign state-of-the-art assembly operations use technological support from abroad rather than develop them domestically. Also the critical stages in the value-added chain of major export-oriented firms have continued to remain at foreign sites.

Table 7.7 Research and development statistics

	Scientist and technologists per 1000 people, 1986–90	R&D scientists and technologist per 10000 people 1986–9	R&D expenditure as % of GNP, 1987–92
Japan	110	60	2.8
United States	55	—	2.9
Sweden	262	62	2.8
Germany	86	47	2.9
France	83	51	2.3
Canada	174	34	1.4
United Kingdom	90	—	2.3
Korea	46	22	2.1
Turkey	26	4	—
Brazil	30	—	0.6
Malaysia	—	4	0.4
Thailand	1	2	0.2
Indonesia	12	—	—
Jamaica	6	0	—
Kenya	1	—	—
Bangladesh	1	—	—

Sources: UNDP (1995); MASTIC (1994).

Complementary industrial development

A number of institutions and policies were introduced to support industrial development in Malaysia. Examples include the Industrial Master Plans (I and II), the Action Plan for Industrial Technology Development (APITD), the Malaysian Technology Development Corporation (MTDC) and the Malaysia Industry–Government High Technology (MIGHT).

The government even initiated and supported heavy industries such as cement, steel, motor car and motorbike industries. Malaysia had an ambitious programme that included infrastructure development, including cyber infrastructure through the Multimedia Super Corridor (MSC). However, none of the local ventures has yet established international competitiveness. Given the preponderance of employment and investment generation emphasis in industrial policy formulation until the end of the 1980s, labour-intensive firms were preferred (Rasiah and Anuwar, 1995). This trend has continued following the enactment of the Promotion of Investment Act of 1986. It was only when serious labour shortages gripped the western corridor in the 1990s that official emphasis shifted away from employment generation (Malaysia, 1994). However, unlike the Northeast Asian economies, where the creation of an effective enabling environment and government vetting, monitoring and appraisal stimulated substantial diffusion of innovative capacities from home-site national innovation systems (NISs) to host-site NISs, coordination weaknesses have continued to impede effective transfers. The only visible regulatory activity undertaken in Malaysia has been vetting *ex ante.* Even that has been poorly governed, largely owing to the lack of proficient bureaucrats (Anuwar, 1992; Rasiah, 1998a). Furthermore, there has not been a preference for transfers from foreign firms to local firms. Interviews showed that around 90 per cent of technology transfer agreements (TTAs) in the manufacturing sector involved intra-foreign transnational technology transfers.[8] Virtually no monitoring and appraisal *ex post* has been carried out (see Rasiah and Anuwar, 1995). Hence institutions governing TTAs in the country, especially MITI, have hardly grasped the issue of technology transfer, let alone bargained for its transfer from foreign licensors to local licensees.

Thus, despite the initiatives of MTDC, MIGHT, HRDF and specialized institutions such as MIMOS, manufacturing firms in Malaysia still specialize in only original equipment manufacturing (OEM) activities with little participation in original design manufacturing (ODM) and original brand manufacturing (OBM) activities because of coordination problems (see World Bank/MOSTE, 1996; Rasiah, 1998a, 1999a). Coordination failures include the lack of effective government–business networking despite the creation of such institutions from the 1980s. Electronics firms, particularly in the Kelang Valley, Negeri Sembilan, Melaka, Johor, Perak and Kedah, reported that the failure of such mechanisms has thwarted the establishment of effective skills development and designing centres to resolve collective action plans (see Rasiah, 1999b).

RECOVERY PACKAGES

After an initial period of risk-averse contractionary policies, the Malaysian government introduced capital controls on 2 September 1998 to shield the economy from external pressures while it launched policies to revive the economy. Danamodal (capital fund) and Danaharta (asset fund), which were formed earlier, have started to inject capital, acquire non-performing loans and engender mergers. Here some salient features of the recovery package are discussed.

Risk-averse Contractionary Policies

Malaysia had two sets of policies following the financial rupture of 1997. The first took cognizance of the expanded risks facing the financial sector, but was still different in many ways from the IMF packages used in the other crisis affected economies. The first, which was in place until 2 September 1998, followed from the recognition that credit had grown far too much compared with the capacity of the financial sector to support it. Hence interest rates were raised from around 9 per cent to 12 per cent to take stock of the increasing risks of default facing the country. A generally flexible exchange rate mechanism was maintained after the rupture of the quasi-peg following the regional contagion effect in September 1997 despite sporadic interventions by the central bank to prevent a free fall. To prevent a deceleration in industrial production, efforts were made to maintain preferential loans for productive firms, primarily in manufacturing. The justification for offering preferential loans lies primarily in the fact that efficient firms require stable and serviceable interest rates reflecting risks associated with them individually rather than the national economy as a whole. The term 'productive' was confined to manufacturing and essential services.

The period of non-performing loans (NPLs) was reduced from 6 to 3 months and the consequent build-up of bad debts scared the banks away from lending. The accompanying credit squeeze spread to loan-dependent sectors, both essential and non-essential. To prevent such a blanket squeeze in funds, the Finance Ministry did advise banks to use the criteria of productive firms and essential services to offer them preferential loans. Special funds were directed at assisting small and medium firms, low-cost housing and others involved in essential services. Banks and other firms were also encouraged to institute reforms to reduce their reliance on loans. Banks faced with serious problems of default, such as Bank Bumiputera Malaysia Berhad (BBMB) and Sime Bank, were subsequently merged with Commercial Bank and Rashid Hussein Bank, respectively. Big local holding companies such as Renong, Malaysian Airline System (MAS) and Malaysian International Shipping Corporation (MISC) were advised to reform, including instituting a management revamp, before seeking fresh funds from the government. Unlike what happened with the IMF package, insolvent holding companies were spared from closure, but required to reform before government assistance could be approved.

The Finance Ministry also sought greater transparency and civil society participation in economic decision making so that the burden of the crisis would be understood by the masses. Especially with a freeze in the salaries of the civil servants, and cuts involving higher-income earners, this strategy was seen as people-oriented. This perhaps created a sense of burden sharing, and may have contributed to relative calm in the society as opposed to what has happened in Indonesia.

Following the financial rupture, the government also created the Special Functions Ministry and roped in the former finance minister, Tun Daim, to lead an advisory team to help solve the financial crisis. This led to the formation of the New Economic Action Council (NEAC), which constituted members from various constituencies and was coordinated by the Economic Planning Unit (EPU) under the prime minister's department. While significant deliberations were carried out by this group, not many of its recommendations were actually implemented. For example, the NEAC recommended a band to allow the ringgit to fluctuate without volatile movements, but the government chose to peg the exchange rate to the ringgit instead. Nevertheless, representatives from the EPU offered the NEAC a major platform for incisive review and assessment of the causes of the financial crisis in Malaysia.

Capital Controls

The policy shift from 2 September 1998 saw the introduction of capital controls, *inter alia,* fixing the exchange rate at RM3.8 per dollar and the imposition of a year's stay on foreign shares (which was replaced by an exit tax in February 1999). By September 1999, the government had amended controls on the stock market to 10 per cent exit tax on profits. Exchange controls included central bank approval to carry over 1000 ringgit abroad and to maintain a foreign bank account. The ringgit was also made non-transactable abroad. Export-oriented firms were given exemptions on foreign exchange controls so that they were not fettered by the controls. Keynesian style efforts of lower interest rates were adopted to stimulate investment. Interest rates were lowered to 7.50 per cent by early 1999, and to 3.75 per cent by late 1999. Loans to preferred sectors such as housing and car purchases were made easy. The central bank also imposed conditions for banks to expand credit growth to at least 8 per cent a year in 1999. Clearly, the efforts were meant to revive a contracting economy.

Danaharta and Danamodal began buying the NPLs that were affecting a number of large companies. Stabilization seems to have helped restore some confidence, as reflected in the recovery seen in the stock market, but manufacturing declined until mid-1999. Industrial output declined further in 1999, registering a fall of 7.2 per cent in January 1999 and 11.2 per cent in February 1999. In addition the contraction experienced by the East Asian economies and weaknesses in the targeting of loans reduced Danaharta's impact. Nevertheless, car firms have begun to see a recovery. Perodua and Proton especially have seen a rise in sales. The Malaysian Motor Traders Association (MMTA) forecast a growth in motor vehicle sales of 22 per cent in 1999 (*Star*, 30 January 1999).

Efforts to stimulate the economy were pushed aggressively. Danaharta and Danamodal have assumed the central task of acquiring the NPLs and capitalizing the cash-starved firms and institutions. As of 31 December 1998, Danaharta had acquired RM19.3 billion worth of NPLs, exceeding its initial target of RM14 billion (NST, 17 March 1999). Danaharta acquired RM8.2 billion of NPLs from financial institutions and managed RM11.6 billion. The manufacturing sector contributed RM511.8 million and RM3.1 billion, respectively, of total NPLs acquired and managed by Danaharta. Manufacturing accounted for 15.6 per cent of NPLs acquired and managed by Danaharta at the end of December 1998. Broad property (that is, real estate, land and buildings) – which was a major cause of the bubble – was the prime target of the Danaharta acquisitions, contributing 27.7 per cent of the total NPLs acquired and managed.

Efforts to revive the financial sector included bank acquisitions and mergers. The government called for the reduction of the number of banks to six, with the central bank selecting the anchor banks. It was deemed that there were too many banks for their operations to be economic. There appears to be considerable opposition from those banks not among the anchor banks, and hence it is unclear whether reductions will be implemented.

Also the main industrial support institutions, MTDC, MIGHT, Malaysian Institute of Microelectronics Systems (MIMOS), Small and Medium Industries Development Corporation (SMIDEC), Standards and Industrial Research Institute of Malaysia (SIRIM) and the MSC have resumed the promotion of industrial and technological development. Financial restructuring has also enabled a slight recovery in car sales, which had dipped by 52.6 per cent in 1998. Unlike the experience of Indonesia and Thailand, however, Malaysia has avoided the IMF conditions because of its lower external debt servicing problems. A number of programmes have been introduced to assist the cash-starved manufacturing sector. Of the 41 small and medium industries (SMI) support funds made available as of mid-March 1999, the Bank Negara was managing nine, comprising RM7.4 billion (NST, 26 March 1999).

IMPLICATIONS

The selective use of foreign exchange controls did bring some positive effects. The offshore bank in Singapore had to dispense with the ringgit, thereby eliminating external restrictions on the velocity of circulation. Making ringgit transactions abroad complemented this strategy. By preventing Malaysians, other than those engaged in export and other related concerns, from holding bank accounts, and taking cash exceeding 10000 ringgit abroad, the government removed the potential for capital flight. The initial controls on capital brought into Malaysia were removed, thereby stimulating the previously panic-ridden to bring back their money. While neighbouring economies resented these moves, as they shielded Malaysia without providing similar shields for them, they worked to reduce sharply capital flights abroad. The exemptions offered to export-oriented firms ensured that such operations were not deterred. Hence Malaysia did not face the typical problems of black market operations and confusion from controls on foreign exchange reminiscent of economies using multiple exchange rates, such as India and Myanmar.

Also shields imposed on the capital markets, including the banning of the unauthorized stock market counter in Singapore, prevented runs on companies and banks. The acquisition of NPLs helped raise liquidity and pump greater credit to revive a contracting economy. While the other crisis-affected economies of South Korea, Thailand, Indonesia and the Philippines were seriously paralysed by credit controls for a longer period, Malaysia managed to avert such deflationary pressures through a revival of credit flows from late 1998, though the evidence on whether they were directed to productive and efficient ventures is unclear.

Strategies to stimulate investment through lower interest rates did help assist recovery in several sub-sectors, albeit confined more to specific sub-sectors such as passenger cars and housing where the glut was gradually reduced through aggressive government promotion and the reliance on employee salaries as collateral. Unlike the case of Thailand, where interest rates fell to 4.0 per cent against Malaysia's 3.75 per cent, the acquisition of NPLs in the latter helped reduce the default portfolios. The low interest rate did not spark a capital flight from Malaysia to high interest rate havens owing to controls on capital flows abroad.

Malaysia was also fortunate to experience a cyclical recovery in its prime manufacturing industry, electric and electronics, which saw a major resurgence in exports from 1999. Reviving global demand helped Malaysia expand further its trade balance, which was already up from a slump in imports after the currency crash. Also, unlike the other crisis-affected economies, Malaysia benefited considerably from a rise in oil palm prices from 1987 until 1998 which, along with falling export prices and rising import prices, helped overturn the current account deficit. Oil prices – rising by almost three times in the period 1998–2000 – did not affect Malaysia as much as South Korea, the Philippines and Thailand because of its status as a net oil exporter. These developments were driven from factors fortuitous to currency controls.

However, revival efforts seem to reinforce the problems that confronted technological capability building prior to the crisis in Malaysia. Because the government diagnosed the crisis as being caused by speculative attacks, more salient problems inhibiting industrial transformation have not received fresh attention. The resurgence in capital inflows to East Asia and the stability offered by capital controls after 2 September 1998 merely revived capital supply to industry along the channels that were in place prior to the crisis. The broad property sector, which was identified earlier as a major cause of the bubble, has become the prime target of Danaharta. Thus the same problems that plagued industrial transition earlier have remained.

Government projects in Malaysia on the implementation of the Second Industrial Master Plan (IMP) and the promotion of strategic industries have continued to receive strong funding without any strategic review. While industrial investment is both desirable and necessary, as was pointed out earlier, without effective institutional reforms to drive technical change it could only exacerbate the savings–investment gap in the long run. For example, electronics industry policies intended to reverse import dependence, strengthen local participation and stimulate industrial deepening through integration of the value-added chain – for example, wafer fabrication, designing and branding – have not achieved their objectives sufficiently. While state-level development projects have faced a slash in budgets,[9] national projects have continued to enjoy priority. Hence, although an expansionary low-interest policy has enabled an investment revival, the resurgence in industrial development continues to reproduce the innovation deficits generated by policies prior to the financial crisis. Nevertheless, the government has shelved a number of mega infrastructure development activities, which have been viewed as grand, for the moment. For example, the bridge project linking Sumatra and Melaka and the new airport project in Kedah have been frozen, while the Bakun Dam has been continued with far smaller funds.

While the crisis measures have established stability, a number of problems have gone without effective scrutiny. First, the preferential loans required a clear mechanism for identifying productive firms, which was not developed. Second, interviews show that funds meant for the SMIs were not distributed accordingly.[10] Third, the sudden contraction in domestic demand and rise in import prices crippled a number of manufacturing firms. Except for rubber products, industrial output of all other manufacturing industries declined in 1998. The fall involving domestic-oriented industries was sharper. Manufacturing as a whole fell by 10.2 per cent in 1998, while export-oriented and domestic-oriented output declined by 7.3 per cent and 13.5 per cent, respectively. The domestic-oriented transport equipment (−52.1 per cent), basic metals (−29.0 per cent), non-metal mineral products (−26.4 per cent) and fabricated metals (−17.0 per cent) experienced the largest declines. Within the export-oriented industries, electrical (−14.6 per cent) and wood-based products (−11.1 per cent) faced the biggest falls. Nevertheless, as noted earlier, the revival in global demand has helped revive the foreign-owned export-oriented industries in the country. Electronics in particular has picked up strongly from early 1999. The Industrial Production Index (IPI) grew by 8.9 per cent, with manufacturing recording a growth of 12.7 per cent in the period 1998–9 (NST, 10 February 2000: 22). Domestically shielded industries such as cars have also begun to grow rapidly, but these industries have not expanded their export shares, suggesting that they are still heavily dependent on subsidies and tariffs.

Malaysia's prime concerns involve the correction of investment direction to ensure the emergence of efficient institutional support, including the network as well as its translation into rising productivity. Unless these changes take effect, the country will only become a location for low value-added activities where labour shortages and wage rises will be unproductively controlled through labour imports.

Given that the previous structures and coordination mechanisms have remained in Malaysia, it can be argued that similar problems are likely to restrict firms' movement up the technology ladder. Despite launching several programmes to stimulate technological deepening, its support institutions are still weakly coordinated. The negative effect of an FDI slowdown has left a number of foreign ventures in disarray. Negative publicity has affected the implementation of the MSC programme, though it began as a masterfully conceived venture. The MSC was aimed at short-cutting the process of spawning a cluster of local expertise in media-related electronics ventures. It was expected to comprise a range of firms including the Internet, telecommunications, electronics and computers by attracting cutting-edge firms to function with the requisite scientific, technological, legal and infrastructural requirements using both foreign and local ventures to spearhead a revolution in information technology. The modern cyber city of Cyber Jaya, located in the MSC, involved sophisticated information technology infrastructure support for all occupants. Political tensions and clampdowns on dissent from 1997 have raised some doubts.[11]

With the exception of process deepening in Penang, where a combination of effective government–business coordination helped generate the requisite institutional framework for human capital transformation, supplier formation and market-oriented technology development assisted the realization of strong cluster dynamics, the remaining sites in the country still function truncatedly. In Penang, the Penang Development Corporation and the state government played key intermediary roles to build strong government–business networks, which formed the basis for the formation of the Penang skills development and design centres. Driven by both private and public needs, these centres specialize primarily in providing skills training and designing services demanded by firms in Penang (see Rasiah, 2000). Hence a number of firms in Penang have managed to move into designing, although the lack of market support has restricted the extent of their movement in the value-added chain. The recession in the electronics industry has also affected demand seriously. The government has not generated countercyclical measures to ameliorate problems facing local firms in Penang. The rising exchange rates prior to the crisis had already affected sales earlier owing to cheapening of imports.

Rising production costs and tough external competition forced Malaysia to review its export strategies and domestic capabilities from the mid-1990s. Growth in foreign-dominated export processing activities has largely involved expansion of relatively low value-added production. With labour reserves exhausted, especially in the western industrial corridor of Malaysia, firms have had to face serious capacity expansion limits. In industries where changing production technologies have required more high-technology processes, as in microelectronics assembly and testing, demand for skilled workers grew even before labour shortages gripped the Malaysian economy (see Rasiah, 1996). The premium for skilled workers has thus gone up in Malaysia, thereby accentuating a dual or segmented labour market. Especially cheap labour imports to Malaysia from neighbouring countries have held down unskilled workers' wages and slowed down labour-intensive firms' initiatives to upgrade their process technologies (see World Bank, 1995a; Rasiah, 1995; Edwards, 1996). As a consequence a dual regime of multi-skilled and casualized workforces coexists within and between firms (see Rasiah and Osman, 1997).

Although the government took US$300 million of the US$l billion loan from the World Bank to install safety nets, support for small and medium-scale firms and low-cost housing, efforts to assist the poor have not received as much attention. While the absolute decline in incomes involving the rich has far exceeded that of the working class, rising unemployment has also undermined the livelihoods of the poor in Malaysia, albeit far less than in the other crisis-affected economies. For every capitalist affected, hundreds of workers have had to face retrenchment. In addition to 'voluntary resignations' faced by workers following reduced work and salaries involving the motor car and electronics industries until 1999, the National Union of Banking Employees (NUBE) also faces the potential problem of similarly arranged resignations once the mergers are completed. Workers displaced from the job stream have faced a complete loss in income, making their relative losses far higher than those of managers and state bureaucrats. Interviews with officials of the Malaysian Trade Union Congress (MTUC) showed that the safety net loan has been primarily used to meet deficits in government finance.[12] Because workers and the MTUC have not enjoyed sufficient powers, few programmes have been launched to help them.

Bank mergers to ameliorate the financial sector problems still remain unresolved. The pre-crisis strategy of managing banking mergers involving overexposed banks such as Bank Bumiputera with Bank of Commerce and Sime Bank with Rashid Hussein Bank was later extended to reduce the number of banks to six. That strategy hit a snag following complaints by the banks that the selection of anchor banks was not based on performance criteria. The implementation of these measures could also lead to massive lay-offs. While the NUBE has claimed that the unique Malaysian economy has a way to absorb workers following 'golden handshakes', it is unclear whether workers will enjoy the privilege of choosing their options. The NUBE itself is currently devastated by police reports over its deals in the stock market, causing it to lose RM23 million following the stock market crash of 1997–8 (NST, 10 February 2000: 1).

CONCLUSIONS

Malaysia faced serious flaws involving a number of its deeper economic fundamentals. Although the spread of basic education has expanded strongly, Malaysia lagged in skill development. The requisite instruments for effective technology development for improving competitiveness were only launched from the late 1980s. Despite efforts to improve the situation, various limitations have restricted Malaysia's capacity to sustain competitiveness in international markets. Hence, at the time of the crash, the country was already gripped by serious institutional drawbacks that were restricting industrial upgrading that is necessary to offset rising production costs. It must strengthen its second-order fundamentals now that the crisis has been brought under control to avoid a repeat of the slowdown. Such efforts should not be driven by excessive reliance on loans.

Capital controls helped shield the economy, but it is unclear whether effective reforms are under way to prevent the large-scale flow of scarce resources to inefficient firms or whether credit resumption to selected firms has accompanied effective reforms. It seems with the resumption of growth that some old practices of patronage and corrupt business practices have re-emerged. The economic recovery and state-led recovery initiatives have helped rejuvenate a number of large companies; examples include Renong, Bank Bumiputera–Commerce Bank, MISC and MAS. However, the opaque nature of reforms does not offer a clearer assessment of how these organizations will fare once the economy is forced to deregulate further.

Hence recommendations to prevent turmoil of the kind that emerged in 1997 should emphasize legal reforms and accountability. It is necessary to stop short-selling and raise accountability to prevent a colossal transfer of rents and the continuation of subsidies without emphasis on performance standards. Unless the judiciary is given more authority and is seen to function independently of the legislature, the legal instruments created to ensure accountability could be compromised against the interests of efficiency and distribution. Given the divergence in interests and outcomes facing the social utility function of individuals and the imaginary society aggregate, even if perfectly static information is assumed, the incidence of deviation between the former and the latter can be minimized with greater civil society participation.

Capability building that is aimed at the achievement of international competitiveness is critical to reviving Malaysia's industrial and technological development vertically. Only then can Malaysia get onto the path of sustainable industrialization. While the critical mass is a prerequisite for viable ventures, effective capability building rather than capacity expansion is central for establishing competitive industrial development. Malaysia enjoys a far better infrastructure base to support industrial and technological development than Thailand, the Philippines and Indonesia. However, it requires better coordination and management to ensure effective technological governance, which it urgently requires to achieve long-term growth and macroeconomic stability.

NOTES

1. Interviews by author with a vice president of a local commercial bank in 1998.
2. Interviews by author with a vice president of a local commercial bank in 1998.
3. Interviews by the author in 1997.
4. Nevertheless, considering the early stage of growth and rapid structural change, capital

and total factor productivity measures should not be a major source of alarm, as they are generally associated with large intial outlays of lumpy investments.
5. Supporting Krugman's (1997) restatement of Young's (1995) statement of unsustainable growth, that is, growth achieved through perspiration rather than inspiration. While I disagree with Krugman's generalization of this finding to the whole of East Asia, Southeast Asia's second tiers tend to support the finding. I have argued elsewhere that South Korea's débâcle had little to do with growing deficits in productivity and innovation (see Rasiah, 1999a).
6. Computed from Radelet and Sachs (1998: Table 5).
7. This unweighted sample had firms from all industries at the three-digit standard industrial classification (SIC) level, located in all states except for Kelantan, Terengganu, Perlis and the federal territory of Labuan.
8. Interview conducted by the author in 1994.
9. Examples of state-level projects that have faced a cut in budget include the Negeri Sembilan Industrial Master Plan and the Sarawak Industrial Master Plan.
10. Drawn from interviews with 56 SMIs spread over the Kelang Valley, Penang and Johor region in 1999 by the author.
11. Drawn from comments from one of its leading supporters, Alvin Toffler, in 1998, and interviews with 18 electronics multinationals located in the Kelang Valley in 1999.
12. Interviews by the author in 1999.

REFERENCES

ADB (1999), *Asian Economic Outlook*, Manila: Asian Development Bank.

Anuwar, Ali (1992), *Malaysian Industrialization: The Quest for Technology*, Kuala Lumpur: Oxford University Press.

Bank Negara Malaysia (1997), *Quarterly Economic Bulletin,* Kuala Lumpur: Bank Negara.

Edwards, C.B. (1996), 'Foreign Labour in Malaysian Development: A Strategic Shift?', IKMAS working paper no. 6, Bangi.

Gomez, T. and K.S. Jomo (1997), *Political Economy of Malaysia*, Melbourne: Cambridge University Press.

Jomo, K.S. (1998), 'The Malaysian Financial Crisis: From Miracle to Debacle', mimeo.

Kornai, J. (1962), 'Appraisal of Project Appraisal', in M.J. Boskin (ed.), *Economics of Human Welfare: Essays in Honor of Tibor Scitovsky*, New York: Academic Press.

Krugman, P. (1997), 'What ever Happened to Asia?', *Foreign Affairs*, 18 August.

Lall, S, V. Selvaratnam, W. Rees, V. Danaraj and R. Rasiah (1996), 'Review of the Action Plan for Industrial Technology Development in Malaysia', World Bank report submitted to Ministry of Science Technology and Environment of Malaysia, Kuala Lumpur.

Lee, J.S. (1994), 'The Role of the State in Economic Restructuring and Development: The Case of Taiwan', Occasional Paper series, no. 9403, Chung-Hua Institution for Economic Research, Taipei.

Malaysia (1981), *Third Malaysia Plan 1981–85*, Kuala Lumpur: Government Printers.

Malaysia (1993), *Economic Report 1993–94*, Kuala Lumpur: Government Printers.

Malaysia (1994), *Ministry of International Trade and Industry Report*, Kuala Lumpur: Government Printers.

Malaysia (1996), *The Sixth Malaysia Plan 1996–2000*, Kuala Lumpur: Government Printers.

MASTIC (1994), *1992 National Survey of Research and Development*, Kuala Lumpur: Malaysian Science and Technology Information Center.

NST (1999), 'Danaharta Exceeds Target by Buying RM19.73b NPLS', 17 March, p. 21.

NST (1999), 'SMI Funds Campaign Should Also Be Held in Other States', 26 March, p.2.

NST (2000), 'NUBE Lost RM23m', 10 February, p. 1.

NST (2000), 'IPI Shows Robust Growth Last Year', 10 February, p. 22.

Polanyi, K. (1957), *The Great Transforniation,* Boston: Beacon Press.

Radelet, S. and J. Sachs (1998), 'The East Asian Financial Crisis: Diagnosis, Remedies and Prospects', paper presented at the Brookings Panel, Washington, DC, 26–27 March.

Rasiah, R. (1995), 'Labour and Industrialization in Malaysia', *Journal of Contemporary Asia*, 25(l).

Rasiah, R. (1996), 'Institutions and Innovations: Moving towards the Technology Frontier in Malaysia's Electronics Industry', *Industry and Innovation*, 3(2).

Rasiah, R. (1998a), 'The Malaysian Financial Crisis: Capital Expansion, Cronyism and Contraction', *Asia Pacific Economy*, 3(3).

Rasiah, R. (1998b), 'The Export Manufacturing Experience of Indonesia, Malaysia and Thailand', UNCTAD discussion paper no. 137, Geneva.

Rasiah, R. (1999a), 'Assessing the Rescue Packages of Asian Economies Destabilised by Financial Crisis', in Rahman Embong and J. Randolph (eds),

Rasiah, R. (1999b), 'Malaysia's National Innovation System', in K.S. Jomo and G. Felker (eds), *Technology, Competitiveness and the State: Industrial Technology Development in Malaysia*, London: Routledge.

Rasiah, R. (2000), 'Innovation and Cluster Dynamics Development in Malaysia', mimeo.

Rasiah, R. and Ali Anuwar (1995), 'Governing Industrial Technology Transfer', paper presented at the conference on Governance Mechanisms and Technical Change in Malaysian Manufacturing, Bangi, 14–15 July.

Rasiah, R. and S. Ishak (2001), 'Market, Government and Malaysia's New Economic Policy', *Cambridge Journal of Economics*, 25(1).

Rasiah, R. and R.H. Osman (1997), 'Enterprise Training in Malaysia's Manufacturing Sector', IKMAS Working Papers, No. 12, Bangi.

Rowthorn, R. and J. Wells (1987), *Deindustrialisation and Foreign Trade*, Cambridge: Cambridge University Press.

Rugayah, M. (1995), 'Public Enterprises', in K.S. Jomo (ed.), *Privatizing Malaysia, Rents, Rhetoric and Reality,* Boulder: Westview.

Star (1999), '22% Pick-up Seen for Motor Vehicle Sales', 30 January, Business Section, p. 2.

Tham, S.Y. (1998), 'Policy and Productivity', mimeo.

UNCTAD (1997), *Trade and Development Report*, Geneva: United Nations Conference for Trade and Development.

UNDP (1995), *Human Development Report*, New York: United Nations Development Program/Oxford University Press.

World Bank (1994), *World Development Report*, New York: Oxford University Press.

World Bank (1995a), 'Human Resource Development in Malaysia: Demand–supply Mismatch', report submitted to Economic Planning Unit, Kuala Lumpur.

World Bank (1995b), *World Development Report,* New York: Oxford University Press.

World Bank (1997), *World Development Report*, New York: Oxford University Press.

World Bank (1998), *World Development Report*, New York: Oxford University Press.

World Bank MOSTE (1996), 'Review of the Action Plan for Industrial Technology Development', report submitted to the Ministry of Science, Technology and Environment, Kuala Lumpur.

Young, A. (1995), 'Tyranny of Numbers: Confronting the Statistical Realities of the East Asian Growth Experience', *Quarterly Journal of Economics*.

8. The East Asian crisis: the Philippines experience

Joseph Y. Lim[1]

INTRODUCTION

Among the victims of the East Asian crisis, the Philippines was the only one not earlier touted as an East Asian 'tiger' or newly industrialized country (NIC). The significance of the crisis for the Philippines and its impact on it are therefore qualitatively different from that on the other countries.

Unlike its East Asian neighbours, the Philippines followed a boom–bust cycle in its recent history of economic development (see growth rate figures in Appendix, which presents selected macro indicators of the hard-hit countries of the Asian crisis). Not only did the Philippines lag behind its 'tiger' neighbours in terms of economic growth, it also failed to penetrate export markets, achieve technological advancement, eradicate poverty and promote overall social and human development (see Lim, 1998b; Agosin and Ffrench-Davis, 1998).

The Philippines' failure to replicate the earlier successes of the so-called East Asian 'tigers' is thus crucial in studying the impact of the East Asian crisis on it. Its domestic savings rate was low compared with those of its East Asian neighbours (see Appendix). It suffered growing trade and current account deficits during periods of growth and boom. On the other hand, the growth of the other East Asian countries in the second half of the 1980s – when their 'tiger' or NIC reputation was at its height – was accompanied more or less by high export growth and manageable trade and current account deficits. This meant that high foreign exchange earnings matched their import needs and sustained their high growth as 'tigers' or NICs. The high domestic savings of the East Asian 'tigers' also pointed to their ability to finance high investments domestically, whereas both the Philippines' domestic savings rate and the percentage share of capital formation in GDP were much lower in the 1980s and 1990s (see Table 8.1).[2]

However, in the early 1980s and in the prelude to the East Asian crisis in the 1990s, the other East Asian economies affected by the crisis, like the

Table 8.1 Some macro indicators of the Philippines, 1981–99

Year	GDP growth rate	GNP growth rate	GNP per capita (1985 price)	Unempl. rate (%)	Labour productivity (GDP/empl)
1981	3.4	3.2	12.643	8.7	38.002
1982	3.6	2.8	12.633	9.4	38.878
1983	1.9	1.5	12.526	7.9	37.419
1984	−7.3	−8.8	11.110	10.6	33.729
1985	−7.3	−7.0	10.086	11.1	31.533
1986	3.4	4.2	10.205	11.1	31.399
1987	4.3	4.6	10.476	9.1	30.785
1988	6.8	7.7	10.971	8.3	31.058
1989	6.2	5.6	11.385	8.4	31.927
1990	3.0	3.7	11.661	8.1	32.446
1991	−0.6	0.4	11.456	9.0	31.270
1992	0.3	1.3	11.382	8.6	30.340
1993	2.1	2.8	11.151	8.9	30.111
1994	4.4	5.3	11.456	8.4	30.616
1995	4.7	4.9	11.734	8.4	31.269
1996	5.8	7.2	12.298	7.4	31.209
1997	5.2	5.3	12.663	7.9	32.168
1998	−0.5	0.1	12.362	9.6	31.841
1999	3.2	3.6	12.535	9.4	31.635

Table 8.1 (cont.)

Year	Exchange rate	Growth of exchange rate	Inflation rate	T-bill rates (91 days)	M3/GDP	Growth of M3/CPI (in %)	Money multiplier
1981	7.90		17.3	12.55	0.2931	13.32	3.82
1982	8.54	8.10	8.6	13.78	0.3029	7.20	4.07
1983	11.11	30.13	5.3	14.26	0.3095	12.84	3.34
1984	16.70	50.27	47.1	28.24	0.2334	−27.10	3.05
1985	18.61	11.43	23.4	25.87	0.2346	−11.25	2.86
1986	20.39	9.56	−0.4	15.63	0.2370	8.08	2.57
1987	20.57	0.89	3.0	11.51	0.2370	8.82	2.59
1988	21.10	2.56	8.9	14.67	0.2483	12.56	2.76
1989	21.74	3.04	12.2	18.64	0.2744	14.06	2.61
1990	24.31	11.84	13.2	26.67	0.2790	3.67	2.44
1991	27.48	13.03	18.5	21.11	0.2781	−2.67	2.47
1992	25.51	−7.15	8.6	16.02	0.2851	1.92	2.51
1993	27.12	6.30	7.0	12.45	0.3258	15.82	2.73
1994	26.45	−2.47	8.3	12.71	0.3589	16.02	3.10
1995	25.70	−2.84	8.0	11.30	0.3995	15.95	3.32
1996	26.21	1.98	9.1	12.40	0.4058	6.81	3.36
1997	29.47	12.44	5.9	13.10	0.4398	15.08	3.50
1998	40.89	38.76	9.8	15.30	0.4291	−2.33	3.62
1999	39.09	−4.41	6.6	10.20	0.4567	12.70	3.95

Source: National Statistical Coordination Board.

Philippines, suffered high or deteriorating current account balances. This indicated a tendency for the investment–savings gap to widen in these countries. They used up more foreign exchange than they could earn. This translated during the latest crisis into 'overborrowing' of financial capital in the form of foreign unhedged short-term debt and overspending on 'wrong' investments (such as real estate and overpriced equities which created 'bubbles').

For the Philippines, the crisis reflected a similar 'overborrowing' and 'overspending'. The main difference was that the true 'tigers'[3] had a higher capacity to save and had higher export earnings. But this also meant that they were trying to grow too fast with respect to their savings and foreign exchange earnings capacity. As long as their currencies were not too overvalued and their savings and export earnings continued at their high levels, one could imagine these economies growing at 4 per cent to 6 per cent per annum (as Taiwan has been doing since the 1990s) without much need of foreign exchange inflows. But very high growth rates and significant overvaluation of the currency in the 1990s necessitated foreign capital inflows to finance the investment–savings and foreign exchange gaps. And because foreign investors had great confidence in these countries, this financing, until the eruption of the latest crisis, was easy to obtain.

The Philippines, however, suffered from a structural defect whereby, to be able to grow respectably at, say, 5 per cent per annum, considerable trade and current account deficits would have to arise because of its low savings rate and low export capacity vis-à-vis imports. Trade deficits exceeded 13 per cent of GDP before the crisis, much larger than those of any East Asian country (see Table 8.2a and Appendix). What prevented the current account deficit from reaching alarming levels was the remittances of Filipino overseas workers.

The present crisis in a way could be seen as a continuation of the boom–bust cycle in Philippine economic history. A boom, which increased trade and current account deficits, could be sustained only if there was enough foreign financing. Unfortunately, this financing was easily withdrawn and depleted as fundamentals weakened (which further widened the trade and current account gaps) and as confidence in the economy waned.

BOOM–BUST CYCLES IN THE 1980S AND EARLY 1990S

The bust part of the cycle is partly reflected in the sharp economic decline in the mid-1980s. It was an economic crisis comparable to the decline of Indonesia in 1998. It included political instability, massive foreign debt problems and overhang, sharp devaluation, high inflation and high interest rates. The years 1984 and 1985 alone set the Philippines back more than ten years in terms of GNP per capita (see Table 8.1). The worldwide foreign debt crisis and political chaos during the twilight years of the Marcos regime made sure that foreign credit and capital inflows ceased and that capital flight by both domestic and foreign residents and investors took place. The IMF 'rescue' programme, which was a programme of draconian monetary and fiscal belt tightening, ensured economic collapse just as it would do to Indonesia around a decade and a half later.

The economy recovered from 1986 to 1990 under the Aquino regime, but this was short-lived as the foreign debt overhang wiped out foreign exchange reserves and as military coups against the Aquino government killed the 'animal spirits' of both domestic and foreign investors. Whereas massive foreign direct investments from Japan went to the ASEAN countries as a result of the Plaza Accord and the yen appreciation, during this period, the Philippines missed out on the East Asian 'take-off' of its Southeast Asian neighbours.

Further stagnation was to occur in 1991 and 1992, a period accompanied again by some initial devaluation, high inflation and high interest rates. The foreign exchange depletion and political instability (marked by a serious coup in late 1989 that almost toppled the Aquino government) brought a downturn in 1991, aggravated once more by tight monetary and fiscal policies dictated by the IMF programme. The economic stagnation lasted up to 1993 as crippling power shortages (a result of economic mismanagement) prevented any quick recovery. This stagnation, together with the economic collapse in the mid-1980s, set the Philippines back 15 years in terms of GNP per capita. In 1997 – the year when the crisis hit – the Philippines was just at the level of GNP per capita of the early 1980s (see Table 8.1).

The Philippines' East Asian neighbours all this time continued their unprecedented growth and the gap with the Philippines widened considerably.

PROCESSES LEADING TO THE CRISIS

The Macroeconomy in the 1990s

When the Ramos government came to power, things began to improve. The country's debt burden was significantly reduced with the implementation of the Brady Plan. The increased remittances of Filipino overseas contract workers (OCWs) – already a growing item in the 1980s – intensified in the 1990s. The fast tracking of the construction of hydroelectric plants under the Ramos administration (1992–3) resolved the energy crisis. The Ramos government was able to inject political and economic stability and confidence into the system. This was further amplified by the dissolution of the debt-strapped central bank and its recreation as the Bangko Sentral ng Pilipinas (BSP), the liberalization of bank entry to domestic and foreign banks, and the liberalization of the foreign exchange and capital accounts.

The Ramos administration deepened the market liberalization and privatization processes started by the Aquino government. On the domestic front, the deregulation of key industries (telecommunications, oil, banking) was undertaken in earnest, with the telecommunications industry subsequently exhibiting significant improvements in productivity and growth.[4] On the external front, the government locked the country into trade liberalization by joining the World Trade Organization (WTO), the ASEAN Free Trade Area (AFTA), and the Asia–Pacific Economic Cooperation (APEC). The Philippines reduced its tariffs unilaterally ahead of the schedule it was bound to by international agreements and way ahead of its neighbours. The economy exhibited extreme confidence, impressed foreign investors and looked as if it was ready for a strong economic take-off.

Strong confidence in the Philippines was first manifested in the sharp rise of the local stock exchange as foreign and domestic investors scrambled to enter the 'emerging market' set for high take-off. The stock index jumped severalfold in 1993. From then on, volatility and large volumes in short-term portfolio inflows and outflows characterized the external capital accounts. Net direct foreign investments and net medium- and long-term borrowings, though, did increase significantly (see Tables 8.2a and 8.2b) owing to the greater confidence in the Philippines as an 'emerging' market and to the final resolution of the foreign debt crisis with the conversion of foreign debts to long-term bonds.

Perceived Strong Economic Fundamentals

Indeed, the macroeconomic fundamentals looked as if they were going to lead to an economic take-off. The inflation rate – which was very volatile and going to very high levels during stagflation and bust periods – was tamed. It fell to single digits in 1992 and continued to fall until 1998, when the country was already well into the financial crisis (see Table 8.1). GDP growth rates picked up, rising by more than 4 per cent in 1994 and 1995 and more than 5 per cent in 1996 and 1997. The national government deficit went into surplus from 1994 to 1997, while the consolidated public sector deficit turned positive in 1996 and 1997.[5]

Interest rates – which were raised as part of the stabilization measures to stave off external deficits and which had made recessions quite severe in the mid-1980s and early 1990s – started to go down towards 11 per cent to 13 per cent. Meanwhile, liquidity increased tremendously but did not cause inflationary pressures as income velocity decreased and the money multiplier expanded (see Table 8.1). This initially seemed to indicate financial deepening but later proved to be a symptom of the 'overborrowing' syndrome of the McKinnon–Pill type.

The trade sector – both exports and imports – started to explode, with annual growth rates surpassing 15 per cent for most years. While import growth still exceeded export growth, the high growth rate of exports was unprecedented in the economic history of the Philippines. This resulted in exceedingly high confidence, spurred partly by the government propaganda that a 'tiger cub' was in the making. Indeed, the 'overexuberance' due to the credible reforms and stability introduced by the Ramos government brought about a McKinnon-style overlending by foreign short-run creditors and overborrowing by domestic borrowers.

The above picture unfortunately concealed some important figures. Starting in 1993, the trade deficit in merchandise goods as a percentage of GNP shot up to more than 11 per cent from 1993 to 1995 and increased to around 13 per cent in 1996 and 1997. Lower foreign debt and interest payments and, more importantly, large remittances of overseas workers kept the current account deficit low but still significant at substantially more than 4 per cent of GNP in the 1994–7 period (see Tables 8.2a and 8.2b). This happened at a time when the currency was appreciating in nominal terms between 1992 and 1995 and, prior to the financial crisis hitting East Asia, was kept very stable.

The stable and appreciating currency was a result partly of the net external inflows brought about by the exuberance during this period and partly of the conscious policy by the Bangko Sentral ng Pilipinas (BSP) to have a stable currency as part of macroeconomic stability.

The appreciating currency accompanied by growing trade and high current account deficits was the single most damaging evidence to show that economic fundamentals were not as rosy as the government and private investors had painted them. Furthermore, the twin effects of currency appreciating in real terms and substantial tariff reductions in the mid-1990s made imports exceedingly cheap and increased import intensity. The ratio of imports to GDP increased from 40 per cent of GDP in 1992 to 64 per cent of GDP in 1997. (Exports grew from 33.6 per cent of GDP in 1992 to 52 per cent of GDP in 1997.) This, as we have seen, contributed to the growing trade deficits.

In addition, the composition of exports showed that much of export growth was attributable to only one commodity, electronics and electrical equipment/parts and telecommunications, which in 1992 comprised less than a third of dollar-denominated exports of merchandise goods but

Table 8.2a Balance of payments, 1992–9 (US dollars mn)

Item	1992	1993	1994	1995	1996	1997	1998	1999
I. Current account, net	−858	−3016	−2950	−3297	−3953	−4 351	1 546	7 188
(as % of GNP)	−1.6	−5.5	−4.5	−4.3	−4.6	−5.1	2.3	9.0
A. Trade, net	−1675	−3715	−3886	−4179	−4542	−5431	1111	6707
(as % of GNP)	−3.1	−6.7	−5.9	−5.5	−5.2	−6.3	1.6	8.4
Goods, net	−4695	−6 222	−7850	−8944	−11 342	−11 127	−28	4306
(as % of GNP)	−8.7	−11.2	−11.9	−11.7	−13.1	−13	−0.04	5.4
Services, net	3020	2 507	3964	4765	6800	5696	1 139	2401
B. Transfers, net	817	699	936	882	589	1080	435	481
II. Capital and financial account, net	1850	2820	4547	3393	11075	6593	478	590
A. Medium & long-term loans, net	633	2455	1313	1276	2841	4824	2740	4716
B. Trading of bonds in the secondary market				−37	−676	−1083	102	
C. Investments, net	737	812	1 558	1 609	3 517	762	1 672	1 218
D. Change in the NFA of KBs	289	299	674	564	4214	1 188	−1 330	−1 836
E. Purchase of collateral	469							
F. Short-term capital, net	660	148	1002	56	540	495	−1 521	−3 610
III. Others	657	544	254	81	−5	−360	96	280
A. Monetization of gold	130	113	154	177	198	105	118	198
B. Revaluation of adjustments	527	431	100	96	−203	−465	−22	82
IV. Net unclassified items	−157	−514	−49	454	−3010	−5245	−761	−4219
V. Overall BOP position	1492	−166	1802	631	4107	−3363	1359	3839
(as % of GNP)	2.8	−0.3	2.7	0.8	4.8	−3.9	2.0	4.8

Source: Bangko Sentral ng Pilipinas (BSP).

Table 8.2b Foreign investments, 1992–9 (US dollars mn)

Item	1992	1993	1994	1995	1996	1997	1998	1999
Investments, net	737	812	1558	1609	3517	762	1672	1218
A. Non-resident								
Investments in the Philippines	931	2135	2492	2944	3621	843	2016	1589
Direct investments	776	1238	1591	1459	1520	1249	1752	1077
Portfolio investments	155	897	901	1485	2101	−406	264	512
B. Less: resident investments abroad	194	1323	934	1335	104	81	344	371
Direct investments	101	374	302	98	182	136	160	206
Portfolio investments	93	949	632	1237	−78	184	184	165

Source: Bangko Sentral ng Pilipinas.

increased to more than 50 per cent of merchandise exports in 1997. This lack of diversification of export growth could perhaps be explained partly by an appreciating currency and partly by the low growth in labour productivity, which brings up an important point. Labour productivity in the Philippines has been on a long-run decline partly because of the booms and busts and the stagnant growth (see Table 8.1). Moreover, the latest growth period – from 1994 to 1997 – did not show any significant improvement in labour productivity except for a small increase in 1997.

Looking at the growth rate of the economy by sectors, one could see that, although manufacturing grew respectably (more or less near the GDP growth rate) in 1994–7, the biggest growth rates came from construction and finance (followed by transport/communication/storage and electricity/gas/water). It should be clear in hindsight that the lead sectors in the growth process were the non-tradeable sectors rather than the tradeables in agriculture and manufacturing. This again may be an indication that the appreciation of currency and tariff reductions in the 1990s made relative prices of non-tradeables more attractive than those of tradeables.

The Financial Conditions before the Crisis

As mentioned earlier, the high 'animal spirits' that pervaded the 1994–7 period were accompanied by a looser monetary policy. Money supply grew by more than 15 per cent annually in real terms for most years from 1993 to 1997. The high monetary expansion was accompanied by a 'boom' lending spree marked by a growing money multiplier and sharp declines in reserve requirement ratio (as prescribed by the monetary authorities) and currency deposit ratio (a sign of increasing volume of lending). The liquidity to income ratio (M3/GDP) increased significantly (Table 8.1).

Interest rates of various instruments fell significantly in pace with inflation. Treasury or T-bill rates for 91 days (the most circulated) fell from 16 per cent in 1992 to 11 per cent and 12 per cent in 1995 and 1996, respectively. Average bank lending rates fell from 19.4 per cent in 1992 to less than 15 per cent in 1995 and 1996. Easy money and easy credit became the name of the game.

The annual growth rate in loans outstanding for banks (in nominal terms) from 1993 to 1996 was more than 30 per cent. The biggest increase was in the years from 1995 to 1996. While loans outstanding for manufacturing grew tremendously from 1994 to 1996, these were outpaced more and more, especially from 1995 to early 1997, by loans to finance/real estate/business service; construction and transport/storage/communication and electricity/gas/water (see Table 8.3). Again the growing attractiveness of non-tradeables was manifested in 1995 and intensified in 1996 and early 1997.

Even if the domestic interest rate was going down from its 1992 levels, it

Table 8.3 *Loans outstanding of commercial banks, 1990–99**

(As % of total) Classified by economic activity	1990	1991	1992	1993	1994	1995	1996	1997	1998	1999
1. Agriculture, fisheries forestry	11.20	13.31	11.82	10.65	9.18	8.08	5.66	4.99	4.67	4.35
2. Mining and quarrying	2.59	2.11	2.10	2.49	1.03	0.77	0.85	1.15	1.49	1.22
3. Manufacturing	38.51	33.97	34.42	33.03	34.90	34.40	32.27	29.94	26.51	28.23
4. Electricity, gas & water	1.32	1.33	1.24	2.43	2.43	2.23	2.80	2.97	3.51	3.93
5. Construction	2.66	2.63	2.52	3.15	3.32	3.36	3.85	3.64	4.08	3.94
6. Wholesale & retail trade	14.47	16.81	16.26	15.71	17.52	17.71	16.09	16.29	15.59	15.00
7. Transport, storage & communication	3.76	3.44	3.38	3.90	4.79	6.06	6.12	7.15	7.32	6.72
8. Fin. inst., real estate & bus. service	16.86	18.28	20.06	16.71	18.30	16.81	21.82	24.60	25.76	25.30
9. Community, social & personal services	8.63	8.12	8.21	11.94	8.53	10.15	10.53	9.28	11.08	11.31
Total	100.00	100.00	100.00	100.00	100.00	100.00	100.00	100.00	100.00	100.00

(Growth rates) Classified by economic activity	1991	1992	1993	1994	1995	1996	1997	1998	1999
1. Agriculture, fisheries & forestry	30.61	10.07	19.10	8.14	19.58	6.43	11.46	−11.00	−6.47
2. Mining and quarrying	−10.54	23.22	56.91	−48.12	2.24	66.85	70.33	23.51	−17.87
3. Manufacturing	−3.03	25.63	26.87	32.50	33.88	42.55	17.34	−15.75	6.94
4. Electricity, gas & water	10.63	15.43	159.50	25.68	24.71	90.58	33.97	12.52	12.67
5. Construction	8.76	18.48	65.31	32.31	37.40	74.20	19.61	6.56	−2.89
6. Wholesale & retail trade	27.65	19.93	27.75	39.85	37.31	38.07	28.00	−8.92	−3.34
7. Transport, storage & communication	0.52	21.88	52.76	53.78	72.03	53.34	47.69	−2.58	−7.72
8. Fin. inst., real estate & bus. service	19.19	36.11	10.07	37.38	24.78	97.20	42.57	−0.33	−1.34
9. Community, social & personal services	3.43	25.37	92.07	−10.42	61.78	57.59	11.44	13.58	2.52
Total	9.91	23.99	32.19	25.41	35.83	51.95	26.47	−4.84	0.45

Note: *Peso and foreign accounts, but excluding transactions of local banks' foreign offices.

Source: Commercial banks' monthly statements of conditions, BSP.

was still significantly higher than the dollar interest rates. The significant interest rate differential could have been due to the following: (a) higher inflation rates in the Philippines compared with those in the United States and other developed countries; (b) a risk premium which had to be added owing to an overvalued currency that was not consistent with the levels of trade and current account deficits; and (c) the central bank policy of sterilizing external monetary inflows to keep the peso stable or appreciating. The probable causes of the interest rate differential (particularly the third one mentioned above) were quite controversial and triggered intense debates between the BSP and mainstream economists, particularly from the University of the Philippines (UP).

Whatever the reasons for the interest rate differential, the semblance of a very stable currency over the medium term encouraged, vis-à-vis domestic peso borrowings, unhedged dollar borrowings. As long as the currency remained stable (or appreciated) and was backed up by a credible central bank, borrowing in dollars at a lower interest rate and then converting to peso to invest in higher-yielding domestic assets or investments brought about windfall gains. The expectation that foreign inflows would continue and the general belief that the BSP would defend the peso and keep it from depreciating caused many of the dollar borrowings to be unhedged.

It is notable in Table 8.4, which gives us the foreign currency deposit unit (FCDU) loans by borrower, that the sharp borrowings from FCDUs occurred in the second half of 1995 and accelerated in the first half of 1996. The growth rate declined but remained at high levels in the second half of 1996. In terms of composition, we can see that, starting in 1996, commodity exporters (the naturally hedged borrowers) decreased their share of the loans. The category 'others' instead took an increasing share. It turned out that 'others' was made up of mostly unhedged borrowers investing in real estate and speculators out to make a quick killing.

Table 8.5 gives us the foreign exchange liabilities by various breakdowns. It must be pointed out that the share of the commercial banks' foreign exchange liabilities to total foreign exchange liabilities increased from 5.66 per cent in 1993 to 18 per cent in 1997. Private firms' liabilities increased from 15 per cent in 1993 to 27.5 per cent in 1997. The banking and private firms' combined share of foreign exchange liabilities increased from less than 21 per cent in 1992 to more than 45 per cent in 1997.

In terms of institutional creditors, foreign banks and other financial institutions' share of foreign exchange lending increased from 14.6 per cent in 1993 to 22.4 per cent in 1997. 'Other' institutional creditors (mostly private) increased their share from around 13 per cent in 1993 to 24.1 per cent in 1997. All these evince the drastic shift towards private borrowings by financial institutions and private firms as growth in private foreign debt

Table 8.4 Foreign currency deposit unit (FCDU) loans, by borrower (US dollars mn)

End of quarter	1993 Q4	1994 Q1	Q2	Q3	Q4	1995 Q1	Q2	Q3	Q4	1996 Q1	Q2	Q3
Commodity exporter	1108.817	1037.354	1267.316	1399.026	1715.786	1849.357	2220.752	2656.492	2985.804	3565.016	4535.652	5288.46
%	55.03	50.72	52.84	53.67	55.44	54.08	59.92	59.54	59.32	57.62	58.62	57.2
Service exporter	44.076	32.611	51.792	69.740	56.311	62.086	50.402	95.793	107.500	177.772	198.019	245.48
%	2.19	1.59	2.16	2.68	1.82	1.82	1.36	2.15	2.14	2.87	2.56	2.6
Producers/ manufacturers	18.535	20.573	12.109	13.554	14.603	48.531	47.296	62.557	56.606	60.417	63.595	65.27
%	0.92	1.01	0.50	0.52	0.47	1.42	1.28	1.40	1.12	0.98	0.82	0.7
Oil companies	492.368	432.054	490.417	587.744	538.739	613.980	340.750	284.059	400.276	423.483	487.038	514.11
%	24.44	21.12	20.45	22.55	17.41	17.95	9.19	6.37	7.95	6.84	6.29	5.5
Public utilities	335.045	439.634	482.754	432.898	448.623	599.315	699.785	744.571	869.567	885.930	1140.542	1197.63
%	16.63	21.49	20.13	16.61	14.50	17.52	18.88	16.69	17.27	14.32	14.74	12.9
Others	16.111	83.07	94.106	103.785	320.518	246.550	317.080	618.149	614.026	1075.005	1313.180	1928.67
%	0.80	4.06	3.92	3.98	10.36	7.21	8.56	13.85	12.20	17.37	16.97	20.8
Total	2014.952	2045.296	2398.494	2606.747	3094.580	3419.819	3706.065	4461.621	5033.779	6187.623	7738.026	9239.64

Source: BSP.

outpaced growth in public foreign debt. Table 8.5 also shows the shift towards short-term foreign debt, with the increase coming mainly from non-trade short-term debt.

Based on the central bank's data on non-performing loans, the Philippine banking system before the crisis exhibited no very alarming trends in non-performing loans (which stood at around 3 per cent or lower). There was a small jump, though, in the ratio of non-performing loans to total loans for commercial banks in the first half of 1997 right before the crisis (from 2.8 per cent in December 1996 to 3.4 per cent in June 1997). Another disturbing trend was the decline in the ratio of loan loss provision to total loans from 1993 to 1996, when domestic credit expanded at a very rapid rate. Still, overall, the ratios of non-performing loans remained low.

The Setting of the Crisis

In summary, the lower inflation, the much higher growth, the improved fiscal performance, and the large capital inflows and growing international

	1997				1998				1999		
Q4	Q1	Q2	Q3	Q4	Q1	Q2	Q3	Q4	Q1	Q2	Q3
5867.985	6081.205	6005.915	5989.271	5171.175	4362.917	3832.573	3339.050	2939.692	2777.111	2878.825	2845.419
55.48	54.85	50.39	50.99	49.71	46.85	44.53	40.04	37.10	37.65	39.08	48.70
285.588	288.296	301.288	389.941	351.086	333.650	346.172	307.808	304.483	271.142	268.516	261.740
2.70	2.60	2.53	3.32	3.37	3.58	4.02	3.69	3.84	3.68	3.65	4.48
89.278	97.439	153.694	166.826	150.470	136.372	138.564	129.059	117.123	95.877	116.171	133.582
0.84	0.88	1.29	1.42	1.45	1.46	1.61	1.55	1.48	1.30	1.58	2.29
448.702	378.320	418.672	450.740	402.127	246.592	159.014	117.594	303.733	215.012	270.896	301.643
4.24	3.41	3.51	3.84	3.87	2.65	1.85	1.41	3.83	2.91	3.68	5.16
1484.504	1399.071	1453.528	1484.115	1614.646	1632.405	1637.277	1723.993	1814.437	1749.143	1752.651	1733.000
14.04	12.62	12.20	12.64	15.52	17.53	19.02	20.68	22.90	23.71	23.79	29.66
2400.772	2843.377	3585.806	3264.532	2713.457	2600.071	2493.122	2720.865	2443.259	2268.294	2078.978	567.000
22.70	25.64	30.09	27.79	26.08	27.92	28.97	32.63	30.84	30.75	28.22	9.70
10576.829	11087.708	11918.903	11745.425	10402.961	9312.007	8606.722	8338.369	7922.727	7376.579	7366.037	5842.38

reserves of the Philippines were seen as strong economic fundamentals that would supposedly cause the birth of a 'baby tiger' in the East Asian region. Thus the financial 'earthquake' that hit the region in mid-1997 caught most policy makers and businessmen by surprise. It took them several months to accept the gravity of the crisis and the strong negative impact it would have on the economy.

Yet the Philippines' financial sector on the eve of the crisis was not in as dire shape as, say, those of Thailand and South Korea, although there was a general perception that the current account deficits might have been understated owing to overestimation from foreign currency deposit unit (FCDU) estimates of exports and remittances of overseas workers. The Philippines by itself would not have gone into a crisis in mid-1997. However, as explained above, it was very vulnerable in both the real and financial sectors to a strong, negative external shock, as indeed happened in mid-1997.

In the case of the Philippines, the East Asian crisis was simply a continuation of its boom–bust cycle. The specificity of this crisis for the

Table 8.5 Total foreign exchange liabilities (end of period as % of total)

Item	1992	1993	1994	1995	1996	1997	1998	1999
By type of debt	100.00	100.00	100.00	100.00	100.00	100.00	100.00	100.00
Medium and long-term	83.62	85.83	86.58	86.59	82.79	81.43	84.97	87.03
Short-term	16.38	14.17	13.42	13.41	17.21	18.57	15.03	12.97
Trade	15.39	9.84	8.78	6.79	9.78	8.87	5.33	4.09
Non-trade	0.99	4.33	4.64	6.62	7.43	9.70	9.69	8.89
By borrower	100.00	100.00	100.00	100.00	100.00	100.00	100.00	100.00
Banking system	14.67	9.28	10.70	13.85	20.61	23.47	23.45	21.02
Bangko Sentral	7.28	3.62	2.21	3.08	3.38	5.50	7.19	6.42
Commercial banks	7.39	5.66	8.49	10.77	17.23	17.97	16.27	14.59
Government banks	2.88	4.19	5.96	5.69	4.39	4.81	4.95	5.31
Private banks	4.51	1.47	2.53	5.08	12.85	13.16	11.31	9.29
Foreign banks	1.88	1.19	0.97	0.66	0.83	1.34	1.03	0.71
Domestic banks	2.63	0.28	1.56	4.42	12.01	11.82	10.28	8.58
Public and private	85.33	90.72	89.30	86.15	79.39	76.53	76.55	78.98
Public	69.82	75.81	71.59	67.73	57.63	49.02	51.25	53.48
Public–National Government & others	69.82	71.18	67.18	63.94	54.79	47.09	49.83	52.18
Central Bank – BOL	0.00	4.63	4.41	3.79	2.84	1.93	1.42	1.31
Private	15.50	14.90	17.71	18.42	21.76	27.51	25.29	25.50
of w/c export advances (export advances means trade credits)	3.28	3.09	1.31	1.08	1.01	1.09	0.69	0.67

By institutional creditor	100.00	100.00	100.00	100.00	100.00	100.00	100.00	100.00
Banks	16.73	13.72	12.11	12.97	17.71	19.53	17.95	16.88
Other financial inst.	1.01	0.85	2.17	3.15	2.29	2.87	2.28	2.48
Subtotal	17.74	14.57	14.28	16.12	20.00	22.40	20.23	19.35
Suppliers	9.23	8.96	9.17	6.57	6.18	5.19	3.27	3.32
Multilateral	25.94	25.90	25.46	24.43	20.62	19.01	21.03	19.77
of which:								
IBRD	12.91	12.94	12.54	12.69	11.17	9.13	8.99	7.74
IMF	3.69	3.69	2.94	2.07	0.97	1.96	3.27	3.63
ADB	8.10	8.14	6.61	6.71	7.44	6.80	7.30	6.86
Bilateral	35.30	37.62	38.82	36.56	32.09	29.29	31.21	31.70
Export agencies	10.44	11.25	11.59	10.01	11.17	10.38	13.20	11.26
Others	24.86	26.37	27.23	26.56	20.92	18.90	20.11	20.45
Others	11.79	12.95	12.27	16.32	21.11	24.11	24.26	25.86
By country profile	100.00	100.00	100.00	100.00	100.00	100.00	100.00	100.00
Country	62.36	61.25	62.33	59.81	58.55	57.58	55.53	55.79
of which:								
USA	22.30	19.88	9.87	9.58	10.01	10.06	9.53	11.11
Japan	28.70	31.27	32.75	30.91	26.53	22.66	24.86	26.54
UK	2.00	3.65	0.94	1.55	1.22	0.98	0.83	0.88
France	2.65	2.04	1.84	2.44	3.77	4.18	3.65	2.84
Germany	2.18	2.09	2.29	2.46	3.10	3.60	4.44	4.44
Multilateral agencies	25.94	25.90	25.46	24.43	20.62	19.01	21.03	19.77
Bondholders/noteholders	11.70	12.85	12.21	15.76	20.84	23.40	23.44	24.44

Source: BSP.

Philippines was that foreign capital inflows ceased, not primarily because of internal causes, but because of 'contagion' – from the Thai, Indonesian, South Korean and Japanese economic crises. The internal weaknesses of the Philippine economy – such as large trade and current account deficits, unhedged dollar borrowings and bubbles in the stock and real estate sectors – made it very vulnerable to the regional 'contagion'.

Another special feature of the crisis for the Philippines was that the foreign financing it had become so dependent upon turned exceedingly volatile (see Table 8.2b) following the liberalization of the foreign exchange and capital accounts in 1992. While net foreign direct investments increased as a result, short-run portfolio flows – at first going to domestic Treasury bills but later pouring heavily into the domestic stock market, starting in 1993 – dominated the volumes of the external inflows and outflows. Unhedged short-run foreign borrowings also increased significantly in 1995 and up to early 1997. Together with the significant external deficits, the nature of the capital flows in the latest growth period of the Philippines made it vulnerable to the financial turmoil that would erupt in mid-1997.

THE IMPACT OF THE EAST ASIAN CRISIS

Contagion and Responses by the Monetary Authorities

The contagion from Thailand actually occurred as early as May 1997, when the asset bubbles (in the stock market and in the real estate market) in Thailand started to burst and the baht came under tremendous pressure to depreciate. These events affected the external accounts of the Philippines. As can be seen in Tables 8.2a and 8.2b, net portfolio investments turned largely negative in May 1997 and continued negative for most of the succeeding months of 1997. Net unclassified items registered large negative outflows, starting as early as March 1997, and lasted throughout the year. These unrecorded accounts could be actual capital flight moving from domestic currency to dollars in the spate of speculations on the dollar. In May and June of 1997, the peso also came under speculative attack just as the baht underwent tremendous pressure to depreciate. The BSP increased the overnight lending and borrowing rates in May and June of 1997. The overnight rate set by the BSP had gone down close to 10 per cent (its lowest ever) before the BSP raised it to an average of 15 per cent in May and June of 1997.

When the baht finally caved in on 2 July 1997, the BSP still tried vainly to shore up the peso by raising overnight rates to an average of 25 per cent in July 1997. When this did not succeed, the BSP used up somewhere between $1.5 billion and $2 billion to defend the peso. This was equivalent to at least 13.4 per cent of the gross international reserves of the BSP (around $11.2 billion) as of the end of June 1997. When this measure still failed, the BSP on 15 July 1997 finally allowed the peso to float on a wider band, effecting a more than 10 per cent depreciation (from P26.37 to more than P29 to a dollar). The pressure on the region's currencies increased in the succeeding months as portfolio investments continued their outward flow and unhedged dollar borrowings aggravated the speculation on the peso. The BSP kept overnight rates above the 20 per cent level until August. The inter-bank call loan rate replicated the high BSP overnight rates.

When high overnight rates still failed to keep the peso from depreciating, the monetary authorities used another tactic. Before the baht depreciation, the total reserve requirement ratio was 15 per cent made up of 13 per cent for the statutory reserve requirement plus 2 per cent for liquidity reserves (which were allowed to be invested in market-yielding government securities). The liquidity reserve ratio was increased to 4 per cent at the end of July 1997 as part of the attempt to reduce liquidity in the system in order to discourage speculation on the dollar. In August this tactic was used to the hilt and the liquidity reserve ratio was further raised to 8 per cent, which brought the total required reserve ratio to 21 per cent. The total reserve ratio was kept high in September. Again this strategy failed to reduce speculation and the peso continued to deteriorate. But the strategy aggravated the rise in interest rates that had resulted ever since overnight rates were raised. There was an increase in the Treasury bill rate starting in August 1997. Bank lending rates increased dramatically from August 1997 onwards.

The squeezing out of liquidity in the system brought another risk to the system. The high interest rates produced new fears of high defaults on loans, especially from the real estate and construction sectors, which borrowed heavily on variable interest rates. The real estate bubble followed the stock market bubble and burst in August 1997.

The gradual realization of the extent of unhedged dollar borrowings, the high exposure of the financial sector to real estate and financial sector loans, the high interest rates and the effect of the peso depreciation on import-dependent firms all increased the perceived risk of defaults in the system. It became obvious that many firms previously doing well had become troubled because of their dollar borrowings and/or their diversification into real estate.

In October, the monetary authorities tried one last attempt to reduce liquidity in the system. This took the form of direct mopping-up operations in order not to exceed an IMF-imposed liquidity target. The mopping-up operation jacked up inter-bank call loan rates to more than 100 per cent for a few days in October, with the monthly inter-bank rate averaging at 34 per cent. Bank lending rates again increased significantly, which further rocked the system. Bank failure rumours started to circulate; bank withdrawals hit many banks which were seen as small or medium-sized (that is, with shaky loans) and therefore would not be bailed out by the BSP. Rumours of bank failure and sporadic withdrawal of funds persisted until February 1998.

The effects of high interest rates and very tight monetary policies on the financial sector were disastrous. Loan portfolios began to deteriorate, the property and equities markets slumped (when collateral values fell) and a genuine credit crunch set in.

The resulting instability in the financial system finally convinced the BSP that a very tight monetary policy would not stem the peso depreciation and was in fact counter-productive. Liquidity reserve requirements were lowered, together with overnight BSP rates. The continued currency instability, however, kept interest rates high even with the laxer monetary stance of the BSP. The East Asian currencies started to plunge again in December 1997 and January 1998, when South Korea became embroiled in the crisis and the Indonesian crisis took a turn for the worse. The average bank lending rates remained high. And the figures were underestimated since there was significant credit rationing (especially of small and medium firms) owing to the high risks of default, the weakness of domestic sales and the high costs of production.

The Currency Market and the External Sector

Between July 1997 and January 1998, the volume of transactions in the foreign exchange market shrank as dollar holders (except, in the beginning, the BSP) refused to release the money into the system (anticipating further peso depreciation) while speculators, importers and dollar debtors exhibited strong demand for dollars. This caused the currency to depreciate at a high rate. When regional currencies stabilized temporarily between February 1998 and April 1998, transaction volumes increased to normal levels. When currency instability started again in May 1998 – beginning with the release of poor first quarter earnings throughout the region simultaneous with the Indonesian riots and violence and the change of government, and culminating in the rapid deterioration of the Japanese economy and the sharp yen depreciation – volumes did not contract to the previous levels, which cushioned somewhat the impact of this latest round of currency instability. Exchange rate stability finally became more permanent starting in the last quarter of 1998, but by this time the battering of 'animal spirits' had already taken its toll and the country entered a deep recession.

Tables 8.2a and 8.2b show us that the crisis and recession effected a drastic reduction in imports, so that the high current account deficits swung strongly to current account surpluses at the end of 1998 and even more so in 1999. The current account surplus was also higher was a consequence of continued high inflows of remittances by overseas workers. On the capital account of the balance of payments, the high net inflows in 1996 and 1997 were cut drastically in 1998 as there were high net outflows of short-term capital and changes in the net foreign assets of commercial banks. Overall, though, the balance of payments still registered positive in 1998 and 1999 owing to the high current account surplus. Gross international reserves increased from $8.65 billion at the end of 1997 to $14.9 billion in early December 1999.

The Financial Sector

After the unsuccessful experience with high interest rates to stave off currency speculation, the interest rate (measured mainly by the Treasury bill rate and the bank lending rate) started to decline from February 1998 onwards. It finally settled to a historical low of under 9 per cent starting in mid-1999. Although the average bank lending rate had also declined, it is a fact that most banks were still rationing loans because of the high risks and bearish outlook in the financial system. A serious credit crunch and 'liquidity trap' had set in. Loan growth moved from very high levels between 1992 and 1997 to negative territory in 1998, especially affecting loans to manufacturing, agriculture and trade. Table 8.4 also shows the rapid decline of FCDU loans to all types of borrowers (commodity exporters, service exporters, manufacturers, oil companies and others). Loans denominated in both domestic and foreign currency fell drastically. Table 8.5 shows clearly that foreign exchange liabilities in the form of trade credits also contracted significantly, affecting the production of traded goods.

The crisis, as already emphasized, weakened the financial sector. This is seen in the deterioration during the crisis of the share of non-performing loans in total loans for commercial banks, thrift (savings) banks and rural banks. The official non-performing loan ratio (to total loans) of commercial banks steadily deteriorated, from 3.4 per cent in June 1997 to 13.4 per cent in January 2000, with no tendencies for significant improvement. A similar story can be told for the smaller sectors of thrift banks and rural banks.

Stricter Rules by the Central Bank

The worsening financial conditions brought the BSP to a quandary. It is clear that, for financial liberalization to effect further financial deepening and improvement in financial intermediation, the financial house will have to be made strong. Confidence has to be restored to the system. The former can be done partly by strengthening prudential and supervisory regulation. One way to go about this is to insist on tighter loan loss provisioning, higher capitalization requirements and capital adequacy ratios. But imposing these at a time of general financial weakness will further weaken some banks and discourage further loan expansion, which of course will deepen the credit crunch that became a root cause of the protracted recession.

The BSP's quandary was reflected in the changes it made to the rules, described as follows:

1. Loan loss provision was increased from 1 per cent of total loans to 2 per cent. The schedule for full compliance was moved to October 1999 to allow banks some more time for the required adjustment and profit loss. The rules concerning allowance for probable losses were also made stricter.

   This provision for loan losses proved to be a tremendous burden for most banks. It discouraged loans from being undertaken during the crisis, so that in April 1999, the BSP relaxed the loan loss provision requirement and applied it only to loans incurred before the cut-off period of 31 March 1999. This meant that incremental loans granted over and above the loan portfolio level of banks starting on 31 March 1999 were no longer subjected to these rules.
2. While the definition of past due and non-performing was made stricter right after the outbreak of the crisis, it was relaxed later on. For loans to be made in quarterly, semi-annual and annual instalments, loans not made within three months were considered non-performing. This used to be six months before the crisis. For monthly and lump sum loans, any failure to pay on time would make the loan non-performing. Because of the rapid deterioration in non-performing loans and required loan loss provisions being a burden to the banks, the rule was relaxed on 27 May 1999 by Circular No. 202. The BSP now allowed a 30-day grace period before a loan would be considered non-performing. This was applicable to loans payable in lump sum, quarterly, semi-annual or annual instalments. In the case of loans payable in monthly instalments, they would be considered non-performing if three or more instalments were overdue. In addition, restructured loans on which payments had been received would no longer be considered as non-performing or past due. The issuance of this directive effectively reduced the amount of money that banks needed to set aside as provisioning for bad debt, which allowed them to increase funds available for relending.
3. The banks' loan exposure to real estate was limited to 20 per cent. So

far this has been achieved (the exposure to real estate declined to 12.3 per cent in June 1999) but there were loans categorized as loans to manufacturing or commercial firms that were used by firms in real estate projects. These might not have been captured by the figures and the BSP is now correcting these possible loopholes.

4. The capital requirements of troubled banks were increased. The capital adequacy ratio was maintained at 10 per cent and strictly monitored. On top of this, a directive issued on 19 March 1998 increased the minimum capitalization of new banks by 20 per cent for universal banks, 40 per cent for regular commercial banks and 60 per cent for rural and thrift banks compared with the banks' capitalization requirement for 1998. Existing banks were given two years (until 2000) to comply with this minimum capital build-up.
5. The foreign exchange mismatch was reduced. The BSP issued Circular No. 1389 dated 13 April 1998 which stipulated that dollar lending to borrowers without dollar returns requires the BSP's approval or else repayment for these loans cannot be sourced from foreign exchange purchased from the banking system.
6. There was a shift in supervision focus from a compliance-based process to a forward looking and risk-based framework. The BSP has started its risk-based consolidated approach to on-site examinations of banking groups. There would also be close monitoring of banks identified as potentially in distress on the basis of a set of forward- and backward-looking indicators. These indicators include capital deficiency, reserve deficiency, sharp changes in credit and deposits, operating losses and a rise in past due loans.

The stricter rules in loan loss provisioning and capital requirements, together with the deteriorating non-performing loan ratios of weaker banks, have led to a trend of mergers among big banks starting in the second half of 1999. Although the surviving banks may have become stronger with higher capitalization, there are concerns that this will reduce competitiveness in the banking sector and will possibly lead to cartel-like behaviour, which will unduly harm financial intermediation and efficiency.

As late as April 2000, when this chapter was being written, the stricter capital requirements have caused serious runs on banks that could not meet these requirements (mostly medium-sized banks). The increasing possibility of bank runs in the financial system has deepened the vulnerability of the Philippine financial system. This could bring the recovery of the entire economy into jeopardy.

At the same time the financial sector cannot fully recover and credit lines cannot be re-established until 'animal spirits' are brought back into the system. However, the perception of government mismanagement and cronyism in the Estrada administration, the growing budget deficit resulting from weak revenue collection and an escalating war with Muslim rebels and insurgents in Mindanao hinder the return of confidence.

Economic Growth, Employment and Income Distribution

Given the turmoil in the second half of 1997, the growth rate for that year was rather respectable: 5.1 per cent for GDP and 5.8 per cent for GNP, around 1 per cent short of that achieved in 1996. In 1998, the full brunt of the crisis was felt. Gross domestic product fell by 0.5 per cent and GNP per capita by 2.4 per cent. Agriculture fell by 6.64 per cent as the El Niño and La Niña phenomena wreaked havoc on the countryside. Industry fell by 1.74 per cent, with construction falling 8.14 per cent and manufacturing by 1.07 per cent. Only services managed to grow at a respectable 3.5 per cent. Capital formation fell by a whopping 17.14 per cent. The unemployment rate jumped from 7.4 per cent in 1996 to 9.6 per cent in 1998.

Some signs of recovery were shown in 1999, with the preliminary figures showing GDP growth at 3.6 per cent. But the recovery was mostly a blip in agricultural production due to significant improvements in the weather. Industry growth was still nil even if manufacturing seemed to have slightly recovered. Construction, moreover, continued to decline strongly.

Not surprisingly, the crisis had a significant impact on unemployment, seen as early as October 1997 in urban areas. Male unemployment rates in urban areas went up from 9.6 per cent in October 1996 to 11 per cent in October 1997 and to 13.1 per cent in October 1998. Correspondingly, female unemployment rates in urban areas went up from 8.9 per cent in October 1996 to 9.9 per cent in October 1997 and to 10.7 per cent in October 1998. In October, unemployment rates were higher for males in urban areas, and this gap widened as male employment was hit harder by the crisis. Rural unemployment rates also went up, from 7 per cent to almost 9 per cent for females and from 4.7 per cent to 6.6 per cent for males in October 1998. In 1999, urban males continued to be increasingly unemployed, while the employment rates of rural males, urban females and rural females improved slightly as the weather improved.

Unemployment in 1998 grew for both females and males in all age groups. Most especially hit in urban areas were young people, particularly those youths aged 15 to 19, followed by those aged 20 to 24, and then by those aged 25 to 34. Male youths were especially affected, with the unemployment rates of those aged 15 to 19 going up from 19.4 per cent in October 1996 to 30.5 per cent in October 1998 to 31.4 per cent in October 1999. The female unemployment rate for those aged 15 to 19 went up from

16.4 per cent in October 1996 to 22.3 per cent in October 1998 and to 22.6 per cent in October 1999.

Urban unemployment increased even in 1999 for all urban males below 45 years of age and for urban females aged 15 to 24, and 65 and over. Urban employment in 1999 improved for females aged 25 to 54, and for males above 45 years of age.

While male unemployment in urban areas was higher, female and male unemployment were equally affected in rural areas because of weather disturbances in 1998. The male unemployment rate in rural areas went up from 4.7 per cent in October 1997 to 6.6 per cent in October 1998, while the female unemployment rate rose from 7 per cent in October 1997 to 8.9 per cent in October 1998. Again, hardest hit were young people aged 15 to 19 and 20 to 24, especially females. Unemployment for young females in rural areas went up from 15 per cent in October 1997 to 19.4 per cent in October 1998 for those aged 15 to 19. Those aged 20 to 24 saw their unemployment rate shoot up from 18 per cent in October 1997 to 25.4 per cent in October 1998. It is the unemployed women in both rural and urban areas, as well as the unemployed males in urban areas, who look for work abroad or in large urban conglomerates. Rural unemployment, however, generally decreased when the weather improved in 1999.

Labour participation among the young (those aged 15 to 19) and among women also increased. The higher labour force participation rates for young women and men during the crisis was accompanied by data showing significant declines in enrolment rates in high school for school year 1998–9. While the number of high school enrollees was growing by around 2 per cent during the good years, the 1998 figures show a decline in the number of high school enrollees of 7.68 per cent for females and 6.63 per cent for males. This explains the increased labour force participation rates and high unemployment rates of youths of high school age during the crisis.

There was also a significant increase in child labour participation rates for males (aged 10 to 14) in both urban and rural areas (with female child labour participation rates increasing only marginally). This was partly because of adult males leaving the agricultural sector because of bad weather and leaving the work to unpaid family labour, and partly due to the high drop-out rates in high school, leading to male children participating in the labour market. Female children dropping out from school might be relegated more to housework as adult women participated more in the labour market.

Data from a rapid household appraisal survey by the government show that per capita household income declined by 12.1 per cent in real terms in 1998. The real income of the richest decile increased, while that of the other deciles fell. The real income of the lowest decile declined by a whopping 29 per cent and 17 per cent of families surveyed experienced declines in real wages. These figures imply a certain deterioration in the poverty situation and income distribution of the country.

The picture sketched above is very clear. The impact of the crisis on employment, child labour, school enrolment, poverty and income distribution was extremely adverse.

Inflation

The inflation rate for 1997 was a meager 5.9 per cent, the lowest since 1987. Based on the consumer price index, the inflation rate, however, is well-known to be biased. Food accounts for almost 60 per cent of the basket while import-intensive goods have a low share. Inflation increased to an average of 9.8 per cent for the whole of 1998. Apart from the significant depreciation of the currency, one cause of the higher inflation was the weather disturbances which brought food prices up significantly.

The year 1999 saw a recession and a slump in demand, which cut inflation to around 6.6 per cent. However, a series of oil price increases rocked major urban and industrial centres in early 2000. This caused some economic instability and dissatisfaction as wages failed to keep pace with higher prices. Thus, even if published inflation rates are currently low (less than 4 per cent in April 2000), the perception of the public (especially after the series of oil price increases) of lagging real wages will put a lid on demand expansion which is needed for an early recovery.

The Fiscal Bind

Another victim of the crisis was the fiscal sector. The national government posted surpluses from 1995 to 1997. In 1998, the government (still under Ramos) imposed a 25 per cent mandatory saving (a euphemism for cutbacks) in government expenditures for all departments of the government in order to comply with the IMF programme of achieving a fiscal surplus of 1 per cent of GNP. The decline in revenue collection during a period of serious recession forced the government and the IMF to relax the fiscal targets and to allow a budget deficit in 1998. The year ended with a national government deficit of around 3 per cent of GNP.

In 1999, the Estrada government decided to go into pump-priming activities to spur some growth. But the continuing slump reduced revenue collections way below targets. In that year the economy may have accumulated a deficit of around P100 million, which is more than 3 per cent of GNP. The growing budget deficit in the midst of the current attempts to recover economically has raised serious alarm.

More serious than a possible increase in interest rates is the state of the confidence factor. As higher budget deficits than those sought are announced, investors withdraw and fears of incurring the IMF's wrath spread.

Loss of Business Confidence

Perhaps one of the biggest economic victims of the crisis was 'animal spirits'. The credit crunch persists and little private investment is taking place as poor economic performance and financial weaknesses continue. The perceived weak performance of the Estrada administration contributes to the bearish feeling of investors and reduces the impact of the pump-priming activities, which are themselves waning as a result of fiscal problems. Periodic charges of cronyism, government 'flip-flopping' in policies, and the heightening war with Muslim rebels in Mindanao reduce the possibility of an early and credible recovery.

Although there are some early signs of positive movements in the manufacturing sector, the climb out of the recession is still a difficult one. Two things need to happen before full recovery can take place. First is the resumption of credit lines and the end of the credit crunch. But non-performing loans refuse to decrease and the recent bank runs foretell difficulties in the financial sector. Second, economic growth should include the investment, construction and manufacturing sectors before it can become credible and sustainable. Both require a strong return of business confidence and 'animal spirits' which had been shattered by the crisis, the recession and the perceived poor performance of the government.

OTHER LONG-TERM EFFECTS OF THE CRISIS AND LONG-TERM ISSUES

Natural Resources and Environmental Impact of the Crisis

The crisis came just when environmental conditions had been deteriorating for more than a decade (see Intal, 1998). Forest cover has dwindled significantly; air pollution in Metro Manila has worsened; pollution of lakes continues; depletion of marine resources increases as overfishing intensifies. As real incomes declined and unemployment rose, the threat of intensive exploitation and extraction of natural resources became very real. The upland ecosystem, with six million hectares of public land, might be severely disrupted if the unemployed and disenfranchised moved to these lands for survival. There were indications that intensified exploitation of coastal and artisanal fisheries occurred in the previous recession of the mid-1980s (ibid.). What prevented widespread migration from urban areas (where lay-offs are growing at a fast rate) to rural areas and open public lands during the crisis was the El Niño phenomenon, which reduced productivity and yields of agricultural and forest crops in 1998. If the unemployed and the victims of the crisis, who are so far largely urban-based, remain in the urban areas, there will be increased problems there of urban congestion, inadequate waste disposal and sanitation, and squatting on private and public lands, especially as the incomes of the urban poor decline substantially.

What we had in 1998 was an urban problem of rising unemployment and rising prices and a rural problem of decline in rural output and incomes as well as food shortages due to weather disturbances, aggravated by the crisis-generated higher prices and weaker demand for rural outputs from the urban areas.

Many reforestation and conservation programmes may be affected by the continuing fiscal tightness. Even foreign-funded programmes may be reduced, as the Department of Environment and Natural Resources (DENR) is unable to provide counterpart funding because of the fiscal bind.

High interest rates and uncertainty during the crisis period would also have an adverse effect on the environment. High interest rates discourage private (and often expensive) investments in natural resources conservation (reforestation, marine conservation and breeding programmes), pollution control and more modern and environmentally friendly equipment (especially for wood processing). Uncertainty limits people's horizons to the short term and encourages overextraction and overutilization of natural resources and overproduction of pollutants.

The results of simulation done by the Philippine Institute for Development Studies (PIDS) (Intal, 1998) predicted that trade liberalization and currency depreciation would reduce industrial pollution (most likely as a result of the reduction in the capital-intensity of firms and the bigger incentives for small and medium firms). However, currency depreciation would give economic incentives to the mining industry and forestry as well as to the other firms that might damage the environment. Perhaps one good illustration of this was the government's lifting of the log ban during the crisis to help alleviate it (by stimulating some export of Philippine wood products). The subsequent rescinding of the lifting of the log ban again emphasized the controversy on whether (a) there is a trade-off between environmental protection and economic growth, and (b) regulatory frameworks and correct incentives (such as taxation of environmentally damaging activities) are effectively in place to ensure that utilization of natural resources (such as forest wood) is done in an environmentally non-damaging manner.

It was unfortunate that the current economic and financial crisis was accompanied by the El Niño drought. The near famine in parts of Mindanao due to the destruction of food crops was very serious and might well have caused Indonesia-size riots. The government's response showed up some inherent problems. Though rice stocks were adequate and were available in the warehouses, the famine victims' lack of income made it difficult for them to gain access to food stocks on a continuing basis. As long as people do not have the entitlement to the food stock – which involves livelihood and sustained income-generating potential – an adequate supply alone is not sufficient to solve any food crisis.

Social Safety Nets

The sharp fall in high school enrolment and the resulting rise in child labour participation indicated the possible medium- and long-term effects of the crisis on both social and economic conditions. The deterioration in social conditions highlights, especially during times of economic hardship and fiscal tightness, the lack of safety nets in the Philippines.

The traditional safety net in developed countries for unemployment and for declines in incomes is the social security system. In the Philippines, the social security system is handicapped by very limited funds, which cannot even adequately meet the emergency health needs of its members. Even less is it able to provide unemployment and other benefits to those displaced by the crisis.

Additionally, as mentioned earlier, the fiscal tightness and expenditure cutback are sure to severely constrain the public sector's ability to provide safety nets with the expected increase in poverty and the decline in social and human development. What is certain is that the bulk of safety nets will have to be provided by the extended family system. Because of the economic decline and large devaluation of the peso, overseas contract workers' contribution to their families' income will become even more urgently needed.

The use of the extended family system as a safety net, however, generates its own social impact. The increased dependency burden will further drain the resources of many families as laid-off and deprived individuals and families pass on part of their problems to their relatives. At the micro level, this is one reflection of the decreased savings rate that results from stagflation. The higher dependency burden adds to the plight of the family head (and other income-generating members of the family) as reduced real income (because of the crisis) is further diminished by more persons relying for subsistence on this reduced income. Also usually not considered is the additional burden placed on the housewife and mother who has to find ways to accommodate more people on meagre resources while her family care and household work multiply (with the increase in the members of the extended household). And then there is the added pressure for her to join the labour force in order to supplement the income of the family. We can imagine the tremendous stress, fatigue and unhealthy pressures that many women become subject to. Pressure on overseas contract workers will also be heavier as family members increasingly rely on their remittances as a main means of coping with the present crisis.

All the above shows the important need to design an effective social insurance scheme (involving both private and public funds) to mitigate painful social damage wrought by economic crises and recessions. Given the current shortage of private and public funds for social insurance, there may have to be temporary reliance on foreign sources for immediate social alleviation. However, once economic recovery and growth resume (and private and public funds become available), it is crucial to institutionalize the social insurance scheme, with bigger mandatory payments from employers and through progressive taxation.

Labour Rights and Conflict Management

There was a big rise in firm closures, retrenchment and rotation of labour staff during the crisis year (Lim, 1998b). There was also increased casualization and informalization of labour employment during the economic downturn (Lim, 2000). These responses to the crisis led to higher incidences of strikes and illegal casualization of many employees.

On paper, the Philippines initially tried to solve labour problems peacefully in late 1997 and early 1998 by instituting the Social Accord for Industrial Harmony and Stability between employers' groups and labour unions. However, this was not able to stop the increased strikes and labour–management conflicts due to the resulting unemployment, the casualization process and the lagging real wages of workers. The conflicts were aggravated by the lack of social insurance and safety nets.

Fortunately, labour unrest and social anarchy due to economic dislocation did not become serious problems, unlike what happened in the mid-1980s under the Marcos dictatorship. The higher tolerance of labour and its rights in the present context shows that democratic institutions, as long as they are well-entrenched, handle conflict management better than repressive and tyrannical ones in times of economic hardship and dislocation. (Contrast the Philippine experience with that of dictatorial Indonesia in 1998.)

LESSONS LEARNED AND POLICY IMPLICATIONS

The crisis has revealed the unreliability of foreign short-run capital flows – particularly short-term unhedged debts and portfolio investments – and the potential damage that they can inflict on even strong economies. There is therefore a pressing need to restructure the international financial architecture to help the more vulnerable countries, a subject which is tackled elsewhere in this volume (see Chapter 13). The other lessons that should be learned and the necessary changes in the effected policies are taken up in the next section.

Evaluating the IMF Response

The Philippines was on an IMF programme when the crisis hit in July 1997. Because the BSP spent around $1.5 billion to $2 billion of reserves defending the peso from the speculative attacks, the government borrowed, almost immediately, nearly the same amount from the IMF to beef up its international reserves. At the end of March 1998, the Philippines left the old IMF programme, only to enter into a 'precautionary arrangement' for a standby facility of $1.37 billion. This programme pretty much represents the ideology of the IMF. It differed from the packages of the more hard-hit countries only in the extent of the financial rehabilitation and financial prescriptions (inasmuch as the financial sector of the Philippines had not been as severely damaged) and in the degree of opening up of the economy to market forces and foreign investments (inasmuch as the Philippines had already opened up much ahead of these countries) it prescribed.

In the end, the IMF programme failed to address the ultimate causes of the crisis. Moreover, it contained some disturbing elements and it even bailed out some of the culprits, particularly foreign portfolio investors and the foreign commercial banks. The objectionable features of the programme are detailed below.

1. It relied a lot on increasing interest rates to stave off currency speculation and to effect 'current account adjustment' to offset the capital outflows. This weakened an otherwise healthy financial sector and, together with currency depreciation, increased non-performing loans and brought about loss of confidence in the financial sector.
2. The IMF and the BSP also called for immediate (that is, without a sufficient grace period and phasing) stricter loan loss provisioning and higher capitalization requirements without regard for the short-run instability and weaknesses (combined with adverse economic and

liquidity conditions) of financial institutions. This led to what was earlier described as a paradoxical situation wherein attempts to achieve long-run financial strength resulted in short-run weaknesses such as a credit crunch, unnecessary mergers and loss of competition in the banking sector, and increased bank runs and loss of confidence in small and medium-sized banks.

3. There was a strong concentration on achieving fiscal surpluses in the crisis years of 1998 and 1999. This completely ignored the objective conditions whereby currency devaluation would cause drastic cuts in imports and would thus substantially reduce import tax revenues. The massive currency depreciation was also stagflationary and reduced the government's revenue-generating capacity on direct and indirect taxes. All this should have pointed to the inevitability of fiscal deficits and a policy of allowing a reasonable deficit in order not to drastically reduce basic social services and essential infrastructure spending. Instead, the fiscal surplus targets gave wrong signals. As soon as it became clear that significant deficits were real, confidence was shattered. The currency depreciated even more.
4. The IMF programme was also insistent on retaining the policy of complete capital liberalization, even for short-run portfolio inflows and short-run foreign lending. In an earlier section, it was made very clear that portfolio investments created undue volatility in the system. The money was for mere speculation and, unlike foreign direct investments (FDI), had no commitment to a medium- and long-term productive investment in the country. More importantly, these unnecessary flows led to the overvaluation of the peso, which jointly with tariff reduction[6] increased the import intensity of the economy and led to higher current account deficits. It was also the overvaluation of the peso (again together with lower tariffs) that made non-tradeables (real estate, financial instruments, the trade sector) attractive vis-à-vis tradeables and the manufacturing sector. This created the real estate and financial bubbles which brought the property and financial sectors into trouble. Thus it was not just the lack of prudential regulation (a point which everyone agrees with and which the IMF concentrates on) that caused the crisis. More importantly, it was relative price distortions that gave concrete economic incentives for financial capital to flow into the wrong sectors. Many of the mistakes the IMF blamed on the East Asian countries – such as high current account deficits and overinvestment in the wrong sectors – could be traced back to the capital liberalization policy.

There are many proposals on how to discriminate between the good foreign inflows (foreign direct investments) and the bad ones (portfolio investments and short-term foreign lending). There are of course the strict quantitative restrictions on portfolio flows and foreign borrowings, as in China. There are the exchange and capital controls being successfully implemented in Malaysia. There is, as in Chile, the use of deposit requirements (30 per cent in Chile, and not to be withdrawn for at least a year) for all financial and portfolio inflows (including foreign lending, financial investments in local financial instruments and stocks, foreign currency deposits[7] and bond issues). There is the Tobin transaction tax imposed on foreign currency exchange transactions (with those earmarked for FDIs possibly exempted). There is also the disallowance of interest payments for foreign loans as expenses for tax purposes, as suggested by Stiglitz.

The problem is that the Philippines, with the IMF programme, cannot implement any of these. Even if the assurance of complete capital liberalization were not in the IMF programme, it would be difficult for the Philippines to implement some capital regulation on its own in this part of the world for fear of becoming the pariah of the region – which would cause it to lose the good direct foreign investments as well. It is precisely the IMF style of presenting a unique package individually to each country that precludes some regional and international solution to the crisis, including some regional and international effort and cooperation to stave off the harmful rounds of currency depreciation and contagion.

5. It is also clear that, in all the IMF packages for the region, foreign banks that were guilty of 'overlending' were not made to share in the burden. None of the IMF packages in East Asia had a Brady-like plan for partial debt forgiveness. Especially in the Philippines, much of the recession and credit crunch was caused by liquidity problems as short-term foreign credit lines were cut. Strong work-out arrangements and debt rollover could have kept confidence afloat in a period of intense currency speculation. It is, however, the IMF belief and ideology that a country has to be the one to undertake the reforms since it was the one that committed a mistake. Unfortunately, the poor of that country more likely than not are the ones who suffer most.
6. The IMF seemed to be little concerned about the social and human impact of the financial crisis and of the required painful reforms. Nor did it see the more long-lasting effects of a strong recession on human capital (education, health and self-esteem).

The experience with the IMF of the Philippines and the other affected countries demonstrates the strong need either to radically change the orientation of the institution or to replace it with a better and more humane set of institutions.

The Lack of a Regional and Coordinated Response

It is disappointing that the countries themselves hit by the crisis have not so far tried to coordinate some kind of regional response. Except for some lip service to trading with one another's currencies, there has been no attempt to unify financial policies and capital regulation in the region, and in the immediate future, to mount a regional and international effort to stave off the currency attacks on the region, in case this happens again. Perhaps the lesson is that united and coordinated policies among East Asian countries may not be forthcoming in periods of extreme weakness and crisis. Countries which have to defend their currencies every day, for example, cannot implement the idea of a common fund. Japan actually proposed the idea of an Asian Fund at a time of extreme weakness in the Japanese economy, but it was quickly shot down by the United States. The idea is useless without concrete support from countries with very strong currencies and very large reserves – which means that some kind of international effort is needed towards this. The IMF's strategy of concentrating on stringent individual programmes for hard-hit countries rather than coordinating regional and international efforts contributed to the lack of a genuine and quick solution to the crisis.

Another disappointing thing is that the hard-hit countries have still not put themselves in the forefront to call for changes in the international financial architecture, having started to recuperate from in mid-1999. These changes should in the future enable the system to protect vulnerable countries from the vagaries of short-term capital flows. It is to be hoped that, if and when such initiatives are undertaken, the affected countries will give their help and support.

Maybe when their economies have fully recovered and are strong again, the East Asian countries could look back to the current crisis and implement, cooperatively and in consultation with each other, common financial and capital regulation policies, and call for a new system in international finance.

Reflating Aggregate Demand

Employment-generating programmes will have to be strenuously undertaken to stimulate job creation and aggregate demand in the economic system, as was done in 1986 and 1987. This is crucial as a domestic policy in the recovery stage of the economy. The problem, however, is that such programmes require a significant amount of funds and the terribly tight fiscal bind at present (which threatens social services and safety nets as well) is a major obstacle to their full implementation. Continued availability of international funds at concessionary rates and with no strings attached is thus vital in cushioning the possible negative impact of higher fiscal deficits.

Breaking the Reliance on External Short-term Flows

The Philippines should avoid dependence on unreliable short-term financial inflows. Even if portfolio inflows and speculative capital (such as short-run debt) return, they should not be seen as stable sources of foreign exchange to fund the import needs of the country.

And if foreign inflows do not go back to the large magnitudes of the mid-1990s, it should be all right if GDP increase more slowly than before – say between 4 and 5 per cent – as long as large current account deficits and foreign debt are not incurred. A lower but more manageable and less volatile growth may also be more environment-friendly, especially if it is more equitably dispersed and not highly concentrated on growth areas. Such growth is also more gender-friendly, as it leads to less uprooting of families as labour, both male and female, is put under less pressure to migrate to urban and high-growth areas to search for jobs.

For long-run purposes, the boom–bust cycles will have to stop. Recall that the IMF has deepened crises in the country three times in the last two decades by imposing harsh stabilization policies. A first step towards the stoppage of boom–bust cycles therefore is to avoid the harsh conditionalities and stabilizing policies imposed by the IMF. This is why a new international financial and economic architecture is crucial for the growth of countries like the Philippines.

On the domestic front, there will have to be improvements in domestic savings and export capacity so that domestic investments and import needs, respectively, can be met. This of course is easier said than done. They require improvements in productivity and competitiveness, which are not only price-determined, but also depend on human and social capital, industrial organization, the quality of the state bureaucracy, and governance and institutions. The Philippines will have to retrace the 'miracle' route – *à la* East Asia – from the very beginning.

DEMOCRATIC INSTITUTIONS AND GOVERNANCE

The question has often been asked whether democracy and democratic institutions have anything to do with the rise and fall of the East Asian countries. The present author believes that authoritarian and corrupt governments can well manage to grow economically since cronyism and corruption thrive together with everything else when the pie becomes bigger. Common sense suggests that good economic policies can be quite independent of democratic institutions, as Malaysia's astute imposition of capital controls as a response to the crisis demonstrates.

Consequently, the charge of lack of transparency during the latest Asian crisis should be directed as much at foreign creditor banks as at individual country governments. The foreign creditor banks had the most information on the size and magnitude of unhedged dollar borrowings, much more than the central banks of the afflicted countries. Lack of transparency and undemocratic practices may have contributed to aggravating the Asian crisis, but they were just feeding on the effects of the root causes of the crisis. These were the volatile short-run speculative capital that flowed into the affected countries after significant foreign exchange and capital liberalization and the absence of regulatory devices to control and supervise these flows.

However, when the going got rough and the pie shrank, as the cases of the Philippines and Indonesia clearly showed, this was when authoritarianism and cronyism reared their ugly heads. The powers that be tried to protect their turf and their wealth very conspicuously. The virtue of democratic institutions and fair play seem to be appreciated more in times of extreme economic hardship than in times of growth and boom. In the former case, people are more intolerant of greed and lust for power. Thus an angry people was forced by crisis and economic instability to get rid of its despots, as the examples of the Philippines and Indonesia during the twilight years of the Marcos and Soeharto regimes, respectively, showed. This also happened on a smaller scale in Thailand and South Korea during the first year of the Asian crisis.

As the country least damaged by the crisis, it is ironic that rating agencies and multilateral agencies (such as the Asian Development Bank) have projected the lowest growth for the Philippines in the year 2000 and beyond. This is because, even while the economy has hardly shown signs of a credible recovery, cronyism and 'lack of fair play' have become the rule under the Estrada government, at least in the public's perception. A 'wag the dog' war that is getting more serious by the day has also broken out in Mindanao. If the crisis taught us anything, it is that 'animal spirits' are downright important. But a stable political and economic environment is crucial for the return of 'animal spirits'. And to achieve this, good governance and good institutions are needed.

The Philippines was able to effect a certain degree of improvement in political and economic conditions after the worst years of the Marcos dictatorship. This achievement, unfortunately, is again in jeopardy.

NOTES

1. The author would like to thank Mr Alvin Firmeza for research assistance and for editing the manuscript.
2. Except in 1998, when the Philippines experienced a higher capital formation to GDP ratio compared with the collapsing economy of Indonesia.
3. Compare also the export to GDP ratio of the Philippines with the four other countries in the Appendix.
4. Not all deregulation was successful. The oil deregulation was very controversial and will take years before its full impact is seen. The attempt at deregulating the shipping industry is known to be largely unsuccessful.
5. Actually, the old central bank liabilities being funded by the national government were put 'below the line', which made national government accounts in surplus (since these did not include the old central bank liabilities) but made public sector borrowing requirements (PSBRs) high.
6. In fact, the overvaluation of the peso subverted the potential beneficial impacts of tariff reduction.
7. A reserve requirement for foreign reserve deposits was originally proposed for the IMF programme, but the BSP was able to lobby successfully against it.

BIBLIOGRAPHY

Agosin, Manuel R. and Ricardo Ffrench-Davis (1998), 'Managing Capital Inflows in Chile', paper presented at the UNU/WIDER seminar on Short-Term Capital Movements and Balance of Payments Crises, held at Sussex, on 1–2 May 1997.

Akyüz, Yilmaz (1998), *The East Asian Financial Crisis: Back to the Future?*, Geneva: UNCTAD.

Fischer, Stanley (1998), 'The Asian Crisis: A View from the IMF', speech at the Midwinter Conference of the Bankers' Association for Foreign Trade, Washington, DC, 22 January 1998.

Fischer, Stanley (1998), 'How to Avoid International Financial Crises and the Role of the IMF', International Monetary Fund.

Intal, P. (1998), 'The East Asia Crisis and Philippine Sustainable Development', paper for the Forum on the Asian Financial Crisis and Sustainable Development as part of the Sixth Session of the United Nations Commission on Sustainable Development, ECOSOC Chamber, UN Headquarters, New York, 22 April.

Lim, Joseph (1998a), 'The Philippines and the East Asian Economic Turmoil', in K.S. Jomo (ed.), *Tigers in Trouble*, Kuala Lumpur: University of Malaysia.

Lim, Joseph (1998b), 'The Social Impact of and Responses to the Current East Asian Economic Turmoil: The Philippine Case', United Nations Development Programme.

Lim, J. (1999), 'The East Asian and Child Labour in the Philippines', a paper commissioned by the International Labour Office, Geneva.

Lim, J. (2000), 'The Effects of the East Asian Crisis on the Employment of Women and Men: The Philippine Case', *World Development*.

McKinnon, Ronald and Huw Pill (1997), 'Credible Economic Liberalizations and Overborrowing', *American Economic Review*, 87(2).

McKinnon, Ronald and Huw Pill (1998), 'International Borrowing: A Decomposition of Credit and Currency Risks', *World Development*.

Montes, Manuel F. (1998), *The Currency Crisis in Southeast Asia*, Singapore: Institute of Southeast Asian Studies.
Montes, Manuel and Joseph Lim (1996), 'Macroeconomic Volatility, Investment Anemia and Environment Struggles in the Philippines', *World Development*, 24(2).
Ranis, Gustav and Frances Stewart (1998), 'A Pro-Human Development Adjustment Framework for the Countries of East and Southeast Asia', UNDP.
Reyes, Celia, Rosario Manasan, Aniceto Orbeta, Jr. and Generoso de Guzman (1999), 'Social Impact of the Regional Financial Crisis in the Philippines', discussion paper, series 99–14, Philippine Institute of Development Studies.
Stiglitz, Joseph (1998), 'Sound Finance and Sustainable Development in Asia', keynote address to the Asia Development Forum, Manila, Philippines.
World Bank (1996), 'Strengthening Philippine Resiliency: A Country Paper', World Bank.

9. Singapore in the aftermath of the Asian crisis

Chia Siow Yue

INTRODUCTION

Since the outbreak of the Asian currency and financial crisis (Asian crisis for short) in July 1997, there has been a proliferation of literature examining its causes and effects and the actions and non-actions on the national, regional and international fronts. There is growing consensus that the Asian crisis originated from the capital accounts, triggered by large inflows of private and unhedged short-term capital and their sudden and massive reversals. Channels for the regional contagion were trade and financial flows and herd behaviour of investors and creditors. The severity of the Asian crisis was aggravated by the coincident downturn of the global electronics cycle (which affected the export performance of several regional economies), asset bubbles and overinvestment in key sectors, structural weaknesses in banking and corporate sectors (particularly weaknesses in prudential regulations and governance) and slow and/or inappropriate policy responses.

The East Asian economies are quite heterogeneous in the openness of their capital accounts, size of their foreign reserves in relation to short-term external indebtedness, soundness of their banking and corporate sectors, development of their regulatory and supervisory institutions and practices, and quality of political governance and public economic management. These differences are reflected in the differential impacts of the Asian crisis.

Singapore's experience with and responses to the Asian crisis makes for an interesting case study. First, Singapore has a very open current account and capital account, yet the impact of the crisis has not been as severe as in several East Asian economies which have been less open. Second, despite sound macroeconomic and financial fundamentals and policies, it could not escape the regional contagion, which adversely affected its exchange rate, asset values, financial and corporate sectors, economic growth and employment. Third, the economic recession was shorter than anticipated; after two quarters of negative growth in the second half of 1998, the economy rebounded in 1999 with a growth rate of 5.4 per cent. Fourth, Singapore's policy responses are not to shift away from economic liberalization and globalization, but to press ahead with economic reforms towards an innovation and knowledge-based economy, so as to meet the challenges and exploit the opportunities of globalization. Fifth, the crisis has not led to pressures for political and administrative reforms, as the quality of political and economic governance has helped shield the economy from being devastated.

IMPACTS OF THE CRISIS

Singapore is one of the most open economies in the world which, together with its small size, renders it highly vulnerable to external shocks. The economy is continually subject to the discipline of the international market and international investor sentiment and has to maintain strong macroeconomic and financial fundamentals, pursue sound public management and rule of law, and ensure continuing political, economic and social stability. Total trade in goods and services reached US$327 billion in 1997, or more than triple the GDP in size, and external demand accounted for two-thirds of total demand. Singapore was ranked thirteenth in 1997 as both exporter and importer of goods and services, among the 133 economies listed in the World Bank's Selected World Development Indicators. Foreign investment penetration has been extensive: the stock of inward foreign equity direct and portfolio investment reached US$70 billion or 81 per cent of GNP in 1995, while companies with over 50 per cent foreign equity accounted for nearly 60 per cent of total corporate assets in Singapore. Being a financial centre, foreign participation in the Singapore financial sector is probably among the highest in the world – Singapore plays host to some 140 foreign banks and non-bank financial institutions, while the total assets of the Asian Dollar Market (ADM), the world's eighth largest offshore lending centre, reached US$375 billion by end-1997. Singapore caught the regional contagion through trade and investment channels and the herd behaviour of portfolio investors.

Exchange Rate and Asset Prices

In the first year of the Asian crisis, the Singapore dollar depreciated against the US dollar by about 15 per cent, but rose sharply against the devalued currencies of Indonesia, Malaysia, Thailand and South Korea. The Monetary Authority of Singapore (MAS) reported that the Singapore dollar had not been subjected to strong speculative attacks. MAS reiterated that Singapore would not restrict the movement of short-term capital but would continue to maintain careful watch over the exchange rate. The increased market volatility necessitated a wider band for the management of Singapore's trade-weighted exchange rate (1997/98 Annual Report).

Heavy investments by local and foreign capital in the stock and property markets from the early 1990s led to market overheating and asset bubbles. Stock and property prices peaked in mid-1996, with the subsequent decline reflecting the increasing caution on the part of investors and buyers and Singapore government's corrective measures aimed at cooling the markets. The regional crisis accelerated the downtrend; the stock price index fell by over 60 per cent from its peak by the 1998 third quarter, while the property price index fell by over 30 per cent by mid-1998. Falling asset values undermined the balance sheets and profitability of property companies and financial institutions.

Financial and Corporate Sectors

In contrast to the buoyancy of earlier years, the financial services sector contracted marginally in 1998. While growth in domestic lending slowed to 5.9 per cent, activities in the offshore ADM contracted sharply from 1998, second quarter and by 9.8 per cent for the whole year, reflecting loan contractions to crisis economies as investment projects were postponed or cancelled, and as Japanese banks in Singapore consolidated their regional lending activity in the face of mounting non-performing loans (NPLs) and the need to meet the Bank for International Settlements' (BIS) capital adequacy requirements back home.

Local financial institutions were weakened by NPLs from their regional and domestic operations and deteriorating balance sheets. But there were no bank failures, bank runs or major debt defaults. In the early months of the Asian crisis, the concern was more with the regional exposure of local banking groups; by end-December 1997, the loan and investment exposure of these banks amounted to S$37.2 billion or 16 per cent of their total assets in the five crisis economies of Indonesia, Malaysia, the Philippines, Thailand and South Korea, of which classified loans (that is, substandard, doubtful or bad) amounted to S$2 billion or 5.7 per cent. By 1998, there was emerging concern over NPLs within Singapore itself, reflecting falling stock and property asset values and the sharp economic slowdown, and the local banks' NPLs reached S$18.4 billion. Total cumulative loan provisions of these banks reached S$8.1 billion or 44 per cent of reported NPLs, causing net profits to plunge 32 per cent to only S$1.2 billion in 1998. However, balance sheets remained fairly healthy, and capital adequacy ratios (CAR) remained substantially above the 12 per cent minimum specified by MAS and well above the 8 per cent minimum specified by BIS.

Business slowdowns and uncertainties led to a fall in corporate earnings and 'downsizing' of business operations. Deteriorating demand conditions and provisions for NPLs and bad debts reduced the profits of the 190 companies listed on the Stock Exchange of Singapore. Financial prudence led to a growing number of companies making record provisions for NPLs, as well as providing for reduced values of their investments and potential losses on their projects. In particular, listed property companies wrote down the values of assets by some S$1.5 billion. The corporate sector was also adversely affected by tight liquidity conditions. The domestic prime lending rate, steady at 6.3 per cent since August 1995, rose to 7.8 per cent by May 1998 and, concerned over rising NPLs, banks tightened their loan criteria. Interest rates started to trend downwards only from the 1998 third quarter.

Trade and Capital Accounts

Exports of goods and services to the region declined, reflecting both price effects from exchange rate realignments and negative wealth and income effects. Of Singapore's total goods exports, East Asia accounted for over half, with the bulk going to ASEAN, Hongkong and Japan. Fortunately, the large declines in goods exports to the region were compensated by continuing buoyancy of the US and EU markets. Service exports are more regionally oriented and so were more severely hit by the regional crisis. Singapore functions as a regional trading, transport, business and financial hub. Entrepôt trade in consumer and capital goods with ASEAN slowed down sharply in 1998, first quarter and turned negative in 1998, second quarter. Visitor arrivals from the region declined sharply with the fall in wealth and incomes and a more expensive Singapore dollar.

With imports falling much more sharply than exports, the current account surplus rose to S$29.5 billion in 1998 or 20 per cent of GNP (against S$22.3 billion in 1997). Net outflow of funds escalated from S$6.0 billion in 1997 to S$29.9 billion in 1998. There was a dramatic reversal in the flow of funds, from an inflow of S$53.6 billion in 1997 to an outflow of S$26.5 billion in 1998. Foreign banks in Singapore, which had traditionally relied on funding from head offices and ADM for their credit activities in Singapore and the region, sharply scaled back such funding and credit activities. Apart from the outflow of bank funds, there was also a net repayment of offshore loans. The balance of payments surplus fell from S$11.7 billion in 1997 to S$5 billion in 1998, with a corresponding slowdown in growth of official foreign reserves.

GDP and Employment

The Singapore economy remained buoyant up to 1998, first quarter, after which the regional contagion and the coincident global electronics downturn led to GDP growth plummeting in the second quarter and negative growth in the next two quarters. In addition to falling external demand, domestic consumption demand weakened in the face of plunging stock and property prices, falling incomes and job retrenchments, while investment demand was affected by excess capacity, economic uncertainties and tight liquidity. Contrary to all earlier forecasts and expectations, the economy managed to rebound in 1999 with a growth rate of 5.4 per cent, reflecting the upturn in the global electronics cycle, some recovery of regional demand and the cost-cutting measures undertaken in 1998–9.

Reflecting the economic downturn, Singapore's unemployment rate rose from 2.4 per cent in 1997 to a high of 4.4 per cent by December 1998, with 29 100 job retrenchments for the year. Job losses were concentrated in manufacturing, commerce and construction. Unemployment fell to 2.9 per cent by December 1999 and the number of job retrenchments for the year fell to 14 600.

GOVERNANCE ISSUES

In explaining the Asian crisis, many analysts and critics have pointed at weak governance as one important factor. The IMF rescue packages arranged for Thailand, South Korea and Indonesia have included structural and institutional reforms aimed at improving governance.

Strong governance is an important factor in explaining Singapore's mild susceptibility to the regional contagion. Singapore's record of economic and political governance has been lauded internationally, as exemplified by the World Economic Forum's *The Global Competitiveness Report* and the IMD's *The World Competitiveness Yearbook.*

Economic and Financial Fundamentals

Singapore's sound fundamentals are seen in the following macroeconomic, microeconomic and financial performance indicators. Real GDP growth has been high and sustained, averaging 9 per cent in the 1990–97 period; per capita GNP in 1997 was the fourth highest in the world; there is low unemployment and low inflation; there are very high savings and investment rates, with the national savings rate averaging over 45 per cent of GNP in recent years; strong current account surpluses, reaching 15 per cent of GNP in

1997; there is a strong balance of payments position, resulting in official foreign reserves which reached US$81 billion at end-1997, one of the highest in the world and which acted as a deterrent to concerted attacks by currency speculators; there has been no official foreign debt since 1994; Singapore is an attractive location for foreign direct investment and multinational corporations; there are strong government budgetary positions with budget surpluses for most years; there is low leveraging in the corporate sector, with a shareholder–debt ratio of 0.25 and a high current assets–liabilities ratio of 1.08 for the financial and corporate sectors; and a sound banking system with MAS maintaining strict prudential and supervisory controls.

Macroeconomic Policies

Singapore's sound economic and financial fundamentals reflect in part prudent, efficient and accountable public economic management. As a small open economy, the task of macroeconomic management has been rendered more difficult by rapidly changing external economic circumstances and external shocks. On the other hand, smallness and a single-tier government made for speedier policy responses.

Except for a short period in the early 1960s, when import substitution was introduced temporarily to jump-start industrialization before the switch to an export-oriented strategy, Singapore has pursued a free trade policy with minimal restrictions on imports and exports. Together with the large presence of foreign investments, these have ensured domestic competition and international competitiveness. In addition, macroeconomic stability, as reflected in low inflation, a stable exchange rate and sound budgetary and balance of payments positions, has been achieved through commitment to fiscal and monetary prudence.

On fiscal prudence, the government has had a consistent current (operating) as well as overall (operating and development) surplus since 1975, although the public sector budget (that is, including statutory boards) showed deficits in the development budget. Development expenditures are financed from government savings and domestic borrowings, with no resort to external borrowings. Disallowing fiduciary issue of money helps impose fiscal discipline. In addition, a 1993 constitutional amendment constrains the ability of an elected government to use the economy's accumulated official reserves to finance budget deficits. Fiscal expenditures have been moderated by the People's Action Party (PAP) political leadership eschewing the Western welfare state, arguing that

> the end result of indiscriminate welfare state policies is bankruptcy . . . [as] money to pay for welfare state expenditure must come either from taxes or from the printing press. Increasing taxes, which mainly affects the rich, reduces the

> amount of money available for investment, thereby slowing down economic growth. Printing paper money to avoid unpleasant tax increases merely results in more inflation. (Goh, 1977)

Singapore has no system of unemployment benefits or of retirement benefits (except for a limited number of elite civil servants). The social safety net is provided by robust economic growth and full employment, and a self-funded Central Provident Fund (CPF) of compulsory savings for old age, housing and medical needs. By 1997, the CPF provided cover for 2.8 million in the population, and contributed to Singapore's over 85 per cent home-ownership rate. With a buoyant economy and fiscal prudence, the government has been able to invest heavily in infrastructure and education and to reduce the income tax burden on corporations and individuals over the years, falling to 26 per cent and a 28 per cent ceiling by 1999.

On the monetary front, the Currency Board issues and redeems currency, while MAS performs other central banking functions. Without fiduciary issue, changes in the money supply depend on net capital inflows and MAS open market (swap) operations in the foreign exchange market. Monetary policy is focused on maintaining price stability to secure sustained economic growth. With free trade and capital mobility, government and public sector budget surpluses and CPF savings, the role of monetary policy is constrained.

Exchange rate policy is to achieve a low inflation rate and a strong and stable Singapore dollar. Singapore has been on a managed floating regime since June 1973. With the lifting of all exchange controls by 1978, the policy responses to the large capital inflows have been through management of the exchange rate, a sound financial system capable of intermediating the capital inflows, and strong fiscal discipline. A low inflationary environment has enabled MAS to manage the exchange rate more flexibly. MAS intervenes in the foreign exchange market to keep the exchange rate within an undisclosed target band. In 1998, the Singapore dollar weakened against the US dollar, appreciated against most currencies in the region and appreciated slightly against the trade-weighted basket of currencies.

Financial Sector Supervisory and Regulatory Framework

The Asian crisis has highlighted financial sector weaknesses in several East Asian economies and the imprudence of capital account liberalization without first strengthening the domestic financial sector and putting in place an adequate prudential supervisory and regulatory framework.

For Singapore, financial liberalization had been progressive since the early 1970s, marked by decontrol of exchange rates and interest rates: in 1972, abolition of the cartel system of exchange rate quotation by commercial banks; in June 1973, the floating of the Singapore dollar; in July 1975, abolition of the cartel system of interest rate setting by commercial banks; in June 1978, the lifting of exchange controls, so that residents could borrow or lend in all currencies, including participation in Singapore's offshore ADM, merchant banks could freely engage in foreign exchange transactions, offshore banks could deal with resident non-bank customers, and non-residents could hold Singapore dollar denominated assets. Internationalization of the Singapore dollar has been discouraged to preempt destabilizing currency speculation.

The MAS is Singapore's de facto central bank. With an open capital account, direct control of capital flows has been replaced by close supervision and regulation of financial institutions. MAS has been noted for its strict prudential regulations and supervision to maintain a sound domestic banking and financial sector, which helped contain NPLs during the Asian crisis. The regulatory framework provides explicit walls between different kinds of financial institutions and activities – banks, finance companies, insurance, securities, futures trading, development loans, Treasury bills. Each piece of legislation contains provisions empowering MAS to act in areas such as management oversight, capital adequacy, regulation of portfolio and equity, and regulation of offshore markets. Montes and Tan (1999) note that such extensive prudential regulation and supervision increases the cost of financial intermediation as well as creating a moral hazard.

On management oversight, MAS approval is required for the appointment of directors and senior executives. MAS also requires fortnightly reports on capital funds of foreign banks and inter-bank indebtedness with banks outside Singapore (including Asian Currency Unit (ACU) operations) and monthly reports on loans and advances to bank directors. On capital adequacy, Singapore banks have capital adequacy ratios (CAR) that well exceed the BIS standard: banks that operate internationally are required to conform with the BIS capital adequacy standard of 8 per cent of risk-weighted assets, half of which must come from shareholders' funds and minority interests. Singapore incorporated banks must have a minimum of S$150 million in shareholders' funds while finance companies must have a minimum capital requirement of S$50 million. Reserve requirements have been set at 6 per cent and commercial banks and finance companies are required to keep liquid assets at 18 per cent and 10 per cent, respectively. On loan regulations, credit to any individual or group of individuals cannot exceed 25 per cent of a bank's capital; specific regulations cover loans for property and car purchases and unsecured loans of banks, merchant banks and finance companies. Equity investments of banks are also restricted; banks can invest only up to 40 per cent of their capital funds, except for shareholdings in other banks and subsidiaries, and are not allowed to own more than 20 per cent of any company's capital without MAS approval.

Various policies insulate the domestic economy from the financial centre's offshore activities. The latter operate under Asian Currency Units (ACUs), which are demarcated from domestic banking units (DBUs), enabling the official monitoring of the use of ACU funds, especially the extent to which they are lent to domestic operations. ACU activities are confined to non-Singapore dollar transactions. By 1997, ACU assets, denominated largely in US dollars, stood at US$479 billion, much larger than the domestic banking system. To pre-empt potentially destabilizing currency speculation, MAS discourages 'internationalization' of the Singapore dollar: lending to non-residents in Singapore dollars is restricted, requiring MAS approval for loans exceeding S$5 million to non-residents or to residents where the Singapore dollar is to be used outside Singapore. Since October 1996, there has been some relaxation; as part of efforts to promote the Stock Exchange of Singapore (SES) and the fund management industry, foreign shareholdings are allowed in stockbroking firms and the 40 or so foreign currency-denominated stocks on SES are allowed Singapore-dollar listing.

Political Governance and Rule of Law

Singapore has a parliamentary democracy but the same political party (People's Action Party) has been repeatedly returned to power in contested elections since 1959. Critics have charged that there is no true democracy as the government is autocratic and intolerant of opposition. However, even the critics have to concede that the rule of law prevails in Singapore, unlike the case of many countries with democratic or undemocratic governments. The dramatic political changes that have been sweeping much of East Asia with increased public demands for accountability are unlikely to be repeated in Singapore in the near term, as the 41-year-old government has continued to demonstrate competence, integrity and accountability and took much credit for Singapore not being devastated by the Asian crisis.

The pioneer generation of PAP political leaders were men of exceptional ability, commitment and integrity. With Singapore handicapped by small geographical and demographic size, dearth of natural resources and threats of communism and communalism, they successfully steered Singapore into sovereign statehood, transformed the stagnating entrepôt economy into a showcase of economic development, and brought social cohesion into the multi-ethnic and multi-religious society. On the principles and practice of government, Lee Kuan Yew, the father of independent Singapore, stressed that leaders must have a sense of trusteeship. In 1990, Lee Kuan Yew voluntarily stepped down as prime minister. His successor, Goh Chok Tong, reiterated the PAP principles and practice of government in a 1995 speech at Williams College in Boston:

> As a custodian of the people's welfare, it exercises independent judgement on what is in the long-term interests of the people and acts on that basis. Government policy is not dictated by opinion polls or referenda. This has sometimes meant overriding populist pressures for 'easier' economic policies. Indeed, implementing the right policies has on occasion meant administering bitter medicine to overcome economic challenges . . . Good governance is built on three inter-related beams and pillars. They are democratic accountability, long-term orientation and social justice. (*Sunday Times*, 24 September 1995)

Integrity and accountability are the hallmarks of the PAP political leaders. Distrusting the ability of the democratic process to throw up future political leaders of calibre and integrity, they adopted a meritocratic and rigorous selection process in choosing their candidates for parliament and cabinet, stressing qualities of competence and integrity. They planned systematically for political renewal. With each general election, older and weaker performers in the parliament and cabinet were retired and replaced by younger candidates of potential. Concerned that over time Singapore might not be able to attract political leaders with commitment, competence and honesty, Lee Kuan Yew advocated paying cabinet ministers well. To ensure a competent and honest political leadership and efficient public service, in 1994 he further proposed a long-term formula to link the pay of ministers and senior bureaucrats to incomes of top professionals in the private sector. Also, out of concern that a future 'profligate government' could squander Singapore's hard-earned foreign reserves, a 1988 White Paper introduced the constitutional amendment providing for an elected president to perform a custodial role in protecting Singapore's official foreign reserves.

The Singapore bureaucracy is also noted for its competence and integrity. The best and ablest are attracted into the bureaucracy through a meritocratic reward system of attractive salaries and benefits and accelerated promotion based on performance. Terms and conditions of service are periodically reviewed and improved so as to recruit and retain the best and to minimize corruption. A scholarship system ensures adequate recruitment of the best young minds.

In sum, Singapore's success in combating political and bureaucratic 'corruption and cronyism' may be attributed to several factors: the high moral code of the PAP political leadership and their determination to stamp out corruption in public service; severe penalties for corrupt practices; reduced discretionary power of the public service and its ability to 'dispense favours' in an economic system characterized by openness, transparency and minimal restrictions and regulations; also an efficient public service reduces the need for businesses and individuals to pay 'facilitation' money. Finally, paying the public service well reduces the need to engage in moonlighting or corrupt practices to make ends meet.

CRISIS AND POST-CRISIS RESPONSES

Responding to the Asian Crisis

At the outset, so as to maintain investor confidence and strong country credit ratings, the Singapore government reiterated that it would continue to rely on market forces, maintain free capital flows and foreign investments, and remain plugged into the global economy. It eschewed capital controls and competitive currency devaluation and continued to manage the exchange rate against a trade-weighted basket, albeit with greater flexibility around an undisclosed band.

The 1998 economic recession resulted from the global cyclical downturn in electronics and the sharp fall in regional demand for goods and services. With the heavy dependence on external demand and the high import leakage of domestic demand, government pump priming was largely eschewed. Instead, policy measures focused on cost cutting and tax reliefs to reduce operating costs of business enterprises to help offset the loss in competitiveness posed by the massive depreciation of regional currencies, and to lower the living costs of individuals and households in the face of falling incomes and job retrenchments. Three 'relief packages' were announced in 1998: the budget delivered in February 1998, the off-budget package in June 1998 and the additional package in November 1998.

The government budget presented in February 1998 contained minimal relief measures as it anticipated no major fall-out from the regional crisis. But as the economic downturn worsened, a $2 billion off-budget package of cost cutting and stimulus measures was announced in June. A further round of cost-cutting measures aimed at job maintenance was announced in November. A major feature of the cost-cutting measures has been the cut in wages and benefits, involving halving of the 20 per cent compulsory CPF contributions by employers as well as a 5–8 per cent wage cut recommended by the tripartite National Wages Council; together these amounted to a 15 per cent reduction in the earnings of workers and wage costs of businesses. Other elements of the cost-cutting package include lower tariffs and user charges of government agencies and tax rebates for businesses and individuals. The various cost-cutting measures were estimated to reduce business costs by about 15 per cent.

Financial Sector Reforms

While Singapore's stringent prudential supervisory and regulatory framework helped shield its financial sector from the full brunt of the Asian crisis, there had been growing pre-crisis concerns that overregulation had stifled the development of the financial centre, particularly vis-à-vis the more *laissez faire* Hongkong. In view of the growing global integration of financial markets arising from advances in information technology, falling regulatory barriers and mergers among financial institutions, Singapore would need a radical change in approach to thrive as a financial centre. The main thrusts of financial sector reforms are for MAS to create a more conducive regulatory environment, and to play a more proactive role in financial centre development. A three-pronged strategy was developed: to build a strong and competitive banking industry, to promote a vibrant asset management industry, and to develop deep and broad capital markets in debt, equity and derivatives.

Banking reforms

In May 1999, MAS introduced a five-year banking liberalization and local bank upgrading programme. First, to liberalize access by foreign banks to Singapore's domestic market, MAS issues a new category of full banking licence known as Qualifying Full Banks (QFBs), with up to 6 QFBs to be issued over 1999–2001; incumbent foreign full banks not awarded QFBs will retain their existing privileges. MAS also increases the number of restricted banks, and gives offshore banks greater flexibility in Singapore dollar wholesale business. The 40 per cent limit on foreign investors' total shareholding in local banks has also been lifted. However, to ensure that control of the local banks rested with individuals or groups who would act in a manner consistent with national interest, MAS requires bank boards to have a majority of Singapore citizens and permanent residents and tightens safeguards on the accumulating of significant ownership in a local bank.

A second aim was to improve corporate governance of local banks. For years, local banks had been protected from competition. However, to survive in the new liberalized environment, they need to improve efficiency, shareholder returns and quality of service, and to attract talents. MAS requires local banks to appoint Nominating Committees to ensure that bank boards and key posts have capable individuals; board appointments and reappointments require MAS approval. MAS will review all regulations concerning local banks so as to give them greater flexibility in their operations without compromising prudential objectives, such as allowing local banks greater autonomy in organizing their operations, including overseas ventures and strategic alliances with foreign banks.

Banking supervision

With banking liberalization comes the need for more effective banking supervision. First, the capital adequacy ratio (CAR) of Singapore incorporated banks has been fine-tuned. While previously local banks had to maintain a CAR of 12 per cent comprising entirely Tier 1 or equity capital (higher than the BIS 8 per cent comprising 4 per cent Tier 1 capital and 4 per cent Tier 2 capital), from December 1998 they are required to have at least 10 per cent Tier 1 capital, while the remaining 2 per cent may consist of Upper Tier 2 capital, and the definition of Tier 1 capital is also widened to include equity-like capital instruments in line with BIS recommendations. Second, also effective from December 1998, MAS allows banks to use internal models for calculating market risk capital, providing them with an incentive to improve their risk management systems.

Third, MAS has raised the prescribed minimum standard of disclosure for banks and merchant banks. Fourth, in line with the plan to develop the securitization market, MAS has provided prudential guidelines for asset securitization activities by financial institutions. Fifth, the minimum cash balance of finance companies has been aligned with that of banks and reduced from 6 per cent to 3 per cent. Sixth, with globalized financial activities and blurring of distinctions between banking, securities and insurance activities, there is need to develop a consistent and common risk framework. MAS has established a general set of principles to enhance the effectiveness of financial regulation and supervision.

Other developments

Measures have also been introduced to develop the securities industry, debt market, the fund management industry, the futures industry and the insurance industry. Measures for the securities industry include enhancing the competitiveness of the Stock Exchange of Singapore (SES); demutualizing and merging SES with the Singapore International Monetary Exchange (SIMEX) so as to reduce the potential conflict of interests between members who are owners and other users of the exchanges and to provide greater transparency and more efficient and flexible funding from the capital markets; more flexible listing requirements for growth enterprises; more flexible rules on foreign listings in Singapore dollars; reduced capital requirements for securities firms; complete freeing up of commissions by 1 January 2001; and free access to trade on the Singapore Exchange (SGX) by January 2002.

On developing the debt market, restrictions on borrowing in Singapore dollars are being relaxed, so as to enable foreign players to issue Singapore dollar-denominated bonds. An Approved Bond Intermediary scheme is established to encourage the origination, placement and management of debt issues in Singapore. To create a more liquid government bond market, issuance of Singapore government securities has been increased and the maturity profile extended to ten years.

Measures for the fund management industry include greater access to the large pool of CPF funds as well as government funds farmed out by MAS and the Government Investment Corporation. To attract more foreign fund managers to operate in Singapore, tax incentives and more flexible licensing requirements have been put in place. Measures for the futures industry include revising the financial requirements for futures brokers and abolishing the minimum commission structure. Measures for the insurance industry include reducing capital requirements for captive insurers; granting blanket approval for captives to write certain non in-house risks; enhancing the regulatory framework for investment-linked policies under the CPF Investment Scheme; reviewing amendments to the Insurance Regulations 1997; clarifying regulations on derivatives transactions; reviewing regulations on financial reinsurance; and reviewing the distribution of personal financial services.

Global Competitiveness

Competitiveness factors

The World Economic Forum (WEF) *Global Competitiveness Report* and the Institute of Management Development (IMD) *World Competitiveness Yearbook* have consistently ranked Singapore as the most competitive or second most competitive economy in recent years. Some key determinants of Singapore's competitiveness are discussed below.

First, of Singapore's factor resources, which have enabled it to develop competitive advantages in several areas of manufacturing and services, only its strategic geographical location is an inherited factor. This natural resource has been enhanced over the years by efficient networks of sea and air transport and telecommunications. Together with free cross-border movement of goods, services and finance, it has enabled Singapore to become a regional entrepôt, financial centre and transport and communications hub.

Second, competitiveness of a stable and predictable business environment, as exemplified by political stability, social cohesion,industrial peace and rule of law, are important elements in Singapore's positive business environment. Political legitimacy not only through the ballot box but also through the ability to deliver on the promise of a rising standard of living, full employment, clean and competent government, and peaceful relations with neighbouring countries has contributed to political stability. An even-handed policy on communalism and religion has contributed to ethnic and religious harmony. Social equity has been maintained with rapid disappearance of poverty and unemployment, equal opportunities in education and employment, and upward social mobility. A social safety net is provided by full employment, compulsory savings under the Central Provident Fund and subsidized public housing with 85 per cent of the population enjoying home-ownership (and thus asset-owning). Singapore has enjoyed industrial peace for three decades. A tripartite National Wages Council, with representatives from workers, employers and government, has been providing annual wage guidelines since 1972. There is a well established legal framework, and the legal institutions and practices protect property rights, mete out justice and adjudicate industrial and commercial disputes.

Third, there is policy competitiveness and policy coherence. The economic policies pursued since the mid-1960s have created a strong macroeconomic environment and robust economy, albeit one that remains vulnerable to external shocks. There is policy coherence over time and across government ministries and departments, so that policies work towards common objectives and businesses can plan and operate in a predictable environment. Prudent monetary and fiscal policies contribute to macroeconomic stability, encourage savings and build up sizeable fiscal and foreign reserves. A free trade environment provides domestic competition and encourages exports unencumbered by tariffs and non-tariff barriers. Singapore leveraged on its limited factor resources and markets by attracting foreign direct investment with its accompanying foreign skills, technology and markets. The effective tax rate is low, with only one layer of taxation (no separate federal, provincial and municipal taxes), no import duties, low consumption taxes (except for tobacco products, alcoholic beverages and petrol), low corporate and individual income taxes, and generous tax incentives.

Fourth, Singapore has at its disposal world-class physical infrastructure and educated, skilled and English-speaking human resources. Land, sea and air transport, telecommunications and power supply provide the basic support system for the manufacturing base and services hub. In the 1960s, so as to provide a workforce that meets the needs of the rapidly growing industrial sector, the educational system was revamped to emphasize technical and vocational education at the secondary level and specialized industrial training institutes were established to turn out qualified technicians and craftsmen. In the 1970s, all schools adopted bilingual teaching in the English language and the mother tongue from the first year of schooling;

the Skills Development Fund was established, with levies on employers to provide financial resources for training and skills upgrading; tertiary education expanded rapidly to provide professionals and managers in engineering, business and computer education; measures and campaigns sought to improve labour productivity and work attitudes. In the 1980s and 1990s, the emphasis has been on increasing the skills and talent pool, with a target of 60 per cent of each age cohort receiving tertiary education by year 2000 and with rapid expansion of engineering, science, business and computer education. In recent years Singapore also introduced a policy of active recruitment of foreign talent for both public service and the corporate sector. More than 20 per cent of Singapore's workforce is foreign.

Competitiveness strategies

Singapore officials have long resisted efforts by international agencies to classify Singapore as a developed economy despite a per capita income that clearly ranks among the highest in the world. A key argument has rested on the heavy dependence of the Singapore economy on foreign capabilities, unlike developed economies in North America, Western Europe and Japan; more particularly, Singapore lacked indigenous innovative and technological capability and indigenous world-class business enterprises.

The Asian crisis heightened Singapore's concern over eroding economic competitiveness. Singapore had been finding it increasingly difficult to compete on a cost basis with regional economies enjoying abundant land and labour resources and the sharply depreciated regional currencies worsened Singapore's competitiveness. The cost-cutting measures instituted in 1998 could only provide temporary respite. At the same time, Singapore finds itself lacking the capabilities of advanced industrial economies in technology, innovation and creativity to succeed as a knowledge-based economy.

In November 1996, and prior to the Asian crisis, the government announced the need to review Singapore's economic competitiveness over the next decade. This review followed the 1986 Economic Committee Report to pull the Singapore economy out of the 1985 recession, and the 1991 Strategic Economic Plan charting economic strategies for the 1990s. The Committee on Singapore's Competitiveness (CSC) released its final report in November 1998. The vision is to develop a competitive knowledge-based economy (KBE) with high-end manufacturing and exportable services as the twin engines of growth. To be a KBE, Singapore will need capabilities and intellectual capital to absorb, process and apply knowledge, a strong technological capability, an entrepreneurial culture, ability to attract global talent and connectivity to other global knowledge nodes. A worrisome feature is whether Singapore's political and social cultures are able to transform and provide the enabling environment for innovation and creativity.

The CSC recommended eight key long-term strategies: maintain manufacturing and services as twin engines of growth; strengthen the external wing to complement the domestic economy as a source of growth; build world-class companies with core competencies to compete in the global economy; nurture and strengthen local enterprises; develop human and intellectual capital with cost-competitive and outstanding capabilities; leverage on science, technology and innovation as competitive tools; optimize resource management by promoting alternative supply and efficient usage; and use government as a facilitator of the private sector by providing sound economic policies and regulatory environment for the conduct of business.

Manufacturing and services as twin engines

Singapore is a manufacturing platform and a regional services hub. The CSC has recommended that manufacturing and services remain the twin engines of growth for Singapore, exploiting the linkage between manufacturing and services, reducing vulnerability by providing a broader economic base, and balancing a globally-oriented manufacturing sector with a regionally-oriented services sector. Singapore will continue to maintain a proactive industrial policy to achieve these aims.

Cost competitiveness in manufacturing has been a growing problem and was aggravated by the 1997–8 regional currency realignments. To remain competitive, Singapore will have to move beyond cost competition to capability competition. This requires movement along the value chain into research and development (R&D) and design, logistics, marketing and sales; manufacture of high value-added products; and the provision of manufacturing-related services to companies in Singapore and in the region. The CSC recommended having a balanced mix of manufacturing activities; building strong manufacturing capabilities in niche areas; developing strong competitiveness in other parts of the value chain; using greater application of science and technology; embracing innovation; providing an entrepreneurial environment; and grooming world-class companies. Strength in manufacturing has to be reinforced by development of hub services, and integration into the regional and global economies. The CSC recommended strengthening of existing hub services such as financial services, international trading, international exhibition, transport and logistics and tourism, as well as developing new high-growth services in health care, education, media, communications and information technology services and e-commerce. Singapore can leverage on its strategic location and excellent infrastructure and talent pool and exploit information technology and telecommunications.

The Economic Development Board (EDB) has launched I21, the industry vision for the 21st century. The vision is to develop a vibrant and robust global hub of knowledge-driven industries, with emphasis on technology, innovation and capabilities; to encourage foreign multinationals to locate more of their key knowledge-intensive activities in Singapore; and to encourage local companies to embrace more knowledge-intensive activities and become world-class players. EDB identified five broad strategies to achieve the I21 vision: diversify among and within industry clusters for a balanced and robust mix of industries and markets; build up world-class capabilities and global coverage; promote innovation; develop local talent and attract foreign talent; and create a conducive business environment and world-class infrastructure. EDB is nurturing the following industry clusters and development programmes: electronics, chemicals, life sciences, engineering, education and health care, logistics, communications and media, headquarters, world class companies and promising local enterprises, innovation, international business, resource development and coinvestment.

The Trade Development Board (TDB) is spearheading the development of Singapore's trade capabilities through both trade facilitation and promotion. TDB monitors trade policies of trading partners and their impact on Singapore's trade, recommends trade policy responses and participates in international trade negotiations, and goes on trade missions to seek new markets. TDB seeks also to leverage on information technology and position Singapore as an e-commerce hub. To encourage companies to set up their regional e-commerce trading centres in Singapore, tax incentives are offered under the Approved Cyber Traders scheme.

Inward and outward investments

Singapore plays host to over 5000 international companies, many of whom are listed in Fortune Global 500. Various international business surveys, including those of the World Economic Forum (WEF), International Institute of Management Development (IMD) and Business Environment Risk Intelligence (BERI) have consistently ranked Singapore as one of the most attractive investment locations in the world.

Inward foreign direct investment (FDI) has played a critical role in Singapore's economic development. In the early years the capital inflow from FDI helped to close the savings–investment gap and to cover the current account deficit. By the mid-1980s, however, savings exceeded investments and Singapore emerged as a net capital exporter. Yet Singapore's reliance on FDI has not diminished, leveraging it for entrepreneurship, management, technology and markets, as domestic enterprises continued to lag behind in international competitiveness. The inward FDI policy is characterized by a holistic approach to make Singapore an attractive investment location through an enabling business environment that minimizes risks and costs: ensuring political stability and industrial peace; providing an efficient public service that minimizes approval and processing procedures and transaction costs; providing ready access to imported inputs at world prices, world-class physical infrastructure, financial services and labour and skill resources; a low tax environment, including generous tax incentives; and national treatment and minimal imposition of performance requirements. Singapore's policy competitiveness towards FDI has been eroding since the mid-1980s, as attitudes and policies towards FDI have undergone radical changes in most developing countries, resulting in more liberal FDI policy regimes and aggressive FDI promotion. Further, as Singapore moves up the development and technology ladder, its competitors for FDI are not only fellow newly industrialized economies (NIEs) but also the OECD countries. Hence the government and investment promotion agencies are continually reviewing the business environment and FDI policy regime to ensure that Singapore remains attractive to FDI, both for new investments and for reinvestments.

Singapore adopted the strategy of outward investment in the region in the early 1990s with the objective of building an external economy to enhance its domestic economy. The strategy was driven by three factors: it would help Singapore overcome its shortages of land, natural resources and labour; the booming East Asian economies would provide business opportunities for Singapore investors; and it would enable Singapore to forge closer ties with its neighbours and ensure its economic and political security in the region. The Asian crisis has temporarily slowed down outward investments, as Singapore businesses which have expanded into the region experienced sharp demand contractions in host markets, currency volatility and non-performing loans. However, continuing regional investments are essential to enable Singapore to expand beyond the confines of the city state and tap the region's resources and markets. Regionalization will provide domestic firms with vital experience in outward investment and progression into global companies. Singapore firms also can exploit new opportunities when regional economies recover, as policies toward FDI, including mergers and acquisitions, have become liberalized.

The CSC recommended several strategies on outward investment: overseas affiliates to generate linkages with the home economy through trade flows through Singapore, consolidating Singapore's headquarters, high-tech operation and R&D functions; Singapore companies to pool their resources in venturing overseas, particularly forming clusters and tie-ups to maximize collective leverage; to promote strategic flagship projects; to promote tripartite cooperation, enhancing its role as a partner country for foreign investors in the region; to develop global and regionally minded managers and investors; and the tapping of foreign talent to overcome domestic manpower constraints.

Development of local enterprises

Although Singapore has played host to thousands of foreign multinational corporations (MNCs), it has so far failed to produce an indigenous multinational in the category of 'Fortune Global 500'. Aspirations to advanced-economy status with economic depth and resilience include producing indigenous world-class companies with core competencies and able to exploit the opportunities and compete effectively in the regional as well as global markets. Notwithstanding nearly four decades of industrialization and robust economic growth, Singapore's numerous local small and medium enterprises (SMEs) continued to play a secondary role to foreign MNCs and remained an Achilles heel. Singapore's earlier industrial policy focused on attracting foreign enterprises and neglected the nurturing of domestic enterprise. Since the mid-1980s, however, the Economic Development Board (EDB) has been more proactive in local SME development, promoting SMEs in supporting industries and linking them with foreign MNCs to facilitate technology transfer and market networking, particularly in the electronics industry.

The CSC recommended the following strategies to strengthen local enterprises: consolidate and pool resources among local enterprises to achieve synergy and competitiveness, such as through linking private sector companies with government-linked companies (GLCs), as the latter have advantages of size, financial resources, core capabilities and experience in venturing abroad; improve the supply of engineering and managerial manpower through expanded education and training facilities; promote innovation and technology, such as through government provision of funding and facilities and incentives for commercialization of innovation, acquisition of technology, and technological upgrading; build indigenous products and brand names; and expand international and regional orientation.

Singapore aims to build at least 50 local world-class and knowledge-based enterprises by 2010, in product, service or capability, to serve MNC clients or to create their own niche markets. This complements the EDB's Promising Local Enterprises programme which aims to develop at least 100 local enterprises, each with an annual turnover of S$100 million, by the year 2005. SME 21 is the new ten-year plan to upgrade and transform the SME sector. Programmes include SME Circles to provide the firms with learning partners; a mentoring scheme to help them map out strategic directions; business support centres to offer an array of support services and advice; a technology incubator programme to provide hands-on management assistance and access to finance; and even a pool of managers to help transform SMEs into professionally run organizations. A promising development in recent years has been the increasing number of emerging 'technopreneurs' and information technology-based small and medium enterprises.

Development of human resource and technological capabilities

Despite an economy with one of the highest per capita incomes in the world, Singapore remains acutely short of human resources because of its small population base and its historical legacy of colonial neglect of education and large-scale immigration of unskilled labour. Even in the first two decades of political independence, inadequate resources were channelled into education and training, so that by the 1990 population census only 25 per cent of the non-student population had completed secondary education and only 14 per cent had post-secondary and tertiary education. However, the educational flow has improved quite dramatically since the early 1980s and, by the end of the 1990s, some 60 per cent of the college-aged cohort are receiving polytechnic and university education.

To become a competitive knowledge-based economy, Singapore has adopted a two-pronged strategy to upgrade its own pool of human resources and to augment it with foreign talent. For the latter, Singapore must leverage on international talent and networks to overcome its limited size and resources. A systematic policy of recruiting foreign talent has been put in place, with EDB given the task of promoting inflow of foreign talent as well as inflow of FDI. Measures to attract foreign talent include promoting a more cosmopolitan living environment in Singapore, establishing an Internet-based international talent recruitment website, developing programmes to enable talent to work in overseas operations of Singapore companies, and cultivating a wide network of 'Friends of Singapore'. Responding to concerns of the citizenry over competition for high-end jobs, the government has gone to great lengths to explain the rationale, that the foreign talent pool will enable Singapore to remain competitive and that a larger robust economy means an absolute gain for Singaporeans.

For the former, funds for education and training have grown rapidly in the past two decades and have been directed to formal education from primary to tertiary levels, continuing education and skills training. With the need for rapid industrial restructuring pressured by both technological change and maintaining international competitiveness, the future jobs profile will require more top-end professional, managerial, technical and specialist personnel. The anticipated workforce profile would have 65 per cent with post-secondary education, 20 per cent with secondary education and the remaining 15 per cent with primary education or below. The resources being poured into education will ensure that new job market entrants have the requisite skills. The educational curriculum and teaching methods in schools, polytechnics and universities are being revamped to emphasize 'learning to learn' and analytical, creative, entrepreneurial, good problem-solving and interpersonal skills. A major problem, however, is with those already in the workforce, particularly those still below 40 years of age, who do not have even secondary school qualifications; these workers have to be upgraded and reskilled to prevent structural displacement. Manpower 21 (M21) outlines several strategies for a globally competitive workforce, including integrated manpower planning to identify and enhance the short- and long-term fit between manpower demand and supply, lifelong learning for lifelong employability, and transforming the work environment towards more flexible work arrangements and job redesign to keep pace with the nature of knowledge-based work and increase participation rates of women and older persons.

While Singapore has depended heavily on foreign MNCs introducing advanced and sophisticated technology and know-how through the FDI process, it needs also to develop its own science, technology and innovative capabilities. The first National Technology Plan in 1991 encompassed the developing of technology infrastructure, encouragement of R&D activities by the private sector and the formulation of a human resource plan to complement the science, technology and innovation needs of Singapore. In 1996, the second National Science and Technology Plan (NSTP 2000) was launched. The NSTP maintained the core strategies of the first plan and provided for improvements in strategic development of research institutes and centres, gross expenditure on R&D, the number of research scientists and engineers, and the number of patents. The R&D expenditure–GDP ratio rose from a mere 0.8 per cent in 1990 to 1.5 per cent by 1997. Likewise, the R&D manpower–labour force ratio jumped from 0.28 per cent to 0.60 per cent. And, reflective of the growing focus on science and technology, of total student admissions into polytechnics and universities in 1997, over half were into science and engineering courses. Notwithstanding these sharp improvements, it should be noted that absolute numbers are very small, reflective of Singapore's small population base, when compared with those of bigger economies, and the ratios are still behind those of South Korea and Taiwan and many advanced industrial countries. Hence the need to recruit foreign talents and further encourage inward FDI by foreign MNCs.

The recommendations of the CSC for Singapore to leap-frog into the next stage of R&D include the following: focus on research areas in which Singapore has already built up reasonable world standing; focus funding on the provision of continued competitive capabilities to the industry; promote transfer of technology, spin-off and start-up companies as well as technology acquisition; nurture more indigenous high-tech enterprises; enhance links to other global technology centres to facilitate the transfer of technology; use government-based venture capital as seed capital to promote investments in technology-based industries and help create networking links with overseas technology companies; introduce human resource development programmes to encourage R&D and innovation activities; create an innovative environment conducive to intelligent risk taking and entrepreneurship.

Singapore is also pushing for further development in information technology (IT) as a business enabler, particularly as Singapore aspires to be a hub for IT in the Asia–Pacific region. For a start, Singapore is focusing on the development of IT in the three areas of communications and media, e-commerce and IT innovation. A 1999 study called the Information Society Index by International Data Corp and World Times Inc noted that Singapore will be the world's second most dominant information economy by the year 2002, behind only the United States (*Business Times*, 8 April 1999). The study tracked data from 55 countries which account for 97 per cent of global GDP and 99 per cent of global IT expenditures. Currently, Singapore ranks first in Internet usage and infrastructure, third in computer usage, and tenth in access to information.

CONCLUDING REMARKS

Singapore has not been as seriously affected by the Asian currency and financial crisis as several countries in the region. For the latter, the crisis has necessitated not only stabilization measures and structural reforms to restore investor confidence and financial health, but has been complicated by or resulted in political and social turmoil. There have been growing demands for greater government transparency, accountability and responsibility and for social safety nets for the poor and unemployed.

Regional contagion has sucked Singapore into the Asian crisis. General business and consumer sentiment in Singapore's domestic economy has been adversely affected by the regional downturn and the Singapore growth rate plummeted in 1998. However, there had been no collapse of the Singapore currency, or financial and corporate sectors, nor political and social unrest. The relatively mild negative outcomes reflected Singapore's strong economic and financial fundamentals and good governance, as manifested in sound macroeconomic and financial policies, strict prudential regulation and supervision of the financial sector, and the accountability and responsibility of politics and government.

At the dawn of the 21st century, the Singapore economy has come a long way. It has achieved political stability, social cohesion, a high quality of life and a highly competitive economy. It has been driven by a strong sense of political and economic vulnerability arising from its geopolitical position in Southeast Asia and its small physical size. The pursuit of a stakeholder society and good governance have enabled Singapore to achieve its goals. For the next lap, with globalization providing intense competition, Singapore's continuing economic prosperity will largely depend on its ability to compete on capabilities rather than costs. The vision is a knowledge-based economy and many strategies and policies are being developed and implemented to achieve this objective, including a large and continuing role for foreign MNCs and a growing importation of foreign talent to enable Singapore to grow beyond the limits of its small physical size and small demographic base. The political leadership and policy makers have the challenging task of convincing the Singaporean business community and the Singaporean workforce that this is a shared vision and a positive sum game, as well as convincing the highly mobile international investors and international professionals to put their stakes in Singapore.

The forward-looking government is putting in place longer-term measures to ensure Singapore's continuing competitiveness in the era of globalization and information technology. The 1998 report of the Committee on Singapore's Competitiveness (CSC) envisions Singapore as 'an advanced and globally competitive knowledge economy . . . [having] a strong technological capability and a vibrant entrepreneurial culture . . . an open cosmopolitan society, attractive to global talent . . . [with] a critical mass of Singaporeans who are risk-taking entrepreneurs, innovators and arbitrageurs'. Such a vision requires a modification of the 'Singapore Inc' model. It requires a change in mind-sets and attitudes of government and people, to be less conforming and risk-averse and to be more innovative and creative. Changing the 'software' is harder than investing in the 'hardware', but the Singapore government and people have a long and successful track record of rising to challenges.

BIBLIOGRAPHY

Business Times, Singapore, various issues.

Campos, Jose Edgardo L. and Hilton Root (1996), *The Key to the East Asian Miracle: Making Shared Growth Credible*, Washington, DC: Brookings Institution.

Chia Siow Yue (1998), 'The Asian Financial Crisis: Singapore's Experience and Response', *ASEAN Economic Bulletin*, 15(3), December; reprinted in H.W. Arndt and H. Hall (eds) (1999), *Southeast Asia's Economic Crisis: Origins, Lessons and the Way Forward*, Singapore: Institute of Southeast Asian Studies.

Chia Siow Yue (1999), 'Singapore's Responses to the Asian Financial Crisis and Globalisation Challenges', paper presented at the AT10 Researchers' Meeting, January, Tokyo.

Chia Siow Yue (1999), 'Singapore: Governance Before and in the Wake of the East Asian Crisis', paper presented at the International Conference on Reform and Recovery in East Asia: The Role of the State and Economic Enterprise, Australian National University, September, Canberra.

Chia Siow Yue (2000), 'Singapore: Towards a Knowledge-Based Economy', paper presented at the AT10 Researchers' Meeting on East Asia's Industrial Restructuring for the 21st Century, January, Tokyo.

Committee on Singapore's Competitiveness (1998), *Report*, November, Singapore: Ministry of Trade and Industry.

Department of Statistics (various years), *Yearbook of Statistics*, Singapore.

Economic Committee (1986), *The Singapore Economy: New Directions,* Singapore: Ministry of Trade and Industry.

Economic Development Board (various years), *Yearbook*, Singapore.

Economic Planning Committee (1991), *The Strategic Economic Plan: Towards a Developed Nation*, Singapore: Ministry of Trade and Industry.

Goh Keng Swee (1977), *The Practice of Economic Growth*, Singapore: Federal Publications.

Institute of Management Development (various years), *The World Competitiveness Yearbook*, Geneva.

Ministry of Trade and Industry (various years), *Economic Survey of Singapore*, Singapore.

Monetary Authority of Singapore (various years), *Annual Report*, also MAS website.

Montes, Manuel and Tan Khee Giap (1999), 'Developing the Financial Services Industry in Singapore', in Seiichi Masuyama, Donna Vandenbrink and Chia Siow Yue (eds), *East Asia's Financial Systems: Evolution and Crisis*, Tokyo and Singapore: Nomura Research Institute and Institute of Southeast Asian Studies.

Straits Times and *Sunday Times*, various issues.

Tan Khee Giap and Chen Kang (1999), 'Economic Outlook for Singapore: Forecasting the Singapore Economy for 1999–2000', paper presented at the 1999 Regional Outlook Forum, organized by the Institute of Southeast Asian Studies, 8 January.

World Bank (1992), *Governance and Development*, Washington, DC: World Bank.

World Bank (1993), *The East Asian Miracle: Economic Growth and Public Policy*, Washington, DC: World Bank.

World Bank (1998), *World Development Report 1998/99: Knowledge for Development*, New York: Oxford University Press.

World Economic Forum (various years), *The Global Competitiveness Report*, Geneva.

10. Weathering the Asian financial crisis: the experience of Taiwan

Tain-Jy Chen

INTRODUCTION

The Asian financial crisis came as a major setback to the rapidly growing East Asian economies, whose performance had been described only a few years earlier as 'miraculous'.[1] So sudden was the crisis that it prompted many critics to interpret it as the 'death throes of Asian state capitalism' and to consider it as the evitable outcome of state intervention (Wade, 1998), whilst sympathizers considered East Asia to be the victim of an attack on the region's undersupervised and underregulated financial institutions, as a result of international financial panic (Radelet and Sachs, 1998). These two opposing views seem to suggest, however, that there is something in common, that is, that discretionary policies affecting resource allocation are dangerous, and that it is useful to adopt rule-based regulations that aim to protect the orderly functioning of the economic system, particularly the financial system.

The crisis revealed several shortcomings within the economies of East Asia, caused both by excessive intervention and by inadequate regulation, including overinvestment, excess capacity, relational lending by financial institutions (that is, bank lending based not on commercial grounds, but on special status of the borrowers, such as good relations with the government, bank owner and so on), and lending against inflated asset values. Excessive and unwarranted lending pointed to the problem of moral hazard for which governments must assume responsibility, whilst inflated asset values pointed to the phenomena of asset bubbles which have plagued East Asian countries throughout the 1990s.

Although not completely immune from the domestic financial turbulence, Taiwan set itself apart from the rest of East Asia by being particularly successful in weathering the crisis. A series of corporate failures in late 1998 and early 1999 had posed a serious threat to Taiwan's financial system, a system which had already been weakened by the fall-out from the financial crisis, but swift action by the government ensured that these troubles did not develop into a full-blown crisis. So this raises the question, what was it that accounted for Taiwan's success in resisting the contagion, that most other countries in the region had felt, from the Asian financial crisis?

Most observers have pointed to Taiwan's large reserves of foreign exchange, low levels of foreign debt and consistent current account surpluses, both before and after the crisis. But apart from these distinctive factors pertinent to foreign trade and finance, in all other respects, Taiwan resembled most other East Asian countries that had fallen victim to the crisis. In the 1990s, much like these other countries, Taiwan had liberalized its banking sector, deregulated interest rates and opened its capital account to the flow of international funds. Asset bubbles had rampaged through Taiwan during the late 1980s, in the same way that they had been experienced in Korea, Japan and Thailand. And, likewise, real estate was the favourite asset for collateral against bank borrowings, so that the credit market was susceptible to the fluctuations in real estate prices. If, or when, the bubble collapses, the value of the collateral shrinks, with bank loans becoming insufficiently secured and setting off a subsequent process of credit squeeze (Blanchard and Watson, 1982; Krugman, 1998). Furthermore, despite liberalization, the state still retained control over the banking sector, with government-administered incentives guiding industrial development. The Kuomintang (KMT) party had ruled Taiwan since 1945, and this long-term clinging to power by a single political party had tended to breed crony capitalism, as exemplified by the case of Indonesia. In fact, 'anti-cronies' was the slogan used by Taiwan's opposition party during the year 2000 presidential election campaign. So why have these internal weaknesses, which look so familiar to those of other East Asian nations, not made Taiwan succumb to the Asian disease?

In this chapter, we argue that financial liberalization in Taiwan has introduced competition into the market, resulting in greater stability rather than increased volatility. The effect of liberalization was to dismantle market segmentation, extending the reach of formal financial institutions and undermining the activities of the underground financial institutions. And although the level of government regulation was not stepped up, the integrated financial market made existing regulations more effective. Competition among creditors resulted in credit being extended to less privileged borrowers, making the loan portfolios in the entire system more diversified. This also forced the less efficient financial institutions to embrace high-risk borrowers, with greater potential for default in the event of a market downturn. Although Taiwan's mini-financial crisis of 1998 appeared to come about as a result of fall-out from the Asian financial turmoil, it was simply a natural process created by the removal of uncompetitive creditors from the market.

As in the rest of East Asia, Taiwan's problems of crony capitalism were clearly revealed by the 1998 mini-financial crisis. But crony capitalism was prevented from doing more serious damage in Taiwan because the vehicles used by the cronies to extract profits, namely the state-owned enterprises, were greatly constrained under democracy. This stands in stark contrast to Indonesia, or Korea for that matter, where large private enterprises were the major vehicles for rent generation, and which could become even more pervasive under democracy.

It is clear that the single most important reason for Taiwan's immunity from the effects of the financial crisis was its extreme prudence in the management of its foreign assets and liabilities. We argue that such prudence was prompted by Taiwan's precarious external relationships, particularly its adversarial stance towards China. The China factor affects not only Taiwan's position in its choice of foreign assets and liabilities, but also its foreign exchange policy and foreign investment strategy. The threat stemming from China underscores Taiwan's strong preference for liquidity and portfolio diversification, which in turn enables it to resist external financial shocks.

The rest of this chapter is arranged as follows. The development of Taiwan's foreign exchange market, and its economic performance following the Asian financial crisis are documented in the next section. In the third section we review the process of financial liberalization, and the evolution of government regulations in Taiwan, to present background reasons for the financial institutions' ability to remain sound, despite the intensified competition. In the fourth section we discuss Taiwan's crony capitalism and its role in the 1998 mini-financial crisis, with the following section giving an appraisal of the role of the state under democracy and an explanation as to why state intervention did not cause serious moral hazard problems in Taiwan. In the sixth section external relations are described and associated with Taiwan's attitude towards the management of foreign assets and liabilities. Concluding remarks are presented in the final section.

SAILING THROUGH THE STORM

The currency crisis which erupted in Thailand in July 1997 quickly sent ripples through Taiwan's foreign exchange market, where depreciation pressure on the local currency, the New Taiwanese Dollar (NT$), forced Taiwan's central bank to intervene. During the period from July to October of 1997, the central bank injected reserves of approximately US$5 billion into the market in its efforts to defend the NT$, persistent intervention which helped to maintain the exchange rate at NT$28.43 to the US dollar by 16 October, only slightly above the level of NT$27.76 on 2 July, when the Thai baht collapsed. However, the mounting selling pressure on the NT$ eventually forced the central bank to reverse its policy, and on 17 October it temporarily pulled out of the foreign exchange market.[2] Within two weeks, the NT$ exchange rate soared from NT$28.43 to NT$30.90 against the US dollar and continued this upward spiral during the following months. By the end of January 1998, it had climbed to NT$33.87, amounting to a 22 per cent depreciation since early July (see Figure 10.1).

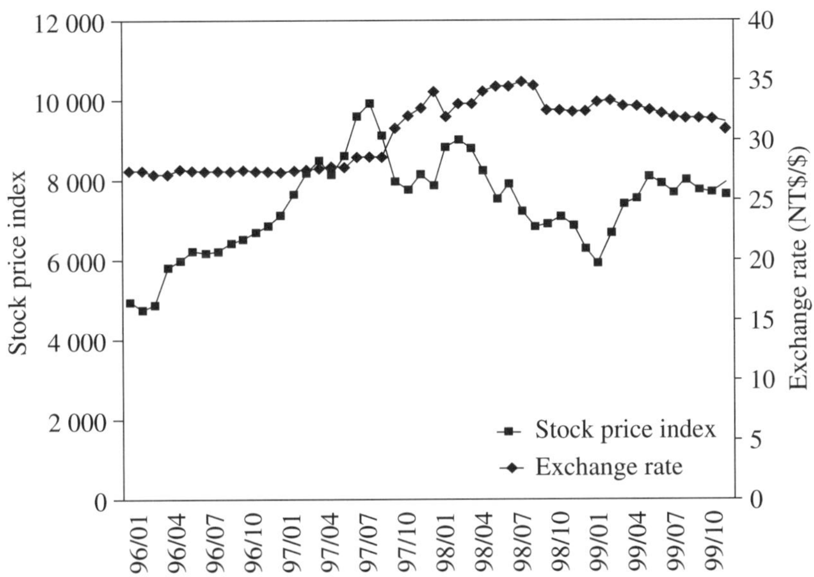

Figure 10.1 Stock price index and exchange rate, Taiwan, 1996–9

The October reversal of policy drew criticism both from inside and outside Taiwan. In a US Congressional testimony, some congressmen interpreted Taiwan's reluctance to continue to defend its currency as a conspiracy, aimed at passing the exchange rate domino to the Hong Kong dollar (HK$), which was pegged to the US$. This, it was suggested, would force a depreciation of the currency there and humiliate the Chinese government, since Beijing had pledged itself to defend the Hong Kong currency.[3] However, such an accusation was based on imagination rather than reality. In fact, the reversal of the policy was driven solely by the fear that the continuing loss of foreign exchange reserves through futile interventions might undermine market confidence and even cause panic, in recognition that no international institutions would come to Taiwan's rescue in the event of a foreign exchange shortfall. In addition, on the day before the policy reversal, the overnight inter-bank loan rate had shot up to 17 per cent, placing tremendous deflationary pressure on the domestic economy. A credit crunch would have caused much more severe damage than a rapid currency depreciation in Taiwan's financial institutions, where foreign indebtedness was limited.

Once the pressure for depreciation was defused in October, the NT$ exchange rate remained relatively stable for the remainder of 1997, and economic performance in the second half of 1997 was satisfactory, despite the Asian financial crisis. GDP grew by 6.8 per cent for the whole year (1997) and the consumer price index increased by just 0.9 per cent from the previous year. The economy started to slacken, however, in the first quarter of 1998, driven mainly by declining exports to Southeast Asia, Korea and Japan. As a result of these falling exports, there was a resurgence in selling pressure on the NT$ during May 1998. However, on this occasion, instead of direct intervention to support the local currency, on 22 May the central bank announced that it would forbid domestic financial institutions from engaging in the trading of non-deliverable forward (NDF) contracts – which were considered to be the culprit of market volatility – or from lending local currency to foreign institutions for such trade. Although foreign financial institutions were allowed to continue to offer NDF contracts to their clients, the shortage of local currency hampered their ability to hedge their forward position on the spot market. This effectively foreclosed the speculative NDF trading in which foreign bank affiliates in Taiwan were most active.

Nevertheless, there were also substantial costs involved in the closure of NDF trading. Since they were now being denied access to a low-cost instrument to cover their exchange rate risk, foreign investors in Taiwan shares started to withdraw funds from the local stock market and remit them abroad, creating increased selling pressure on both the foreign exchange and the stock markets. The NT$ depreciated sharply in late May and early June 1998, to reach a low of NT$34.90 on 10 June, its lowest level since 1987. The local stock price index (Taiex) also fell sharply from 8304 at the end of April, to 7117 on 12 June 1998 (see Figure 10.1).

As the economy continued to slide in the second and third quarters of 1998, along with sluggish exports and consumer expenditure, the central bank was forced to re-enter the foreign exchange market and sell its US$ reserves. Such action squeezed the money supply and raised domestic interest rates, adding further deflationary pressure to the economy. In order to sterilize the contractionary effect on the money supply, on 1 August the central bank lowered the required reserve ratios for bank deposits and, on 28 September, it further lowered the rediscount rate (Shea, 1999). However, these efforts failed to revitalize the struggling economy, and there was a steady increase in the number of corporate failures, severely denting the banking sector with ballooning non-performing loans.

Many of the failing businesses were closely connected to the ruling Kuomintang (KMT) party politicians, with some even owned directly by the KMT party itself. They had borrowed heavily from the KMT-affiliated or KMT-controlled financial institutions, using stock shares as collateral, but, as stock prices fell, the value of their collateral shrank and parts of their loans were recalled. In order to avoid such a recall, many attempted to prop up the price of the stocks which had been entrusted to the banks as collateral by injecting company cash into the stock market to buy their own stocks. Those who chose this tactic simply ended up in a liquidity trap as the bear market rolled on.

Cases of business failure culminated in November 1998 when, as a result of cumulative loan defaults, two bills finance companies (as defined on p. 265), both of which were owned by KMT politicians, became insolvent. There was also a serious run against a major regional bank in central Taiwan, the Taichung Small Business Bank. All of these incidents came at the time of the parliamentary election, forcing the ruling party to come to the rescue. The Ministry of Finance (MOF) acted swiftly to remove the management of the crippled Taichung Small Business Bank and organized a team of commercial banks to take over the two insolvent bills finance companies. It also put forward proposals for a relief package to aid the defaulting corporations, including a six-month extension on loan repayment schedules, and a temporary delisting of their company shares from the Taiwan stock exchange to freeze the value of their collateral. In order to qualify for the relief measures, the troubled enterprises had to apply to a review committee consisting of government officials, commercial bank representatives and experts.

As a means of compensating the banks for revenue losses resulting from deferred payments, the MOF lowered the business transaction tax for commercial banks from 5 per cent to 2.5 per cent, and the central bank also raised the interest rate paid on the reserve-B accounts of commercial banks from 2.4 per cent to 2.7 per cent to help increase their earnings (Chu and Lee, 1998). Despite these government rescue efforts, the ratio of non-performing loans (NPLs) in the commercial banks rose to an average of 4.8 per cent at the end of 1998, a year in which 19 of the 94 commercial banks in Taiwan recorded losses.[4]

It was fortunate that most of the distressed enterprises were medium-sized corporations with strong ties to the ruling party. Taiwan's large business groups were unscathed by this mini-financial crisis, and although the financial sector was seriously damaged by the crisis, the major commercial banks remained financially sound. As GDP recorded dismal growth of 4.8 per cent in 1998 – against the government's rosy forecast of 6 per cent at the beginning of the year – and as exports continued to fall in the first quarter of 1999, some observers, for example Rohwer (1999), predicted that Taiwan would eventually succumb to the turmoil of the Asian financial crisis. Nevertheless, Taiwan survived.

From the beginning of the second quarter of 1999, as the economy slowly began to pick up, boosted by rejuvenated exports, the pressure on the financial sector began to subside, and the review committee for applications for loan roll-overs was subsequently disbanded in April 1999. The post-crisis experience in Taiwan demonstrated that democratic institutions are effective in dealing with external shocks and managing domestic troubles. As Rodrik (1999) points out, the democratic institutions of Thailand and Korea performed much better than the autocratic regime of Indonesia in producing the requisite policy adjustments in response to the crisis. Rodrik credited democracy for facilitating the smooth transfer of power from a discredited set of politicians to a new group of leaders in Thailand and Korea that effectively managed the crisis, whilst, in Taiwan, democracy prompted the swift and decisive government actions which enabled Taiwan to weather the financial storm. Nevertheless, the mini-crisis of 1998 had severely damaged the support base of the ruling KMT party. Financial scandals, exposed during the crisis, brought to the attention of the public the crony capitalism that had been engaged in by the KMT party, a factor which partly accounts for the party's dramatic defeat in the presidential election, held in March 2000.

FINANCIAL MARKET LIBERALIZATION AND REGULATIONS

Many pointed to the lax financial institutions, particularly the commercial banks within the region, as the root cause of the Asian financial crisis. They claimed that these institutions, while ready to compete through liberalization, were inadequately supervised owing to the absence of sufficient expertise within the regulatory agencies. Moreover, these institutions were heavily distorted by various government incentives and directives in the allocation of funds, and were steadfastly protected in the case of insolvency. Government-directed lending resulted in the inefficient use of funds, and government protection resulted in moral hazard problems (Krugman, 1998). Taiwan was not completely free from these problems.

In 1989, Taiwan had amended its banking law to allow for the establishment of private banks, whose entry into the market had been denied since the 1960s, and as a result, following their licensing in 1991, 15 new private banks commenced their operations. Additional private banks emerged to join the market, following their conversion from credit cooperatives and investment trusts, and, along with the entry of these new banks, branching restrictions were also relaxed, thus breaking the regional segmentation of commercial banking. Competition intensified as the number of commercial bank branches (including foreign bank branches) increased from 1063 to 2247 between 1990 and 1997. Nevertheless, the state-owned banks remained the dominant force within the market, still accounting for 60.5 per cent of total bank loans in 1997.

This competition brought credit to the less privileged, but was probably also responsible for increasing the numbers of risky borrowers. In 1986, state-owned enterprises accounted for more than 13.2 per cent of bank loans but, by 1996, this ratio had fallen to just 3.7 per cent.[5] Along with the increased competition amongst commercial banks, the booming equity and bond markets of the 1990s had provided multiple sources of financing to the corporate sector, but since access to direct financing tended to favour the large enterprises, the growth in their demand for bank loans slowed. This forced the banks to seek new clients amongst the small and medium-sized enterprises (SMEs) and individual customers. The increased availability of bank loans to SMEs squeezed the operating space for the informal financial market, which had previously been an important financier for Taiwan's SMEs (Shea, 1994).

In 1986, borrowings from the informal sector accounted for 25.7 per cent of the total liabilities of private enterprises; that ratio subsequently fell to 12.5 per cent in 1997.[6] It is even more remarkable to note that bank loans now account for a higher percentage of total liability within SMEs than in the large enterprises, since the large enterprises have better access to equity and bond markets; thus banks and other lending institutions are now forced to take better care of the SMEs. Throughout this period, the gradual shrinkage of the informal financial sector greatly enhanced the effectiveness of banking regulations, bringing more stability to the market.

The increasing number of banks, and the dismantling of regional barriers to banking activities, placed many small-sized regional banks in a position of distress. For example, at the end of February 1999, the lowest point in Taiwan's indigenous financial crisis, three of the regional banks specializing in SME financing in Taiwan – each of which had been established prior to the 1989 Banking Law amendment – were amongst Taiwan's worst-performing commercial banks, judging by their NPL ratios.[7] Seven nationwide state-owned banks, which were the dominant firms in the market, also had mediocre performances with five of them recording NPL ratios above 5 per cent. Among the 16 private commercial banks established since the

1989 Banking Law, three recorded NPL ratios above 5 per cent, but, with the notable exception of Pan Asia Bank, in which non-performing loans exceeded 10 per cent, the private banks performed as well as, if not better than, the state-owned banks. However, the state-owned banks are known for their conservatism. Employees within these banks are public employees who are subject to disciplinary action if there is default in the loans that they have reviewed and approved. The prudence shown by the newly established private banks was partially explained by the stringent capital requirement that the government had imposed upon them at the time of their establishment: a minimum of NT$10 billion capital was required in order to gain government approval for the establishment of a new commercial bank. As a result of these stringent capital requirements, as of December 1998, the average capital adequacy ratio for Taiwan's commercial banks was 12.6 per cent, well above the BIS (Bank of International Settlements) requirement of 8 per cent.

The Taiwanese government also imposed strict regulations on bank portfolios. Many East Asian and Southeast Asian banks suffered from excessive lending in real estate and, wary of the burgeoning bubble in the real estate market, Taiwan's central bank imposed selective credit control measures on real estate lending in 1988, which resulted in significant cooling off in real estate trading. In addition to these control measures, a statutory cap was also imposed on real estate lending, at a level of 20 per cent of the combined value of the bank's savings and time deposits. The selective credit control measures have been gradually relaxed since October 1990, but the real estate market has never recovered from its serious glut. Between 1990 and 1997, the price of residential housing in Taipei City increased by a mere 2.9 per cent in real terms, after adjusting for consumer price changes.[8] The bursting of the real estate bubble in Taiwan, around 1990, had left many lending institutions awash with bad loans and they were thus forced to restructure their portfolios some five years earlier than their counterparts in Thailand. This ensured that Taiwan's real estate market was immune to the shocks of the Asian financial crisis because it had been dormant for some time prior to the onset of the turmoil.

Along with the bursting of the real estate bubble, the central bank also tightened its grip on the money supply in order to contain price inflation, which has a tendency to follow in the footsteps of asset inflation. Starting from 1992, the central bank set as its official operating target 'money growth rate'; the target for the growth rate of M2, for example, was set at between 6 per cent and 12 per cent in 1998. This effectively controlled the money supply and prevented a resurrection of the sort of asset bubbles that had ravaged the economy in the late 1980s. With inflation contained, and interest rates running at low levels, the interest rate spreads between Taiwan and the United States or Japan were minimal. This, together with the government's regulatory controls over commercial banks' exposure to overseas borrowings denominated in foreign currencies, made Taiwanese banks relatively free from exchange rate risks. By the end of 1997, overseas borrowings accounted for a mere 1.7 per cent of the total liabilities of Taiwan's commercial banks. Most of Taiwan's foreign debt had been incurred by private enterprises which had issued convertible bonds in Europe to take advantage of their high-value equity shares in Taiwan.

In addition to the liberalization of the banking sector, the government in Taiwan also opened the bills financing market to new entrants in 1994. Bills finance companies underwrite or guarantee short-term corporate debts, mainly commercial papers, and, as a result of the opening up of the market, 13 new bills finance companies joined the existing three incumbents that had previously monopolized the market. Most of these 16 bills finance companies were owned by commercial banks, who are major buyers for commercial papers, but two of them were owned by construction companies and politicians affiliated to the KMT. Both of these companies went belly-up in 1998 during the mini-financial crisis.

Since the bursting of the real estate bubble in 1990, construction companies have been entrenched in recession. The early bursting of the bubble may have insulated the major commercial banks from the Asian crisis fallout, but it wreaked havoc on bills finance companies and small banks that had lent heavily to the construction industry. Construction companies that invested in two of the failing bills finance companies, Central and Hung-Fu, raised funds by issuing short-term corporate debts guaranteed by the affiliated bills finance companies. These funds were then reinvested in new businesses or stock speculations, but this overdiversification, and unwarranted investments, resulted in failure. The Central Bills Finance Company, which commenced operation in 1996, went bankrupt in 1998. With capital of NT$2.5 billion, the company offered guarantees on NT$22.5 billion worth of short-term debt, of which NT$10.3 billion was in arrears at the time of bankruptcy. Most of these bad loans had gone to related companies; in fact, the failed bills finance companies resembled Korea's merchant banks, owned and controlled by the large conglomerates (chaebols).[9] Fortunately, the enterprise-controlled bills finance companies constituted only a small proportion of the industry in Taiwan.

In reality, the government's supervisory expertise over the financial institutions is just as inadequate as in the rest of East Asia; nevertheless, Taiwan is fortunate that the banking institutions are generally solid. The state-owned banks, which dominate the banking sector, are run by professionals with good discipline. Relational lending does exist, but it is not pervasive. State-owned banks may be susceptible to corruption, but they are relatively free from moral hazard problems. Taiwan also has a tradition of bailing out failing financial institutions, but it is limited to small-scale credit cooperatives and investment trusts. As alluded to earlier, the financial liberalization which succeeded in enhancing the level of competition also made government regulations more effective. The rapid development of instruments for direct financing forced commercial banks to seek new clients in Taiwan's SMEs and, although the government may come to the rescue of large enterprises to protect the bank's loan portfolios, no such scenario can be imagined for SMEs in the case of bankruptcy. All of which explains why the problems of moral hazard have not been so serious in Taiwan.

CRONY CAPITALISM IN TAIWAN

Although the government in Taiwan has traditionally distanced itself from the major enterprises (Gold, 1986), Taiwan is not free from crony capitalism. Because of the symbiosis between state enterprises, there was relatively little damage to Taiwan's economy as a result of crony capitalism. Ever since the mid-1980s, the power of the state enterprises has been restrained under democracy. KMT politicians and the KMT itself have been the major beneficiaries of crony capitalism within Taiwan. Before democratization was firmly set in motion, during the mid-1980s, KMT politicians sought financial benefits from the procurement and construction projects of government agencies and government-owned enterprises. Rent-seeking activities were mostly small-scale and short-lived, and rarely grew into big business. Politicians, or cronies, who wanted to establish large-scale businesses with the blessing of the state power, usually had to work within the KMT party, which itself operated a major business organization.

The KMT owned several holding companies with investments in a wide range of industries, the total assets of which amounted to an estimated NT$200 billion in 1998 (Chang, 1999). These KMT-owned businesses were extremely profitable because they were mostly monopolies, a position that was obtained in one of two ways: either through government licensing or through entry barriers erected by the state enterprises. For example, prior to 1989, the KMT owned a TV broadcasting company, a major bank and three bills finance companies, all areas of business in which the application for licences had been frozen. The KMT also owned several petrochemical companies that effectively monopolized the production of petrochemicals as a result of their exclusive access to raw materials supplied by the state-owned China Petroleum Company (Baldwin *et al.*, 1995).

The market opening of the mid-1980s, which coincided with democratization, had the effect of removing the licence protection for these KMT enterprises, and although the KMT remained in power until May 2000, under the system of democracy, their enterprises were not systematically favoured in the licensing procedures. For example, when the government resumed licensing for private banks in 1991, although the KMT-invested bank, Sinopac, was granted a licence, this was only one of 15 new licences granted. And even in the competition for government procurement projects, the KMT-owned enterprises no longer held the upper hand. One example is provided by the competition for Taiwan's massive high-speed railway project, in which the KMT-led consortium suffered a humiliating defeat at the hands of a private consortium which supported the opposition party. The state-owned enterprises also lost their power as a magnet for resources. Their business expansion plans were scrutinized by parliament and were, at times, blocked. Some of them were privatized and ended up in the hands of KMT cronies, but, when that happened, the subsequent privatization plans were blockaded by filibustering within parliament.

Lacking government protection and the patronage of state-owned enterprises, the KMT-affiliated businesses and their cronies sought their profits from speculation in the real estate and stock markets. They also provided venture capital for investment in high-tech start-ups, an area that involved little government favouritism except for the statutory tax concessions applied to high-tech industries in general. Nevertheless, this speculation in the real estate and stock markets by the KMT is essentially the root cause of the mini-financial crisis of 1998.

Real estate speculation was an important channel for politicians to garner economic income, and a typical formula was to buy low-priced agricultural land and resell at greatly inflated prices after rezoning the area as industrial or commercial land. Such land speculation activities subsided after 1990, as Taiwan's real estate market entered a prolonged period of recession; the construction industry suffered along the way and share prices of the construction companies listed on the stock exchange dwindled, sometimes to sub-par values.

The KMT business organization and its cronies, which invested extensively in the real estate and construction industries before 1990, were caught in dire financial straits. In 1995, the KMT-owned financial institutions held 5 per cent of the total financial assets, whilst the non-KMT private financial institutions held 28 per cent, with state-owned institutions holding the remaining 67 per cent (Chang, 1999). The KMT turned to stock speculation in an attempt to recover their wealth and, with the backing of the affiliated financial institutions, they were able to obtain substantial funds in spite of their shaky financial status. Their tactics were as follows.

First of all, through illicit trading, they inflated the share price of the listed companies in which they owned major shares, then borrowed money from the financial institutions using the inflated share prices as collateral; they then reinvested the money in new businesses or other company shares. There were two ways to inflate the share price. One was by beautifying the financial statement of the target company through transfer pricing in intra-group trading; the other way was by setting up subsidiaries with borrowed funds to purchase the shares of the parent company. The key to this process is that stocks were entrusted to the creditors as collateral. However, as their collateralized stock prices fell continually during 1998, the value of their collateral declined substantially, and they were required to remit further assets as collateral; otherwise, their loans would have been recalled. In their futile attempts to prop up the price of their collateralized shares to avoid a recall, these borrowers drained the cash on the stock market and ended up in illiquidity.

Politics and regulatory slackness played an important role in the Asian financial crisis. In an examination of the cases of Indonesia, Korea, Malaysia, the Philippines and Thailand, Bongini *et al.* (2000) found that connections with industrial groups or influential families greatly increased the likelihood of distress for financial institutions, suggesting that the supervisors within the financial institutions had granted forbearance from regulations in relational borrowing. However, such connections with industrial groups also increased the likelihood of the distressed financial institutions being closed rather than rescued, which further suggests that the closure processes themselves were transparent in these countries. In the 1998 mini-crisis in Taiwan, all of the distressed financial institutions were owned by KMT cronies, amongst whom relational lending was rampant. Amongst these, two distressed private banks were taken over by the Central Depository Insurance Corporation, awaiting liquidation or merger with the other commercial banks,[10] and three distressed bills finance companies were taken over by state-owned commercial banks under the direction of the government.

Nevertheless, crony capitalism within Taiwan was manageable, for three reasons. First of all, there was relatively autonomous authority in carrying out monetary policy without the influence of cronies. This is exemplified by the central bank's determination to burst the real estate bubble, a policy which went completely against the interests of the cronies. In consequence, even the KMT itself was saddled with devalued real estate. Second, the state did not divert significant financial resources into the hands of the cronies; thus the cronies were also unable to control Taiwan's major financial institutions. Although they may have been favoured in the procedures for the licensing of financial institutions, their managerial inefficiency and relational lending activities quickly brought their institutions to the brink of bankruptcy. Third, the major business groups remain outside the scope of crony capitalism. Some of them were even suppressed by the government under the prior autocratic regime. It has been mainly the KMT politicians and KMT-affiliated businesses, not the big businesses, that have engaged in rent-seeking activities.

THE ROLE OF THE STATE UNDER DEMOCRACY

The Asian financial crisis threw up a debate on the role of the state. Some viewed the crisis as an inevitable consequence of excessive government intervention within the markets, especially the financial market. Government-directed investment, in which finance plays a key role in carrying out state objectives, leads to excess capacity and inefficient production. Thus a moral hazard crisis can easily arise as a result of banks being allowed to borrow or lend funds on the basis of implicit or explicit public guarantees (Akerlof and Romer, 1993; Krugman, 1998). Some commentators have taken the opposite view that the crisis was caused by inadequate government supervision in domestic financial institutions, along with a lack of regulations on international credit creation and short-term capital movements (Wade, 1998). The former group viewed the economic growth in East Asia as input-driven at the expense of allocative efficiency (Krugman, 1994), while the latter group viewed it as a reward for government for remedying market failures, say, in coordinating investment decisions (Rodrik, 1995; Wade, 1998).

In fact, amongst the high-performing East Asian countries, there was significant diversity in terms of the chosen paths and the underlying policies for economic development (Rodrik, 1997). The Asian financial crisis made the contra-distinction even more apparent. For example, the contrast has now been indicated on numerous occasions between the dominance of large conglomerates in Korea and the prevalence of SMEs in Taiwan (for example, Feenstra *et al.*, 1999). Economic development is path-dependent and policy options available to the government are often conditioned by the structures built up during the course of development. For example, the high debt-to-equity ratio of Korea's enterprises made them susceptible to depressive shocks; thus, in Korea, the banks and enterprises need to cooperate in order to buffer the system shocks, and the government must also support their cooperation (Wade, 1998). No such constraints are placed upon the government in Taiwan, since Taiwan's enterprises are much less leveraged in comparison with their Korean counterparts.

With business conglomerates representing the major vehicles for Korea's economic development, and since this remained unchanged after financial liberalization in the 1980s, the Korean government found it necessary to control the banks in order to control the large enterprises (Leipziger and Petri, 1997). The fact is that this 'alliance capitalism', based on the nexus between state, banks and enterprises, made the large conglomerates the lowest-risk borrowers; even without government direction, banks would have lent to them anyway (Chen and Ku, 2000). In contrast, the major mechanism that the Taiwanese government employed to direct resource allocation was through the state-owned enterprises (SOEs). There was no need for Korean-style 'alliance capitalism' in Taiwan since the government directly owned these enterprises! Moreover, since the mid-1980s, democratization has greatly reduced the role of Taiwan's SOEs. In 1980, they accounted for 14.5 per cent of manufactured output, a ratio which had fallen to 7.9 per cent in 1998.

Since 1990, the Taiwan government has, to a large extent, abandoned the policy of industrial targeting (that is, choosing particular industries to receive government assistance). Even where it does pursue such policies, as in the promotion of the high-tech industry, start-ups are favoured over large business groups, and tax incentives, rather than the allocation of funds, are generally used as the main policy instrument. Industry-specific fiscal incentives were phased out by the 1990 expiry of the Statute for Encouragement of Investment. In its place, the Statute for Industrial Upgrading adopted activity-based incentives, such as tax concessions for R&D, pollution control and production automation. Ever since 1990, the Ministry of Economic Affairs (MOEA), which oversees economic activities and distributes tax incentives, has adopted 'the removal of barriers to investment' as its policy focus. This was a reactive move aimed at assisting private enterprises encountering difficulties in the implementation of investment projects, rather than a proactive move aimed at dictating the flow of resources.

'Barriers to investment' encompasses difficulties in land acquisition, shortages of labour, water and electricity, resistance from local residents and even the threat of flooding or landslides. Large-scale investment projects with the potential risk of environmental hazard are more likely to face such barriers and thus receive government assistance. Therefore the policy is tantamount to an effort to coordinate large-scale investment, which thus threatens to crowd out resources for other sectors of the economy.

But, even in this respect, the government has often failed to deliver. One prominent case in point was the large investment project proposed by Bayer of Germany in 1995. The project was aimed at large-scale production of tolylene diisocyanate (TDI) in the Taichung area, with an estimated capital contribution of NT$49.2 billion to the Taiwanese economy. Nevertheless, despite a strong lobby by the central government, it was rejected by local officials; local residents in Taichung strongly objected to the investment plan because TDI was known to be toxic. This indicates, as stressed by

Rodrik (1995), that the government's ability to coordinate investment, as the major contribution to economic development in East Asian states, has been significantly reduced under democracy.

On the financial front, the government in Taiwan did succeed in introducing a long-term investment fund offering subsidized loans to 'essential' investment projects. Established in 1994, and run by the Council for Economic Planning and Development, the fund was mainly furnished by the nation's resourceful postal savings. The purpose of the fund was to stimulate domestic investment, but it only cofinanced the projects that had already been screened and approved by commercial banks. In a typical case, the fund would cofinance up to one-third of the capital requirement for the project, and charge borrowers the going interest rate (which is flexible) on a one-year time deposit of postal savings, but it would share no risk of the loans. The commercial banks petitioning the fund for cofinancing had to bear all the default risks. Cofinancing by the fund made the normal commercial loan packages more attractive only to the borrowers, but it had the added advantage of creating no moral hazard problems. Up to May 1998, a total of 75 investment projects had been cofinanced by the fund, with the total funding reaching NT$534 billion.[11] Government-sponsored infrastructure projects and large private investments, including petrochemical complexes in Yunlin and silicon wafer fabrication plants in Hsinchu, have been the major beneficiaries. Subsidized loans extended to private investments by the fund amounted to NT$250 billion, accounting for 6.5 per cent of cumulative private investment for the period 1995 to 1998.[12] The subsidized private projects typically involved substantial sunk costs, but the funding showed no consistent industry bias.

Even after the new private banks joined the financial market in 1991, the government still controlled about two-thirds of financial resources through public-owned institutions. The MOEA, which formulates industrial policy, if there is any, nevertheless has little power over the allocation of financial resources. State-owned banks, which are supervised by the MOF, have complete autonomy over their lending decisions. On several occasions, the MOEA has failed to persuade state-owned banks to finance investment projects that it was seeking to promote,[13] since, unlike the state-owned enterprises, which are staffed by retired government officials, the state-owned banks are run by professionals.

As it lacks the ability to affect the allocation of financial resources, tax incentives are one of the few powerful policy instruments at the disposal of the MOEA. Under the authority of the Statute for Industrial Upgrading, the MOEA holds the power to screen private R&D projects applying for tax credits. It also operates a matching fund to subsidize private R&D proposals, the aims of which are to develop 'pioneering' products. This fund can subsidize up to 50 per cent of the R&D costs without subsequently claiming property rights or repayment from the subsidized firms. In addition, the MOEA itself operates a large research institute carrying out R&D on industrial technologies by means of public funding. Any technologies successfully developed by the MOEA are transferred to the private sector at low cost.

Most tax incentives, R&D subsidies and public-funded research projects have apparently favoured the high-technology industries, and support for the electronics sector has been particularly fruitful, with electronics and information products accounting for 26.7 per cent of total exports in 1997.[14] But although such concentration of industrial output in the electronics sector has raised concern over the volatility of export earnings, fortunately, the electronics sector itself is fairly diversified, with products ranging from traditional passive electronics components, such as resistors, capacitors and diodes, to newly emerging computer and semiconductor products.

For two decades, Taiwan has managed to avoid a current account deficit; this is not because Taiwanese enterprises and its citizens saved more than their East Asian neighbours, but because their investments did not become excessive and were not misguided by artificially low interest rates. The government's complete removal of interest rate controls in 1989, together with the entry of private banks, served to integrate the formal financial institutions and the black market money shops, and private investors were guided by market interest rates that truly reflected the cost of funds. If they were to fail to deliver a return comparable to the cost of funds, many Taiwanese enterprises would face merciless elimination by market forces. In contrast, the large business groups in Korea and Japan could endure uneconomically low returns with cross-subsidies (Chen and Ku, 2000).

It is interesting to note here that the leading companies in Taiwan's newly emerging computer and semiconductor sectors were all new entrants to the markets in the 1980s and 1990s. This stands in stark contrast to the position in Korea and Japan where spin-offs of the large consumer electronics firms remained at the helm of the industry. Easy entry and exit characterizes Taiwan's industrial structure where turnover contributes to growth in productivity (Aw *et al.*, 1997). This phenomenon indicates that, in Taiwan, there is no systematic bias in accessibility of productive resources based on government–business relationships.

EXTERNAL RELATIONS AND DEFENSIVE FINANCE

A factor that sets Taiwan apart from the rest of East Asia is its external relations; indeed, no country in East Asia recognizes Taiwan as a sovereign state. Taiwan currently remains outside the membership of major international financial institutions such as the IMF and World Bank. Worse still is Taiwan's persistent adversarial position with China. Under such an isolated and adversarial environment, Taiwan was continually mindful of the state of financial distress.

Taiwan's central bank held more than US$80 billion worth of foreign exchange reserves at the onset of the Asian financial crisis. At the end of June 1997, public borrowing from international banks was virtually zero, whilst borrowing from these banks by private enterprises was estimated to amount to US$ 25163 million, around 9.2 per cent of 1996 GDP. This figure was significantly lower than in Korea (21.3 per cent) and Thailand (38.1 per cent) (Komine, 1998). But, despite massive foreign reserves, Taiwan's central bank was wary of the danger of a liquidity crisis. It was extremely bold in its intervenions in the foreign exchange market in 1986–8, when the NT$ was appreciating in the aftermath of the Plaza Accord, but proved rather timid in its interventions in 1997, following the Asian crisis. The former interventions led to an accumulation of foreign reserves, whilst the latter led to a diminution of these reserves. Even though excessive holdings of foreign reserves are costly in terms of resource utilization, this decline in foreign reserves led to a certain amount of insecurity in the central bank. But with large foreign exchange reserves, a strong balance of payments position and little foreign debt, Taiwan was able to escape the contagion of the financial panic that is said to have ignited the Asian financial crisis (Radelet and Sachs, 1998).

The adversarial relations with China also put Taiwan on constant financial alert. In March 1996, as Taiwan held its first popular presidential election, China conducted military exercises in the East China Sea and fired several ballistic missiles towards the island. The manoeuvres were an attempt to intimidate the presidential candidates who strongly advocated Taiwan's independence, and this provocative action sent the Taipei stock exchange tumbling. The MOF had to deploy public pension funds in order to withstand the selling pressure, as jitters amongst private investors also prompted them to remit their funds abroad. This placed downward pressure on the NT$, and the central bank was forced to intervene in the foreign exchange market in order to support the NT$ exchange rate. The 1996 missile crisis led the government of Taiwan to establish a permanent fund, known as the National Stabilization Fund, which is available for mobilization to intervene in the stock exchange in the event of non-market-related external shocks, such as further Chinese aggression.

The continuing threat from China has also had the effect of sensitizing the government to any domestic financial instability which might cause social unrest, since this might also invite opportunistic activity from China.

In the mini-financial crisis of 1998, set off by bankrupt businesses, the MOF acted swiftly to bail out and take over the management of the troubled financial institutions in order to pre-empt any ensuing bank runs. The ministry proclaimed 'saving banks and leaving enterprises' as the principle of its rescue operations during this crisis, thus reflecting the government's fear of overall financial chaos much more than individual business failures. Since Taiwan's economy is dominated by SMEs, any failure of a particular business group would only stifle a small proportion of economic vitality, but the failure of any of Taiwan's banks might well have resulted in a domino effect on the whole financial system. Even now, the government continues to prohibit the setting up of branches in mainland China by any Taiwanese banks, despite repeated pleas from the private banks, and funds originating in China are also denied access to investment in Taiwan's stock market. The government in Taiwan continues to be wary of closer financial ties with China which may make Taiwan vulnerable to financial disruption initiated by China.

Ever cautious of Chinese dominance, the Taiwanese government also restricted direct investment in China by Taiwan's enterprises, whilst generally encouraging direct investment in Southeast Asia. Such investment in China requires prior approval, whereas direct investment in the rest of the world requires only to be reported to the government after its execution. There was also a limit placed on the maximum amount of capital each company may invest in China, and some particularly sensitive industries, such as semiconductors, are completely banned from entry into China.

The majority of Taiwan's outward investments, whether in China or elsewhere, are export-oriented, and although some investment projects aimed at the local markets of Southeast Asia have been stricken by sluggish local demand in the aftermath of the financial crisis, most of the export-oriented investment projects have benefited from a lower currency valuation in the Southeast Asian countries. In comparison, the value of the Chinese currency has remained stable at a comparatively high level following the crisis, placing Taiwanese subsidiaries in China in an unfavourable competitive position in the export markets. Diversification of Taiwan's foreign investment, partially forced upon investors by the government, did in fact create a bonus during the Asian crisis, protecting domestic production from further decline.

Despite government restrictions, between 1991 and 1997, an amount equivalent to US$18.4 billion was invested in China.[15] In 1997, exports to China accounted for 23.5 per cent of Taiwan's total exports, with direct trade with China producing a surplus of US$26.7 billion.[16] However, the adversarial position between China and Taiwan has not been softened by the increasing level of investment and trade. During Taiwan's second popular presidential election, in March 2000, China once again repeated its intimidation of Taiwanese voters, warning them not to vote for pro-independence candidates, a threat which again backfired. Taiwan's voters went on to elect as president the most anti-China candidate of the DPP opposition party, which emblazoned Taiwanese independence on its party platform, and tensions between Taiwan and China have been elevated since the election outcome was determined on 18 March 2000. Following the election, the president-elect, Chen Shui-Bian, pledged not to antagonize China by declaring independence; China, on the other hand, has insisted that Chen recognize China's sovereignty over Taiwan, a demand which was rejected.

Chen seemingly pinned his hopes on the ensuing negotiations between the two countries, establishing direct shipping, telecommunication and postal service links, following their joint accession to the World Trade Organization (WTO), apparently relying upon these increasing trade relationships to deflate the tension. But China has demonstrated lukewarm enthusiasm towards the prospect of three direct links that had always been taboo during the KMT regime. This precarious Taiwan–China relationship, if not stabilized, is likely to discourage future private investment in Taiwan, which will probably bring the government back into the market, not only in the financial sector, but also in the business sector; even the role of the state enterprises can be reconstituted if policy initiatives fail to stimulate private investment.

CONCLUSION

The Asian financial crisis raised the debate on the merits and demerits of the East Asian model of economic development. Those who oppose the model have pointed to excessive state intervention, excessive investment, overcapacity, problems of moral hazard and crony capitalism. Those who support the model have pointed to the inherent advantages of large savings, an educated labour force and the outward-looking nature of East Asian economic policies. The former have blamed governments for the crisis; the latter have blamed the international financial system for doing a great injustice to East Asia's immature financial institutions.

Taiwan's experience is useful in pointing out that all East Asian economies are not the same, and that there are, in consequence, ways of avoiding financial turmoil. This suggests that the management of a country's overall risk may well be just as important as all the other macroeconomic policies. The liberalization of the financial market, in the same way as the liberalization of other markets, needs to be undertaken with proper and sound institutional arrangements. Regulations which aim to protect a country's competitive mechanisms are important to the success of liberalization and should not be considered as intrusions in the market.

The Taiwan experience also indicates that liberalization of the political market, that is, democratization, reinforces rather than jeopardizes free competition in the financial market. Democracy has also constrained the operations of crony capitalism by limiting the power of the political cronies' agents. The key to the prosperity of crony capitalism seems to be the coexistence of economic income along with the limitations that the government imposes upon competition. Market liberalization eliminates economic income through freer competition. A liberalized and non-manipulated financial market also ensures that relational lending becomes much more transparent, with a clear indication that any financial institutions which indulge in relational lending will become susceptible to failure.

The Asian financial crisis indicates that there is no short-cut to economic growth. Economic development by rapid capital accumulation with borrowed funds may produce admirable growth figures in the short run, but it is not sustainable in the long run. The Taiwanese experience, and for that matter the experiences of Korea and Japan, suggest that sustainable economic growth needs to be supported by domestic-financed investments and the advancement of technological capabilities.

NOTES

1. See, for example, World Bank (1993).
2. See Corsetti *et al.* (1998) in which it was argued that, in October 1998, the mounting pressure on the NT$ was precipitated by the earlier decision in Singapore – whose export structure was similar to that of Taiwan – to allow its currency to depreciate.
3. See *The China Times*, 15 November 1997.
4. See *Common Wealth*, 31 May 1999.
5. See: Central Bank of China, *Annual Reports on Financial Institutions* (1986 and 1996).
6. Borrowings from the informal financial sector include borrowings from individuals and other private enterprises. Data are taken from the *Survey Report of Financial Conditions of Public and Private Enterprises*, Central Bank of China.
7. These were the Taichung, Kaohsiung and Taitung Small Business Banks, each of which had NPL ratios above 10 per cent. Data are from *Taiwan Hsin Pao*.
8. See *The Annual Report on Real Estate Industry in Taiwan* (1999).
9. See *Tzai Hsun*, May 1999, p.196.
10. A third private bank, Chung-Hsing Commercial Bank, was plunged into trouble in April 2000, after the revelation of its mounting non-performing loans. A large portion of these loans had been granted to a real estate speculator without the due process of auditing and evaluation. Chung-Hsing, which was established in 1991, was owned by a veteran KMT politician in Kaohsiung.
11. See Council for Economic Planning and Development (1998).
12. The realized figure of gross fixed capital formation by the private sector was NT$3873 billion in 1995–8. Some of the loans approved by the Long-Term Investment Fund may not be actually disbursed due to cancellation of the investment projects, or rejection by the borrowers.

13. In 1992, for example, the state-owned Chiao-Tung Bank led a consortium in the evaluation of an MOEA-proposed project, which aimed to acquire the ailing US aircraft manufacturer, McDonnell Douglas, and turned up a negative report. The acquisition plan was subsequently abandoned for lack of funding.
14. See the *Taiwan Statistical Data Book* (1998).
15. The amount of US$18.4 billion was realized investment; the value of approved investment projects was US$38.3 billion. Data are from the *China Statistical Yearbook* (1999).
16. See the *Taiwan Statistical Data Book* (1999).

REFERENCES

Akerlof, G. and P. Romer (1993), 'Looting: the Economic Underworld of Bankruptcy for Profit', *Brookings Papers on Economic Activity*, 0(2), 1–60.

Aw, B.-Y., X. Chen and M. Roberts (1997), 'Firm-Level Evidence on Productivity Differentials, Turnover, and Exports in Taiwan's Manufacturing', working paper, Pennsylvania State University, Department of Economics.

Baldwin, R., T.-J. Chen and D. Nelson (1995), *Political Economy of US–Taiwan Trade*, Ann Arbor: University of Michigan Press.

Blanchard, O. and M. Watson (1982), 'Bubbles, Rational Expectations, and Financial Markets', in P. Wachtel (ed.), *Crisis in the Economic and Financial Structure*, Boston: Lexington.

Bongini, P., S. Claessens and G. Ferri (2000), 'The Political Economy of Distree in East Asian Financial Crisis', World Bank Working Paper, 2265.

Chang, C.-H. (1999), 'The Reform of the Business Service Sector: The Case of Taiwan's Financial System', mimeo.

Chen, T.-J. and Y.-H. Ku (2000), 'Different Approaches, Different Outcomes: Industrial Priorities, Financial Markets, and the Crisis in Korea and Taiwan', in K. Sun and P. Chou (eds), *Weathering the Storm: Taiwan, Its Neighbors, and the Asian Financial Crisis*, Washington, DC: Brookings Institution.

Chu, Y.-P. and T.T. Lee (1998), 'From Bubbles to New Rounds of Asian Monetary Cooperation, with Reference to the Taiwan Experience', mimeo.

Corsetti, G., P. Pesenti and N. Roubini (1998), 'What Caused the Asian Currency Crisis and Financial Crisis? Part I: A Macroeconomic Overview', National Bureau of Economic Research, working paper no. 6833.

Council for Economic Planning and Development (1998), 'Review of the Long-Term Investment Fund', unpublished project report.

Feenstra, R., T.-H. Yang and G. Hamilton (1999), 'Business Groups and Product Variety in Trade: Evidence from South Korea, Taiwan and Japan', *Journal of International Economics*, 48(1), 71–100.

Gold, T. (1986), *State and Society in the Taiwan Miracle*, New York: M.E. Sharpe.

Komine, T., (1998), 'Currency Crisis and Financial Turmoil in Asia and the Potential for Future Growth', Economic Research Institute working paper, Economic Planning Agency, Japan.

Krugman, P. (1998), 'What Happened to Asia?', mimeo.

Leipziger, D.M. and P. Petri (1997), 'Korean Industrial Policy, Legacies of the Past and Directions for the Future', in L.-J. Cho and Y.H. Kim (eds), *Korea's Political Economy: An Institutional Perspective*, Boulder: Westview Press.

Radelet, S. and J. Sachs (1998), 'The Onset of the East Asian Financial Crisis', mimeo.

Rodrik, D. (1995), 'Getting Intervention Right: How South Korea and Taiwan Grew Rich', *Economic Policy: A European Forum*, 0(20), 53–97.
Rodrik, D. (1997), 'Trade Strategy, Investment and Exports: Another Look at East Asia', *Pacific Economic Review*, 2(1), 1–24.
Rodrik, D. (1999), 'The Asian Financial Crisis and the Virtues of Democracy', *Challenge*, 42(4), July–August.
Rohwer, J. (1999), 'Why Taiwan may be Next to Fall', *Fortune*, 15 February.
Shea, J.-D. (1994), 'Taiwan: Development and Structural Change of the Financial System', in H. Patrick and Y.-C. Park (eds), *The Financial Development of Japan, Korea and Taiwan: Growth, Repression and Liberalization*, Oxford: Oxford University Press.
Shea, J.-D. (1999), 'Economic Policies After the Asian Financial Crisis: Comments' (in Chinese), *Economic Forecast and Policies*, 30(1), 161–4. Academia Sinica, Institute of Economics, Taipei.
Wade, R. (1998), 'The Asian Debt-and-Development Crisis of 1997–?: Causes and Consequences', *World Development*, 26(8), 1535–53.
World Bank (1993), *The East Asian Miracle*, Oxford: Oxford University Press.

11. Why financial crisis may come to China but not Taiwan

James W. Dean[1]

INTRODUCTION

If the East Asian financial crisis of 1997–8 sparked One Great Debate, it was a debate over 'Asian' versus 'Western' capitalism. Or, more precisely, it sparked a debate about whether the root cause of the crisis was a failure of Asian capitalism or a failure of Western capitalism (Dean, 2000a, 2000b). Western economists were prone to vacillate, and the most influential of them changed his mind mid-crisis (Krugman, 1998a, 1998b, 1999).

In my own case, it took a trip to the People's Republic of China (hereinafter called China), followed by a stop in the Republic of China (hereinafter called Taiwan) to clarify my mind. Both Taiwan and China embrace so-called 'Asian' capitalism – in Taiwan's case, perhaps not so closely as the hardest-hit crisis countries, Indonesia, South Korea, Malaysia and Thailand – but in China's case much more closely. Had practising the evil arts of Asian capitalism been sufficient to trigger a crisis, China should have been Asia's leading candidate for Armageddon. Taiwan too should have been brought low, much like its arch-rival, South Korea. But the two Chinas survived, while the Southeast Asian 'tigers' did not.

This chapter will argue that the two Chinas averted crises precisely because of their distinctive, 'Asian' suspicion – paranoia might be more precise – of Western capital markets. Neither was seduced by the sirens of Tokyo, Wall Street and Frankfurt. But there the similarity ends. While Asian capitalism in Taiwan shows every sign of being sustainable, in mainland China it is not.

ASIAN CAPITALISM

For purposes of this chapter, Asian capitalism will be defined very crudely, characterized as a governance style involving three-way symbiosis between government, finance and industry. This can be depicted as an 'Asian governance triangle', with government, *G*, on the top corner, and finance and industry, *F* and *I*, on the bottom two corners (Figure 11.1).

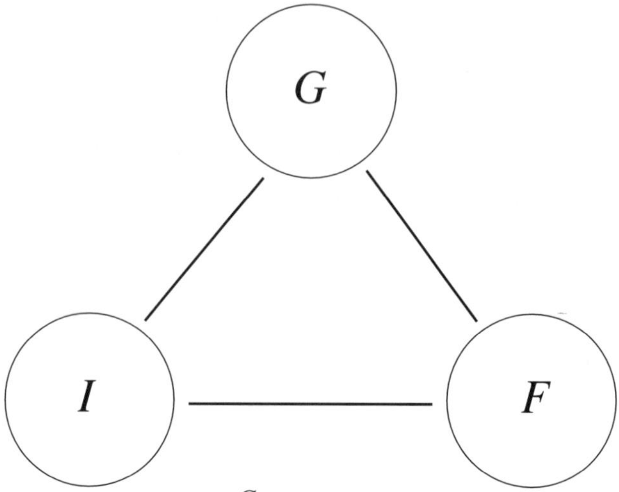

G: government
I: industry
F: finance

Figure 11.1 *Asian governance triangle*

Albeit with very different details, the economies of South Korea, Indonesia, Malaysia, to some extent Thailand, and certainly China, are governed with state support for finance and industry and vice versa.[2] Taiwan's economy does not quite fit this governance style, but as we shall see it shares with mainland China a measure of government-enforced insulation from international capital markets. This insulation played an important role in shielding China (and, arguably, Taiwan) from the financial crises that hit their neighbours.

Asian Capitalism in China: the 'Socialist Market Economy'

Asian capitalism as currently practised in China is bleeding its economy badly. Although real GDP growth for the year 2001 is forecast to be almost 8 per cent, this is in the context of a continuous slowdown since 1992, when the rate was 14 per cent. Moreover, experts estimate that these growth statistics are at least 2 per cent too high by conventional accounting standards. And a recent survey by the Chinese central bank suggests that every three dollars lent by the banks – largely to state owned enterprises (SOEs) – has increased output by only two dollars. In other words, the SOEs have destroyed one-third of the capital they have received.

China's leadership has been acutely aware of this for some time – at least since the early 1990s. But the leadership has no plans for a decisive and final leap towards Western capitalism since it judges, probably rightly, that this would trigger a profound crisis, not just economic, but social and political as well. The plan instead is to 'restructure' the most palpably unsustainable aspects of Asian capitalism – notably the loss-making SOEs – while continuing to move gradually and judiciously closer to Western capitalism.

The final destination envisaged by the Chinese Communist Party is *not* Western capitalism. Rather, it is a state of being that the 14th Party Congress called, in October 1993, the 'socialist market economy': an oxymoron which stuck and is still today very much part of official rhetoric. Nevertheless, the East Asian crisis has raised more doubts than ever about the sustainability of the 'socialist' part of China's emergent market economy, not least, one suspects, in the minds of many in the top ranks of the Communist Party. Put politely, the socialist market economy is a moving goal-post. Put less politely, China's policy makers are increasingly schizophrenic.[3]

The schizophrenia is both about making a final leap toward a market economy internally (whether to privatize the SOEs) and about embracing the market economy externally (whether to permit unrestricted access to foreign goods, services and capital). To complicate matters, internal and external liberalization are intertwined.

In summer and early autumn of 1999, schizophrenia was just below the political surface, as China waffled about joining the World Trade Organization (WTO). Rumour had it that Premier Zhu Rongji was so frustrated with his conservative colleagues, who oppose opening China further to the West, that he contemplated resigning. For his part, President Jiang Zemin waited for President Clinton to telephone three times before returning his calls and ultimately agreeing to resume negotiations.

In negotiations with the United States, Zhu and his liberal constituency prevailed. But the liberalization that will be mandated by the WTO poses far greater risks to financial and political stability than most Western observers appreciate. For example, the terms of putative admission to the WTO cede greatly enhanced access to foreign banks. However, all that forestalls the collapse of China's domestic banks is patient forbearance by Chinese depositors. Should deposits move *en masse* to foreign banks, the SOEs would collapse too.[4]

In late March, 2000, the drama of WTO negotiations with the United States was repeated when the European Union's negotiators left Beijing without a deal. The Chinese were unwilling to grant majority-ownership entry by European firms to China's insurance, telecommunications and car sectors.

China seems prepared to sacrifice some of the efficiency of pure Western capitalism along the path to reform in order to avoid crisis. While the rhetorical goal-posts will shift, what is certain is that China has chosen for the moment to eschew 'big-bang' reform in favour of stability. But China's governance is increasingly fragile, and its insulation from the world's capital markets is wearing thin. China's governance triangle has turned into what I will call a 'triangle of woes'. It is China's Achilles heel.

WHY FINANCIAL CRISES MATTER

To understand why China has thus far been willing to pay a high and rising price to avert financial crisis, we begin by characterizing a 'financial crisis', and explaining why it might be costly to the real economy (see Box 11.1). A financial crisis typically involves sharp, negative and unexpected drops in the prices of financial assets, such as currencies and stocks, a sharp rise in interest rates, and often widespread bank failures.

BOX 11.1 SEVERITY OF FINANCIAL CRISIS INDEX

A quick and easy index of the severity of a financial crisis is the sum of changes over a short period of time in a country's exchange rate and its stock market prices. Over the severest period of crisis, between June 1997 and March 1998, Indonesia's crisis index measured −96 per cent, South Korea's −69 per cent, Malaysia's −65 per cent and Thaliand's −52 per cent. By contrast, China's crisis index was only −11 per cent, since the Renminbi held firm and the stock market fell only 11 per cent.

The reason for financial crises being costly is not simply that wealthy holders of the wrong currencies, stocks or bank shares lose money. Rather, it is that sharp price changes in the financial sector typically spread to the real sector. Currency, stock market and banking crises usually lead to sharp declines in exports and in investment and consumption spending, which in turn result in sharp drops in output, incomes and employment. Contraction in the real sector inevitably causes misery for millions of people. Consider the massive unemployment, malnutrition and displacement of populations in Indonesia resulting from a crisis that began simply as an attack on their national currency.

Crisis in China?

In China's case, a financial crisis might evolve something like this. China's banks are kept alive only by massive indirect government subsidies.[5] By continuing to keep banks alive, the Chinese government implicitly guarantees bank deposits. The average Chinese household saves about 40 per cent of its annual income and hundreds of millions of ordinary Chinese hold the bulk of their savings as bank deposits. Should the government's willingness to bail out even one Chinese bank come into doubt, or should foreign banks become an easy alternative after China joins the WTO, millions of ordinary Chinese might pull their deposits out of banks – including banks that were previously sound but would become unsound as a result. There could easily be a 'run' on the banks.

The core business of Chinese banks is lending to the SOEs, which still produce almost 30 per cent of China's national output. Many SOEs make losses rather than profits and rely on a continuing flow of new loans to stay afloat. A bank run would force a large number of SOEs to close their doors. Since more than half of China's city-dwellers work for SOEs, massive unemployment would ensue. And such a crisis would entail more than just unemployment, since for millions of Chinese an SOE is their only source of medical, health, housing and education benefits.

In short, what began as a banking crisis would quickly become a massive real crisis, with severe economic and social consequences. Worst of all, the crisis could have dire political consequences, the direst of which could be popular revolt against the Communist Party's monopoly of power. The crudest interpretation of the party's willingness to pay a high price to avoid financial crisis is that it must pay that price for its very survival.

CHINA'S TRIANGLE OF WOES

The relationships between the Chinese government, Chinese banks and Chinese SOEs can be characterized as an unhealthy and fragile version of the 'Asian governance triangle'. Figure 11.2 depicts the government's fiscal deficit, *D*, at the top of the triangle. This feeds in to the banks, *B*, on the bottom right corner and then to the SOEs on the bottom left. This is China's 'triangle of woes'.

Each corner of the triangle is vulnerable to crisis *on its own account*. Hence crisis could erupt at the *D* corner if the government found itself no longer able to finance its deficit by selling bonds or printing money, at the *B* corner if people lost confidence in the banks and began withdrawing deposits (or even if deposits stopped growing), or at the *SOEs* corner if

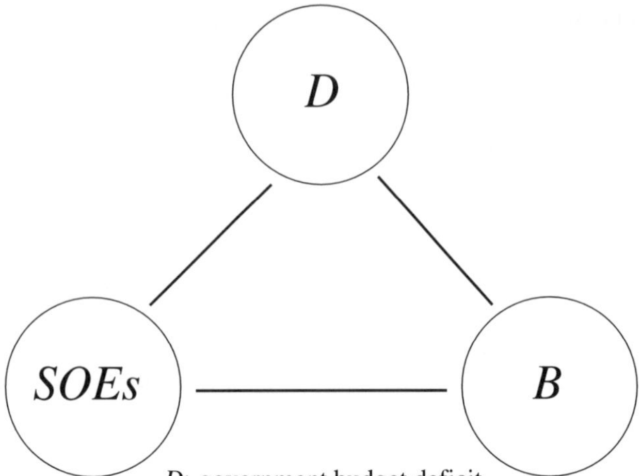

D: government budget deficit
B: banks
SOEs: State-owned enterprises

D + (borrowing by *SOEs*) = public sector deficit

Figure 11.2 *China's 'triangle of woes'*

expenses finally overwhelmed cash flow from sales revenues and new borrowing.

Moreover, *crises are interdependent.* Crisis in any one corner could lead readily to crisis in the others. Consider a crisis originating at the apex. A crisis at *D* could result in the end of the government bond interest paid to banks, government subsidies to SOEs, or to both. Were banks cut off from government bond income, they would likely find themselves unable to retain deposits. The crisis would have spread from *D* to *B*.[6] Or if subsidies to SOEs ceased, the banks would likely find themselves hard put to earn loan revenues, and again the fiscal crisis would spread to *B*. Similarly, crises in the *B* or *SOEs* corners might spread to the *D* corner: if banks or SOEs were the initial source of crisis, the resulting rise in subsidy spending might so bloat the government deficit as to cause a crisis there too.

The Chinese leadership has been sensitive to this fragile symbiosis since fiscal deficits first appeared in the early 1990s. But their awareness was heightened with the onset of East Asia's crisis in mid-1997, so much so that an extraordinary meeting (a 'National Financial Work Conference') was convened in Beijing, on 17 November 1997, to devise prophylactic measures. Its neighbours' crises threatened China both on its external trade account and on its external capital account. On the trade account, much-depreciated currencies and plummeting incomes in Southeast Asia hurt

China's exports. On the capital account, foreign investment dried up, particularly from Hong Kong, China's main source of foreign investment, which was mired in its own serious recession.

The effect of China's deteriorating trade and capital accounts was an outflow of foreign exchange reserves, a decline in the monetary base and a decline in both foreign and domestic spending on Chinese goods and services. Even before the slowdown in spending, China had been systematically overproducing goods for domestic consumption, as predictable by-products of artificially-supported SOEs. When spending slowed down, inventories quickly built up, output growth slowed down and unemployment rose. Most ominously, prices began to fall. By late 1999, the East Asian crisis countries (except Indonesia) had recovered, but China's malaise persists. China has averted crisis, but at the price of persistently slower growth and broad-based deflation.

Fragile SOEs

Central to the economic dilemma facing China is how to phase out the loss-making SOEs without precipitating massive unemployment. The past two years' downturn in foreign and domestic spending has moved this dilemma to the top of the policy agenda. And putative admission to the WTO, which foreshadows much more foreign competition, has brought the dilemma to a head. The leadership has now moved 'restructuring' the SOEs to the top of its economic priorities.

'Restructuring' seems to mean turning the SOEs into profit-making enterprises wherever possible, rather than phasing them out. Ominously, it seems also to mean keeping them state-owned wherever possible, rather than privatizing them. The government is keenly aware of its growing deficit and the difficulties of tax collection. It would be convenient to turn the SOEs into cash cows, but that is probably a pipe-dream.

Fragile Banks

The problems of the SOEs do not bode well for the banks. Hence much of the leadership's attention, articulated best by Premier Zhu Rongji, the so-called 'economic czar', has turned to them. Beijing bankers point out that less than 10 per cent of their SOE loans are in arrears. This ignores the fact that interest payments continue to flow largely because of new loans from the very banks that collect interest on the old loans, not to mention the more direct ways in which the SOEs are subsidized.

The bulk of the banks' SOE loans are still performing only because of implicit government guarantees on banks, and government subsidies of SOEs. Were these to cease, interest payments on SOEs would cease, rendering the banks illiquid. Worse, the prospects for eventual repayment of principal would plummet, rendering the banks insolvent. Not only would the Chinese banking sector collapse were government guarantees and subsidies to end, it would collapse even if they were widely expected to end.

Bank Debt into Equity?

A conventional and very capitalist technique to avert debt payments crises is to swap debt into equity. Recently, China has begun swapping bank debt – more precisely, bank loans to the SOEs – into equity holdings in the SOEs. This would relieve the SOEs of their scheduled interest obligations, in effect converting them into performance-contingent dividend payments that the SOEs would be expected to pay to the banks if and only if they began to show profits.

Such swaps certainly relieve the SOEs of a major cash flow obligation, but they compound the banks' liquidity problems. Stripped of a flow of interest income from SOEs, banks would be even more dependent for their survival on a flow of new deposits, or on interest income from government bonds. In effect, loan-for-equity swaps are a technique to shift the burden of crisis-avoidance from the SOEs to the banks. More importantly, they are a technique to shift part of the burden from explicit government subsidization of SOEs toward a contingent guarantee of the banking sector that is potentially even more costly than what already exists. The new guarantee must provide for the added probability of bank failure should dividends on their new equity holdings never materialize. Moreover, the new guarantee must be credible enough to assure depositors that their money will continue to be safe and, beyond that, credible enough to induce them to keep adding to their deposits.

In short, swapping bank loans into SOE equity should not be misconstrued as a technique to save the banks. Quite the reverse: it is a technique to shift the burden of crisis avoidance from the SOEs and the fiscal deficit, onto the banks. It will reduce the extent to which the SOEs are subsidized from the government budget, and thereby reduce pressure on the budget deficit. Far from helping the banks, it will compound their cash flow problems, since they will lose interest income. And it will not move them any closer to solvency, since the value of their new equity will be no larger than the expected value of their old debt (unless the swap changes the incentives of the SOEs to generate profits: see Bowe and Dean, 1993, 1997a). The sole virtue is that it shifts the burden from a highly explicit drain on government revenues to a less transparent contingent guarantee on the banks.

A Dearth of Lending Opportunities

Another technique that is currently in favour with the government is encouraging the SOEs to issue marketable debt (bonds) and then encouraging banks to buy those bonds by guaranteeing them. But this technique depends for its immediate success on an explicit government guarantee as well as government pressure to buy the bonds, and (like the swap technique) for its ultimate success on an implicit government guarantee that banks will not fail, or at least that depositors will not lose money. Or, to put it another way, it depends ultimately on the continued willingness of ordinary Chinese to save at world-record rates, and to hold those savings in the banking system.

The only fundamental way to rescue the banks is to increase their holdings of commercially viable, performing loans. This is a particular problem at present since most commercially viable enterprises in China are joint enterprises with foreigners. But foreign direct investment (FDI) has fallen sharply since the onset of the Southeast Asian financial crisis. This leaves bankers with the challenge of finding potentially profitable indigenous investment projects. This challenge is compounded by their almost total inexperience with the art of modern risk assessment. The authorities have moved moderately to engender this art by allowing banks for the first time to adjust their interest rates on loans within a modest band – as of late 1999, this was between 3.2 per cent and 4.8 per cent, with a median regulated rate of 4 per cent.

But, in reality, Chinese banks face a dearth of commercial lending opportunities. This is not helped by legislation that threatens imprisonment for loan officers who make bad loans (although the bankers I interviewed in September 1999 dismissed this as a threat that has never been enforced and is likely to be idle in practice). Consumer and household mortgage lending might offer alternative (and collateralized) opportunities, but Beijing bankers claim that convincing their customers to borrow for personal or family purposes is an uphill battle. Chinese savings habits, and the associated reluctance to borrow, are deeply engrained.

The macroeconomic manifestation of a dearth of lending opportunities is that the central bank finds it difficult to increase the money supply. It can pump cash into the banking system, but if the banks are loath to make loans, no new deposits – that is, no new money – will be created. Students of the anachronistic field called 'money and banking' will recognize this as the 'pushing on a string' problem: the central bank can push, but unless the so-called commercial banks pull, no new money will result.

Fragile Fiscal Deficit

The reason for the Central Bank of China trying to pump up the money supply is to generate spending. As already mentioned, China now literally suffers from deflation: that is, prices are falling. Despite the 'pushing on a string' problem, the Chinese money supply *is* increasing (at about 15 per cent annually), but this is not enough to generate spending. In other words, the ratio of spending to money – the so-called 'velocity' of money – is low and falling. The conventional cure for this (credited in the Western world to Keynesian thought) is for the government to do the spending, since the private sector will not. Over the past year, the Chinese have explicitly adopted this economic strategy: what Western macroeconomics calls 'expansionary fiscal policy'. Hence the growing deficit at the apex of our triangle of woes, which began as a by-product of subsidies to the SOEs and the banks, is now growing even faster as the result of a new strategy to encourage spending.

HOW CHINA AVOIDED A CURRENCY CRISIS

The thrust of the argument thus far is that China is *internally* fragile at each of the three corners of its triangle of woes, and that a crisis at any corner could quickly spread to crisis at the others. Over the past two decades, financial crises in other parts of the world have often also been rooted in similar fragility. Latin America's international debt crisis of 1982–9 had much to do with fiscal deficits (Bowe and Dean, 1997b; Dean, 1998b); Mexico's crisis of 1994–5 had much to do with bad banking; and East Asia's crisis of 1997–8 had much to do with an unhealthy symbiosis between bad banking and loss-making enterprises.

But in each of these cases, internal fragility led to a crisis on the countries' *external* capital accounts, a crisis that manifested itself most dramatically as a collapse in their currencies' external values. And it was these collapsing exchange rates that led to sharp and sudden declines in real economic activity – in output and employment – setting up a vicious circle that fed back to further currency declines, further output drops, and so on. In short, the internal problems became a full-blown crisis with catastrophic real consequences only after they turned into external problems.

More precisely, there were full-blown crises because external, borrowed capital dealt punishing blows. This did not happen in China. It did not happen for the simple reason that China was not, and is not, vulnerable to sharp withdrawals of external capital. Despite capital inflows during the 1990s that dwarfed those to any other developing country, China did not borrow as heavily relative to its foreign exchange reserves as its crisis-prone neighbours, nor did it borrow in the same form. Even though in 1997 China's external liabilities as a percentage of GDP were (and still are) higher than South Korea's, the bulk of these take the form of direct investment, mostly joint ventures, that are highly illiquid and difficult to withdraw quickly. By contrast, nearly all of Korea's external exposure was in so-called 'portfolio' form (mostly bank debt and bonds), some two-thirds of it short term: that is, due to be repaid fully within one year. China is not vulnerable to an external capital account crisis because the bulk of its external liabilities are in the form of highly illiquid joint ventures; its remaining liabilities, which take the form of foreign-held portfolio debt, are a small fraction of its foreign exchange reserves. For 2001, short-term debt is estimated at 11% of foreign exchange reserve.

Nevertheless, in 1997 China did face a serious problem of capital flight. A significant percentage of export receipts were being retained abroad: although Chinese foreign exchange controls require all export revenues to be brought home, double invoicing had become endemic. Some estimates suggest that in 1997 China's entire trade surplus was matched by capital flight of the same magnitude. Moreover, China's exports to the region were in jeopardy. And not only did foreign investment inflows plummet, foreign firms began to pick up stakes and leave.[7] Pundits speculated that devaluation was imminent.

After the emergency meeting of 17 November 1997, China mounted a concerted campaign to close the loopholes in its capital controls. The most effective measures centred on a consolidation of computer records between customs and other authorities. By some estimates, remitted export receipts in 1998 virtually doubled as a result. This re-enforcement of capital controls probably played a key role in averting a run on the Renminbi (RMB).

Currency inconvertibility and related capital controls were reinforced by a heavily regulated domestic financial sector that severely cramps the style of any would-be speculator who tries to borrow RMB and sell short. China restricts the convertibility of the RMB into external currencies, enforces strict limits on borrowing for speculative purposes (for example, borrowing RMB to buy hard currency) and discourages the development of broad and deep forward and futures markets for the RMB. In short, China, unlike its crisis-prone neighbours, did not dismantle capital controls or currency inconvertibility during the 1990s, and was less prone to capital flight and currency speculation as a result.

WHY THE CRISIS BYPASSED TAIWAN[8]

Unlike China, Taiwan is not undermined by a 'triangle of woes'. There is no growing fiscal deficit, no insolvent banking system and no large, money-losing state-owned sector. In fact, Taiwan was and still is fundamentally healthier than the three Southeast Asian crisis countries as well. Leading up to their crises Thailand, Indonesia and South Korea all had rotten banking systems making rotten loans to rotten enterprises: Taiwan did not. Hence the reason for Taiwan avoiding crisis may seem too obvious to discuss.

But the facts are that the three crisis countries were not nearly rotten enough to deserve the punishment they received. Nor can Taiwan's fundamental virtues fully explain why it averted crisis. The most fundamentally virtuous of the three crisis countries was South Korea. Before November 1997, most observers would have put Korea's fundamentals roughly in the same quality category as Taiwan's: no fiscal problems, no obvious banking problems and no money-losing state enterprises. Yet Korea's currency collapsed, and Taiwan's did not. To be sure, post-crisis pundits belatedly recognized that great chunks of South Korea's government-underwritten conglomerates, the chaebol, were indeed unprofitable, as were the banks that were keeping them alive. But it would be hard to argue that Korea's international creditors attacked the Korean won for these reasons.

A much more plausible argument is that Korea's currency was attacked because short-term international exposure was very high relative to international currency reserves. In fact, Korea was so financially fragile that by December 1997, foreign-currency reserves were down to about $10 billion, with almost that much short-term debt coming due every month. In short, Korea, though far from insolvent, was temporarily illiquid vis-à-vis its foreign creditors (Dean, 1998a, 1998b, 1999). Between June 1997 and March 1998, the won dropped by 36 per cent and the stock market by 34 per cent, for a total 'financial fall' of 70 per cent.

The New Taiwanese dollar, by contrast, lost only 15 per cent over the same nine-month period, and that was largely the result of a deliberate central bank decision (on 17 October 1997) to move from a managed float to a clean float. There was no prolonged period of free fall. And the stock market actually rose by 10 per cent, for a net financial fall of only 5 per cent.

The determining difference between Taiwan and South Korea is that the former ran an extremely conservative and cautious foreign exposure policy, whereas the latter did not. Foreign exposure has two aspects: balance sheet exposure and balance of payments exposure: that is, exposure of stocks and exposure of flows. On the stock front, Taiwan entered 1997 with foreign exchange reserves of about $85 billion, in contrast to Korea's reported reserves of less than $35 billion (part of which turned out to have been offset by unreported liabilities of Korean bank branches abroad). Relative to its smaller GDP, Taiwan's reserves looked even better. But the more startling contrast is between debt figures: in 1997, Taiwan's foreign debt was negligible, whereas Korea's was over $150 billion. This sum is not an excessive debt obligation for an economy as large as Korea's, but the real problem was that about two-thirds of it was short term: $100 billion came due within 12 months. Hence Korea was utterly reliant on the willingness of its creditors to relend or 'roll over' its short-term debt. Taiwan had very little such exposure. Since 1997, Korea's position has improved and Taiwan's has deteriorated. Their estimated ratios of lost-term debt to reserves for 2001 are 38% and 22% respectively.

Taiwan's flow exposure, on its balance of payments, was also extremely conservative. In 1996 and 1997, it was running substantial current account surpluses (5 per cent and 2 per cent of GDP, respectively), allowing it to be a net international lender rather than a net borrower. Correspondingly, Taiwan's domestic saving has long exceeded its domestic investment. Even when the current account deteriorated in 1997, Taiwan's balance of international payments was not dependent on a flow of loans from abroad.

It is therefore tempting to argue that Taiwan's survival was entirely due to its long run of export success, manifested in a continuous trade and current account surplus – export success that not only relieved it of the need to borrow abroad but allowed the build-up of huge foreign exchange reserves. But not just free market forces were at work. Taiwan has long regulated the access of its firms to foreign borrowing and, indeed, to domestic borrowing. Taiwan enforces a rigid ceiling on the debt–equity ratios of its firms. The average debt–equity ratio across all firms is about 40 per cent (in contrast to more than 300 per cent in South Korea). Moreover, Taiwan's huge stock of foreign exchange reserves – the fourth largest in the world, after Japan, China and the United States – is the result of deliberate central bank purchases of foreign currency export receipts. In other words, Taiwan's near-zero foreign debt and extravagant foreign exchange provisioning is no accident; rather, it is very much a matter of government policy.

That said, government policy seems to be quite consistent with the private preferences of individuals and firms. The Taiwanese have one of the highest savings rates in the world, and that is the result of free choice, not government coercion. Moreover, Taiwanese firms' 40 per cent debt–equity ratio is below the regulatory ceiling, again the result of free choice. Taiwan's extraordinarily cautious public and private choices seem to be rooted in fear of crisis. Since its post-1949 political conception as the Republic of China, Taiwan has lived on the edge of one form of crisis or another – economic, political or military. It has been systematically sanctioned economically and politically, and is perennially threatened by invasion from the mainland. Its concerted efforts to minimize vulnerability to international capital markets are shaped by that experience. It is not that the Taiwanese foresaw the generic fickleness of global portfolio capital any more clearly than others; rather, they engineered their capital–market autarky in response to the specific fickleness of foreign good will towards them.

All this cautious debt and payments management notwithstanding, Taiwan's currency might well have been brought down by speculators. Indeed, it was attacked several times, but not successfully. In principle, domestic holders of New Taiwanese dollars might have moved massively into foreign currency, or domestics or foreigners might have speculated massively by borrowing NT$ and buying foreign currency, and successfully forced the NT$ into a free fall. But this did not happen.

Arguably, speculation on a massive scale did not occur because of one final element of Taiwan's cautious exposure policy: capital controls. Capital controls, unlike the other elements of Taiwan's exposure policy, are not conventionally thought wise or necessary, particularly for such a fundamentally solvent and liquid economy. Taiwan's capital controls are mild, but nevertheless no firm or individual can convert more than NT$5 million into foreign currency without special dispensation. This may or may not have played a role in deterring massive currency flight in the autumn of 1997. It does seem implausible that even the wealthiest speculator would have taken on the Taiwanese central bank with its massive reserves. But the NT$ did suffer repeated attacks during the first nine months of the regional crisis, and arguably the attacks would have been more severe had the capital controls not been in place. As it was, the central bank was bled of about US$7 billion in reserves between June and October of 1997 (Wu, 1998).

INSOLVENCY, ILLIQUIDITY AND CAPITAL CONTROLS

To analyse the desirability of capital controls, it is helpful to review a conventional distinction for analysing a firm in financial difficulty: the distinction between *insolvency* and *illiquidity*. Roughly, insolvency means that the firm has a long-term 'stock' or balance sheet problem. Its net worth is zero or negative: its liabilities are at least as large as its assets. Illiquidity means that the firm has a current 'flow' or payments problem: its current expenses exceed its current revenue. Insolvency means that the firm has a permanent problem and must close its doors; illiquidity may only be temporary.

Applying these concepts to entire economies is at best an imprecise exercise, since even the poorest or most internationally indebted economies cannot really be permanently insolvent. But for all practical purposes their governments can be internationally insolvent for the foreseeable future if they are unable or unwilling to extract foreign debt payments from the population at large.

It is much less likely that a country's entire private sector can be internationally insolvent. For that to be true the firms that together account for the bulk of private sector output would have to have negative net worth. In other words, the present value of firms' liabilities – the current dollar value of their expenses for the foreseeable future – would have to exceed the present value of their assets. It is a very rare circumstance that all or most of a country's producers can find themselves so in debt to foreigners that they can never again show a profit.

Hence it would have been nonsense to classify Thailand, South Korea or even Indonesia as internationally 'insolvent', even at the depth of their despair, especially since the bulk of their debt was private-sector (Dean, 1998a, 1999). Certainly many of their large firms, and the banks that financed them, *were* insolvent: the rot ran deep in all three countries. But the rot certainly did not extend throughout their entire private sectors, nor were all the rotting firms doomed to subtract value from the economy in perpetuity. For most, there was and is a good chance of turnaround if they seriously restructure.

However, the three worst-hit economies – Indonesia, Thailand and South Korea – *were* internationally 'illiquid'. Their public and private sectors found themselves almost overnight facing international payments obligations that vastly exceeded their immediate ability to pay. This was not because their rotten banks and firms had suddenly and sharply deteriorated further, but rather because they faced sudden and sharp withdrawals of financial capital. Wealth holders and investors, both domestic and foreign, made the collective judgment that they could exhaust the countries' foreign exchange reserves if they sold liquid domestic currency assets and bought foreign currency. They precipitated 'currency crises'.

The currency crises would not have happened had the countries in question held sufficiently larger foreign currency reserves, or had they saddled themselves with sufficiently smaller liquid liabilities to foreigners, or finally, if they had had the will and ability simply to block conversion of domestic currency into foreign currency. The first two, goodly stocks of foreign exchange reserves and relatively little short-term foreign debt, are conventionally considered the two *sine qua non* of a prudent balance of payments policy. In all probability such policy would have averted the crises.

But in principle the crises could have occurred even with large reserves and little short-term foreign debt if *domestic* wealth holders had sold large quantities of domestic currency assets for foreign currency assets: that is, if they had undertaken massive 'capital flight'. Hence the final and sufficient policy to prevent currency crises is simply to prohibit – or rather, *successfully prevent* – capital flight by implementing what are commonly called 'currency controls' or, more generally, 'capital controls'.

Most market-oriented economists, that is to say most economists, instinctively reject capital controls. The facts that both Taiwan and China had capital controls in place and both averted the currency crises that hit their neighbours has softened some economists' attitudes recently, and the conventional wisdom, even at the IMF, has become that financial liberalization should be a sequential rather than 'big-bang' process (Dean, 1998c). In Taiwan's case, the banking system is strong enough to withstand external liberalization, and the role played by capital controls was probably marginal at best. But in China's case, with its extremely fragile banks, external capital controls may have been critical.

DOES CHINA FACE CRISIS NOW?

China's 'fundamentals' look far worse than Thailand's, Indonesia's or South Korea's ever did. Its SOEs and banks are insolvent if free market accounting standards are applied, and its government finances are not in superlative shape either. Thus far, China has averted crisis for three reasons.

First, China remains willing to pour public funds into the SOEs and the banks. Partly as a result, hundreds of millions of ordinary Chinese people keep adding to their bank deposits, deposits that enable the banks to sustain their flow of non-repayable loans to the SOEs. More cynically, Chinese people have nowhere else to hold their savings, except as cash. [9] The Southeast Asian crisis countries, with a similarly sick symbiosis between government, banks and industry, were unwilling to persist with loss-making subsidies. For example it may have been Thailand's willingness to let a major bank – Finance One – fail in May of 1997 that precipitated the domestic and foreign run on Thailand's banks and ultimately its currency. But China persists with the subsidies.

Second, China remains shielded from crisis by the structure of its external balance sheet. China has massive foreign exchange reserves and relatively long-term foreign liabilities. The proportion of short-term debt is low enough for it to be easily repaid out of foreign exchange reserves should external creditors decide not to roll it over. And although there has been an exodus of direct foreign investment, foreign exchange reserves are hardly threatened with exhaustion from that quarter either.

Third, China remains shielded by capital controls. Whether in the Southeast Asian crisis countries capital controls could have been applied *ex post* effectively enough to stem the attacks on their currencies, given contractual obligations to repay short-term debt, is doubtful, although a mutually agreed temporary moratorium on debt repayment might well have worked. But in China's case capital controls were already on the books, as were the will and the means to enforce them.

China's 'triangle of woes' *would* collapse in crisis if any of its three corners collapsed: if the government could no longer finance its deficit, if the public pulled their deposits out of banks, or if the SOEs collapsed. None of these cataclysmic events is likely to happen as long as the Communist Party keeps control. Indeed, to ensure its own survival, which would be severely threatened were a financial crisis to occur, the party will continue to pour funds into the banks and the SOEs as long as necessary. And the sobering reality is that China is a 'party-state': the Communist Party both governs and administers. Were the party to collapse, the civil service would collapse with it, much as happened in post-Soviet Russia.[10]

This said, the potential for crisis is probably higher now than ever before in China's post-revolutionary history. First, China is poised to become more vulnerable internally, as *each corner of its triangle of woes* is opened to international competition under the WTO. Both the SOEs and the banks will face competition, but so too, in a sense, will the fiscal deficit, as Chinese government bonds lose the luxury of unchallenged Chinese banks as monopsony buyers. Taxes may also be harder to impose as profit-oriented firms increasingly demand useful goods and services for their tax dollars. In other words, current expansionary fiscal policy, involving as it does large and often wasteful infrastructure projects, may prove harder and harder to sell to taxpayers.

Second, *the links between the three corners of the triangle* are vulnerable. The glue that holds the triangle together, the Communist Party, is increasingly vulnerable to a competition of ideas. China is opening up to the rest of world through the Internet. For example, in March 2000, under pressure from US firms, China backed off from regulations banning foreign-designed encryption software.[11] Not only will this protect the privacy of foreign firms, it will also protect the privacy of Chinese citizens who exchange politically subversive opinions. In effect, the party is open to public scrutiny as never before.

Third, and finally, currency inconvertibility and capital controls, *the prophylactic that shields the triangle from the rest of the world*, have become, in effect, China's Achilles heel. China's capital account is increasingly uncontrollable. Flows to and from Hong Kong and Taiwan are almost impossible to monitor. Capital flight will become even easier as China's financial autarky is eroded when WTO conditions allow foreign financial institutions to compete for bank deposits. E-commerce will undermine financial autarky still further.

The bottom line is that direct and indirect subsidies to the SOEs and the banking system are now costing China some 10 per cent of its GDP. In the current context of declining output growth and plummeting foreign investment inflows, this strategy is unsustainable. So too are currency inconvertibility and capital controls. China's window of opportunity for reform and crisis avoidance is still there, but it has narrowed substantially over the past two years.

NOTES

1. I am grateful to the China Institute of Contemporary International Relations in Beijng, which arranged many helpful interviews during my visit in September 1999. I am also grateful to the Chinese Academy of Social Sciences, People's University in Beijing, Beijing University and the Shanghai Academy of Social Sciences. This chapter benefited greatly from a reading of Lardy (1998), which is surely the definitive study of Chinese economic reform. And I am most grateful of all for very helpful comments from Charles Adams of the International Capital Group at the IMF, Margaret Cornish-Kehoe of Scotia Capital Markets, and my Western Washington University colleague Allan Sleeman. None of them is even remotely implicated by the argument of this chapter.
2. For sympathetic explication of modern Asia's symbiotic style of economic governance, see Wade (1998) and Wade and Veneroso (1998).
3. By schizophrenic I do not mean crazy. As individuals, China's leaders are far from crazy; they simply face a dilemma that has understandably led to splits in the ranks and collective schizophrenia.
4. China's agreement with the USA states that two years after joining WTO, foreign banks will gain substantial access to Chinese borrowers: hence they might be able to 'cherry pick' the better SOE loans, which would further weaken domestic banks. Then, after another three years, foreign banks will be able to take general retail deposits. It is not clear at this early point how vigorously foreign banks will compete for that business, so that the vision of a massive run on domestic banks may well prove excessively Apocalyptic. Interestingly, within days of the WTO agreement with the USA, Chinese academics began advocating granting foreign banks quick and early joint venture access to the state-owned domestic banks.
5. These 'subsidies' take the form of interest income on government bonds and government-guaranteed loans, as well as the continued flow of new deposits that constitute contingent liabilities of the government since the government is unlikely to allow the banks to fail.
6. Russia's financial crisis of August 1998 began this way. Russian banks were implicitly government-subsidized: they were dependent for most of their interest revenue on government bonds. When the Russian government found itself unable to raise enough tax revenue to service its own bonds, it defaulted, leaving the banks in the lurch. This in turn led to widespread losses by depositors, to a freezing up of banks' and Russia's credit lines to the West, and to a free-fall collapse in the foreign currency value of the ruble.
7. The exodus of foreign firms accelerated in 1999. For example, Caterpillar, Pittsburgh Plate Glass, Fosters and the Royal Bank of Canada all pulled out of China: see *The Economist*, 25 September 1999, pp. 71–3.
8. This section benefited from discussions with Rong-I Wu, President of the Taiwan Institute of Economic Research in Taipei, and from Wu (1998).
9. The pent-up demand for other outlets is evident from the popularity of 'stamp markets' in major Chinese cities, where ordinary Chinese can buy limited edition stamps for saving and speculative purposes. Pent-up demand is also evident in the sporadic frenzy surrounding trading of so-called 'A-shares', ownership of which is restricted to Chinese citizens.

10. However, the long reign of the party-state in China has resulted in deeply entrenched corruption that can only be rooted out by separating party and state, and also removing the political monopoly of the Communist Party. Hence China finds itself between the devil and a hard place. For an excellent analysis of this dilemma, see Pei (1999).
11. The original regulations were issued by the State Encryption Management Commission, which works in conjunction with China's spy service (*Wall Street Journal*, 13 March 2000).

REFERENCES

Bowe, Michael and James W. Dean (1993), 'Investment Incentive Effects of Debt–Equity Swaps', *Oxford Economic Papers*, 45 (April), 130–47.

Bowe, Michael and James W. Dean (1997a), 'Debt–Equity Swaps and the Enforcement of Sovereign Loan Contracts', *Journal of International Development* 9(1), Jan./Feb., 59–83.

Bowe, Michael and James W. Dean (1997b), 'Has the Market Solved the Sovereign Debt Crisis?', *Princeton Studies in International Finance*, 83 (August).

Dean, James W. (1998a), 'Why Left-Wing Moralists and Right-Wing Academics Are Wrong About Asia', *Challenge*, 41(2), March/April, 44–60.

Dean, James W. (1998b), 'Asia's Crisis in Historical Perspective', *Journal of the Asia Pacific Economy*, 3(3), Fall, 267–83.

Dean, James W. (1998c), 'Can Financial Liberalization Come Too Soon?', *Social and Economic Studies*, 47(4), 47–59.

Dean, James W. (1999), 'Was East Asia Illiquid or Insolvent? With Special Reference to South Korea', *Multinational Business Review*, VII(2), Fall, 60–7.

Dean, James W. (2000a), 'Which Failed: Asian Capitalism or International Capital Markets?', in Jay Choi (ed.), *Asian Financial Crisis*, vol. 1 of *International Finance Review*, JAI Press/Elsevier.

Dean, James W. (2001), 'East Asia Through a Glass Darkly: Disparate Lenses on the Road to Damascas', in Geoffrey Harcourt, Hank Lim and Ken Park (eds), *Essays in Honor of Mark Perlman*, Routledge.

Krugman, Paul (1998a), 'What Happened to Asia?', January, http://web.mit.edu/krugman/www/.

Krugman, Paul (1998b), 'Bubble, boom, crash: theoretical notes on Asia's crisis', January, http://web.mit.edu/krugman/www/.

Krugman, Paul (1999), 'Balance sheets, the transfer problem, and financial crises', January, http://web.mit.edu/krugman/www/.

Lardy, Nicholas R. (1998), *China's Unfinished Economic Revolution*, Washington, DC: Brookings Institution Press.

Pei, Minxin (1999), 'Will China Become Another Indonesia?', *Foreign Policy*, Fall, 94–109.

Wade, Robert (1998), 'The Asian Debt-and-Development Crisis of 1997: Causes and Consequences', *World Development*, August.

Wade, Robert and Frank Veneroso (1998), 'The Asian Crisis: The High Debt Model vs. The Wall Street–Treasury–IMF Complex', *New Left Review*, March–April.

Wu, Rong-I. (1998), 'Taiwan's Role in the Asian Financial Crisis', *Review of Pacific Basin Financial Markets and Policies*, 1(4), 529–44.

Other Information Sources

China Daily, various recent issues.

China Monthly Report, September, 1999. Produced and published by HSBC (Hong Kong and Shanghai Bank Corporation) China Services Limited, Hong Kong.

China Economic Quarterly, third quarter, 1999. Produced in Beijing in cooperation with the Center for Economic Analysis and Forecasting (CEAF) at the Chinese Academy of Social Sciences (CASS), and published in Hong Kong.

The Economist, various recent issues.

12. Marketization, democracy and economic growth in China

Leong H. Liew[1]

INTRODUCTION

Interest in China's political change and its progress towards democratization[2] is strong. There is a considerable literature on this topic. The bulk of it is written largely from a political science perspective that examines the impact of Chinese economic reform on the development of civil society (for example, He, 1997; Unger, 1996; White *et al.*, 1996), legal reform (for example, Pei, 1997; Tanner, 1994) and political governance (for example, Kelliher, 1997; O'Brien, 1994). Possibly because the literature is largely written from a political science perspective, its primary focus is on how economic reform and the resulting economic growth have affected the process of democratization in China.

The cross-country evidence that democracy is positively correlated with economic growth is overwhelming (Diamond, 1992: 466; Przeworski and Limongi, 1997: 156). But does the positive correlation between democracy and economic growth mean a causal relationship between the two variables? And if it does, what is the direction of this causality? Does economic growth promote democracy or does democracy promote economic growth? Or is the relationship symbiotic?

This chapter explores these questions with regard to contemporary China. It argues that early moves towards democratization in the post-Mao reform era were due more to a specific cause of economic growth – marketization of the economy – than to economic growth per se. Since marketization[3] is responsible for the impressive growth rates in the reform era, it can easily be mistakenly concluded that economic growth is driving the process of democratization forward. This chapter further argues that the impressive economic growth rates achieved in the post-Mao reform era were due to effective government more than to democratic government. It argues that democracy is both growth-enhancing and growth-impeding and, at China's current level of economic development, the optimal political system for China in the sense of maximizing economic growth will differ from the Western liberal democratic model. The chapter concludes that, in the post-industrial society, the happiness of the Chinese people may be independent of higher incomes and therefore democracy should be a goal for China for its capacity to improve the lives of the Chinese people, beyond what it can do for economic growth.

MODEL OF DEMOCRATIZATION AND ECONOMIC GROWTH

The Chinese leaders' decision to reform and to marketize the economy from the late 1970s was first and foremost a political decision – an act of political liberalization. But beyond this stage of political liberalization, marketization is driving the democratization process in China. The form of progression from a highly authoritarian state to a potential democracy in China is illustrated in Figure 12.1.

The first step in democratizing a highly authoritarian society is enlarging the private space of the individual. Without private space, there can be no autonomous political space from which society can contest state power. By private space, I mean an autonomous sphere that is free from intrusion by the state. Although private property creates private space, having private space is not the same as having private property. A slave possesses no private property. Nevertheless, he or she may have some private space because of the inability of the slave owner to monitor completely his or her behaviour all the time. A person possessing private property nevertheless may have his or her private space curtailed because of the existence of a system of collective monitoring similar to the one that existed in Maoist China. So, instead of focusing on private property as the prerequisite for a liberal democracy like some scholars,[4] I choose to focus on the somewhat more encompassing concept of private space.

Marketization in China has expanded the private space of the individual. The significant withdrawal of the state from the lives of citizens and the resulting weakened state authority necessitates political and legal reform to give legitimacy to the efforts of the state to re-establish political authority and to arbitrate disputes among actors in the economic sphere. This enlarges the political space available. The expansion of private space also directly enlarges the political space for citizens. Individuals, no longer dependent on the state for their livelihoods, are better able to contest state power. The expansion of their political space increases their capacity to work for political and legal reform and enhances the prospect of democracy. Political and legal reform introducing the principle of 'rule by law' lowers business transaction costs, which will promote economic growth.

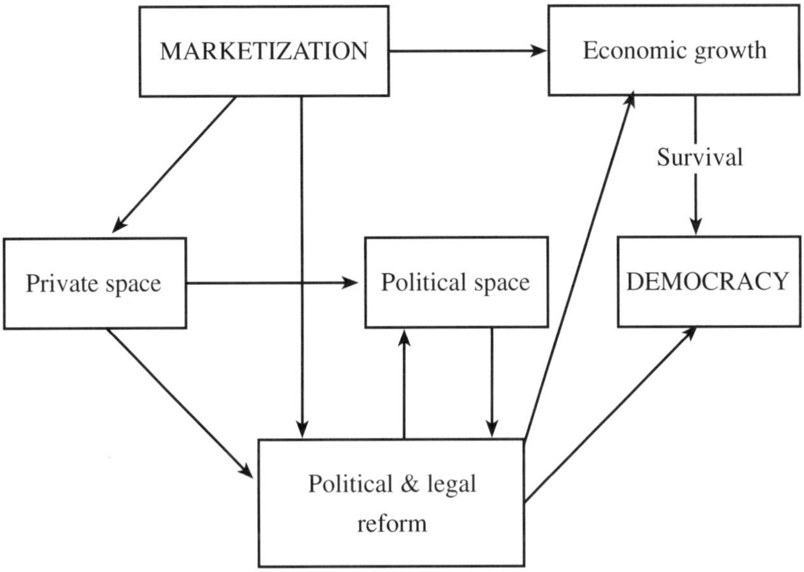

Figure 12.1 China's route to a potential democracy

Marketization promotes economic growth but, according to Przeworski and Limongi (1997), economic development is a deciding factor in the survival rather than the birth of democracy.

In the literature on the process of democratization, the important step of expanding private space before the opportunity of expanding political space is often overlooked. This may have to do with the literature's focus on the countries of Latin America, where the existence of the market and private property is taken for granted and political control was not as absolute as in pre-reform China. Hence the question of the existence of private space does not exist.

Political liberalization has lagged behind economic reform in China. The reason is that mature industrialized economies depend more on democratic process for further economic growth than do economies at an early stage of economic development. Moreover, while marketization can drive the democratization process forward in authoritarian socialist countries, democratization in these countries may slow down the process of marketization because of resistance from losers of market reform. Hence the sustainable type of democracy for China at its current level of marketization and economic development will not be the 'ideal' liberal democratic model. Instead of democracy, what is crucial for a country like China to develop economically is effective government.[5]

MARKETIZATION AND PRIVATE SPACE

Marketization in the Chinese economy has reduced the control of the state over the economy and expanded the private space available for the individual. In pre-reform China, the amount of private space granted to an individual was very small. Needless to say, the means of production were largely in state hands and the economy was highly centralized. Jobs were allocated by the state and private exchange was curtailed. But the state was not content merely to control the economy. Leisure activities were highly regulated and, 'with politics in command', the individual was even expected to share his or her private thoughts.

In 20 or more years of Chinese economic reform, agriculture was decollectivized and the economy transformed from one where the plan was the main instrument for allocating resources, and the market played only a secondary role (*jihua wei zhu, shichang wei bu*) to what the Chinese called a 'socialist market economy' (*shehui shichang jingji*). Socialism in China was originally defined by the Communist Party of China (CPC) in terms of state ownership and the use of administrative planning. This perspective changed at the Third Plenum of the Twelfth Central Committee of the Party in 1984. At that plenum, state ownership continued to be regarded an essential characteristic of socialism, but not of administrative planning. The CPC had deemed the market to be compatible with socialism. Later in the reform process, even state ownership was relinquished as the defining characteristic of socialism, replaced by public ownership through the decision of the CPC Fourteenth Central Committee at its Third Plenum in 1993.[6] At that plenum, the role of the market in Chinese socialism was advanced even further. Crucially, it replaced the plan as the main instrument of resource allocation.

The change in the party's attitude to state ownership has transformed the status of non-state business. While the party insists that public ownership has to be the dominant form of ownership, the development of other forms of ownership, including private and individual ownership, is encouraged. Private and individual businesses are not only tolerated but are now considered as making valuable contributions to the economy. The shift in the party's view on ownership is now enshrined in the Chinese constitution with two amendments to the constitution at the Second Plenum of the Ninth National People's Congress in March 1999. The first amendment was to Article 6 of the constitution, with the addition of a clause stating that China is now at its preliminary stage of socialism. This amendment is used to justify having public, instead of state, ownership as the main form of ownership of the means of production. The clause further states that public ownership will develop together with other forms of ownership. The second constitutional amendment was to Article 21, with the addition of a clause stating that individual, private and other forms of non-public ownership are important components of a socialist economy and that they '*supplement* the system of socialist public ownership' (Tian, 1999: 1; emphasis added).

It was not so long ago that private business in China operated in an environment of political insecurity and faced fiat and officially sanctioned discrimination. Private business was revived officially in the late 1970s, but it was only a decade later, in March 1988, that private businesses with more than seven employees were legitimized (Young, 1998: 87). Since then private business has flourished in China and is now an important provider of employment. No longer are citizens dependent on the state or collective business for their livelihood.

Marketization expands the size of private property in two related ways. First of all, marketization generates incomes from non-state directed entrepreneurial activities for the individual, enabling increases in private wealth, which allows the financing of private investment that generates further increases in private wealth. Even in the absence of private entrepreneurial activity, the use of markets by state-owned enterprises (SOEs) can lead to an increase in private property. In China, the policy that allowed SOEs to sell to the market any production above their plan procurement output led many SOEs to incur huge losses because not every firm that sells in the market can make a profit and this has led to many SOEs being restructured internally or privatized (Liew, 1999). Using a different argument to link marketization and privatization, Li *et al.* (1997) showed theoretically that cross-regional competition among SOEs leads to their partial privatization because asymmetric information on SOE managers' effort induces local government officials to cede more of the residual shares of profit to the managers. The expansion of private property reduces the control of the state over the individual and may enhance the prospects for democratizing. It is important, however, to stress that the mere existence of private property does not guarantee private space if ownership of wealth is highly skewed. What if a society's wealth is all private but is concentrated in the hands of only a few family oligarchies? What if the families behave in a tyrannical fashion and have control over the means of state coercion? In such a scenario, individual choice is limited and democracy is compromised. This scenario suggests that the existence of private property is insufficient for democracy. Its ownership must be sufficiently dispersed to provide meaningful choice to individuals. Markets must be competitive to check monopoly power.

The CPC's ability to control and regulate the lives of the people has declined markedly with the decollectivization of agriculture and as the market takes over more and more from the plan. These two factors are more significant for enlarging the private space of the individual than the relative decline of the state sector. In 1978, SOEs were responsible for 77.6 per cent of industrial output. By 1997, this had fallen to 25.5 per cent (GTJ, 1998: 433). But, over the same period, the proportion of employment in industry accounted for by state-owned enterprises only fell from 78.4 per cent to 65 per cent. Furthermore, employment in state-owned units[7] only fell from 18.7 per cent of total employment (GTJ, 1987: 115) to 15.9 per cent (GTJ, 1998: 127). What is therefore significant for the democratization of China is not that proportionately fewer people are in state employment. Rather, it is that the marketization of the economy has forced state-owned and other enterprises to adapt to having economics rather then politics in command and decollectivization of agriculture has weakened the hold the party has over the countryside. Relying on the market and household agricultural production instead of the plan and collective has fundamentally changed the rules of the game, reducing the need for and the ability of the party to command and the incentive for party apparatchiks to intrude on the private space of the individual.

Walder (1986) has described how the Chinese firm under communism was not just an economic but a political and social institution as well. It intruded into many aspects of the lives of its employees. This was the case in all state production and administrative work units, or *danwei*.[8] The *danwei* provided employees with, for example, family housing and health care, child care, recreational facilities and pensions, and sometimes organized deliveries of special foods during festive seasons. The *danwei* was used to enforce China's family planning and moral code governing relations between the sexes. It was also an important linchpin in the household registration system that monitored and controlled population movement. The *danwei* had to grant permission before one could marry and its recommendation was crucial in getting one's children admitted into tertiary education or obtaining employment.

Before reform, production in the firm was secondary to politics and this was reflected in the incentive structure of the firm. Rewards were largely non-pecuniary and granted more on the basis of success in political activism than of competence in production. Although in theory corporate governance was based on democratic management, in practice, workers' participation in management consisted of nothing more than formalistic rituals. It was a system of virtuocracy, rather than meritocracy (ibid.), where people were 'regularly rewarded for the display of behaviour and attitudes that reflect politically defined "virtue"' (Shirk, 1982). This system changed with reform. The higher the firm's profits, the better the benefits enjoyed by its employees. The quest for production efficiencies has meant that politics is no longer in command on the factory floor. Depoliticization of the factory floor and of the wider Chinese society has expanded the private space of individuals. Management now cares more about the productivity of workers than about their political beliefs or what they do during their leisure time.

Crucially, marketization of the economy has increased choice for Chinese people and loosened the hold that the state has over the individual. Chinese people no longer have to put up with poor-quality goods from a state-owned department store or shoddy service in a state-owned restaurant. There are alternatives. Consumer goods are no longer rationed. The state no longer has a monopoly over the modes of long-distance travel. There are many privately run hotels that are willing to accommodate the exhausted traveller. There are other forms of urban housing beyond those provided by *danwei*. There are now private schools and private health clinics. Even more important for the individual is the freedom to choose or change one's job. All these changes have reduced the control that the *danwei* has over the lives of ordinary citizens by offering them alternatives. The process of '*de-danwei-isation*', as You (1998) calls it, has truncated the reach of the state.

As in urban areas, marketization in the countryside has expanded the private space available to the individual. Decollectivization of agricultural production and the introduction of markets for agricultural commodities has reduced the control of the party (and government) over farmers. The collective farm, like the socialist firm, was more than a production unit. It also enforced official political and social policies. For example, it executed the party's policies on family planning, enforced the ban on traditional and religious practices, and 'recruited' members to undertake 'voluntary' labour in constructing public infrastructure.

Marketization has reduced the effectiveness of state propaganda. It has loosened the controls of the state over information by allowing public access to alternative sources. Globalization of the Chinese economy has provided access to information from overseas. Publishers of books, newspapers and magazines now have to make a profit. They have to respond positively to consumer choice. *Nanfang zhoumo* (*Southern Weekend*), a newspaper in the southern city of Guangzhou, doubled its circulation to 1.3 million by running exposés of official wrongdoing on its front page and the highly rated TV programme *Focal Point* made its name for airing stories on official corruption (Wong, 1999: 14). Because of the need to stay internationally competitive, China has embraced the information revolution. Wong pointed out that an additional phone line for Internet access costs only 100 yuan (US$18) and the marginal cost of Internet access is now only 4 yuan (US$0.76) an hour. China has 40 million pager customers and is forecast to have 27 million Internet users by 2001 (ibid.: 15). These developments have made it more difficult for the state to manipulate public opinion to exercise political control.

MARKETIZATION AND THE GROWTH OF CIVIL SOCIETY

In a system of virtuocracy, people are punished for non-conformist behaviour. Those who did not conform to political dictates in pre-reform China were often classified as class enemies, and personal relationships were badly affected by constant political campaigns to root out class enemies. Private space and choice are limited severely in a society with politics in command. It was impossible for a civil society to develop in China in an environment of continuous political agitation, ubiquitous state control and limited private space. This situation changed with economic reform. The expansion of private space resulting from marketization has expanded the political space from which state power could be challenged.

Evidence pointing to enlargement of the political space in China is the growth of civil society. According to Pei (1998: 291), the number and diversity of civic groups in China have increased dramatically since economic reform began. Between 1979 and 1992, the number of these associations that are organized nationally grew by an annual average of 48 per cent a year. The growth of these associations at the provincial and municipal levels was even higher. In the eight provinces and the cities examined by Pei, the annual growth rates averaged 56 and 86 per cent, respectively. Pei's data show that the distribution of national, provincial and municipal civic associations changed significantly between 1978 and 1992, reflecting the depoliticization of Chinese society in that period. In 1978, about half the national, provincial and municipal associations surveyed were involved in the natural sciences, technology and engineering. These associations were involved in 'politically safe' areas and their overrepresentation before the reform period is to be expected. The share of this type of association fell in the course of reform, to about 20 per cent of the total in 1992. Meanwhile, academic associations involved in the social sciences, humanities and management studies rose significantly, to about a quarter of the total. Even more dramatic was the growth in professional and managerial associations and business and trade associations. From being less than 5 per cent of those surveyed in 1978, they had become about a third of the total in 1992.

The civic associations surveyed by Pei spanned the full spectrum – from those that are relatively dependent on the state to those that are relatively autonomous. If enough autonomous associations emerge, they could, according to Okabe (1998: 180), provide 'the foundation for pluralism and the eventual development of a more democratic state'. However, the CPC tolerates autonomous associations only when it considers them not to be a serious threat to its political power. Understandably, the CPC is especially wary of religious sects, student unions and trade unions because of their past challenges to the Chinese state during the Qing dynasty and Guomindang (Nationalist) rule. The CPC itself was active in the student and union movements, which organized demonstrations against the then Guomindang government in the 1920s, 1930s and 1940s. The recent crackdown against the Falungong, a religious sect, is illustrative of current limits the CPC still places on the development of civil society in China. However, if one were to compare the situation now with that at the start of reform in the late 1970s, the evidence of a much-expanded civil society, both in size and degree of autonomy, is unmistakeable.

MARKETIZATION AND POLITICAL AND LEGAL REFORM

Communist Party organizations in many parts of rural China have simply collapsed as a consequence of economic reform. Talented people, who previously sought careers in the party and/or government, now prefer to go into business and have the freedom of choice to do so. Many current party and government cadres are more concerned with making money than with implementing official policies. The result is weakened government authority. Crime rates have risen and the government is increasingly finding it difficult to enforce its taxation and birth control policies in the countryside. Village elections are seen as a way to give legitimacy to their efforts at re-establishing political authority in the countryside.

Another reason for the party leadership's endorsement of village elections is official corruption. Corruption among local officials has increased in the reform period. Local officials are accused of imposing illegal levies on farmers to fund local public infrastructure. Other officials are accused of appropriating funds, earmarked for agricultural purchases, for themselves or diverting the funds to other uses. Rural residents have protested against corrupt officials and in some cases have even rioted. The situation in parts of the countryside is so serious that the party views official corruption in the countryside as a threat to its rule. The party sees village elections as a way of making local officials more accountable, thereby legitimizing its authority.

Direct elections of village leaders began in 1987 and these elections vary in their degree of fairness. But local interest in the elections is high and some research suggests local leaders have become more accountable and responsive in regions where the elections are well organized (O'Brien, 1994). Scholars like Bernstein (1999: 108) are less optimistic. He pointed out that village elections have only a limited impact because the source of many of the abuses of power is in administrative levels above the village level. There are, however, some limited moves to open up the process of selecting top officials at the provincial level. Guangdong Province has led the way. Candidates for official positions, including those of governor and vice-governor, members of the provincial people's congress central committee, the most senior judge and the procurator-general can now be nominated by 30 or more deputies of the provincial people's congress. Before, the party nominated and selected the officials internally with no external input. The motivation behind the reform was to combat official corruption by introducing more competition into the election of officials. The same motivation is behind Guangdong Provincial People's Congress decision to hold open hearings on proposed pieces of legislation. Guangdong Province was the first Chinese province to introduce laws on the tendering of building projects (Ching, 1999: 22).

Village elections are gaining popularity and villagers are putting pressure on county and township leaders to hold multi-candidate village elections (Li and O'Brien, 1999: 144). Although many township leaders are apprehensive about village elections, the fact that elected village leaders have shown themselves to be effective implementers of township policies has led at least some township leaders to appreciate the benefits of having elected village officials (ibid.: 142–4). Support for village elections has come from the very top party echelon; both Party General Secretary Jiang Zemin and the number two in the party hierarchy, Li Peng, the former premier, support village elections.

Another sign of political change in China is the evidence of growing assertiveness by deputies of the National People's Congress (NPC), made possible by the enlargement of political space, as they attempt to create an independent role for themselves in drafting proposed laws, debating national policies and monitoring the bureaucracy (Tanner, 1994). This growing independence of the NPC, according to Tanner (1999: 126), is unlikely to be rolled back because it is backed by powerful CPC leaders, supported by an increasingly policy-focused bureaucracy and emerging elite norms that accept internal debate.

The party's desire to enhance its political legitimacy after the Cultural Revolution led it to implement legal reform (Potter, 1994). Its efforts at legal reform are tied to its quest for economic reform. Learning from the experience of reform in Eastern Europe, there is increasing awareness in the party that workable markets do not simply appear just because the plan is abolished and private property reinstated. There must be a system of laws underpinning markets before they can function effectively. The use of markets requires laws covering contracts and property rights, among other laws (Koslowski, 1992). Moreover, as marketization progresses, we will increasingly see the state as a party to a disputed contract and one indication of the strength of market institutions is the degree of impartiality of courts or tribunals in arbitrating such disputes. Research by Pei (1997) found that significant progress has been made in this regard. He found that about 40 per cent of the legal cases involving the Chinese government as defendant were settled either out of court or in court in favour of the plaintiff. We can even expect those officials who got rich by taking advantage of previous vague property rights governing state assets to support the enactment and enforcement of property rights law. They wish for protection of their illegal 'laundered' wealth because they cannot remain as officials forever and would like to be able to transfer their wealth safely to their children.

The party views political reform in China not necessarily as a desirable end in itself but as a means to economic growth. As the party sees it, political reform is necessary to make markets work more efficiently. It seeks to institute a system of 'rule by law' rather than 'rule of law'. The principle of 'rule by law' specifies that actions must conform with the law and law should be the primary means of social control. This principle does not, however, require political rulers to be accountable. This requirement, in contrast, is embodied in the 'rule of law' (Bernstein, 1999: 95). It is only with 'rule of law' that a country is democratic. Can there be 'rule by law' without 'rule of law'? Bernstein is sceptical that 'rule by law' can be fully established in China without accepting 'rule of law'. His argument is increasingly gaining some support from within the Chinese political leadership and this support is manifested in the village elections that have increased political competition for official posts.

DEMOCRACY: MARKETIZATION OR ECONOMIC GROWTH?

One argument as to why economic growth will lead to democracy is that democracy is a luxury good. As income increases, there is an increase in the demand for democracy; members of the middle class are not content simply with comfortable incomes and want to have a say in how the country is run. It becomes extremely difficult for the government to ignore demands for democracy once those in the ranks of the middle class reach a critical mass. However, although more Chinese are rising to the middle class, the number is still very small. The 1997 per capita GDP of Mainland China remains low, at US$3130.[9] But even if a substantial middle class were to emerge in China, there is no guarantee that it would embrace democracy. Robison and Goodman (1996: 3) have argued that the new rich in Asia are equally likely to 'embrace authoritarian rule' as to 'support democracy'. The middle class in high-income Singapore provides clear empirical support for this observation. Members of this class are ambivalent about democracy. The majority of them are contented with Singaporean 'soft authoritarianism' as long as their material needs are satisfied (Lam, 1999: 274).

Although high incomes may not lead to democracy, the market is crucial to democracy. This is because high incomes do not translate into freedom of choice unless there is a market. When economic choice is tightly circumscribed by the state in absence of the market, private and political spaces are confined.

While the birth of democracy may not depend on the level of a country's income, the survival of democracy definitely does. Przeworski and Limongi (1997) found that, while countries with low incomes can give birth to democracies, survival of the democracies is more likely when per capita incomes are above US$6055 (at 1985 US$). 'While democracy is terribly fragile in poor countries, it is impregnable in the rich ones' (ibid.: 166). Their research suggests that, while China's low level of economic development does not rule out the birth of democracy, consolidation and survival of democracy depends on China having a much higher per capita income than it currently sustains.

The low level of economic development in China also suggests that economic growth is not the major driving force behind the current democratization process. A low-income country like China enjoys a comparative advantage in labour-intensive, low-technology industries. When it is perspiration rather than technical innovation that largely drives production, management style will tend to be authoritarian. There is less need for input from labour into management decisions because product competition is mainly price-driven. In contrast, middle and, especially, high-income countries are less dependent on low-skill jobs. They pay higher wages and provide better working conditions to high-skill workers. As a result, labour–capital tensions in these countries are potentially less antagonistic than those in China and, from the perspective of the state, there is less need for political control over labour in the interest of capital accumulation.

Thus, at China's low level of economic development, it is the process of marketization rather than economic growth that is driving the process of democratization. Marketization is expanding the amount of private space for the individual and promoting the growth of civil society and political reform. All these current processes contribute to the democratization of China. Economic growth is the outcome of marketization but it has little impact on the democratization process because of China's low level of economic development. But the survival of democracy, if it were to be born, depends on China's ability to increase its per capita income significantly.

EFFECTIVE GOVERNMENT AND ECONOMIC GROWTH

The Chinese economy has more than quadrupled in size since reforms began in 1978. Between 1978 and 1995, real GDP and real GDP per capita in China grew at an annual rate of 9.4 and 8 per cent, respectively (World Bank, 1997a: 4–5). This impressive growth performance has made a significant impact on poverty levels. By the end of 1995, less than 6 per cent of the population was living below the poverty line (World Bank, 1997b: 11). While there are losers from reform, the majority has benefited. The World Bank (1997a: 4) estimated that growth in the quantity of physical capital and labour input and improvements in the quality of labour explained just over 50 per cent of China's impressive GDP growth between 1978 and 1995. Another 16 per cent was explained by sectoral reallocation. This left 29 per cent of the growth unaccounted for. Economic reform by definition changes the rules of the game and therefore sectoral reallocation and the significant size of this 'unexplained' residual must be due to technical and institutional change. Economic growth in China has been the result of, not just more inputs, but innovation as well.

Marketization is the primary institutional change (innovation) that has produced China's impressive growth rate. Marketization has enabled resources to flow from sectors of low marginal productivity (agriculture and state-owned industry) to sectors of high marginal productivity (services and non-state industry). Resources were shifted out of agriculture because China does not have a comparative advantage in agriculture. The shift of resources out of agriculture has been possible because decollectivization of agriculture has increased agricultural productivity and produced surplus farm labour, to be absorbed elsewhere in the economy. The pattern of production is now based more on comparative advantage, with a corresponding increase in the division of labour and regional mobility of labour, the latter being made easier by the collapse of the household registration system.

A strong and effective central state is necessary to implement economic reform and this feature of the Chinese state enabled the success of economic reform in China (Liew, 1995). The state in an economy in transition from a plan to a market economy must have the capacity and the political will to establish effective market institutions, like contract and bankruptcy laws, and to ensure that some intermediate level of government does not usurp economic powers that need to be devolved to the firm. The success of economic reform also depends on the ability of the state to maintain macroeconomic stability. Uncontrolled inflation distorts investment and saving decisions and undermines public support for reform. The maintenance of macroeconomic stability depends to a large degree on how successfully the state can moderate the many conflicting demands on resources. In particular, it is imperative for the state not to lose control over monetary policy to regional and popular demands for excessive monetary growth and that it is able to collect sufficient taxes for the provision of public goods and support to the losers from economic reform. There is no doubt that it was the continuing strength of the executive power of the centre that enabled China to re-establish macroeconomic and hence political stability when inflation seriously threatened in 1988 and 1993 (ibid.).

A crucial reason for the relative success of Chinese compared with Russian reform is that the Chinese are able to better manage the transition from one set of institutions to another. The Chinese have an institutional capacity far superior to the Russians'. Presidential and parliamentary elections in Russia have not provided the Russians with institutional capability for reform. In Russia, the institutions of the former Soviet Union were destroyed before new institutions were built to replace them. Nothing demonstrates this more clearly than the prevalence of organized crime in Russia, where the tentacles of organized crime extend to the immediate family of the former president and even involved the laundering of funds provided by the IMF and World Bank.[10] Organized crime flourishes in places where state authority is weakest (Goldsmith, 1997: 37). Property rights are not secured when organized criminal gangs are so strong that they could challenge the authority of the state. When this occurs, legitimate business suffers, with a negative impact on economic growth.

Economic reform in China changes the fundamental rules of the game that alter the behaviour of individuals in a dynamic fashion. Individuals and organizations have to learn to play according to the new rules and the rules themselves are modified or replaced in response to individual and organizational behaviour. New social norms have to be developed and accepted as well, because otherwise imperfect information and compliance costs will make the new economic system non-viable (Liew, 1998: 43). Individual behaviour consistent with the new social norms requires a gestation period before the norms are widely accepted. For example, most citizens in developed market economies respect private property and law of contracts. This was not the case in pre-reform China, which had no need for norms respecting private property and legal contracts because there was little private property and few private transactions in a planned economy dominated by state ownership and where party dictate was law. Respect for private property and legal contracts has to be inculcated in the reform period. Unless there is sufficient respect for private property and legal contracts, transaction costs will be exceedingly high and a market system will be unworkable.

Individual respect for informal norms, such as respect for private property, once it is engrained in an individual, becomes fairly automatic. There must be a conscious effort to inculcate individual respect for informal norms that are consistent with the good running of a market economy to replace those that prevailed under the previous planned economy. Otherwise, the new informal norms that emerge from the destruction of the old planned economy may hinder rather than facilitate the workings of a market economy. One way to look at this is to borrow Maynard Smith's biological concept of an evolutionarily stable strategy (ESS). An ESS is 'a strategy which, if most members of a population adopt it, cannot be bettered by an alternative strategy' (Dawkins, 1989: 69). The strategy in ESS is a 'pre-programmed behavioural policy'; there is no conscious maximizing behaviour. A major environmental change creates a period of evolutionary instability before an ESS eventuates.

According to Dawkins, there is a critical frequency, a knife-edge that, depending on which side the majority of a population falls on, will favour one type of behaviour over another as an ESS (ibid.: 218). Hence, on one side of the knife-edge, the critical frequency of market-friendly behaviour is exceeded and an ESS of informal norms favouring the market is the likely outcome. On the other side of the knife-edge, the critical frequency of anti-market behaviour is exceeded and an ESS of informal norms that work against the market is favoured. At the beginning of reform, an ESS of informal norms that work against the market is likely to be favoured. The need then is for public policy slowly but surely to form local clusters of population with the critical mass that can produce a local ESS of informal norms friendly to the market. The long-term aim for state reformers is to enlarge these clusters so that they spread out and eventually produce an ESS of market-friendly informal norms for the whole population. This step-by-step approach is what China has adopted and it accords the Chinese state a far more dominant role in society during the transition to a market economy than would be the case under liberal democracy. So far, an effective semi-authoritarian Chinese state has managed to guide in the new market norms far better than an ineffective but semi-democratic Russian state.

Huntington (1968) advanced the thesis that an autocratic government is conducive to economic growth because democracy leads to popular demands for high consumption which, if satisfied, affect adversely profits and investment and undermine economic growth.[11] A variant of this argument can be applied to the case of China. In a period of substantial changes in the rules of the game, losers from these changes will inevitably emerge.

Although income inequality in China remains modest by international standards, it has increased significantly in the reform period. China's Gini coefficient rose from 28.8 in 1981 to 38.8 in 1995 (World Bank, 1997b: 7) and is expected to increase with further reforms. The largest contributor to the increase in inequality is the growth in rural–urban inequality. Rural–urban income inequality is large by international standards and accounted for 60 per cent of the growth in inequality between 1984 and 1995 (ibid.: 15–16).[12] Poverty in China is largely a rural phenomenon; there is virtually no urban poverty in China (ibid.: 49). The main factor accounting for the relatively advantageous position of urban residents is the large government subsidies that the state provide for its urban residents and the less than perfect mobility of labour from the countryside to the urban areas, which cushioned unskilled urban labour from competition offered by rural labour. Increasing labour mobility and gradual reductions in urban subsidies as reform progresses will reduce rural poverty and narrow existing rural–urban income inequality, but it will be at the expense of unskilled urban workers.

While it was a political decision to marketize the economy, China is still an economy in transition and its low-level economic and technological development means that there are diminishing returns to political liberalization; the elasticity of economic growth with respect to political liberalization falls with further liberalization. The dilemma for the government is that, while economic reform enlarges the size of the economy, this will create winners as well as losers.

Uncompetitive sectors suffer from reform and highly-organized opposition among the losers from reform could derail the transition to a market economy. Since 1993, with the party's decision to adopt a 'socialist market structure' for China,[13] closing inefficient firms has become a main plank of CPC policy. The People's Republic had seen little unemployment since its formation in 1949, but some estimates claim that, by the end of 1997, 20 million workers had lost their jobs from state-owned enterprise (SOE) restructuring, resulting in an unemployment rate of 7 per cent[14] (Xiao and Xiao, 1998: 218). The rate is expected to rise further. Labour Minister Li Boyong announced in February 1998 that between 8 and 10 million workers would be redundant from SOEs within the next three years (Chan, 1998).

There are many reports of protests by urban workers who have been laid off. This particular grievance is a major source of concern for the Chinese government and is one reason for its caution towards political liberalization. State compensation for losers to produce a Pareto outcome is not a feasible option because of the high transaction costs that must be incurred in a daunting administrative task. It is particularly significant that labour in China is largely unskilled and unorganized as a movement and therefore in a weak bargaining position without effective unions. But effective unions are very likely to deter much-needed local and international investments in the industries that employ unskilled labour and low levels of technology, in which China has a comparative advantage.

Clearly, during the period of transition to a market economy, a major concern of the state is that democracy could force it to succumb to populist demands and weaken its economic reform programme. Moreover, democracy offers no guarantee that income inequalities would be moderated. The United States today is recognized as a liberal democracy, but suffers from large and increasing income inequalities. India too is recognized as a democracy, but its level of economic development is low and suffers from large income inequalities. In contrast, South Korea before its recent democratization had a high degree of income equality while experiencing rapid economic growth under authoritarian rule. Thus one could argue that, since democracy cannot prevent income inequality and since income inequality may cause political instability, democracy cannot guarantee political stability, which is a prerequisite for economic growth. Yet this is not to suggest that an authoritarian system *can* guarantee political stability.

While absence of democracy is no guarantee that economic growth cannot occur, a high degree of authoritarianism will adversely affect economic growth, sometimes with fatal consequences. A.K. Sen (1981) offered a persuasive argument that famines are caused, not by a lack of food but by a lack of food entitlements, and he stressed the importance of adversarial politics and a free press in famine prevention. A similar inference is drawn from Yang's (1996) analysis of the Chinese famine during the Great Leap Forward. He found that an authoritarian system without a free press and a system of checks and balances was responsible for the disastrous economic policies that led to the famine, which claimed the lives of 30 million people.

Environmental protection and proper management of scarce natural resources are important factors determining state capacity, and having an effective state capacity is crucial to the successful management of economic reform. Economy (1999) found that mismanagement of water resources is diminishing the fiscal strength of the state in China as it faces continuous demands for resources to mitigate environmental damage and to invest in new infrastructure projects such as wastewater treatment plants and irrigation systems. She found that part of the explanation for this mismanagement lies in the devolution of state power from the centre to local governments, and in local corruption. Local governments opt for rapid local economic growth without properly accounting for the associated social costs and pay lip-service to environmental protection. Funds from the centre earmarked for preservation or enhancement of the environment are sometimes diverted to other uses by local governments or to the pockets of corrupt officials. Hence making local officials accountable to citizens is imperative if the environment is to be successfully managed and the capacity of the state enhanced. Elections of local officials to make them accountable is an important step towards successful management of the environment, but there is always the possibility that local citizens may choose rapid economic growth in preference to a cleaner environment.

The experience of Chinese reform to date supports the argument that it is effective government rather than democratic government that is responsible for its success. However, the devolution of Chinese state power to local governments, especially at levels of government below the provincial level, has weakened the authority and diminished the coherence of the state and threatens economic reform and the success of marketization. The effects of crime and corruption of local officials are threatening the political stability and future economic growth of China. Village elections are incapable of making local officials publicly accountable as indicated above, because it is officials mainly at the administrative levels above the village level, including officials at the centre, who are the problem. This poses the pertinent question: if officials above the village level are to be held accountable, where does accountability end? The logical answer is that there must be accountability right up to the top leadership. But what is the form of this accountability? Making officials accountable also implies making them respond to pressures from citizens for specific public policies. Some pressures from citizens are market enhancing and promote economic growth, but others seek preferential treatment or to dilute reform policies and have negative impacts on growth. The balancing of these two contradictory forces of official accountability means that, at China's current stage of transition to a market economy, the optimal political system for China in the sense of maximizing economic growth will differ from the Western liberal–democratic model. This is illustrated in Figure 12.2.

Democracy has growth-enhancing and growth-impeding consequences. In Figure 12.2, the economic growth rate is measured along the vertical axis and level of democratization is measured along the horizontal axis. The level of democracy in a liberal democracy is denoted as L^*. The positive curve shows the positive impact on the rate of economic growth of elements of liberal democracy, such as the holding of regular elections, which put a check on official corruption and other abuses of power. The negative curve shows the negative impact of elements of democracy, such as populist pressures to impede the reform of SOEs, on economic growth. The point of intersection of the two curves gives the optimal level of democracy (D^*) and its associated optimal economic growth rate (G^*) at China's current level of economic development. The optimal level of democracy is optimal in the sense that it is the level of democracy that maximizes economic growth at China's current level of economic development, given that democracy has positive and negative impacts on economic growth. The optimal level of democracy is not synonymous with a desirable or an ideal level of democracy. As China's economic development increases, the two curves will shift to the right, resulting in a higher level of democratization. The resulting economic growth rate, however, is uncertain.[15]

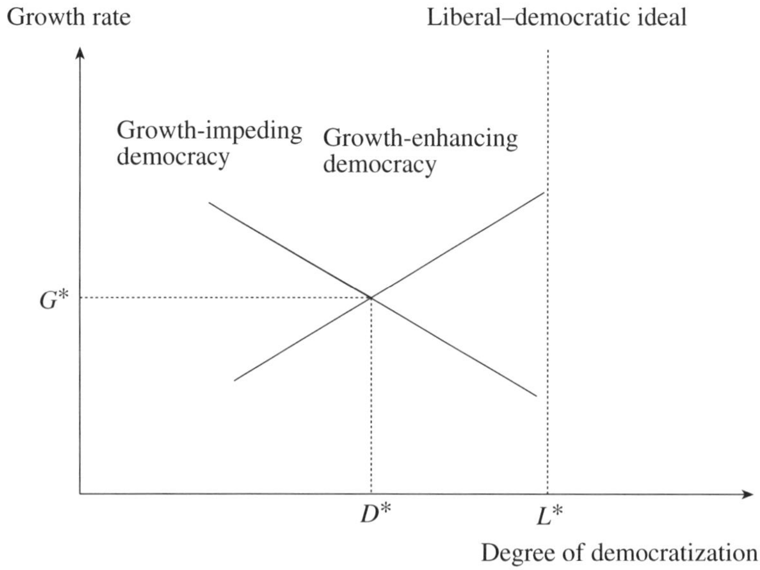

Figure 12.2 China's current optimal level of democracy

FROM INDUSTRIALIZATION TO TECHNICAL INNOVATION GROWTH

A firm is more likely to opt for a numerator rather than a denominator strategy when corporate governance is a form of industrial democracy where workers are treated as stakeholders with equal status to owners. A numerator strategy focuses on improving a firm's competitiveness through research and development and the 'upskilling' of the workforce. This is likely to lead to higher economic growth and a more equal distribution of a country's wealth than a denominator strategy, which focuses on short-term profits through cost reductions. In a firm where workers are treated as stakeholders at par with owners, there is greater participation of workers in decision making. While the presence of workers as stakeholders is restricted mainly to Japanese manufacturing firms, the shift to a flatter, less hierarchical, organizational structure is occurring worldwide, including the structure in Anglo-American firms, where owner sovereignty reigns supreme. In these firms, the hierarchical Taylorite organization is now seen to be inflexible and slow to adapt to new circumstances. But a flatter organization structure compared with a hierarchical one requires a higher degree of trust and social capital (Fukuyama, 1999: 207), which depends on a more democratic workplace.

The participation of workers in decision making, argued Stiglitz (1999: 11), is a requirement for success in a knowledge-based economy. The information revolution has arrived and all countries, including China, have to adapt to the new technological realities. China is now extensively integrated with the world economy and, to remain internationally competitive and sustain rapid economic growth, China has to incorporate and exploit effectively the latest communications capabilities and information technologies (Tipson, 1999: 234). China, like Singapore, is trying to exploit the new technologies for economic development while limiting the political and social impacts that accompany these technologies. While China may be able to moderate these impacts, it will not be able to isolate itself completely. In the realm of human rights, for example, Tipson is optimistic that the new information technology will do more to improve human rights in China than the efforts of external organizations (ibid.: 258).

Chowdhury and Islam (1993: 255) argued that, although the state cannot create a decentralized organizational structure at the firm level, it could encourage the adoption of a decentralized structure through its industry competition policy. Increased industry competition arising from the process of globalization has encouraged the decentralization of organizational structures in firms, but I am less optimistic than Chowdhury and Islam about the impact of this process on innovation. There is a wide range of forms of decentralization, some of which may not involve intra-firm research and human resource development. In recent years, the most common form of organizational decentralization in the Anglo-American business world is 'outsourcing', often to firms in developing countries, without any accompanying significant technical innovation undertaken in the firm of the home country. A competition policy on its own is insufficient to guarantee innovation-driven economic development. Competition may drive a firm to opt for a denominator rather than a numerator strategy.

The post-industrial prospects of workplace democracy for industrial workers with the advent of the information revolution are dim without state intervention. Advances in production technology in mature industrialized economies have reduced the demand for many unskilled and semi-skilled workers, and new information technology has made it easier for management to monitor the intensity of work of employees. Employees have become atomized and this has resulted in the gradual loss of trade union membership and influence. Rapid advances in technology and the growth of the information economy are a double-edged sword. While highly skilled workers will enjoy greater empowerment in their workplaces, workers with a modicum of skill will be subjected to greater control, which is made possible with modern technology. Retraining and 'upskilling' can only moderate, but not prevent, this outcome because the ability to absorb and utilize advanced knowledge varies between individuals and, for some individuals, diminishing returns to learning begin to occur at relatively low levels of knowledge. Not everyone can be a skilled worker in the post-industrial economy.

The current situation in China is different from the situation in mature industrialized countries because it remains an underdeveloped economy, where the pressing concern is economic development. Nevertheless, there are high expectations placed on the new information technology in opening up the Chinese polity. The new information technology will facilitate China's transition to a more open and less hierarchical society but, still, one has to be realistic about how much it could achieve. At China's current level of economic development and comparative advantage in relatively unskilled labour-intensive industries, and with the need to overcome resistance to further economic reform, there is less of an imperative to embrace industrial democracy and a more ready acceptance of Taylorite vertical corporate structures. Moreover, given the current experiences of mature industrialized countries, the link between economic growth and democracy in post-industrial China is unclear.

In the post-industrial economy, a high level of democratization may not increase economic growth because of diminishing marginal utility of income. Citizens may prefer more leisure to higher incomes by voting in state policies that limit market competition. Research by Oswald (1997) on residents in the United States and Western Europe indicates that income promotes happiness, but the effect is small. The suicide rate, for example, is independent of social class. Similarly, Frey and Stutzer (1999) found that, in a sample of Swiss residents, the income impact on happiness is small. What is especially interesting in their study is that, although they found that both Swiss nationals and foreign residents benefit from the same sort of outcomes that are available to all Swiss residents, Swiss nationals are much happier because they can participate in voting on initiatives and referendums while foreign residents cannot. Participation in decision making has a greater positive impact on happiness than income. Hence the issue as to whether democracy promotes growth is perhaps relevant for China only at its current low level of economic development. In the long run, democracy in China should be treated as a desirable end in itself, rather than as an important determinant of economic growth.

CONCLUSION

Several conclusions can be drawn from the analysis in this chapter on the issue of democracy in China. First, it is marketization, rather than economic growth, that is responsible for the current political liberalization in China. Second, Chinese success in economic reform to date has been due more to effective government than to democracy. Despite their imperfections and lack of accountability, institutions in China have shown themselves to be far more effective in promoting economic growth than institutions in Russia operating under the rubric of an imperfect democracy. Third, democracy enhances but can also impede economic growth. While democracy can promote economic growth, it is more important in circumstances of high economic development than in China's current relatively low level. Hence, at China's current stage of transition to a market economy, the optimal political system for China in the sense of maximizing economic growth will take a form different from the Western liberal–democratic model, which may apply after a market economy has been established but not during transition to a market economy. Fourth, in the long run, industry competition alone cannot guarantee a form of workplace democracy in Chinese firms that induces innovation-driven economic growth. Competition may drive firms towards a denominator strategy of cost reduction rather than a numerator strategy of innovation-driven revenue increase. Finally, in the post-industrial Chinese society, happiness may not depend on higher and ever-increasing incomes.

Democracy should therefore be a goal for China for its capacity to improve the lives of the Chinese people, beyond what it can do for economic growth. In the end, we are talking about the lives of 1.2 billion people, not just one national economy, one ruling party or one Chinese polity.

NOTES

1. An earlier version of this chapter was delivered at a seminar organized by The Chinese Management Research Centre, City University of Hong Kong. The author thanks the seminar participants for their perceptive comments, which have helped to improve the arguments in this chapter. The usual caveat applies.
2. Democracy as a concept has many definitions. In this chapter I define democracy according to the Western liberal model, whose components are universal suffrage, free and fair periodic elections, freedom of expression, right to form and join organizations, right to stand for public office, and freedom of the press.
3. Marketization is defined as the process of replacing the plan with the market to allocate resources and increasing the share of private relative to state property.
4. See, for example, Li (1987–8). Li followed a long line of scholars that included John Locke. While they stressed the importance of private property, they did not explore the route, starting with the existence of private property, through which democracy may be realized and institutionalized.

5. An effective government is not a perfect government. It is a government that can provide a critical level of stability and direction for society. This chapter focuses on a critical aspect: economic development.
6. CPC General Secretary Jiang Zemin's report to the Fourteenth Party Congress in October 1992 foreshadowed this decision.
7. All state economic and non-economic units in all sectors of the economy.
8. A *danwei* is a state-owned or affiliated organization. A state-owned enterprise is a *danwei*. So are government departments and universities. Most urban residents were employed by *danwei* before the reform period.
9. Purchasing power parity estimate; UNDP estimate published in its 1998 Report (*Transition*, 1999: 21). Per capita GDP in Taiwan in 1996 was already US$12651 (Ichimura and Morley, 1999: 7).
10. Jonathan Steele, the former *Guardian* correspondent in Moscow, believed that official corruption in Russia was worse under Yeltsin than it was in the former Soviet Union under Brezhnev.
11. Huntington's ideas influenced the development of the Chinese ideology of neo-authoritarianism *xinquanweizhuyi*) in the 1980s. They remain popular in China today.
12. Interregional income disparities are widening but remain moderate (World Bank, 1997b: 20).
13. This was foreshadowed at the Fourteenth Party Congress in October 1992. CPC General Secretary Jiang Zemin's report to the congress spelt out the objective of establishing a socialist market economy.
14. Most economists believe that the figure is much higher.
15. The growth-impeding curve shifts to the right because, at higher levels of economic development, democracy is a lower impediment to economic growth. Labour–capital conflicts are less intense. The growth-enhancing curve shifts to the right because, at higher levels of economic development, democracy becomes a more important determinant of economic growth. Technology is the reason for this and this is discussed in the next section. The size of the shift to the right also depends on the marginal utility of income. Different countries experience different degrees of diminishing marginal utility of income and this explains why the resulting growth rate is uncertain as the two curves in Figure 12.2 shift to the right. The growth rate of countries could be lower at higher levels of economic development and democracy and this is consistent with the wide range of growth rates observed across democratic industrialized countries.

REFERENCES

Bernstein, Thomas P. (1999), 'China: growth without political liberalization', in James W. Morley (ed.), *Driven by Growth*.

Chan, Vivien Pik-Kwan (1998), '10 million jobs to go in state firms', *South Morning Post*, 27 May.

Ching, Frank (1999), 'Seeds of change', *Far Eastern Economic Review*, 30 September, 22.

Chowdhury, Anis and Iyanatul Islam (1993), *The Newly Industrialising Economies of East Asia*, London: Routledge.

Dawkins, Richard (1989), *The Selfish Gene*, Oxford: Oxford University Press.

Diamond, Larry (1992), 'Economic development and democracy reconsidered', *American Behavioral Scientist*, 35(4/5), 450–99.

Economy, Elizabeth (1999), 'The case study of China: reforms and resources: the implications for state capacity in the PRC', occasional paper, Project on Environment Scarcities, State Capacity, and Civil Violence, Cambridge: American Academy of Arts and Sciences and the University of Toronto.

Frey, Bruno and Alois Stutzer (1999), 'Happiness, economics and institutions', unpublished manuscript.

Fukuyama, Francis (1999), *The Great Disruption: Human Nature and the Reconstruction of Social Order*, London: Profile Books.

Goldsmith, Arthur A. (1997), 'Economic rights and government in developing countries: cross-national evidence on growth and development', *Studies in Comparative International Development*, 32, 29–44.

Guojia tongjiju (GTJ) (1987, 1998), *Zhongguo tongji nianjian* (*China Statistical Yearbook*), Beijing: Zhongguo tongji chubanshe.

He, Baogang (1997), *The Democratization Implications of Civil Society in Contemporary China*, London: Routledge.

Huntington, Samuel P. (1968), *Political Order in Changing Societies*, New Haven: Yale University Press.

Ichimura, Shinichi and James W. Morley (1999), 'Introduction', in James W. Morley (ed.), *Driven by Growth.*

Kelliher, Daniel (1997), 'The Chinese debate over village self-government', *The China Journal*, 37, 63–86.

Koslowski, R. (1992), 'Market institutions, East European reform, and economic theory', *Journal of Economic Issues*, 26(3), 673–705.

Lam, Peng Er (1999), 'Singapore: rich state, illiberal regime', in James W. Morley (ed.), *Driven by Growth.*

Li, Lianjiang and Kevin J. O'Brien (1999), 'The struggle over village elections', in Merle Goldman and Roderick MacFarquhar (eds), *The Paradox of China's Post-Mao Reforms*, Cambridge, MA: Harvard University Press.

Li, Shaomin (1987–8), 'The road to freedom: can communist societies evolve into democracy?', *World Affairs*, 150(3), 183–9.

Li, Shaomin, Shuhe Li and Zhang Weiyang (1997), 'Competition and institutional change: privatization in China', Marketing Department Working Paper Series, no. MKT97-18-0, City University of Hong Kong.

Liew, Leong (1995), 'Gradualism in China's economic reform and the role for a strong central state', *Journal of Economic Issues*, 29, 883–95.

Liew, Leong (1998), 'Chinese reform strategy', *Forum for Development Studies*, 1, 39–65.

Liew, Leong (1999), 'Chinese economic reform experience: limits of a Pareto-improving policy', revised version of a paper delivered at the Conference on China, India, and Russia: Progress and Challenges of Economic Transition, Michigan State University, 23–5 October 1998.

Morley, James W. (ed.) (1999), *Driven by Growth: Political Change in the Asia–Pacific Region*, Armonk: M.E. Sharpe.

O'Brien, Kevin (1994), 'Implementing political reform in China's villages', *Australian Journal of Chinese Affairs*, 32 (July), 33–67.

Okabe, Tatsumi (1998), 'China's prospects for change', in Larry Diamond and Marc F. Plattner (eds), *Democracy in East Asia*, Baltimore: Johns Hopkins University Press.

Oswald, Andrew (1997), 'Happiness and economic performance', *Economic Journal*, 107 (November), 1815–31.

Pei, Minxin (1997), 'Citizens v. mandarins: administrative litigation in China', *The China Quarterly*, 152 (December), 832–62.

Pei, Minxin (1998), 'Chinese civic associations: an empirical analysis', *Modern China*, 24(3), 285–318.

Potter, Pitman B. (1994), 'Riding the tiger: legitimacy and legal culture in post-Mao China', *The China Quarterly*, 138 (June), 325–58.
Przeworski, Adam and Fernando Limongi (1997), 'Modernization: theories and facts', *World Politics*, 49 (January), 155–83.
Robison, Richard and David S.G. Goodman (1996), 'The new rich in Asia', in Richard Robison and David S.G. Goodman (eds), *The New Rich in Asia*, London: Routledge.
Sen, A.K. (1981), 'Ingredients of famine analysis: availability and entitlements', *Quarterly Journal of Economics*, 95, 433–64.
Shirk, Susan L. (1982), *Competitive Comrades: Career Incentives and Student Strategies in China*, Berkeley: University of California Press.
Stiglitz, Joseph (1999), 'Participation and development: perspectives from the comprehensive development paradigm', paper delivered in Seoul, Korea.
Tanner, Murray Scott (1994), 'The erosion of communist party control over lawmaking in China', *The China Quarterly*, 138, 381–403.
Tanner, Murray Scott (1999), 'The National People's Congress', in Merle Goldman and Roderick MacFarquhar (eds), *The Paradox of China's Post-Mao Reforms*, Cambridge, MA: Harvard University Press.
Tian, Jiyun (1999), 'Amendments to the People's Republic of China Constitution', *Renmin ribao*, 10 March, p. 1.
Tipson, Frederick S. (1999), 'China and the information revolution', in Elizabeth Economy and Michel Oksenberg (eds), *China Joins the World: Progress and Prospects*, New York: Council on Foreign Relations Press.
Transition (1999), 'UNDP Report exposes transition's dark side – the rise in poverty, crime, disease and mortality', August, 19–22.
Unger, Jonathan (1996), 'Bridges: private business, the Chinese government and the rise of new associations', *The China Quarterly*, 147, 795–819.
Walder, Andrew G. (1986), *Communist Neo-Traditionalism: Work and Authority in Chinese Industry*, Berkeley: University of California Press.
White, Gordon, Jude Howell and Xiaoyuan Shang (1996), *In Search of Civil Society: Market Reform and Social Change in Contemporary China*, Oxford: Oxford University Press.
Wong, Jan (1999), 'Comrades on the net', *Media, The Australian*, 30 September–6 October, 14–15.
World Bank (1997a), *China 2020*, Washington, DC: World Bank.
World Bank (1997b), *Sharing Rising Incomes*, Washington, DC: World Bank.
Xiao Zhou and Xiao Yu (eds) (1998), *98 Liang hui hou: Zhongguo jingji da zoushi (98: China's Major Economic Direction After Two Congresses*), Beijing: Zhongguo jingji chubanshe.
Yang, Dali L. (1996), *Calamity and Reform in China*, Stanford: Stanford University Press.
You Ji (1998), *China's Enterprise Reform: Changing State/Society Relations After Mao*, London: Routledge.
Young, Susan (1998), 'The Chinese private sector in two decades of reform', *Journal of the Asia Pacific Economy*, 3(2), 80–103.

13. The IMF and the new international financial architecture

Elaine Hutson and Colm Kearney

INTRODUCTION

The world financial system seems to be exhibiting an increasing degree of fragility. At the national level, more than a dozen countries have, during the last decade or so, experienced systemic financial shocks that cost more than 10 per cent of GDP to fix. Even amongst the developed OECD economies, which have well-developed financial and regulatory systems, France, Finland, Japan, Norway, Spain, Sweden and the United States experienced major financial problems. At the international level, the world has witnessed four financial crises of varying degrees of seriousness in the last two decades: the Latin American 'Southern Cone' crisis of 1981–2, the European Exchange Rate Mechanism (ERM) crisis of 1992, the Mexican tequila crisis of 1994 and the Asian crisis of 1997–8.

The Asian crisis has been the most serious, having not only catastrophic effects on the countries directly involved, but also threatening the systemic stability of the global financial system. The scale of the Asian crisis – amounting to a capital outflow equivalent to 11 per cent of the affected countries' combined GDP – makes it the worst crisis since the Southern Cone crisis in Latin America, where there was a net private capital outflow of 8 per cent of the combined GDP of Argentina, Brazil and Mexico.

It is crucial that we develop an understanding of the causes of these crises, how their occurrence can be minimized, and how they can most appropriately be managed when they occur. We address two issues in particular. First, can capital controls assist in reducing the likelihood and extent of financial crises? While many commentators have argued that the flight of capital from the East Asian economies was a symptom rather than a cause of the crisis, others have advocated capital controls to reduce short-term capital flows. Second, we address the issue of crisis management by the International Monetary Fund (IMF). Criticism of the IMF's crisis management policies has been simmering for some time, but it increased in the wake of the Mexican crisis, and has mushroomed since the Asian crisis.

The fundamental criticism of the IMF is that it has extended its sphere of economic and political influence far beyond its mandate. It has done this with the support and backing of the US government in a way that has been seen to promote the interests of the United States, rather than those of the international community generally. We discuss how the IMF can be changed so that it can better assist in reducing the likelihood of financial crises and improve the management of crises when they occur.

The chapter is structured as follows. The next section reviews the main explanations that have been advanced for the Asian financial crisis. The third section discusses the question of controlling short-term capital flows. The fourth section summarizes the role played by the IMF during the crisis, and points to the tensions that arose from the broadening of its loan conditions. The fifth section summarizes the recommendations of two recent high-level reviews of the 'international financial architecture', and in the sixth section we present our recommendations for changes to the role and functions of the IMF. The final section summarizes the argument and draws together the conclusions.

THE ASIAN CRISIS

A voluminous literature has emerged since the Asian crisis (see *inter alia* Heillner, 1998; Mathieson *et al.*, 1998; Kearney, 1999; and Hutson and Kearney, 1999) for reviews) which attempts to explain its genesis and extent. In this section, we summarize and assess the various explanations for the Asian crisis. Box 13A.2 documents the major events in the unfolding of the crisis.

What Caused the Asian crisis?

Broadly speaking, there are two main explanations. The first is that the crisis resulted primarily from fundamental weaknesses in the Asian economies, such as crony capitalism, poor corporate governance, inadequate financial regulation and inappropriate exchange rate policies. The second explanation is that it resulted mainly from international financial market failures; in particular, informational asymmetries and moral hazard.

Did fundamental weaknesses in the Asian economies cause the crisis?

The term 'crony capitalism' refers to the process whereby those in power ensure that resources are directed to family members, friends and political allies, rather than to the most efficient users. Such munificence is often accompanied by implied government guarantees. The crony capitalism argument has had a considerable run in the literature, but it probably plays only a small part in explaining the Asian crisis. First, it cannot explain the timing of the crisis, because cronyism was widely recognized to occur in the worst affected countries for many years. Second, cronyism by definition is selective, and so cannot explain the depth of the crisis; nor can it explain its contagion to markets that were subsequently affected, including those as far afield as Latin America and Russia. Third, cronyism is recognized to exist in other Asian economies that have not been affected by the Asian crisis – and even in some Western countries!

It is well recognized that the East Asian countries had *lax corporate governance standards and poor regulatory systems.* In particular, financial institution regulation was seriously deficient. The East Asian governments had not adopted the Bank for International Settlements' (BIS) recommendations on capital adequacy (which have had widespread acceptance in OECD countries). Risk management practices were inadequate and in many cases absent. Poor regulation of the financial sector has been singled out as a major contributor to the massive growth in risky, undiversified lending. When the crisis came, the inadequate (or, as in Indonesia, absent) bankruptcy laws prevented the orderly work-out of debts.

Again, however, such factors cannot explain the timing of the crisis, as it had been well understood for some time that many East Asian economies lacked such basic legal and regulatory infrastructure. On balance, therefore, poor corporate governance and financial regulation in the affected economies cannot fully explain the crisis. These factors can, however, contribute to explaining its severity after the initial exchange rate and capital withdrawal shocks put pressure on the region's financial systems, exposing their weaknesses.

According to most commentators on the crisis, among the major culprits are the exchange rate policies of the East Asian countries, most of which pegged their currencies to the US dollar. Many of the countries exhausted their foreign currency reserves early in the crisis, trying vainly to keep their currencies at unrealistically high levels. The massive decreases in the value of the East Asian currencies fed rapidly through to the financial sector and the real economy because most bank and corporate debt was denominated in foreign currencies. Firms quickly became insolvent as the local currency value of their debt multiplied.

Most financial institution and corporate borrowing had been unhedged, partly because of poor risk management practices, but mainly because of the mistaken perception that their currencies would remain stable against the dollar. A couple of events leading up to the crisis exposed the flaws in this approach to exchange rate management. In 1994, China devalued its yuan vis-à-vis the US dollar by 35 per cent. This was with the goal of enhancing its competitiveness in the US market, which it succeeded in doing at the expense of the East Asian economies. Second, between April 1995 and April 1997 the yen depreciated vis-à-vis the US dollar by 60 per cent. Because the exchange rates of many of the former 'tiger' economies followed the dollar, intraregional trade was curtailed, reducing exports and making it increasingly difficult for East Asian-based companies to service their large foreign borrowings.

Did international financial market failures cause the Asian crisis?

Informational asymmetries We have seen that the corporate sector in many East Asian economies had operated under poorly developed accounting standards and risk management practices, while financial supervision had been hampered by the failure to implement international capital adequacy standards and to properly monitor developments in the financial institutions' balance sheets. This resulted in a serious informational asymmetry whereby foreign investors and lenders had significantly less information relative to the managers of the region's institutions. When the crisis hit, the uncertainty resulting from insufficient or incorrect information contributed to the risk aversion that induced the suppliers of capital to withdraw so emphatically from the region. This sudden withdrawal has been described in terms of herd behaviour, and has been used by some commentators as evidence of market non-rationality. In any event, the existence of informational asymmetries of this type can intuitively explain why herd-like behaviour might follow from the receipt of bad news in the market place.

An informational asymmetry that needs attention from regulators around the world relates to the over-the-counter (OTC) market in financial derivatives. This off-balance sheet activity attracts insufficient monitoring. The BIS (Bank for International Settlements, 1996) estimates that the total amount of derivatives in the world's OTC markets amounted to US$45 trillion at the end of 1995, a tenfold increase on three years earlier, and that transactions in these instruments during 1995 amounted to US$8 trillion. Although it is suspected that a significant amount of derivatives trading was involved in placing capital in the East Asian economies, we do not know even the approximate extent to which this occurred. Further, Savona and Maccario (1998) make the point that modern intermediaries now primarily use derivatives to alter their short-term exposure in response to crises.

Moral hazard Moral hazard occurs when the existence of insurance against risk encourages the insured to engage in riskier behaviour. Examples of situations where moral hazard can arise include the provision of 'lender of last resort' facilities to banks, and the deposit insurance scheme which contributed to the Savings & Loan débâcle in the United States in the late 1980s. This issue has received considerable attention in the context of the Asian crisis, most notably from Corsetti *et al.* (1998), Fischer (1998), Greenspan (1998), Krugman (1998) and Meltzer (1998). The moral hazard here resulted from implicit or explicit guarantees from national governments, and also from the likelihood of assistance from international agencies such as the IMF in the case of crisis. Krugman (1998) is a strong proponent of the argument that moral hazard resulted from implicit government guarantees. He cites guarantees to the South Korean chaebol that contributed to their overborrowing and overinvestment in high-risk initiatives. This is denied by Chang *et al.* (1998), however, who point out that no chaebol was bailed out during the 1980s and 1990s, while three of the biggest 30 went bankrupt.

The moral hazard argument has been directed against the international agencies' role in financial crises. For example, it has been suggested that the large transfer of US government funds to rescue the Mexican economy provided a credible guarantee to American suppliers of capital to Asia. Vasquez (1998) argues that the near doubling of capital flows to East Asia in 1995 can be traced to the IMF and US Treasury bail-out of Mexico in 1994. The most serious allegation of moral hazard during the Asian crisis is directed toward the IMF. One of the most telling criticisms of the IMF is that its bail-outs serve foreign creditors at the expense of the local population. Further, as foreign lenders perceive an implicit IMF guarantee, they are less careful about assessing the risks of lending to developing economies.

A related criticism of IMF bail-outs is that they may increase the frequency of financial crises around the world. Loriaux *et al.* (1997) and Matthews (1998) describe the process of growth in developing countries that relies on the existence of the IMF to come to their rescue when things go wrong. Rapid expansion of industrial development and export-led growth is financed largely by foreign capital. This process is bound to come unstuck at some time, perhaps from domestic overheating or deteriorating external conditions. The existence of an external agency that comes to the rescue acts as insurance against excessive damage while the economy recovers, ready for the next period of rapid expansion. The process has systemic moral hazard; the IMF has become an unwitting insurer, and contributes to the propagation of financial crises.

What Caused the Asian Crisis? A Summary

There is an emerging consensus that crony capitalism, poor corporate governance, inappropriate exchange rate systems and inadequate financial regulation contributed to the build-up in unsustainable financial flows to the East Asian economies. These factors, however, cannot alone explain the timing of the crisis and its contagion to other markets. There is also a consensus that international financial market failures – in particular, informational asymmetry and moral hazard – contributed to the crisis. The consensus view was aptly summarized by former US Treasury Secretary Robert Rubin (1998):

> While each of these countries enjoyed decades of strong growth and rising standards of living for their people, they also had deep-seated common and individual problems. At the core, for all of them, close links between governments, banks and corporations led to fundamentally unsound investments by corporations funded by unsound lending by banks. Their financial systems lacked transparency, which masked the extent of the problem. They had inadequate financial regulation and supervision . . . Additionally, several economies had large current account deficits, fixed exchange rates and inadequate monetary policies – an unsustainable combination.
>
> Foreign investors injected an extraordinary amount of capital into these flawed systems without due weighting of the risks involved . . .
>
> No single factor that I have described would likely have produced a financial crisis. While economies usually adjust in a relatively orderly fashion to market swings, in this case the combination of factors proved combustible. (Rubin,1998: 2–3)

ARE CAPITAL CONTROLS THE ANSWER TO FINANCIAL CRISES?

In most commentaries and discussions about the causes of the Asian crisis, the issue of the flight of capital – the factor that actually precipitated the crisis in the middle of 1997 – is not directly addressed. Implicit is the notion that capital flight is a response to underlying fundamental economic weaknesses, and the perception amongst lenders and investors that risk has increased. It has been noted, however, that countries with capital controls in place, such as India and China, have been unscathed by the crisis. Those that were hit hardest – Indonesia, Thailand and South Korea – had relaxed their capital controls in the early 1990s.

Under the post-war Bretton Woods system, where free trade in goods and services was seen as important, free flows of capital were seen as disruptive and cross-border capital transactions were controlled. The IMF's Articles of Agreement (VI (3) and VI (1)) included provisions allowing members to regulate international capital flows and giving the IMF the power to request capital controls. Since the collapse of Bretton Woods and the adoption of floating exchange rates, and since the more recent trends towards deregulation of domestic capital markets, capital controls around the world have gradually been lifted. It is increasingly argued by economists that capital account liberalization is important for economic prosperity, particularly for emerging economies that require high levels of investment but have a low capital base and low savings rates. The IMF and other agencies have, since at least the 1970s, been encouraging capital account liberalization.

Since the Mexican and Asian crises, however, many mainstream economists have acknowledged that controls on short-term capital flows may be appropriate in certain circumstances. The foremost proponents are Barry Eichengreen and James Tobin (see Eichengreen *et al.*, 1995), who argue that short-term capital flows – 'hot' money – can have a destabilizing influence on exchange rates. Controls on short-term capital controls throw 'sand in the wheels of international finance', reducing the volatility-enhancing effect on exchange rates, and thereby assisting in the promotion of export growth. This position implies that even countries with sound fundamentals could be adversely affected by the vagaries of short-term international capital flows. Other important proponents of controls on short-term capital flows are Joseph Stiglitz, former chief economist of the World Bank, and MIT's Paul Krugman.

Many economists, however, oppose capital controls in any circumstances. If the fundamentals were right, they argue, capital controls would be unnecessary. Mishkin (1999), for example, argues that capital flight is a symptom rather than an underlying cause of financial crises. He points to empirical studies showing that capital flows do not have predictive power in forecasting foreign exchange crises, but such factors as banking sector problems do.

The middle position is that capital account reform should not be fully implemented until the financial sector has been fully liberalized and good regulatory and supervisory systems are in place. This principle is illustrated in many of the East Asian economies which rushed to liberalize their capital accounts in the late 1980s and early 1990s, but had vastly underdeveloped and underregulated banking systems. For countries considering tightening controls, short-term capital controls should be used only as an interim measure while other economic reforms are put in place. This argument is summarized by Guitian (1998):

> The experiences of the Asian economies demonstrate the need to proceed with caution in opening the capital account, to anticipate and minimise the risks involved. Capital account liberalisation needs to be undertaken as an integral part of economic reforms and coordinated with appropriate macroeconomic, exchange rate, and financial sector policies. The issue relates more to the sequence of reforms than to their speed. (Guitian, 1998: 16)

The commonly cited success story for short-term capital controls is Chile, which imposed controls following a severe capital crisis in 1982, and removed them in 1998. Chile imposed three types of controls. The most well-known was a requirement that 30 per cent of all non-equity capital must be deposited, interest-free, in the central bank for one year. Coupled with this requirement was that foreign money coming into Chile stay for at least one year. Lastly, Chilean firms were restricted from tapping international capital markets unless their debt had a rating as high as Chilean government paper. One of the architects of the Chilean controls, former central banker Roberto Zahler, has argued that capital controls should be used only by countries with solid macroeconomic and exchange rate policies in place (*Wall Street Journal*, 4 September 1998).

THE ROLE OF THE IMF DURING THE ASIAN CRISIS

The Causes of the Asian Crisis: the IMF Perspective

The IMF has played down the 'international market failure' explanation, and emphasized the 'fundamental weaknesses' argument. The IMF slant on this issue is summarized by Fischer (1998):

> Macroeconomic adjustment is not the main element in the programs of Thailand, Indonesia and Korea. Rather financial sector restructuring and other structural reforms lie at the heart of each program – because the problems they deal with, weak financial institutions, inadequate bank regulation and supervision, and the complicated and non-transparent relations among governments, banks, and corporations, lie at the heart of the economic crisis in each country. It would not serve any lasting purpose for the IMF to lend to these countries unless these problems were addressed. Nor would it be in the countries' interest to leave the structural and governance issues aside . . . the Fund has been accused of encouraging countries to move too quickly on banking sector restructuring: we have been urged to support regulatory forbearance, leaving the solution of the banking sector problems for later. This would only have perpetuated these countries' economic problems, as experience in Japan has shown.

The second sentence of this quotation asserts that the Asian crisis can be blamed on the first of the causes discussed in the second section of this chapter; that is, fundamental weaknesses in the East Asian countries. Interestingly, the issue of inappropriate exchange rate policies is not mentioned here (although it is in other published comments) and neither are the international market failure problems of asymmetric information and moral hazard. These countries operated very successfully for three decades, with economic performance that was the envy of the world, while many Western countries performed relatively poorly and several experienced serious financial crises of their own.

In other forums, the IMF (1998) has demonstrated awareness of the problem of moral hazard in its role in the Asian crisis. It has, however, played down the moral hazard argument by suggesting that imprudent lending is more likely to reflect irrational exuberance that leads investors and lenders to underestimate risks, rather than moral hazard. At the root of investors' 'irrational exuberance' is informational asymmetry, it argues, so improved information should eliminate the problem. In advancing this position, the IMF is placing all the blame at the feet of the East Asian economies, and none on the Western lenders. Better information, however, would not necessarily improve matters. It is widely acknowledged that many sophisticated financial institutions continued to lend to the region long after the increased riskiness became obvious. In fact, as Lipsky (1998) argues, the build-up in short-term debts before the crisis reflects this perception amongst lenders.

The Broadening of the IMF's Loan Conditionalities

The role played by the IMF during the Asian crisis has been the focus of much comment and criticism. Much of the IMF's unpopularity has stemmed from the perception that its rescue funds have protected the domestic and international lending institutions, rather than assisting the citizens of the stricken economies who had to bear a large part of the burden of adjustment to the harsh conditions. These conditions have been referred to by Sachs (1989) as being 'all head and no heart', and have, according to Salvatore (1998), led to 'riots and the toppling of governments'.

More recently, however, and particularly regarding the IMF's response to the Asian crisis, the institution has been subject to extensive criticism regarding the broadening of its loan conditions. This has involved a move away from the traditional macroeconomic stabilization policies, to the inclusion of requirements for microeconomic restructuring as well. These include an extensive set of financial and real sector reforms, ranging from the closure of banks and changes to pension systems, to agriculture, energy and transport, the ending of monopolistic practices and subsidies and even the operation of labour markets. This broadening of conditionalities significantly raises the hurdles that recipient countries have to negotiate in order to secure rescue funds. Microeconomic restructuring is typically harder to implement than macroeconomic reforms, and can take considerably more time. Heillner (1998) points out that the extended conditionality requirements slowed the pace of the disbursement of funds to the East Asian economies. He argues that monies supplied in response to negotiated conditions, and released in stages in response to perceived compliance, is not the way to inject liquidity into a financial system in crisis.

A further issue that has received considerable attention is that the appropriate sequencing of the reforms is a notoriously complex problem. The fact that the conditionality reforms are generally required during a crisis makes the problem even more complex. The IMF's attempts to push through its broader reform programmes in Asia may have worsened the crisis. Its support package to Thailand, for example, had conditionality measures including the freezing of a number of finance companies. This caused panic amongst uninsured depositors. In Indonesia, a similar panic occurred when the IMF required the closure of several domestic banks. Sachs (1998a) has referred to these measures as the IMF's 'screaming fire in the theatre'. Another condition imposed on Indonesia was that it unwind its food and fuel subsidies. The resulting increase in consumer prices imposed great hardship on the Indonesian people. This was interpreted in Indonesia and beyond either as IMF arrogance or as an attempt to bring down a government that it did not believe would deliver on its preferred reforms.

The IMF's bail-out packages have traditionally been conditioned on the recipient government's willingness to enact macroeconomic stabilization policies, such as the reduction in fiscal deficits and rates of monetary growth. The funds were then released only after compliance with these conditions, a requirement that was designed to fulfil the 'adequate safeguards' required by part (v) of Article 1 of its Articles of Agreement in which its role is specified. This reads as follows:[1]

> (v) To give confidence to members by making the general resources of the Fund temporarily available to them under adequate safeguards, thus providing them with opportunity to correct maladjustments in their balance of payments without resorting to measures destructive of national or international prosperity.

The inclusion of the new conditionalities constitutes a very significant rise in the 'safeguards' that it considers 'adequate' in order to comply with the intent of part (v) of Article 1 of its Articles of Agreement. Why did the IMF consider that this was necessary? It is not obvious that the traditional macroeconomic stabilization conditionalities proved to be inadequate, and it is equally unclear that broadening them to include a wide range of microeconomic restructuring policies would necessarily improve the safeguards. The answer to this question, however, is not known. The IMF has not provided an explanation as to why loan conditions have been broadened over the years. Although it has persistently called for greater accountability and transparency in corporate governance amongst the East Asian economies, the IMF does not practise what it preaches. This point has been made forcefully by some eminent economists. For example, Sachs (1998b) states:

> While it pays lip service to 'transparency', the IMF offers virtually no substantive public documentation of its decisions, except for a few pages in press releases that are shorn of the technical details needed for a serious professional evaluation of its programs . . . The world accepts as normal the idea that crucial details of IMF programs should remain confidential, even though these 'details' affect the wellbeing of millions. Staff at the Fund, meanwhile, are unaccountable for their decisions. The people most affected by these decisions have little knowledge or input. In Korea, the IMF insisted that all presidential candidates immediately endorse an agreement they had no part in drafting or negotiating – and no time to understand. The situation is out of hand.

The Increasing Politicization of the IMF

Many commentators have argued that the IMF has become too politicized. It has been claimed that the expansion of conditionality requirements in the East Asian and also the Mexican bail-outs served the interests of wealthy nations, in particular the United States, and that the IMF has become a stooge of US foreign policy. In a speech in 1998, former US Treasury Secretary Robert Rubin discussed the importance of the Asian economies as a destination for US exports. Some 30 per cent of US exports go to Asia – more than to Europe – as do more than half the exports of California, Oregon and Washington state (Rubin, 1998: 3).

The broadening of its loan conditionalities is the lever with which the IMF has increased the scope of its activities beyond those specified in Article 1. It understands the political reality that, when countries are in economic and financial strife, they are at their weakest, and maximum influence can be exerted. This is no conspiracy theory. It was for precisely this reason that Malaysia refused any IMF assistance during the Asian crisis. Further, it received confirmation in the speech by Robert Rubin cited above. Before a crisis, he said, 'We have the capacity to advocate but not to force sovereign countries to take actions they do not believe to be in their interest', but, during times of crisis, pressure can be exerted: 'our approach requires that these countries take the concrete steps necessary to reform their economies . . . If countries don't take these steps, no financial assistance is made available.'

Concern about the IMF's expanding role, and its increasing politicization, has been expressed by a number of eminent economists. Perhaps most notable amongst these has been former president of the Council of Economic Advisors, Martin Feldstein (1998a):

> The fundamental issue is the appropriate role for an international agency and its technical staff in dealing with sovereign countries that come to it for assistance. It is important to remember that the IMF cannot initiate programs but develops a program for a member country only when that country seeks help. The country

> is then the IMF's client or patient, but not its ward. The legitimate political institutions of the country should determine the nation's economic structure and the nature of its institutions. A nation's desperate need for short-term financial help does not give the IMF the moral right to substitute its technical judgements for the outcomes of the nation's political process.

And elsewhere, he has stated (Feldstein, 1998b):

> IMF Managing Director Michel Camdessus has said that if the IMF had only wanted to deal with the countries' liquidity and debt problems, it would by now have succeeded. He then [said] that the Asian crisis was really a 'blessing in disguise' because it gave the IMF the leverage to force structural policy changes that the national governments would not otherwise adopt. This is a remarkable confession of the arrogance and inappropriateness of the IMF policies. Even apart from whether the IMF has any legitimate right to usurp these sovereign responsibilities, the attempt to remake an economy in the midst of a currency crisis made it likely that there would be neither fundamental restructuring nor a rapid resolution of the crisis itself . . . The IMF should commit itself publicly to avoiding a repetition of its recent mistakes . . . The world will be watching closely to see if the IMF can redefine itself as a valuable institution.

One of the most notorious incidents during the Asian crisis was the IMF's reaction to Indonesia's proposal for a currency board. Following the failure of the IMF's Indonesian support package to stabilize the rupiah, the government proposed a currency board in order to contain the damage and buy time to implement real sector reforms. The IMF, however, interpreted this proposal as an attempt to postpone real sector reforms. On 8 January 1998, a strongly worded letter from the IMF, addressed to the Indonesian government, was leaked to the press. In the letter the IMF threatened to withhold disbursements of the rescue package if the currency board proposal was pursued. On 14 February 1998, the IMF's First Deputy Managing Director Stanley Fischer was reported in *The Jakarta Post* as having criticized the currency board proposal and using uncharacteristically blunt language about political issues when he remarked that the rupiah had been hit by suggestions that the country could select a vice president whose 'devotion to new ways of doing things is limited'.

These events were widely interpreted as attempts to exert political pressure on the Indonesian government to sequence its reforms according to the IMF's preferences. They certainly did not help to stabilize the rupiah (see Box 13.2, 8 January and 16 February 1998), and as such were in conflict with part (iii) of Article 1 of the Fund's Articles of Agreement. Also the threat of withholding the loan package did nothing to assist the government in its task of stabilizing the economy with minimum destruction to national and international prosperity, and as such its outcome sits uncomfortably with the intent of part (v) of Article 1.

It should be understood that the upshot of these developments was to raise a considerable amount of mistrust within Asia about the motives and behaviour of the world's most important international financial institution. It was interpreted as having stepped beyond its brief in a manner that constituted political interference. The governments of the East Asian economies developed a more sophisticated understanding of the political–economic dynamics involved in this process and, although they did not succeed in doing so, they became aware of their potentially greater bargaining strength if they could act cooperatively when dealing with the IMF. Philippine Finance Secretary Salvador Enriquez articulated this on 13 February 1998, when he stated: 'The Philippines, Indonesia, Thailand and Malaysia should deal with the IMF collectively as a group and adopt a common stance to share the burden of adjustments between the creditors and the debtors.' This statement reveals a great deal about how the IMF was perceived to operate during the Asian financial crisis. This ill-feeling and mistrust continues today as these economies struggle to get back on their feet.

THE NEW INTERNATIONAL FINANCIAL ARCHITECTURE

In response to the extensive criticism of the IMF and other international financial institutions (IFIs) such as the World Bank, there have been several high-level reviews of the 'international financial architecture'. The two most important have been the G22-sponsored review, whose report appeared in 1998, and the US government's Council for Foreign Relations (CFR) review which was published in September 1999. While the IMF has made some changes to its operations, such as improving the provision of information (under pressure from the US Congress), it has ignored many of the recommendations of these review groups. The CFR task force, for example, recommended that the IMF and the World Bank go 'back to basics', with the IMF concentrating on monetary, fiscal and exchange-rate policies, and banking and financial sector surveillance and reform, and the World Bank focusing on the longer-term structure and social aspects of economic development. In a speech at the Bretton Woods Committee Meeting on 4 April 2000, IMF acting managing director Stanley Fischer described the IMF as including '*structural policies* that underlie the monetary and fiscal systems and the financial system' (emphasis added).

The G22 Recommendations

In response to the Asian crisis, the finance ministers and central bank governors from 22 systemically significant economies met in Washington,

DC in April 1998. The countries represented were Argentina, Australia, Brazil, Britain, Canada, China, France, Germany, Hong Kong SAR, India, Indonesia, Italy, Japan, Korea, Malaysia, Mexico, Poland, Russia, Singapore, South Africa, Thailand and the United States. The objective of the meeting was to begin the process of designing the new international financial architecture. Three working groups were set up to examine the following issues:

- the enhancement of transparency and accountability,
- the strengthening of domestic financial systems, and
- the management of international financial crises.

Each of these working groups included senior staff from the relevant agencies, and the proceedings were observed by the heads of the BIS, IMF, OECD and the World Bank. Each group presented a report recommending actions to strengthen the international financial system, published as the World Bank Reports (1998). These reports were endorsed by a meeting of the G7 in October 1998.

The working group on the enhancement of transparency and accountability
This highlighted the necessity for improvements by the private sector, national authorities and the international financial institutions. With regard to the private sector, it recommended the adoption and enforcement of national disclosure standards including timeliness, completeness, consistency, risk management, and audit and control processes. It also recommended that better data should be compiled on the international exposures of investment banks, hedge funds and other institutional investors, and that countries should upgrade their data provision to the BIS. With regard to the national authorities, it recommended that more timely and accurate information should be made public on fiscal stances and foreign liquidity, including forward positions. With regard to the international financial institutions, it recommended that the presumption of the public release of information rather than its restriction should be adopted. Special attention was given to the IMF in this regard. Chapter 4 of the report discusses at length the historical lack of transparency and accountability of the IMF, and makes clear its view that improvements are needed.

The working group on the strengthening of domestic financial systems
This highlighted the necessity to develop strong prudential regulation and supervision of banks, to initiate better deposit insurance schemes, and to improve corporate governance in the financial sector.

The working group on the management of international financial crises

This working group highlighted four issues. First, it sought to limit the scope of explicit or implicit government guarantees and to ensure that any guarantees that are offered are properly priced to reflect the inherent risks. Second, it sought to expand the use of innovative financing arrangements that provide emerging markets with greater insurance against periods of market volatility. It proposed arrangements that could provide greater flexibility in payments and better risk sharing between creditors and debtors. Amongst its recommendations were the development of pre-negotiated options to extend repayments automatically, debt instruments that include repayment reductions under specified circumstances, and contractual access to additional finance in certain circumstances. Third, it examined the maintenance of appropriate exchange rate regimes and suggested that regime changes should be incorporated into risk assessments. Finally, it examined the implementation of more effective insolvency and debtor–creditor regimes. It proposed the international adoption of a set of principles, and it also proposed the adoption of collective action clauses in sovereign bond issues that would better coordinate creditor behaviour in the event of a crisis.

The G7 countries met in October 1998 and committed themselves to implementing the recommendations of the World Bank Reports (1998). They also went further in recommending reform of the IFIs such as the IMF, better coordination amongst countries, and further research projects such as on the growth and implications of derivative markets. In addition, they suggested the establishment of a new precautionary short-term credit facility that could apply to countries which have basically sound policies but have been hit by contagion from other markets. These countries would have to be undergoing 'strong IMF-approved policies' (1998c: 285).

The Council on Foreign Relations Task Force Recommendations

In September 1998, US President Bill Clinton suggested that a private-sector group should review the need for a new international financial architecture. The Council for Foreign Relations (CFR) sponsored the Independent Task Force on the Future of the International Financial Architecture. Members of the task force included business people, bankers, academics and politicians. Much was made at the time of putting together a broad group of people, who were not seen as 'the usual suspects' on the international financial architecture issue, that is, central bankers, and IMF and World Bank officials. In September 1999, the group published their report: *Safeguarding Prosperity in a Global Financial System: The Future*

International Financial Architecture. The CFR task force made recommendations that were more specific than those of the G22 working group. Another feature distinguishing the CFR task force report from that of the G22 working groups was the importance the task force assigned to the moral hazard problem associated with IMF bail-outs. The crux of their recommendations was that, if future crisis prevention was to improve, the onus must be put 'back where it belongs: on emerging economies themselves and on their private creditors who dominate today's international capital markets'. Six principles guided the committee:

1. Encourage emerging economies to intensify their crisis prevention efforts.
2. Permit savings to flow to the countries and the uses where they have the best return.
3. Promote fair burden sharing among private creditors, official debtors and official creditors when a crisis does occur.
4. Increase the role of market-based incentives in crisis prevention and resolution.
5. Make reform of the architecture a two-way street, with the major industrial countries also doing their part.
6. Refocus the mandates of the IMF and the World Bank on areas they are best equipped to address.

The task force made seven key recommendations. They are as follows.

Recommendation 1
The IMF should reward countries for 'good housekeeping', such as lending on more favourable terms. 'Good housekeeping' refers to prudent macro- and microeconomic management, and ensuring systems of regulation and disclosure that comply with international standards. The report also suggests that the IMF should publish periodic 'standards reports' of each member country's compliance with international standards.

Recommendation 2
The IMF should advise emerging economies with fragile domestic sectors to impose short-term capital controls, such as the taxes imposed on short-term flows in Chile, in order to moderate the boom–bust cycle. The report, however, warns against controls on long-term capital flows.

Recommendation 3
Fair burden sharing and market discipline should be promoted. The task force recognized the moral hazard problem associated with large official

bail-outs, and the report discusses at length several recent examples (Asia, Mexico, Russia) where bail-outs have allowed private creditors (particularly large commercial banks) to escape from their commitments at little cost. They argued that, 'as with other types of insurance, the appropriate response to moral hazard should be to limit the size of insurance payments and charge risky policyholders more'. When rescue packages are being considered, there must be a balance between limiting systemic risk and encouraging market discipline; however, in recent bail-out packages the balance has been skewed against market discipline.

Rescheduling of debt, rather than bail-outs of creditors, is the more appropriate approach in a crisis. No category of private debt should be exempt. To this end, collective action clauses should be included in government bond contracts. The IMF should encourage emerging economies to maintain comprehensive registers of their creditors, and creditors should be encouraged to form standing committees to help coordinate future debt rescheduling. Finally, the IMF should provide assistance only when there is a good prospect of resolving the country's underlying problems, and it should make 'good faith' discussions on rescheduling a condition of emergency assistance.

Recommendation 4

The IMF and G7 countries should refuse to support pegged exchange rates. The report contains an extensive discussion on the problems with fixed exchange rate regimes, and argues that they are particularly inappropriate for emerging economies.

Recommendation 5

The IMF's rescue packages should be smaller, and be delivered with more speed, than they have been in the recent past. The IMF should return to normal lending limits for countries in crisis. For those threatened by 'contagion', the IMF should supply funds from a special contagion facility, which should be disbursed quickly and be free of policy conditions.

Recommendation 6

The IMF and the World Bank should go 'back to basics'. Both of these institutions have tried to do too much in recent years, and have lost sight of their respective strengths. In particular, the IMF should lend less and concentrate more on encouraging crisis prevention. It should focus on a leaner agenda of monetary, fiscal and exchange rate policies, and of banking and financial sector surveillance and reform. The World Bank should focus on the longer-term structure and social aspects of economic development, but should not be involved in crisis lending or crisis management.

Recommendation 7
The international community should assist in generating political support for the reforms. The emerging economies should be full partners in the reform exercise. Further, with prospects of recovery from the Asian and Russian crises improving, the committee warns against complacency that may stall the reform process.

PROPOSED CHANGES TO THE IMF'S ARTICLES OF AGREEMENT

There is a pressing need for a more wide-ranging review of the IMF's role in the global financial system than it has hitherto considered in deliberations about the new international financial architecture. Since the establishment of the IMF in 1945, the world economy has changed beyond recognition, and the IMF has adapted with it. However, there has never been a full review of the IMF's Articles of Association. Until there is a formal review of its articles the IMF will always be open to criticisms of politicization and operating beyond its mandate. A review of its Articles is essential for a clarification and refocusing of its roles and duties so that it sustains its pre-eminent position as the guardian of global financial stability. Here we suggest some amendments to Article 1.

Part (ii) of Article 1, which aims to assist the expansion of world trade with the aim of promoting members' employment and real incomes, should be reviewed as to the desirability of its removal. The promotion of international trade might be better left to the World Trade Organization (WTO). Part (vi), which aims to reduce the magnitude and duration of payments imbalances, should also be reviewed. Developments in open economy stabilization policy suggest that such an aim is not always appropriate. For example, the US economy is currently experiencing historically high levels of performance alongside continual and large payments imbalances. In a world where most countries have moved to floating exchange rates it is no longer obvious that attempting to minimize either the magnitude or the duration of payments imbalances always constitutes optimal policy.

Parts (iii) and (v) of the Articles, relating to exchange rate stability and adequate safeguards to members, are uncontroversial in their intent but have allowed the IMF to act in ways that are questionable. In Indonesia – the country worst affected by the Asian crisis – the IMF attempted to impose a very broad menu of reforms in their preferred sequence. Many commentators argued that the delays and confusion that resulted from the IMF's heavy-handed approach contributed to a worsening of the crisis in Indonesia. As discussed earlier, its handling of the Indonesian government's proposal for a currency board, when it threatened to withhold emergency assistance if the currency board was pursued, created greater exchange rate instability. This threat, and the delay in payments that resulted, was not in the spirit of part (v) of Article 1, which is supposed to 'assist the economy to adjust without the destruction of national prosperity'.

Part (v) should be redesigned to clarify the IMF's responsibilities in timing the release of emergency funds, and to spell out precisely the meaning of 'adequate safeguards'. The IMF's loan conditionalities should be made explicit, so that countries that need assistance, and their creditors (or potential creditors), know what to expect.

SUMMARY AND CONCLUSIONS

The Asian crisis of 1997–8 took the region and the world by surprise, having a catastrophic effect on Indonesia, Malaysia, South Korea and Thailand and threatening world systemic stability. Following massive capital inflows in the early-to-mid 1990s, speculative attacks on the region's currencies in 1997 led to a dramatic reversal in capital flows. Explanations for the crisis have centred on fundamental weakness in the East Asian economies; fixed exchange rate regimes, poor business regulation and corporate governance, weak and poorly managed financial systems, and crony capitalism have been singled out as major culprits. It is also widely recognized, however, that international market failures played a crucial role in the crisis, in particular the moral hazard engendered by massive IMF bail-outs which have gone largely to international banks.

Since the Mexican and Asian crises, many mainstream economists have advocated controls on short-term capital flows, based on the notion that such flows are highly affected by herd-like behaviour of investors. The explanation for this view is that investors are irrationally exuberant in good times and irrationally pessimistic when crashes occur. An alternative explanation for apparent 'herd-like' behaviour is that it is a rational response to the incentives faced by investors: investors saw an opportunity in East Asia to earn large returns at relatively low risk. Lending short limits risk to lenders, enabling them to withdraw their money out at short notice. Even mainstream international finance text books suggest that the obvious solution to country or political risk is to lend short. The build-up in short-term debt before the Asian crisis is evidence of an increase in perceived risk. The perceived risk was artificially reduced by two other factors. First, exchange risk was limited by fixed exchange rates and, second, investors perceived an implied guarantee from the IMF. The herd-like behaviour amongst Asian creditors is not, therefore, necessarily the result of systematic irrationality amongst lenders. Controls on short-term capital flows may therefore be appropriate, so that the additional costs faced by lenders better equate risk with expected returns, such that resources are properly allocated to the most efficient users. However, moves throughout the region towards flexible exchange rate regimes should assist in making the risk–reward trade-off more appropriate. If reforms to IMF bail-outs that reduce moral hazard are put in place (see the previous two sections) the situation will improve further.

The IMF has also been subject to extensive criticism over the increasing politicization that has been facilitated by the extension of loan conditionalities beyond the traditional macroeconomic policy requirements. We argue that there should be a major review of the IMF's Articles of Agreement, so that its roles and duties can be more tightly defined. This would reduce the likelihood of the Fund appearing to be motivated by political interests. We also advocate that its loan conditionalities should be made transparent so that both debtor countries and creditors know exactly what to expect in the case of a crisis. The problem, however, in making loan conditionalities explicit, is that moral hazard remains a factor. Some commentators have argued that to reduce moral hazard the IMF's loan conditionalities should be left vague, in order to reduce the value of the implied insurance of IMF bail-outs to Western lenders. However, we argue that specifying loan conditionalities is essential to the IMF's overcoming the cycle of mistrust and suspicion amongst emerging economies (particularly apparent during the Asian crisis). Moral hazard can be reduced in the other ways suggested by the Council for Foreign Relations task force: by reducing the size of IMF bail-outs and, instead of bailing out lenders, assisting in the rescheduling of debt repayments.

We also advocate that the IMF be moved out of Washington, DC and be located on a rotating basis in the world's main financial centres, such as Frankfurt, London, New York and Tokyo. In addition to placing geographical distance between the IMF and the US government, and thus helping to ease suspicion that the IMF is an instrument of US foreign policy, such a move would help alter the institution's organizational and policy culture.

APPENDIX

BOX 13A.1 ARTICLE 1 OF THE IMF'S ARTICLES OF AGREEMENT

(i) To promote international monetary cooperation through a permanent institution which provides the machinery for consultation and collaboration on international monetary systems.
(ii) To facilitate the expansion and balanced growth of international trade, and to contribute thereby to the promotion and maintenance of high levels of employment and real income and to the development of the productive resources of all members as primary objectives of economic policy.
(iii) To promote exchange stability, to maintain orderly exchange rate arrangements among members, and to avoid competitive exchange depreciation.
(iv) To assist in the establishment of a multilateral system of payments in respect of current transactions between members and in the elimination of foreign exchange restrictions which hamper the growth of world trade.
(v) To give confidence to members by making the general resources of the Fund temporarily available to them under adequate safeguards, thus providing them with opportunity to correct maladjustments in their balance of payments without resorting to measures destructive of national or international prosperity.
(vi) In accordance with the above, to shorten the duration and lessen the degree of disequilibrium in the international balances of payments of members.

Source: IMF Annual Report, and/or IMF home page at http://www.imf.org/external/index.htm.

BOX 13A.2 THE IMF AND THE ASIAN FINANCIAL CRISIS

1997

14 May The Thai baht is hit by a massive speculative attack based on poor economic performance and political instability. The central bank raises interest rates and intervenes to support the

baht. The Singapore central bank assists. Speculators move on to the Filipino peso.

2 July The Thai central bank introduces a managed float and seeks IMF assistance. The baht devalues by 15–20 percent to a record low of almost 29 to the US dollar.

14 July The Philippines obtains a US$1.1 billion rescue package from the IMF.

5 August The Thai central bank suspends 48 finance firms and announces a revamping of its finance sector in line with the IMF rescue package.

11 August Thailand obtains a rescue package of US$16 billion from the IMF.

20 August Thailand obtains a further US$3.9 billion rescue package from the IMF. Its total rescue package now amounts to US$19.9 billion.

31 October The IMF grants Indonesia a $23 billion financial support package.

3 December Concerns about South Korea's signing of the IMF loan agreement send markets down. The rupiah, baht and ringgit follow the won to all-time lows against the US dollar.

1998

8 January The ringgit and Indonesian stocks hit record lows, raising the spectre of civil unrest. Reports surface that the IMF has written a sharply worded letter to Indonesia in response to the recent budget that was widely condemned as insufficiently austere.

16 February The rupiah plunges after reports that the IMF has threatened to withdraw support if Indonesia adopts a currency board.

2 March Indonesian inflation hits 32 per cent. Escalating food price rises cause civil unrest.

6 March Continuing signs that Indonesian president Soeharto is unwilling to implement reforms worries currency markets, with the rupiah down 25 per cent in the last 3 days. This devaluation exacerbates unemployment and the huge private debt overhang. Riots in the towns continue.

16 March Confidence seems to have been restored in South Korea. Foreign creditor banks have rolled over $22 billion of short-term debt into 2- and 3-year maturity loans.

14 May Rioting and looting in central Jakarta sends the rupiah to 11 700 to the dollar, more than 25 per cent below the level 2 days earlier.

15 May Indonesian markets are virtually abandoned in the aftermath of 4 days of rioting, arson and looting in Jakarta. Banks are closed and most offices deserted. Overseas corporations start closing down operations and evacuating staff. Demands that President Soeharto step down intensify. The death toll stands at more than 500.

19 May Soeharto promises new presidential elections in which he will not run. Jakarta stocks surge 6.4 percent on this news, and the rupiah recovers to 11000 after hitting a low of 16000 to the dollar earlier in the day.

21 May Soeharto announces his resignation, handing over to Vice-President Jusuf Habibie. Regional markets rally on this news.

BOX 13A.3 HISTORY OF THE IMF: 1944–99

1944 The International Monetary and Financial Conference in Bretton Woods, New Hampshire, formulates the Articles of Agreement of the IMF and the World Bank.

1945 The Articles of Agreement are signed by 29 governments, representing 80 per cent of the original quotas.

1947 The IMF commences operations.

1952 Germany and Japan join the IMF.

1962 The Executive Board agrees on the General Arrangements to Borrow (GAB).

1963 The Compensatory Financing Facility (CFF) is established.

1969 The Buffer Stock Financing Facility (BSFF) is established.

1970 The first allocation of SDRs.

1971 The Bretton Woods system collapses as the United States ceases to buy and sell gold to settle international transactions. Par values and the convertibility of the US dollar are replaced by the Smithsonian Agreement which realigns currencies in a temporary regime of central rates with wider margins.

1972 The Board of Governors establishes the Committee of 20 to reform the International Monetary System.

1973 Generalized floating commences as Europe floats its currencies against the US dollar.

1974 The Interim Committee is established and meets for the first time. The Committee of 20 completes its work. The Executive Board adopts Guidelines for the Management of

Floating Exchange Rates together with a new method of SDR valuation based on a basket of 16 currencies. The Extended Fund Facility (EFF) is established to give medium-term assistance to members with balance of payments problems stemming from structural change.

1976 The Interim Committee amends Article IV of the Articles of Agreement.

1978 The second amendment to the Articles of Agreement allows members to adopt the exchange rate arrangements of their choice.

1979 The Supplementary Financing Facility (SFF), established in 1977, enters into force.

1980 The Interim Committee agrees that the IMF should provide more funds over longer time periods to assist the adjustment and financing of payments imbalances. The Seventh General Review raises quotas to SDR 60 billion.

1981 A smaller basket of five currencies belonging to members with the largest exports during 1975–9 (the British pound, French franc, German mark, Japanese yen and US dollar) is used to value the SDR.

1982 The IMF assists adjustment programmes in Mexico and other countries facing severe debt problems.

1983 The Eighth General Review recommends higher quotas. The GAB is revised and extended.

1986 The Structural Adjustment Facility (SAF) is established to provide balance of payments assistance on concessional terms to low-income developing countries.

1987 The Louvre Accord is adopted to enhance policy coordination in order to promote more stable exchange rates. The Enhanced SAF (ESAF) is established to assist low-income members undertaking strong macroeconomic and structural adjustment programmes.

1988 The Compensatory and Contingency Financing Facility (CCFF) is established to compensate members with reduced export earnings owing to circumstances beyond their control, and to help sustain adjustment programmes in the face of external shocks.

1989 The Executive Board adopts guidelines on developing country debt, including the linking of support for debt-reduction strategies to sustained programmes with strong structural reform.

1990 Quotas are raised by 50 per cent. The Interim Committee proposes a third amendment to the Articles of Agreement, suspending voting rights for members that do not fulfil their financial obligations to the IMF.

1992 Many states of the former Soviet Union gain membership. An SDR 719 million stand-by arrangement for Russia is agreed. The Executive Board adopts the third Amendment of the Articles of Agreement.

1993 The Systemic Transformation Facility (STF) is established to assist countries facing balance of payments difficulties arising from transformation from a planned to a market economy.

1994 Three Deputy Managing Director posts are created. The Madrid Declaration is agreed to, which calls on industrial countries to sustain growth, reduce unemployment and prevent a resurgence of inflation, developing countries to extend growth, and transition countries to pursue bold stabilization and reform efforts.

1995 The largest financial commitment by the IMF sets up a stand-by arrangement of SDR 12.1 billion for Mexico.

1996 The largest EFF in IMF history, SDR 6.9 billion, is agreed for Russia. A Special Data Dissemination Standard for member countries having, or seeking, access to international capital markets is established.

1997 The Asian crisis hits, and the Supplemental Reserve Facility (SRF) is established to assist members with sudden and disruptive loss of market confidence. The SRF is activated the next day to support the stand-by arrangement of SDR 15.5 billion for Korea, the largest financial commitment in the IMF's history. The public release of Public Information Notices following members' Article IV consultations is approved. The Executive Board agrees to amend the Articles of Agreement to allow all members to receive equitable shares of cumulative SDR allocations.

1998 The GAB are activated for the first time for a non-participant and for the first time in 20 years to finance an SDR 6.3 billion augmentation of the EFF for Russia.

Source: IMF (1998), *Survey Supplement on the Fund* (September).

NOTE

1. Article 1 of the IMF's Articles of Agreement is reproduced in full in Box 13A.1.

BIBLIOGRAPHY

Aaron, H.J, R.C. Bryant, S.M. Collins and R.Z. Lawrence (1994), 'Preface to the Studies on Integrating National Economies', in B. Eichengreen (ed.), *International Monetary Arrangements for the 21st Century*, Washington, DC: Brookings Institution.

Bank for International Settlements (1996), *Central Bank Survey of Foreign Exchange and Derivatives Market Activity*, Basle: BIS.

Cardenas, M. and F. Barrera (1997), 'On the effectiveness of capital controls: The experience of Colombia during the 1990s', *Journal of Development Economics*, 54, 27–57.

Chang, H.-J., H.J. Park and C.G. Yoo (1998), 'Interpreting the Korean Crisis: Financial Liberalisation, Industrial Policy and Corporate Governance', *Cambridge Journal of Economics*, 22, 735–46.

Corsetti, G., P. Pesenti and N. Roubini (1998), 'Paper Tigers? A Model of the Asian Crisis', National Bureau of Economic Research Working Paper No. 6783, November.

Council of Economic Advisors (1999), *Economic Report to Congress*, Washington, DC: CEA.

Craig, L.E. (1997), 'IMF "Austerity" Measures Aren't Enough', Press Release, 2 December.

Eichengreen, B. (ed.) (1994), *International Monetary Arrangements for the 21st Century*, Washington, DC: Brookings Institution.

Eichengreen, B., J. Tobin and C. Wyplosz (1995), 'Two Cases for Sand in the Wheels of International Finance', *The Economic Journal*, 105, 162–72.

Eichengreen, B. *et al.* (1998), 'Hedge Funds and Financial Market Dynamics', IMF occasional paper no. 66.

Feldstein, M. (1998a), 'Refocussing the IMF', *Foreign Affairs*, March/April.

Feldstein, M. (1998b), 'What the IMF should Do', *Wall Street Journal*, 6 October.

Felix, D. (1999), 'Is the Deepening Asian Crisis the Fault of Japan or the IMF?', http://www.igc.org/coc/bwi071.htm.

Fischer, S. (1998), 'The IMF and the Asian Crisis', Forum Funds Lecture, University of California Los Angeles, 20 March.

Greenspan, A. (1998), 'Remarks before the 34th Annual Conference on Bank Structure and Competition', Federal Reserve Bank of Chicago, 7 May.

Guitian, M. (1998), 'The Challenge of Managing Global Capital Flows', *Finance and Development*, June, 14–17.

Heillner, G.K. (1998), *The East Asian and Other Financial Crises: Causes, Responses and Prevention*, Geneva: UNCTAD.

Hutson, E. and C. Kearney (1999), 'The Asian Financial Crisis and the IMF', *Journal of the Asia Pacific Economy*, 4(3), 393–412.

International Monetary Fund (1998), *World Economic Outlook*, various issues, Washington, DC.

Johnson, C. (1998), 'Economic Crisis in East Asia: The Clash of Capitalisms', *Cambridge Journal of Economics*, 22, 653–61.

Jomo, K.S. (1998), 'Malaysian Debacle: Whose Fault?', *Cambridge Journal of Economics*, 22, 707–22.

Kapur, D. (1998), 'The IMF: A Cure or a Curse?', *Foreign Policy*, Summer, 26–39.

Kearney, C. (1999), 'The Asian Financial Crisis', *Quarterly Economic Commentary*, Economic and Social Research Institute, Dublin, February.

Kregel, J.A. (1998), 'Derivatives and Global Capital Flows', *Cambridge Journal of Economics*, 22, 677–92.

Krugman, P. (1998), 'What happened to Asia?', mimeo, Department of Economics, Massachusetts Institute of Technology, Cambridge, MA.

Lipsky, J. (1998), 'Asia's Crisis: A Market Perspective', *Finance and Development* June, 10–13.

Loriaux, M. *et al.* (1997), *Capital Ungoverned: Liberalising Finance in Interventionist States*, Ithaca: Cornell University Press.

Mathieson, D.J., A. Richards and S. Sharma (1998), 'Financial Crises in Emerging Markets', *Finance and Development*, December, 28–31.

Matthews, J.A. (1998), 'Fashioning a New Roman Model out of the Crisis: The Rebuilding of Institutional Capabilities', *Cambridge Journal of Economics*, 22, 747–59.

Meltzer, A.H. (1998), 'Asian Problems and the IMF', *Cato Journal*, 17(3), http://www.cato.org.

Mishkin, F.S. (1999), 'Lessons from the Asian Crisis', *Journal of International Money and Finance*, 18, 709–23.

Rubin, R.E. (1998, 'Address on the Asian Financial Situation', Georgetown University, Washington, DC, http://www.treas.gov/press/releases/pr 2168.htm.

Sachs, J. (1989), *Developing Country Debt and Economic Performance*, Cambridge, MA: MIT Press.

Sachs, J. (1998a), 'The IMF and the Asian Flu', *The American Prospect*, March–April, 16–21.

Sachs, J. (1998b), 'IMF is a Power unto Itself', *The Financial Times*, 11 December.

Salvatore, D. (1998), 'International Monetary and Financial Arrangements: Present and Future', *Open Economies Review* 9, S1, 375–415.

Savona, P. and A. Maccario (1998), 'On the Relation between Money and Derivatives and its Application to the International Money Market', *Open Economies Review*, 9, S1, 637–64.

Vasquez, I. (1998), 'Why the IMF Should Not Intervene', presentation at a conference on 'The Asian crisis and the reform of the monetary system', Madrid, 25 February 1998.

World Bank (1993), *The East Asian Miracle: Economic Growth and Public Policy*, New York: Oxford University Press.

World Bank Group (1998a), *Report of the Working Group on Transparency and Accountability*, October.

World Bank Group (1998b), *Report of the Working Group on the Strengthening of Domestic Financial Systems*, October.

World Bank Group (1998c), *Report of the Working Group on the Management of International Financial Crises*, October.

Appendix

Macro indicators of the five victims of the East Asian crisis

	GDP growth rate																	
Country	1981	1982	1983	1984	1985	1986	1987	1988	1989	1990	1991	1992	1993	1994	1995	1996	1997	1998
Thailand	5.91	5.35	5.58	5.76	4.64	5.54	9.52	13.29	12.19	11.63	8.18	8.08	8.71	8.90	8.66	6.40	−1.35	−8.04
Korea	6.72	7.30	11.78	10.14	6.23	11.55	11.52	11.27	6.38	9.51	9.13	5.06	5.75	8.58	8.94	7.06	5.51	−5.84
Indonesia	7.93	2.25	4.19	6.97	2.46	5.88	4.93	5.78	7.46	7.07	7.13	6.46	6.50	7.54	8.22	7.98	4.65	−13.68
Malaysia	6.94	5.94	6.25	7.76	−1.02	1.05	5.39	8.94	9.21	9.74	8.48	7.80	8.35	9.30	9.36	8.60	7.70	−6.70
Philippines	3.41	3.63	1.87	−7.32	−7.31	3.41	4.31	6.76	6.13	3.10	−0.58	0.33	2.13	4.39	4.76	5.68	5.07	−0.54

	Inflation rate																	
Country	1981	1982	1983	1984	1985	1986	1987	1988	1989	1990	1991	1992	1993	1994	1995	1996	1997	1998
Thailand	12.77	5.18	3.76	0.88	2.48	1.81	2.49	3.82	5.36	5.93	5.70	4.07	3.36	5.10	5.77	5.85	5.61	8.05
Korea	21.28	7.11	3.53	2.32	2.40	2.73	3.04	7.13	5.74	8.58	9.30	6.22	4.82	6.16	4.49	4.96	4.45	7.48
Indonesia	12.30	9.33	11.87	10.45	4.80	5.73	9.35	8.05	6.42	7.76	9.40	7.59	9.60	8.53	9.43	8.03	6.71	57.73
Malaysia	9.74	5.75	3.66	3.99	0.33	0.77	0.22	2.60	2.74	2.67	4.40	4.69	3.57	3.71	5.28	3.56	2.66	5.27
Philippines	13.33	10.13	10.09	50.40	23.12	0.73	3.76	8.77	12.16	14.16	18.70	8.93	7.58	9.06	8.11	8.41	5.01	9.70

Country	Gross domestic savings (% of GDP) 1981	1982	1983	1984	1985	1986	1987	1988	1989	1990	1991	1992	1993	1994	1995	1996	1997	1998
Thailand	22.59	23.97	22.75	23.68	24.81	26.41	29.22	33.61	35.36	34.28	36.14	36.00	36.05	36.76	36.99	35.83	35.10	39.77
Korea	23.87	25.04	28.59	26.84	33.55	34.83	37.68	39.44	36.54	37.24	37.22	36.29	36.03	35.43	35.65	34.02	33.67	35.68
Indonesia	33.34	27.76	28.96	29.70	29.80	27.27	32.90	31.53	35.44	32.26	33.46	35.32	32.46	32.20	30.59	30.08	31.04	41.46
Malaysia	28.80	28.60	32.61	35.47	32.71	32.08	37.30	36.31	34.63	33.35	33.51	36.46	37.70	38.77	39.48	42.61	43.86	48.73
Philippines	26.78	25.25	27.36	23.89	18.80	19.03	20.96	21.05	20.32	18.69	16.64	14.93	13.76	14.85	14.53	14.60	14.02	13.70

Country	Gross fixed capital formation (% of GDP) 1981	1982	1983	1984	1985	1986	1987	1988	1989	1990	1991	1992	1993	1994	1995	1996	1997	1998
Thailand	27.99	26.94	28.46	28.60	27.17	25.78	27.64	30.68	34.62	40.38	41.63	39.26	39.52	40.02	41.13	41.07	35.60	24.77
Korea	27.96	28.37	29.25	25.41	28.56	28.17	29.06	29.61	31.93	37.30	39.03	36.96	36.16	36.00	36.69	36.79	35.10	29.45
Indonesia	24.32	25.32	25.08	22.40	23.06	24.13	24.82	25.63	26.57	28.34	27.00	25.77	26.28	27.57	28.43	29.60	28.71	20.87
Malaysia	36.03	36.33	35.79	31.92	29.85	26.35	22.96	24.13	29.34	32.40	36.40	36.02	38.35	40.13	43.04	42.28	42.82	25.80
Philippines	27.73	27.52	29.86	23.07	16.47	16.05	16.51	17.79	20.82	23.12	20.04	20.92	23.77	23.63	22.20	23.42	24.50	21.31

Country	Current account balance (% of GDP) 1981	1982	1983	1984	1985	1986	1987	1988	1989	1990	1991	1992	1993	1994	1995	1996	1997	1998
Thailand	−7.38	−2.74	−7.17	−5.05	−3.95	0.57	−0.72	−2.68	−3.46	−8.50	−7.71	−5.66	−5.07	−5.59	−8.05	−7.94	−1.96	12.19
Korea	−6.61	−3.43	−1.84	−1.42	−0.84	4.34	7.38	7.97	2.41	−0.79	−2.83	−1.25	0.30	−1.02	−1.86	−4.75	−1.95	12.48
Indonesia	−0.62	−5.64	−7.42	−2.12	−2.20	−4.89	−2.76	−1.57	−1.09	−2.61	−3.32	−2.00	−1.33	−1.58	−3.18	−3.37	−2.28	4.22
Malaysia	−9.87	−12.77	−11.56	−4.88	−1.92	−0.36	8.15	5.38	0.83	−2.03	−8.69	−3.72	−4.66	−6.23	−9.70	−4.63	−4.90	12.94
Philippines	−5.88	−8.65	−8.34	−4.12	−0.12	3.19	−1.34	−1.03	−3.42	−6.08	−2.28	−1.89	−5.55	−4.60	−2.67	−4.77	−5.23	1.97

Trade balance as % of GDP

Country	1981	1982	1983	1984	1985	1986	1987	1988	1989	1990	1991	1992	1993	1994	1995	1996	1997	1998
Thailand	−5.82	−2.00	−7.34	−5.22	−3.42	0.90	−0.84	−3.36	−4.04	−7.88	−6.07	−3.73	−3.42	−2.58	−4.73	−5.13	1.04	14.58
Korea	−7.02	−3.22	−2.11	−1.52	−0.91	2.88	4.59	4.88	0.41	−1.97	−3.49	−1.67	−0.47	−1.66	−2.20	−4.26	−1.91	12.17
Indonesia	7.40	2.00	1.13	6.51	6.67	3.07	6.16	6.74	7.06	5.04	4.12	5.05	5.21	4.47	3.23	2.62	4.67	19.57
Malaysia	−7.02	−3.22	−2.11	−1.52	−0.91	2.88	4.59	4.88	0.41	−1.97	−3.49	−1.67	−0.47	−1.66	−2.20	−4.26	−1.91	12.17
Philippines	−6.24	−7.12	−7.47	−2.16	−1.57	−0.68	−3.06	−2.86	−6.10	−9.07	−7.07	−8.86	−11.44	−12.25	−12.07	−13.69	−13.53	−0.04

Exports as % of GDP

Country	1981	1982	1983	1984	1985	1986	1987	1988	1989	1990	1991	1992	1993	1994	1995	1996	1997	1998
Thailand	19.81	18.68	16.19	20.17	18.15	20.43	22.94	25.59	27.45	26.64	28.59	28.80	28.99	30.78	32.93	29.40	38.00	47.38
Korea	30.50	29.34	29.54	32.02	32.10	31.96	34.68	33.35	28.08	26.56	26.01	24.89	24.71	25.21	27.40	26.77	30.77	41.25
Indonesia	25.38	20.91	21.89	23.69	21.21	17.98	22.66	23.14	24.32	25.26	25.41	24.29	23.17	22.74	23.48	22.07	26.09	53.50
Malaysia	30.50	29.34	29.54	32.02	32.10	31.96	34.68	33.35	28.08	26.56	26.01	24.89	24.71	25.21	27.40	26.77	30.77	41.25
Philippines	16.05	13.52	15.07	17.16	15.06	16.21	17.23	18.67	18.37	18.47	19.46	18.54	20.92	21.04	23.54	24.80	30.68	45.30

Imports as % of GDP

Country	1981	1982	1983	1984	1985	1986	1987	1988	1989	1990	1991	1992	1993	1994	1995	1996	1997	1998
Thailand	25.63	20.67	23.53	25.39	21.57	19.53	23.78	28.96	31.49	34.52	34.66	32.53	32.41	33.35	37.67	34.53	36.96	32.80
Korea	37.52	32.57	31.65	33.54	33.01	29.08	30.09	28.47	27.67	28.53	29.50	26.56	25.18	26.88	29.61	31.03	32.68	29.08
Indonesia	17.98	18.90	20.76	17.17	14.55	14.91	16.50	16.41	17.27	20.21	21.29	19.25	17.96	18.27	20.24	19.46	21.42	33.92
Malaysia	37.52	32.57	31.65	33.54	33.01	29.08	30.09	28.47	27.67	28.53	29.50	26.56	25.18	26.88	29.61	31.03	32.68	29.08
Philippines	22.29	20.64	22.54	19.33	16.63	16.89	20.29	21.54	24.47	27.55	26.53	27.41	32.37	33.29	35.60	38.49	44.21	45.35

National government fiscal balance (% of GDP)

Country	1981	1982	1983	1984	1985	1986	1987	1988	1989	1990	1991	1992	1993	1994	1995	1996	1997	1998
Thailand	−3.35	−6.36	−3.95	−3.41	−5.24	−4.23	−2.23	0.68	2.95	4.53	4.72	2.83	2.09	1.85	2.93	2.31	−0.87	−2.68
Korea	−3.34	−3.04	−1.03	−1.14	−1.15	−0.09	0.43	1.51	0.19	−0.67	−1.62	−0.49	0.64	0.32	0.29	0.45	0.25	−3.77
Indonesia	−2.02	−1.91	−2.40	1.36	−0.98	−3.53	−0.83	−3.09	−2.01	0.41	0.39	−0.39	0.61	0.94	2.22	1.16	1.39	
Malaysia	−19.12	−17.03	−13.13	−8.89	−7.36	−10.48	−7.73	−4.28	−5.13	−4.76	−1.99	−0.84	0.21	2.32	0.85	0.73	2.41	−3.44
Philippines	−4.32	−4.54	−2.02	−1.90	−1.95	−5.03	−2.45	−2.91	−2.11	−3.45	−2.11	−1.18	−1.48	1.07	0.58	0.29	0.06	−1.89

Real exchange rate (1981 = 100)

Country	1981	1982	1983	1984	1985	1986	1987	1988	1989	1990	1991	1992	1993	1994	1995	1996	1997	1998
Thailand	100.00	100.2	96.5	98.3	110.5	105.0	100.1	94.6	91.0	85.2	80.1	76.5	73.7	69.4	64.8	62.1	73.4	90.9
Korea	100.00	100.2	102.8	104.5	110.2	108.7	98.1	80.2	69.1	66.9	63.1	63.2	61.9	58.2	53.2	52.9	60.2	84.2
Indonesia	100.00	95.4	119.9	122.6	126.9	139.2	165.4	156.3	154.1	148.5	143.2	138.2	128.8	122.4	115.8	111.3	130.8	374.7
Malaysia	100.00	95.6	91.5	88.8	93.7	96.7	94.2	95.5	96.1	93.4	90.9	79.9	77.9	76.5	69.0	66.9	73.0	98.0
Philippines	100.00	98.0	117.6	117.4	103.7	112.9	109.6	102.8	93.5	91.3	86.1	72.3	71.3	63.0	56.2	52.6	56.5	75.8

Import cover

Country	1981	1982	1983	1984	1985	1986	1987	1988	1989	1990	1991	1992	1993	1994	1995	1996	1997	1998
Thailand	2.24	2.33	2.44	2.10	2.50	3.13	4.00	4.00	4.10	5.02	5.40	6.14	6.74	7.22	7.30	6.81	7.09	8.60
Korea	1.32	1.44	1.13	1.21	1.30	1.34	1.11	3.07	3.21	2.73	2.02	2.51	2.90	3.01	2.90	2.72	1.69	6.60
Indonesia	3.64	2.11	2.52	3.81	4.70	4.07	5.35	4.38	4.01	4.17	4.47	4.68	4.76	4.50	4.02	4.95	4.31	9.30
Malaysia	4.14	3.53	3.40	3.29	5.05	6.93	7.38	5.04	4.56	4.45	3.92	5.64	7.57	5.51	3.97	4.44	3.37	5.6
Philippines	3.12	1.39	1.20	1.19	1.44	4.11	1.72	1.48	1.63	0.91	3.23	3.64	3.19	3.38	2.90	3.77	2.40	4.00

Country	External debt (% of GDP) 1981	1982	1983	1984	1985	1986	1987	1988	1989	1990	1991	1992	1993	1994	1995	1996	1997
Thailand	31.14	33.44	34.72	35.90	45.09	43.00	40.33	35.29	32.57	33.00	38.44	37.56	42.09	45.44	49.41	49.94	60.69
Korea	47.32	50.13	49.12	41.06	57.87	50.56	34.81	24.11	18.89	18.59	18.17	18.26	18.17	23.36	23.51	25.32	30.09
Indonesia	28.90	24.75	26.59	35.40	36.56	42.05	53.62	69.14	60.92	58.55	61.07	62.06	63.26	56.43	60.96	61.55	56.70
Malaysia	36.71	49.81	57.83	55.19	64.96	78.89	72.27	53.51	43.04	35.83	35.48	34.33	40.74	41.84	39.33	40.00	48.25
Philippines	58.31	65.73	72.90	77.55	86.66	94.43	89.72	76.37	67.30	69.02	71.45	62.30	66.10	61.50	51.04	48.46	55.30

Country	Long-term debt (% of GDP) 1981	1982	1983	1984	1985	1986	1987	1988	1989	1990	1991	1992	1993	1994	1995	1996	1997
Thailand	20.42	22.82	23.87	25.25	33.98	33.93	33.14	26.43	23.74	23.24	25.73	24.35	24.02	25.23	24.97	29.21	36.48
Korea	30.86	31.75	32.75	28.39	36.99	33.07	22.00	14.25	10.35	9.57	9.66	10.24	10.12	13.38	11.46	12.70	16.48
Indonesia	25.07	21.19	22.77	29.45	29.91	35.07	45.48	59.82	52.64	50.09	50.90	50.76	50.28	45.05	49.96	48.71	42.53
Malaysia	29.33	42.36	46.77	46.97	55.98	69.11	64.85	48.91	37.03	31.38	31.17	28.09	29.91	33.30	31.00	28.84	32.99
Philippines	28.70	32.54	41.24	44.61	53.07	72.17	74.49	63.28	55.25	56.97	58.17	50.30	54.61	50.92	42.93	38.35	39.90

Country	Short-term debt (% of GDP) 1981	1982	1983	1984	1985	1986	1987	1988	1989	1990	1991	1992	1993	1994	1995	1996	1997
Thailand	8.26	8.31	8.25	8.49	8.22	6.59	5.27	7.78	8.46	9.75	12.71	13.21	18.07	20.21	24.44	20.73	22.63
Korea	14.67	16.69	14.72	11.14	19.28	16.06	12.43	9.86	8.54	9.02	8.50	8.02	8.04	9.98	12.05	12.63	11.29
Indonesia	4.33	3.56	3.83	5.43	6.17	6.93	8.08	8.38	7.58	7.86	9.73	11.17	12.98	11.38	11.00	12.85	14.17
Malaysia	6.49	6.43	9.97	7.46	8.61	9.78	7.42	4.60	6.01	4.46	4.31	6.24	10.83	8.54	8.33	11.16	15.26
Philippines	26.43	30.49	28.36	30.12	29.79	18.02	11.44	10.20	9.29	9.99	10.89	9.92	9.26	8.92	7.12	9.62	14.36

Short-term debt (% of international reserves)

Country	1981	1982	1983	1984	1985	1986	1987	1988	1989	1990	1991	1992	1993	1994	1995	1996	1997
Thailand	167.0	197.7	205.7	184.9	146.1	101.3	66.5	78.7	64.2	62.6	71.3	72.3	92.5	99.5	114.2	99.7	133.1
Korea	381.3	442.7	516.3	414.9	633.7	525.5	472.7	145.4	124.7	18.9	183.3	147.4	137.4	156.7	180.5	193.0	264.1
Indonesia	65.3	115.0	124.8	113.3	121.6	159.6	113.7	133.3	146.2	149.3	154.6	172.8	159.7	160.4	189.4	176.6	217.1
Malaysia	39.6	45.7	80.0	68.0	54.7	45.0	31.5	45.2	29.2	19.5	19.1	21.1	25.5	24.3	30.6	41.0	71.9
Philippines	456.0	1275.3	1261.0	1571.4	1488.9	311.5	392.3	385.4	279.0	479.1	152.3	119.4	107.7	95.0	82.9	79.5	162.3

FDI inflows (as % of GDP)

Country	1981	1982	1983	1984	1985	1986	1987	1988	1989	1990	1991	1992	1993	1994	1995	1996	1997
Thailand	0.59	0.84	0.52	0.87	0.96	0.42	0.61	0.70	1.79	2.46	2.85	2.05	1.90	1.44	0.95	1.23	1.26
Korea	0.15	0.09	0.08	0.12	0.25	0.42	0.45	0.56	0.50	0.31	0.40	0.24	0.18	0.21	0.39	0.48	0.64
Indonesia	0.14	0.24	0.34	0.25	0.35	0.32	0.51	0.65	0.67	0.96	1.16	1.28	1.27	1.19	2.15	2.72	2.18
Malaysia	5.06	4.97	4.19	2.35	2.23	1.76	1.34	2.07	4.40	5.45	8.31	8.89	7.80	5.99	4.78	5.12	5.22
Philippines	0.48	0.04	0.32	0.03	0.04	0.43	0.92	0.25	1.32	1.20	1.20	0.43	2.28	2.48	1.99	0.18	1.47

Portfolio investment inflows (as % of GDP)

Country	1981	1982	1983	1984	1985	1986	1987	1988	1989	1990	1991	1992	1993	1994	1995	1996	1997
Thailand	0.30	0.13	0.19	0.27	0.37	2.30	−0.07	0.68	0.86	2.06	−0.04	−0.08	0.83	4.34	1.72	2.43	1.94
Korea	0.03	−0.02	0.66	0.92	1.84	−0.31	−0.22	−0.33	0.00	0.09	0.79	1.61	3.17	2.14	3.04	4.37	2.78
Indonesia	0.05	0.33	0.43	−0.01	−0.04	0.33	−0.12	−0.11	−0.17	−0.08	−0.01	−0.06	1.14	2.19	2.03	2.20	−2.46
Malaysia	4.52	2.14	2.22	3.26	6.22	0.11	0.44	−1.29	−0.28	−0.60	0.35	−1.92	−1.10	−2.27	−0.50	−0.27	−0.25
Philippines	0.01	0.00	0.02	0.00	0.06	0.04	0.06	0.13	0.69	−0.11	0.28	0.29	1.65	1.41	3.53	6.12	0.72

Country	Other investment inflows (as % of GDP)																
	1981	1982	1983	1984	1985	1986	1987	1988	1989	1990	1991	1992	1993	1994	1995	1996	1997
Thailand	5.51	6.28	3.06	4.04	5.00	1.86	−0.49	0.78	3.18	5.12	8.17	9.82	5.81	5.37	6.81	11.51	6.42
Korea	6.68	6.50	2.87	1.79	1.79	−2.04	−6.33	−1.13	−0.64	2.17	2.38	1.60	−0.44	3.58	4.70	5.07	−1.88
Indonesia	1.83	5.38	6.32	3.70	1.73	4.56	4.19	1.96	2.37	3.05	3.30	3.19	1.38	−0.87	1.20	0.11	−1.15
Malaysia	1.98	6.70	11.28	2.53	−2.76	1.91	−4.91	−3.43	−0.68	−0.21	1.03	5.46	11.59	2.63	5.36	4.65	−1.15
Philippines	7.17	8.58	−1.83	2.15	1.01	0.02	−0.02	−1.10	1.20	3.56	5.00	5.55	4.52	5.56	4.10	7.60	5.28

Country	Net other investments (as % of GDP)																
	1981	1982	1983	1984	1985	1986	1987	1988	1989	1990	1991	1992	1993	1994	1995	1996	1997
Thailand	5.57	6.40	3.29	4.31	5.19	2.48	−0.15	0.50	2.74	5.55	8.36	9.46	5.72	7.97	7.52	13.14	4.98
Korea	6.66	5.43	2.21	2.11	0.62	−2.67	−6.41	−1.93	−1.07	1.21	1.36	0.53	−1.82	1.64	1.63	2.29	−4.95
Indonesia	1.83	5.38	6.32	3.70	1.73	4.56	4.19	1.96	2.37	3.05	3.30	3.19	1.38	−0.87	1.20	0.11	−1.15
Malaysia	0.88	6.21	6.40	3.30	−2.26	2.12	−6.58	−6.55	−0.60	−0.69	3.02	8.03	10.14	3.33	4.46	4.71	−2.16
Philippines	5.17	9.53	−1.51	2.47	1.01	0.02	−0.02	−1.10	1.20	3.56	5.00	5.55	4.52	5.56	4.10	9.69	5.79

Source: International Financial Statistics, International Monetary Fund, various years.

Index